Management of Interest Rate Risk

edited by

Boris Antl

Published by Euromoney Publications

Published by
Euromoney Publications PLC
Nestor House, Playhouse Yard
London EC4V 5EX

Copyright © 1988 Euromoney Publications PLC
ISBN 1   870031   32   6

MB

Typeset by Valentine Press Limited, Essex
Printed in Great Britain by Grosvenor Press (Portsmouth) Limited

Contents

Part III   Interest rate futures

Introduction

As this book goes to press, the financial markets around the world are undergoing the biggest crises since the 1930s. The stock market declines in major financial centres around the world in late 1987, coupled with the high US budget and balance of trade deficits and the developing countries', explosive foreign debt situation, all point to an unusually volatile situation in the world financial markets.

This book is concerned with two specific segments of these financial markets: the money markets and the capital markets around the world.

Four major developments in these markets are of great importance. The first is the dramatic increase of interest rate volatility in recent years. Whereas in the 1950s and 1960s annual interest rate movements of one or two percentage points were considered significant, in the 1970s and 1980s we have seen interest rates – whether short or long term – fluctuating by several percentage points on a month-to-month or even week-to-week basis. For example, in the 1970s and 1980s short-term US interest rate levels ranged from 5 to 18%, while long-term rates fluctuated between 5 and 14%. Similar movements took place in most other major countries.

The second development is the proliferation of complex financial products to manage interest rate risk. Interest rate risk today is managed by such instruments as swaps, options, futures, caps, floors, collars, forward rate agreements, forward-forward agreements, interest rate guarantees and swaptions. Volatility subjects corporations to unacceptable swings in financing costs; complex products increase the difficulty of precisely measuring interest rate exposure. These two structural changes have forced corporations to institute comprehensive risk management programmes and become increasingly sophisticated about interest measurement and protection techniques.

The third structural change is the deregulation of financial institutions and the increasing integration and globalisation of the various money and capital markets around the world. Many financial institutions around the world are now permitted to operate in many more markets than in the past and thus provide new and additional services to their customers. The integration of the various domestic and international markets then allows the market participants to trade 24 hours a day on a global basis and take advantage of the many attractive arbitrage opportunities existing between these markets.

The fourth, but seldom mentioned development, concerns the technological change on the trading floors of all the major financial institutions. Some of the most dramatic changes are taking place here, in the heart of the financial system. Whereas about 10 years ago the most advanced commonly available tool was a hand-held calculator, today's technology is the microcomputer or minicomputer loaded with sophisticated software packages, networked locally and globally, and with the power of a mainframe computer worth some US$3 million in 1978. Almost every trader around the world has such a technological marvel on his or her desk. This indeed changes the way the markets operate. As a result, market participants are now paying much closer attention to the issues of timely information flow, speed, accuracy and creativity, as these are – other things being equal – largely a function of the tools available to the trader, money market and capital market specialist.

The impact of these developments is far-reaching. For the creative portfolio manager, the emergence of new techniques and applications is a blessing. Many portfolio managers are now able to hedge some of the risks inherent in their portfolios via an array of newly available instruments, thereby enabling them to take unmatched positions on their books. It is now possible not only to manage risk months or years into the future, but also meet any repayment schedule, whether a straight line amortisation, an annuity, or anything else. And as the number of applications grows and the average size of a transaction decreases, the products and its many attractive attributes become available to an increasing number of institutions and market participants.

None the less, as most market participants are mesmerised by the sheer volume and profitability of these transactions, it is as important to monitor other closely related developments. Indeed, as volume grows, credit considerations, accounting treatment and legal issues become important. All market participants should monitor closely the current attempts of the major central banks around the world to regulate off-balance sheet transactions, including the products covered in this book. The developments in the accounting profession are closely linked to these regulatory issues and are likely to impact the way changes in interest rates are going to impact the profit and loss of an operation.

The developments on the tax side are noteworthy as well. Creative off-market transactions or elaborate cross-border transactions are becoming more and more common, enabling the parties involved to optimise their global tax positions and maximise profits by unique structures. Add to this the current changes in the US and other major countries' tax codes and the number of possible tax driven arbitrage opportunities becomes irresistible. These allow the most sophisticated market participants not only to meet their clients' requirements but also to make significant fees on any single transaction.

This book discusses all these developments in detail. Part I introduces the topics relevant for the manager of interest rate risk. Accordingly, we discuss first the role and determinants of interest rates and briefly outline the various markets and instruments available to the corporate treasurer or portfolio manager. With these definitions in mind, we suggest that the first step in the management of interest rate risk is the definition of exposure to that risk; the second step the development of a scenario for anticipated future interest rate movements and the corresponding appetite for or against risk; and the third step a well defined framework for action.

Part II discusses other elements of interest rate risk management, including accounting treatment, a framework for domestic and international tax rules, and the other relevant regulatory and governmental controls issues.

Parts III through VII focus on the individual products. Each of the sections addresses one individual product, namely interest rate futures, interest rate swaps, options, forward rate agreements, forward-forward agreements, caps, floors and collars. Within each of these sections we first discuss the product and its mechanics in some detail and then look at the accounting treatment in the major countries. Thereafter we discuss the documentation and provide sample contracts and terms of trade on the major exchanges, when applicable. Each part then concludes with one or more case studies, illustrating actual applications.

Finally, in Part VIII three experts, a treasurer, a banker and an accountant, perform a comparative analysis of the various products, listing their pros and cons in terms of economics, practicality and effectiveness. Then, looking into a crystal ball, each of these experts provides their best guess as to what we can expect in the near future in these new and exciting markets.

In conclusion, there seems to be no end to the changes and turmoil in the finance world. The volatility of interest rates, the proliferation of complex financial products and the need to manage risk are likely to stay with us in the years to come. The recent phenomenal growth of these markets, however, is unlikely to continue forever, especially if the forthcoming regulations adversely impact the attractiveness of some of these products or if the current financial crises spills beyond the stock markets. None the less, superior creativity of the market participants coupled with the emergence and growth of secondary markets in many of these instruments are likely to add new fuel to the momentum and possibly drive the markets to new heights. Indeed, all the recent market, regulatory and technological developments seem to point towards a continuing integration of the world's capital and money markets. And given all the most exciting and unexpected developments in the markets in the last five or six years, only those with the greatest imagination and understanding of the current forces at work can foresee things yet to come.

Boris Antl
San Francisco, May 1988

Glossary

Interest rate future   An agreement to buy or sell a standard quantity of a specific financial instrument at a future date and at a price agreed between the parties.

Interest rate swap   A transaction in which two unrelated borrowers or investors agree to make payments either directly, or through one or more intermediaries, to each other based on the interest rate cost of the other's borrowing or investment. Interest rate swaps can be made between one fixed rate and one floating rate instrument or between two floating rate instruments (i.e. basis swaps).

Interest rate option   A financial instrument giving its buyer the right but not the obligation to fix the rate of interest on a loan, a deposit, a swap or another instrument for an agreed amount for an agreed period on a specific future date. Options can be traded on various exchanges or over the counter.

Forward rate agreement (FRA)   A contract whereby the customer can determine the interest rate that will be applied to a loan or a deposit of an agreed amount to be drawn or placed on an agreed future date, the settlement date, for a specified term. On the settlement date the difference between the agreed rate and the prevailing rate will be settled by the customer or the bank. A variation of the FRA is a forward-forward agreement, whereby the customer may place a deposit or borrow funds for a fixed period at an agreed rate commencing on a specified later date.

Caps and collars   A capped (floor) rate provides the customer protection against future increases (or decreases) on interest rates on either existing or prospective debt (or investment). It protects the customer against increasing (or declining) rates on floating rate loans while, at the same time, allowing him to benefit from favourable movements. An interest rate collar provides, in addition to the cap, a floor on the rate, whereby the provider of a collar agrees to limit the borrower's cost of floating rate debt to a band limited by a specified ceiling rate and a specified floor rate. The user of the collar buys the ceiling and sells the floor.

PART I

Market policies and strategies

1   Determinants of interest rates

Horace W. Brock

Introduction

When the present author was in college, he learned that the Federal Reserve Board 'set' interest rates primarily via open market transactions and discount rate adjustments. How things have changed! Consider US credit market developments between September 1985 and April 1986: there was a dramatic rally, yet as Federal Reserve Board Governor Lyle Gramley has pointed out, and as the Federal Open Market Committee (FOMC) minutes make clear, Fed policy was completely passive during this period. The Fed did cut the discount rate twice, but in each case it acted well *after* the market on its own had driven interest rates successively lower.

Those headline events that did roil the markets had little to do with the Fed, or with the money supply whose accelerating growth rate was all but ignored. Rather, what drove the markets were events such as the Gramm–Rudman legislation of December 1985, oil price deflation in early 1986, a soaring US trade deficit, an increased inflow of foreign capital, a 16% decline in the value of the dollar, and disappointingly flat economic growth.

An 'extended' law of supply and demand

How then do we analyse the determinants of interest rate movements in today's deregulated, globalised environment? What paradigm is most appropriate? We shall argue that the complexities of today's environment require that we analyse interest movements in terms of what can be called the 'extended' law of supply and demand in the credit market. Although this approach is both theoretically correct and intuitively appealing, it is surprisingly unfamiliar to market participants as well as to many who construct forecasting models.

Surprisingly, one reason this is true is that most people do not understand what the law of supply and demand *means* in a credit (as opposed to a money) market context. In this regard, shifts in credit supply and demand are often mistakenly identified with changes in economic flow-of-funds. In other instances, supply and demand considerations are incorrectly seen as incompatible with more important 'psychological' factors. The first section of this chapter will clarify the true meaning of supply and demand in today's deregulated credit market. In doing so, it will demonstrate how the extended law of supply and demand is able uniquely to explain numerous dramatic events of the US credit market between 1981 and 1986.

'Forecasting' reconceptualised as 'risk assessment'

Explaining the true determinants of interest rate movements is not sufficient. The second section of this chapter therefore constructs a bridge between this section and the enterprise of making 'useful' interest rate forecasts. We sketch how recent advances in the 'economics of uncertainty' make it possible to reinterpret and improve interest rate forecasting. In particular, we shall show how the very concept of forecasting can be replaced by the more general concept of 'risk assessment'.

More significantly, we shall argue that it is desirable to do so. The events of the past decade –

particularly heightened uncertainty and risk – have *de facto* transformed investment management (and even trading) into risk management. Typical decisions of today's players are: 'How much should I lengthen/shorten my portfolio? How much should I spend to cap/hedge/swap my position?' But it is clearly impossible to answer such questions rationally without first assessing *how likely* different market outcomes are. In short, formal risk assessment should accompany and indeed precede risk management.

Contrast this *desideratum* with real-world practices today: some 'most likely' interest rate levels act as a forecast. On rare occasions, this forecast will be supplemented by some 'market volatility' index masquerading as a risk assessment. Yet neither the most likely number nor the volatility index captures the true interest rate risk an investor faces – the risk stemming from those uncertain front page events that inevitably roil the markets (recall the sources of the 1985–86 rally). What is clearly needed is a link between these front page uncertainties on the one hand and the relative likelihood of future interest rate levels on the other.

Exhibit 1.1   The US credit market, 1988

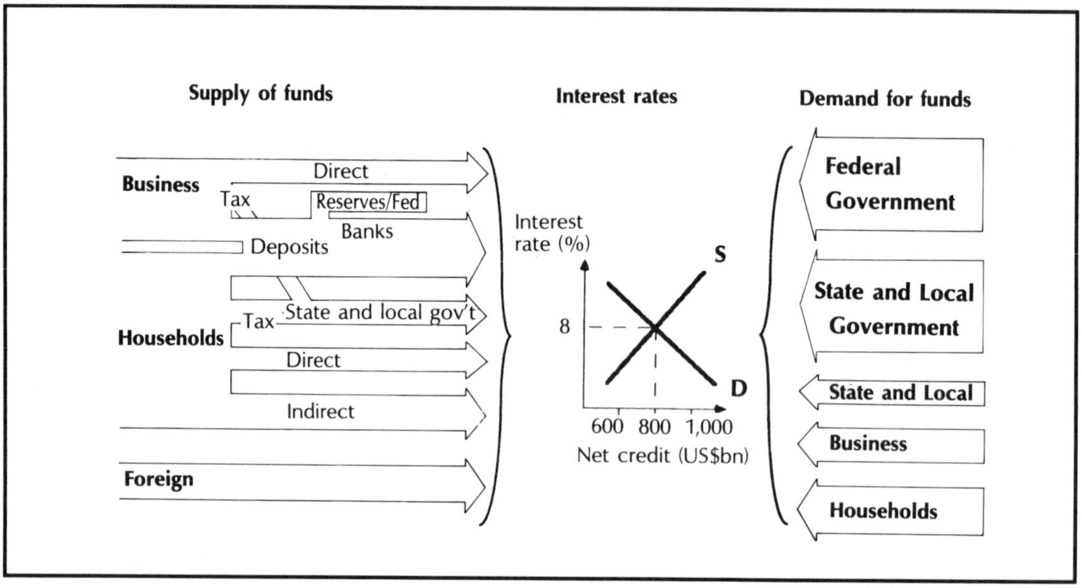

The extended law of credit supply and demand

Exhibit 1.1 shows the workings of today's credit market. On the left are those who 'lend'. Note that the Fed fits in here in a natural way via its open market activities that provide bank reserves to the banking system. As the diagram indicates, it is the banks that provide credit – not the Fed. (Generally, banks are willing to extend 10 dollars of fresh credit for each fresh dollar of reserves, other things being equal, given today's credit multiplier of about 10.)

How do interest rates change within this framework? They change when the behaviour of borrowers and lenders/investors changes. But what do we mean by a 'change of behaviour'? Understanding this concept is the key to everything (see the supply/demand graph in Exhibit 1.1). The 'supply schedule' here can best be thought of as the nation's *aggregate* 'willingness to lend' schedule (foreign lending is included). This schedule depicts the total amount of funds that will be made available at any given nominal interest rate. Naturally, the higher the interest rate, the more credit will be made available, other things being equal. Hence the schedule has a positive slope.

A parallel analysis holds for the demand schedule, although in this case the quantity demanded decreases as the price rises. Equilibrium occurs at the point of intersection of the two schedules. In reality of course, there will be both a short-term and a long-term credit supply/demand schedule. We are momentarily abstracting from this for the sake of simplicity.

Changes in interest rates

As the state of the world changes, the aggregate willingness to lend at any given interest rate (say US$800bn annually at an 8% interest rate) will change. It will either increase or decrease. For example, if inflation escalates, people might only be willing to lend US$700bn at the same 8% nominal rate. But as this decrease will be true for any and every level of interest rates, the *entire schedule* clearly shifts backward. It is this 'functional shift' (of the schedule) that causes interest rates to change.

Why do we emphasise this point? Because it is often misunderstood. For example, suppose you hear that 'mortgage credit demand has increased'. Does this constitute a 'change' that will lead to an increase in interest rates? Not necessarily. If the increased demand is itself simply a response to lower interest rates, then this increase represents a shift 'along' the given demand curve. It is only when demand is greater or lesser at a *given* interest rate that the entire schedule shifts, and thus that interest rates can and do change.

Exhibit 1.2   The US credit market, 1981-85

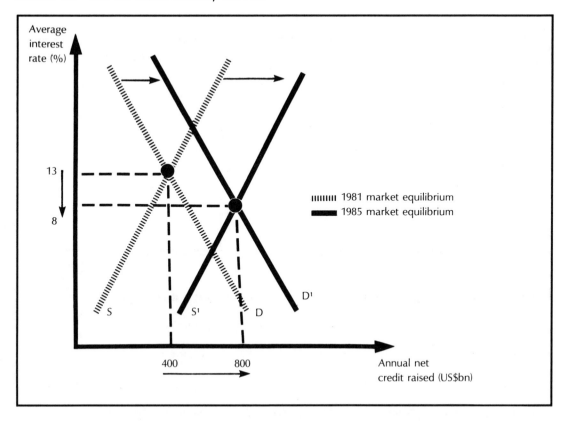

The 'extended' law of supply and demand we have spoken of is simply the law of supply and demand in the credit market extended so as to incorporate the effect of *all* relevant changes in the state of the world upon the borrowing/lending behaviour of *all* parties, whether the sources of behavioural change are psychological (e.g. consumer optimism increases), mechanical (e.g. the Fed tightens bank reserves), business cyclical (e.g. capital investment increases as a recovery gets under way), or international (e.g. foreign capital inflows increase).

Explaining an important market rally

To demonstrate how changes in the environment cause changes in the willingness of various parties to borrow and/or lend, it will be helpful to apply the extended law of supply and demand to a very significant and often misunderstood rally: that of the 1981–85 period when both long- and short-term interest rates fell dramatically.

Exhibit 1.2 contrasts equilibrium in the credit market in 1981 with equilibrium in 1985. For the sake of simplicity, we have lumped short- and long-term credit together. The first thing to note is that the *quantity* of net credit raised on an annual basis doubled from about US$400bn in 1981 to about US$800bn in 1985. However, the average interest rate *dropped* by some 500 basis points. How was this outcome possible? By examining Exhibit 1.2, it can be seen that the only way in which price can fall while quantity increases is for the supply schedule to increase *more* than the demand schedule. This is precisely what happened – and it surprised many in the process.

In the early 1980s, just after President Reagan's tax cuts were announced, many Wall Street commentators expected interest rates to rise. They correctly expected a 'collision' between private and public sector credit demand. In other words, they expected the aggregate demand curve to shift

Exhibit 1.3 Falling interest rates, 1981 versus 1985

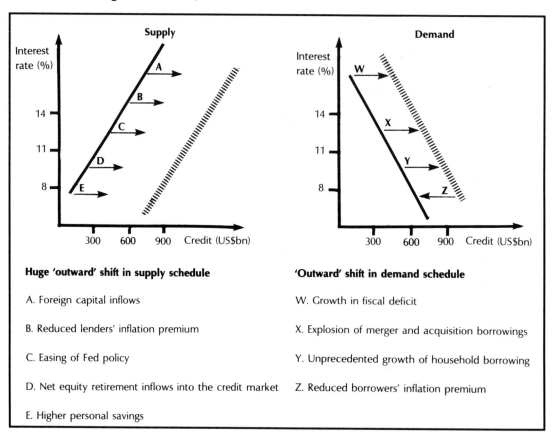

Huge 'outward' shift in supply schedule

A. Foreign capital inflows

B. Reduced lenders' inflation premium

C. Easing of Fed policy

D. Net equity retirement inflows into the credit market

E. Higher personal savings

'Outward' shift in demand schedule

W. Growth in fiscal deficit

X. Explosion of merger and acquisition borrowings

Y. Unprecedented growth of household borrowing

Z. Reduced borrowers' inflation premium

outward. It did – much further than anyone expected. What most observers failed to foresee was that the supply schedule would shift out even further.

Exhibit 1.3 indicates the various 'headline events' that caused these shifts and thus drove the market during these years. The figure shows which side of the market each event impacted, e.g. whether a given event affected the behaviour of borrowers, of lenders, or of both. It also shows the 'direction' of the effect. The factors are listed in order of their relative importance.

Supply side developments

On the supply side of the ledger, the most dramatic development was the increase in the nation's current account balance (i.e. trade deficit) from a US$5bn surplus to a US$160bn deficit (Exhibit 1.3, event A). Now any shift in the current account of US$165bn is automatically mirrored by an equal and corresponding shift in the capital account. Thus the nation enjoyed a net 'foreign capital inflow' of US$160bn in 1986 – a US$165bn increase over the US$5bn *outflow* in 1981. Between 80% and 90% of this capital inflow takes the form of credit market investments such as Treasury bills and bonds, as opposed to equity or real estate investments. Thus, approximately US$140bn of the outward shift in the supply schedule was due to the change in annual foreign capital inflows. The next most important factors were:

- lower lenders' inflation premium, a direct result of falling inflation over the period;
- easing of Fed policy;
- unprecedented credit market inflows of funds from net equity retirements, due largely to leveraged buyouts and mergers and acquisitions; and
- higher personal savings, primarily due to the creation of 10 million new jobs.

The important thing to see here is that each of these real-world developments is properly described by an increased supply of funds at any *given* nominal interest rate, i.e. an outward shift of the nation's credit supply schedule.

Demand side developments

On the demand side, several events took place. First, there was the rapid growth of the fiscal deficit beginning in 1981. Also contributing significantly to the increased demand for credit was the explosion of borrowings for mergers and acquisitions. In addition, households increased their borrowings to unprecedented levels over this period, for a combination of business cyclical and demographic reasons.

The reduced borrowers' inflation premium (again, a direct result of the falling inflation over the period) worked to *decrease* the demand for credit at any given interest rate. However, the factors cited above far outweighed the effect of this lower inflation premium – the only factor working to decrease borrowing we can identify.

Overall, our analysis shows that a judicious use of the law of supply and demand in the credit market can go a long way in explaining how price and quantity change over time – especially when the concept is 'extended' to deal with those contemporary developments that transcend considerations of Fed policy, money supply growth, and the business cycle. But how can these insights be harnessed to help investors better forecast the future?

This question brings us to the threshold of interest rate forecasting – a controversial and difficult undertaking. In the following section, we first discuss limitations of traditional forecasting methods. Thereafter we demonstrate a new approach to forecasting specifically designed to overcome these limitations.

Exhibit 1.4   Standard 'black box' forecasting

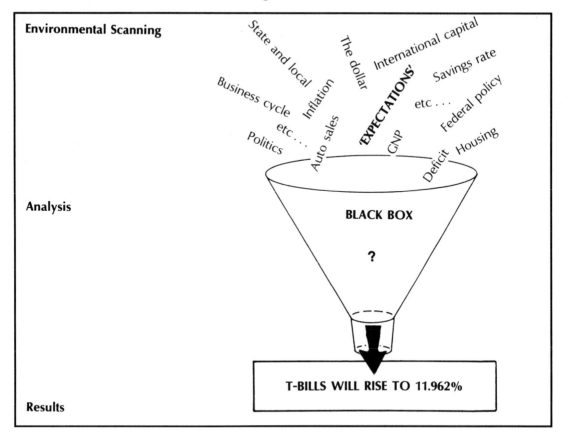

Meaningful forecasting *qua* risk assessment

In answering this question, I would like to begin by offering a candid appraisal of the state of interest rate forecasting based on the reactions of others as well as myself. Exhibit 1.4 summarises the results of a survey my firm carried out on this subject in 1982. Some 100 professional investment managers were asked for their views about interest rate forecasting. The blunt consensus was: 'I don't like betting my Christmas bonus on some overly precise forecast emanating from some black box whose innards I can't and don't understand. Besides, point forecasts are usually wrong.'

As it happens, this reaction is insightful as well as descriptive. Modern rational choice theory instructs us that 'rational' decisions under conditions of uncertainty are those most consistent (in a well-defined sense) with our degree of confidence in our forecast. How can one possess any meaningful confidence in the kind of interest rate forecasts the respondees are referring to? Several important points arise in this context, and they provide motivation for the approach to be set forth below.

Some limitations of traditional forecasting methods

First   As pointed out in the Introduction, most forecasts are uninformative about risk and uncertainty. A financial market participant in today's environment – knowing that no clairvoyant exists – wants an honest assessment of the risks he ineluctably faces. 'How likely are various possible market outcomes? I need to know my risks before I can determine what position to take, much less how much to spend to hedge that position.' Knowing the mean and standard error of econometric forecasts is no substitute for such intelligence. Nor are indices of market volatility. Nor are computations based on various concepts of duration.

All these approaches bypass the assessment of those 'macro-risks' that will be highlighted below, e.g. 'How likely is it that Gramm–Rudman will pass, that the economy will strengthen, and that foreign capital inflows will decline? And what do these probabilities imply about the probabilities for future interest rate levels?'

Second The knowledge base underlying most models is strictly historical. The implicit assumption is that statistical analysis and extrapolation is sufficient for meaningful forecasting. In a non-stationary environment such as that of today's financial markets, it clearly is not. Although history must always be consulted, so must experts. Among other things, a true expert can tell us when to pay no heed to historical experience – and why. This is as true in interest rate analysis as it is in medical research. A particular challenge is to integrate successfully historical and non-historical intelligence.

Third Most interest rate forecasting models are non-behavioural in the sense that they do not explicitly model the way market participants react to changes in the environment, e.g. higher inflationary expectations. Rather, they make use of regression weights to pass directly from the stipulated change in the environment to the resulting change in interest rate levels. (To state this more analytically, most forecasts come from 'quasi-reduced form' as opposed to 'structural' models.)

It is often forgotten that changes in human behaviour underlie any changes in interest rates. Even more surprisingly, it is forgotten that there are two very different kinds of behaviour in any market: that of supplier and demander.

Thus, if one believes, as we do, that interest rate forecasts should reflect explicit assumptions about changing behaviour on both sides of the market, the question arises as to how to model such behavioural adjustment. A way to do so is outlined below.

Summary Fortunately, there exists an alternative to traditional forecasting methods, one consonant with the need for genuine risk assessment, with the need for future-oriented expertise as well as historical analysis, and with the desirability of modelling human behaviour. Moreover, the method can be applied to the entire credit market – not just to a convenient submarket (e.g. the Fed Funds market).

A new approach to price forecasting

Exhibit 1.5 depicts the new approach to forecasting. It stems largely from the 'Economics of Uncertainty' often associated with Harvard–Stanford Nobel Laureate, Kenneth J. Arrow. The premises underlying the approach are as appealing as they are straightforward. We shall discuss each with the aid of the exhibit. (*Note:* this exhibit is redrawn from CRED–INTEL, 1986. It represents an actual forecast for 90-day T-Bills and 30-year T-bonds made in November 1986.)

Premise 1: A need to characterise the underlying risks As Arrow (1964) has pointed out, uncertainty means not knowing which state of the world will obtain in the future. But 'not knowing' does not mean we have no information to work with, and it is usually possible – and rational – to derive a meaningful set of betting odds on future events. (More formally, we should assess a probability distribution on the future state of the world.) Now as a practical matter, this generally calls for us to identify a few 'significant' risks, and to quantify them as best as possible.

Exhibit 1.5   Interest rate risk forecasting and risk analysis, May 1987

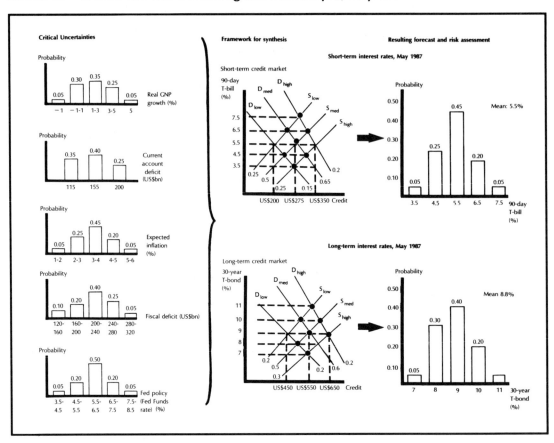

In an interest rate context, much of the uncertainty about market outcomes in today's environment inheres in those events that appear on the left-hand side of the figure. In the present example, the probability distributions shown for these future states of the world were derived from extensive analytical work. The underlying knowledge base was partly historical, and partly expert-based.

Premise 2: A need to model future behaviour   One of the basic premises of the 'economics of uncertainty' is that the behaviour of market participants which ultimately determines market-clearing prices will differ in different states of the world. But what will this uncertain behaviour be, and how can we 'forecast' it? Exhibit 1.5 provides a graphic answer to this question. 'Future behaviour' in a given state of the world can be represented by a pair of supply and demand schedules summarising the willingness of borrowers/lenders to borrow/lend *in that particular state of the world.*

Going one step further, we must ask: What is the probability of such market behaviour? It is simply the probability that the particular state of the world will eventuate, i.e. the 'risk' assessed above in the context of Premise 1. To make all this more concrete, consider the structural model appearing in the middle of the upper portion of Exhibit 1.5. There are three (decimal) probability numbers appearing alongside the three supply schedules, and three accompanying the three demand schedules. (For example, the probabilities of the 'high', 'medium' and 'low' demand schedules are 0.20, 0.65 and 0.15 respectively.)

10

How do we interpret these distributions? They simply summarise the probabilistic impact upon the behaviour of investors and borrowers of those five 'macro-risks' quantified on the left-hand side of Exhibit 1.5. Obviously, very considerable effort is required to pass from the 'key event' uncertainties on the left to the 'future market behaviour' probabilities in the middle. But this is not the place to discuss this issue. One final and particularly interesting step in the analysis remains.

Premise 3: The need to interpret a 'forecast' as a set of 'contingent prices'   Exhibit 1.5 makes clear that any different number of future 'market equilibria' are possible. The actual outcome will depend upon which pair of schedules turn out to be the 'true' schedules. And this in turn will depend upon which state of the world obtains. We are thus led to Arrow's pioneering approach of replacing the notion of a future price with the more general concept of a set of 'contingent prices' – where any given price is explicitly contingent upon some underlying state of the world. How exactly does this work?

To explain matters, let us ask what the probability is of a future T-bill rate of 7.5% in May 1987. To compute this, simply note that this 'highest' yield occurs where the low supply schedule intersects the high demand schedule. The probability of this occurring is, roughly, the arithmetic product of the probabilities that each of these will be the 'true' schedule, namely $(0.25) \times (0.20) = 0.05$. Note that this is the number that appears as the probability of a 7.5% yield in the 'forecast histogram' of the far right-hand side of Exhibit 1.5. (Naturally, it is not necessary to assume that the supply and demand schedules are stochastically independent.) Proceeding in a similar way, the reader can flesh out both of the histograms in detail. He actually sees where the forecast comes from.

Thus we end up *solving* for a forecast of a very new kind: a set of price probabilities implicit in a probabilistic characterisation of the uncertain future state of the world *and* of the 'contingent' behaviour it induces. Should some single number summary be required, the mean or even the 'certain equivalent value' of the distribution can be determined with ease.

Exhibit 1.6   The fundamental strategic decision

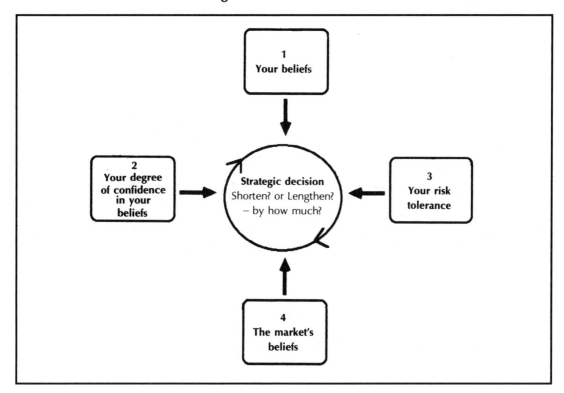

Yet, in general, such a summary will almost never coincide with the forecast generated by traditional models. Not only do the informational bases of the two approaches tend to differ significantly, but the Arrowian approach is significantly more general, in part because it is inherently non-linear. An instance of the latter observation is seen in the fact that a given family of demand (supply) schedules in Exhibit 1.5 do not constitute parallel lines. For more on these matters, see Brock (1987).

Conclusion: Relevance to decision-making

The ultimate appeal of the approach sketched above is its usefulness for real world decision-making under uncertainty. To see how true this is, consider the essence of today's investment management strategy problem, as shown in Exhibit 1.6. The generic strategy question confronting money managers is illustrated in the middle: 'Do I shorten or lengthen, and *by how much?*' (This question can refer to anything from asset allocation to hedging/swapping decisions.) What kind of information is required rationally to make this decision? The answer is shown by the four boxes.

First The investor must specify which market outcome he believes to be most likely? (See box 1.) In terms of Exhibit 1.5 the answer to this question is given by the mean (or mode, etc.) of the histogram on the far right.

Second He must determine how much confidence to place in this forecast, e.g. the degree of risk involved. (See box 2.) This information is given by the full interest rate probability distribution of Exhibit 1.5. (We are implicitly defining risk here in the modern Bayesian sense of 'degree of confidence'. Traditional measures of risk can be shown to be special cases of this one.)

Third He must assess his risk tolerance, that is, his willingness to take a specific risk – once risk has been properly assessed. (See box 3.) It is worth recalling that the concept of 'risk tolerance' is logically distinct from that of 'risk' proper, notwithstanding that one's risk tolerance this year usually depends upon the outcome of the risks one took last year!

Fourth He *may* wish to compare his own views and sense of risk with the market's, to the extent that the latter is measurable. (See box 4.) In many contexts, an optimal strategy will be defined in terms of a deviation from some market index value, or whatever. This is particularly true in an environment where what matters is not whether interest rates (or IBM's earnings) rise or fall, but whether they rise more or less than the market has anticipated. For these latter expectations will be reflected in the price structure at the time a strategy is adopted.

Solution to the problem Technically speaking, the solution to the above strategy problem will be a portfolio duration (or some such measure) that maximises the investor's expected utility in the context we have just sketched.

The present essay will have succeeded in its intentions if it has (1) deepened the reader's understanding of today's determinants of interest rate movements, and (2) sketched a way of integrating such considerations into a coherent interest rate forecast that is truly useful for strategising under conditions of uncertainty.

References

Arrow, K.J. (1964). The role of securities in the optimal allocation of risk-bearing. *Review of Economic Studies*.
Brock, H.W. (1987). Arrow–Bayes equilibria: A new theory of price forecasting. In G. Feiwel (Ed.). *Arrow and the ascent of modern economic theory*. London: Macmillan.

CRED–INTEL (1986). *Interest rate forecast and risk assessment – November 1986*. Strategic Economic Decisions, Menlo Park, California.

Hirshleifer, J. and J.G. Riley (1980). The analytics of uncertainty and information – An expository survey. *Journal of Economic Literature*.

Mascaro, A. and A.H. Meltzer (1983). Long- and short-term interest rates in a risky world. *Journal of Monetary Economics*.

2 Markets and techniques*

Boris Antl

Introduction

The heightened volatility of interest rates, deregulation of financial institutions and the lack of traditional sources of fixed rate funds have made the management of rate risk a growing challenge. Since 1977, a series of financial innovations has been introduced which enable borrowers, issuers and investors to control the risk of interest rate volatility. The growing volume of floating rate debt issuance and the unprecedented volatility of interest rates since 1979 has led to explosive growth in the use of hedging mechanisms to either fix or cap floating interest rates.

A borrower is concerned about the all-in cost of his borrowings and borrowing at the lowest cost is his primary objective. Nevertheless, issues of liquidity, counterparty diversification and availability are also factors the treasurer must consider. An incredibly low borrowing rate might not be enough to justify the disruption of existing relationships and the risk of lack of availability of funds at a later date. Most treasurers have multiple borrowing alternatives from which to choose. Because the purpose of this book is to explore interest rate hedging alternatives this chapter will not address the fund raising decisions that must be made including type of borrowing, currency, etc. Instead, the hedging alternatives applicable to assets and liabilities denominated in US dollars and other major currencies will be discussed.

Floating and fixed rate

The liability manager's dilemma is whether to fix the rate of interest on borrowings or to allow interest rates to float with prevailing market conditions. If a treasurer determines that floating rate exposure best meets his needs either because his forecast for interest rates convinces him that his overall cost of borrowing will be less on a floating rate basis or because he has floating rate assets, the cost of his borrowing will be unknown. He will benefit fully from any drop in interest rates and will be charged on a dollar-for-dollar basis for any increase in interest rates. If the treasurer decides to fix the interest cost, it is known with certainty what the interest expense will be. If rates go up, the interest expense will not be affected, but neither will the benefits of a lower rate environment be enjoyed.

Between the extremes of fixing the interest rate on a debt and allowing the interest rate to float, there are many techniques that are available. When interest rates are fixed, the borrower pays a 'term premium' and removes all interest rate risk and opportunity. When, on the other hand, a borrower chooses to allow the interest on his debt to float with the market, he has the advantage of not paying a term premium but is totally subject to the direction of interest rates. If rates go up sharply, so does the interest expense; if rates go down, the borrower reaps the full benefit.

---

*This chapter was prepared with significant contributions by Leslie Lynn of Citicorp Investment Bank, New York, as well as Richard Hutchison, Cory Strupp, R.D. Bown and Ian Cooper, who have contributed in other parts of this book.

Techniques

There are a variety of exchange traded and over the counter techniques that can be utilised to either alter the interest rate basis of a borrowing or to retain the advantages of floating rates while mitigating some of the associated risks:

- Borrow either in the public or private markets on a floating rate basis and use an interest rate swap to convert the floating rate debt to fixed rate debt.
- Borrow on a floating rate basis and use forward rate agreements (FRAs) to convert the floating rate debt to fixed rate debt.
- Hedge the interest rate exposure in the financial futures market.
- Hedge the interest rate exposure by an interest rate option.
- Limit the floating rate of interest by an interest rate cap or collar.

Once a borrower has decided that it would be beneficial to hedge the interest rate risk, the technique selected will depend on the borrower's access to alternatives based on his credit rating, the tenor of the debt and the relative pricing of the available techniques. Just as a discussion of the fund raising alternatives is outside the scope of this book, a detailed discussion of the credit considerations for each alternative method of fixing is also not included. Rather, we focus on the mechanics, market conditions, and the practicality of each of the techniques outlined above. We then conclude with a analytical framework that may be used for a comparative analysis of multiple hedging alternatives.

Interest rate swaps

An interest rate swap is a transaction in which two parties agree to make periodic payments to each

Exhibit 2.1   Interest rate swap

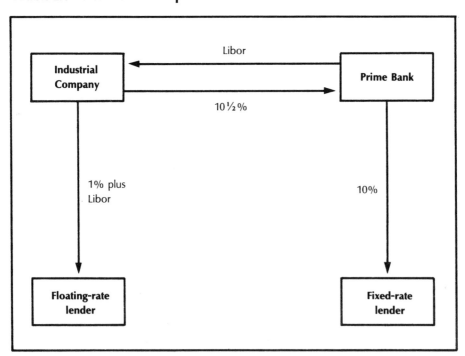

other, calculated on the basis of specified interest rates and a specified principal (or nominal) amount. Typically, the payment to be made by one party is calculated using a floating rate of interest (e.g. Libor, prime, commercial paper), whereas the payment to be made by the other party is determined on the basis of a fixed rate of interest or a different floating basis. The structure of a simple interest rate swap is presented graphically in Exhibit 2.1.

An interest rate swap can be used to transform one type of asset or interest obligation into another and thereby enable a swap participant to tailor its assets and interest obligations to meet its needs in a given rate environment, to reduce its cost of borrowing, or to hedge against future changes in rates.

The interest rate swap market had its inception in 1981. Initially, swaps were viewed as one-off transactions, but that perception was quickly dispelled as their widespread usefulness became apparent and their popularity spread. By the end of 1987, the notional principal amount of interest and currency swaps outstanding was believed by knowledgeable observers to be in excess of US$600bn.

Participants in the swap market are many and varied: any substantial borrower or investor is a potential swap participant. Commercial banks and investment banking firms often act as intermediaries, bringing together counterparties with complementary needs, frequently in complex chains of matching transactions. Commercial banks also enter into swaps as end users, to cover their own funding needs and to establish fixed returns on floating rate investments. Together, acting as intermediaries and end users, commercial banks and investment banking firms constitute the primary swap market.

In addition to the primary swap market, a secondary swap market has also begun to develop. In this market, existing swap positions are traded. For example, an intermediary which is unable to match a particular swap may go into the market and purchase a matching swap from another intermediary. Another method by which swaps may be traded is through assignment, whereby one party assigns a swap (or portfolio of swaps) to another party. Although this market is growing, its development has been impeded by several factors, as discussed in Part IV.

Interest rate swaps have been readily adopted in the corporate world, enabling corporate borrowers to fix floating rate debt (or flat fixed rate debt) for 2 to 10 years. It is estimated that more than 40% of large companies have now used swaps.

Interest rate futures

A futures contract is a form of forward contract in that it conveys that right to purchase or sell a specified quantity of an asset at a fixed price on a fixed future date. Although financial futures are a relatively recent development, the concept of futures markets is well developed, with commodity futures markets having been in existence since the early 19th century.

In the 1950s and 1960s, international and national monetary policies provided insurance against financial risk, in part through fixed exchange rate systems and through interest rate targeting. In recent years, however, there has been a general breakdown in government supplied economic stability. This has resulted in corporations with a sense of survival searching out ways of transferring this new-found financial risk to other parties.

In response to this demand, the International Monetary Market at the Chicago Mercantile Exchange introduced financial futures in 1972. Since their initial introduction financial futures have developed rapidly with increases in both the volume traded and the instruments available. The London International Financial Futures Exchange (LIFFE), which opened in September 1982, now trades in a wide variety of financial futures contracts including gilts, Japanese government bonds, US Treasury bonds, etc. Today, there are financial futures exchanges in most major financial centres around the world.

For hedgers of interest rate risk, the use of financial futures substitutes basis risk for interest rate risk. The actual borrowing costs will not be known with certainty, unless the underlying borrowing resets on the exact quarterly cycle of the corresponding futures and the debt is tied to the same index as the futures, i.e. 3-month Treasury bills, certificates of deposit or Libor.

Although much discussed, it is estimated that interest rate futures have been used by less than one in five companies, probably because of the time, attention and experience required to structure and monitor effective hedges. Use by professional traders, however, has made the financial futures market highly successful.

Part III discusses interest rate futures in greater detail.

Forward rate agreements

Essentially, a forward rate agreement (FRA) is a futures contract without the troublesome elements which have hampered the growth of the futures market as a corporate hedging market. In its interbank form an FRA is a contract between two banks for a stated sum of principal at a stated price of interest for a stated period. Unlike financial futures which have fixed settlement dates, the FRA can be dealt from any date in the future until any other date. Although the most commonly dealt periods are those which start one, two, three or six months from the current spot value date, in fact virtually any dealing period is now readily available.

Forward rate agreements have existed in one form or another for about five years. It was only in 1984, however, that a fully fledged interbank market began to develop and its subsequent growth has been impressive. It is estimated that the daily turnover in London alone has now reached over US$5bn equivalent. In addition, prices are available, admittedly on an *ad hoc* basis, in virtually every currency for which there is an active Euromarket. There has also been a considerable improvement in the periods which can be dealt in, extending easily for up to 24 months.

The FRA market has made it possible for interest rate protection to be taken out on a forward basis which is more adequately tailored to the customers' requirements, more competitively priced, and also more easily defined on a basis which can be understood, than has hitherto been available through either the futures or cash forward/forward market.

A more detailed discussion of the FRA and related topics is presented in Part VI.

Interest rate options

Interest rate options are short-term options on short-term interest rates. They are one part of the debt option market. This market also includes medium-term options on short-term interest rates (caps, floors and collars), short-term options on bonds (bond options), and medium-term options on bonds (bond warrants).

As with other option markets, the market for interest rate options offers exchange-traded contracts and over the counter (OTC) contracts. The difference between the two markets is the usual one that exchange-traded contracts tend to be more liquid but offer a restricted range of contracts. OTC markets offer tailor-made transactions, but often with lower liquidity or higher cost.

The first breakthrough in exchange traded options came with the start of trading in individual stock options in the United States in 1973, followed by other major financial centres shortly thereafter. Since the original success of the individual stock options, however, the emphasis has shifted to options based on more complex financial instruments, with one of the greatest single successes being the Treasury bond futures option traded on the Chicago Board of Trade. Other new products include Treasury bill options and Eurodollar options.

The range of options contracts on financial instruments currently traded is wide, and there is no sign of an end to the proliferation. The highly successful Chicago Exchanges are expected to increase their range of option products over the next few years, and the exchanges in London, Sydney, Toronto, Hong Kong, Singapore and Tokyo are developing their own financial options trading. The commercial and investment banks with their OTC products are unlikely to lag far behind in involvement and innovation.

The holder of a call option benefits if interest rate falls and index price rises. The holder of a put option benefits if interest rate rises and index price falls. Borrowers wishing to hedge future borrowing rates are, therefore, natural holders of put options. For the borrower, the option hedge locks in a maximum borrowing cost at a level higher than the futures hedge; as a consequence, the option holder is able to keep the potential gain resulting from a fall in rates. On the other hand, lenders wishing to lock in a floor on future lending rates are natural holders of the call option.

The price of an option reflects a particular forecast of the future volatility of rates. Standard interest rate option models enable the user to price options using their own volatility forecast or to impute market expectations of volatility from option prices. Actual volatilities and market implied volatilities fluctuate considerably over time, offering possibilities for speculation by those with strongly held views on future interest rate volatility.

For additional material on interest rate options see Part V.

Interest rate caps

An interest rate cap is an agreement between the 'seller' or provider of the cap and a borrower to limit his floating interest rate to a specified level for a period of time. The borrower selects a reference rate to hedge (e.g. Libor, commercial paper), a period of time to hedge (e.g. 2 – 5 years) and the level of protection desired (e.g. 10%, 11.5%, 12.75%). The seller or provider of the cap, for a fee, assures the buyer that its reference rate will not exceed the specified ceiling rate during the terms of the agreement. If market rates exceed the ceiling rate, the cap provider will make payments to the buyer sufficient to bring its rate back to the ceiling. When market rates are below the ceiling, no payments are made and the borrower pays market rates. The buyer of the cap therefore enjoys a fixed rate when market rates are above the cap and floating rates when market rates are below the cap.

Interest rate caps are available in a number of currencies and for a variety of interest rates. The largest market is US dollar denominated, against 3- and 6-month Libor, prime, commercial paper or Treasury bills. There is also considerable business in Deutschmark and sterling based agreements, and the market for yen is expected to grow rapidly. Occasional trades have been reported in Swiss francs, Australian dollars, Canadian dollars, ECUs and Dutch guilders. The market is global and transaction sizes range from US$5m to US$100m equivalent.

Caps provide protection against rising interest rates without fixing rates. With its hedge in place, the buyer continues to borrow at the short-term end of the yield curve. When the yield curve is upward sloping, borrowing short-term results in considerable cost savings compared to fixed rate alternatives, such as interest rate swaps.

To determine whether the cap is economically attractive, the borrower must forecast its all-in cost of financing with the cap in place and compare the results with other alternatives. This is easy to do by calculating costs on a discounted cashflow (DCF) basis under various sets of interest rate assumptions. As cap agreements are generally paid for in a lump sum up-front, these fees must be taken into account when evaluating and quantifying costs of caps. These fees may appear large initially; for a 5-year cap on 3-month Libor, for example, they may amount to anywhere between 2 and 6%, depending where the ceiling is set.

Exhibit 2.2 is an example of an analysis of a 5-year financing, using the DCF method. The example assumes a bullet maturity financing with the front-end fee treated as an up-front discount, impacting the all-in cost of the borrowing. All figures used in this and the following examples, including the forecasts, were invented for illustrative purposes only.

Refering to Exhibit 2.2, a fairly tight cap protected the borrower from a spike in rates in the later years of the financing. Its all-in borrowing cost over the term of the financing was nearly one percentage point lower than if no protection had been bought; the cashflow benefits in years 3 to 5 are apparent.

Interest rate caps are further discussed in Part VII.

Exhibit 2.2 Interest rate caps: 3-month Libor ceiling at 10% for 5 years

Period	0	1	2	3	4	5	IRR
Fee	5.3%						
Forecasted Libor (%)		8.5	10.0	13.0	16.0	14.0	12.3
Ceiling rate (%)		10.0	10.0	10.0	10.0	10.0	
Refund to borrower (%)		–	–	(3.0)	(6.0)	(4.0)	
Borrowing cost hedged (%)		8.5	10.0	10.0	10.0	10.0	9.70
Effective cost of fees p.a. (%)		1.37	1.37	1.37	1.35	1.37	1.37
All-in borrowing cost (%)		9.87	11.37	11.37	11.37	11.37	11.37

Interest rate collars

An interest rate collar is a variation of the cap agreement. Here, the 'seller' or provider of the collar agrees to limit the borrower's floating interest rate to a band limited by a specified ceiling rate and floor rate. The borrower selects a reference rate to hedge (e.g. Libor), a period of time to hedge (e.g. 3 years, 7 years), and the level of protection desired (e.g. 8.25% to 10.25%, 8% to 11%). The seller of the collar, for a fee, assures the borrower that its reference rate will not exceed the specified ceiling rate nor be less than the specified floor rate during the term of the agreement. If market rates exceed the ceiling rate, the collar provider will make payments to the buyer sufficient to bring its rate back to the ceiling. If, on the other hand, market rates fall below the floor, the borrower makes payments to the collar seller to bring its rate back to the floor. When market rates are between the floor and the ceiling, the borrower pays the market rates. The buyer of a collar, therefore, has its borrowing confined to a band or collar, ranging from the floor to the ceiling.

Collars are generally priced so that the all-in cost per annum of borrowing at the ceiling rate will be somewhat more than the fixed rate alternative, whereas the all-in cost at the floor will be considerably less than the fixed rate alternatives. The relative risks and benefits of a collar are illustrated in Exhibit 2.3.

As we can see, the borrower selected a collar with a floor at the then current 7.63% level and a ceiling 250 basis point above it, i.e. 10.13%. We assume that this cap rate level is in accord with the objectives and risk perception of the borrower. Given this scenario, the borrower is likely to achieve

Exhibit 2.3 Interest rate collars (floor–ceiling agreements)

				At floor	At ceiling
Index	=	3-month Libor			
Term	=	5 years	Libor (%)	7.63	10.13
Floor	=	7.63%			
			Effective cost of fees p.a. (%)	0.66	0.66
Ceiling	=	10.13%	All-in cost (IRR) (%)	8.29	10.79
Fee	=	2.60%	Swap cost (%)	10.20	10.20
Cost of interest					
rate swap p.a. (%)	=	10.20%	Difference (%)	(1.91)	0.59

substantial savings compared to fixing rates via an interest rate swap. Only if interest rates run up quickly is he likely to incur an opportunity cost, in this example amounting to a maximum of about $\frac{5}{8}$% per annum equivalent.

For a further discussion of interest rate caps, please see Part VII.

Conclusions

The floating rate borrower or issuer has a number of hedging alternatives available. Each has advantages and disadvantages, and frequently they are not directly comparable. Given this decision-making environment, coupled with imperfect information flow, the treasurer must protect the company against unnecessary risks.

One way to get a fix on this is to compare the per annum all-in cost of borrowing under various hedges at various rate levels at a point in time. Exhibit 2.4 compares the costs of four hedging alternatives on a 5-year, 6-month Libor based obligation. All-in cost calculations do not include the borrowers credit spread, which would be the same in all cases. Front-end fees are converted to per annum equivalents using a discount rate of 11%, and we assume 6-month Libor at 8.81%.

The alternatives are:

- No hedge.
- Interest rate swap (11.68% fixed semi-annually versus 6-month Libor).
- Cap agreement (cap at 11.31%; front-end fee of 5.1%).
- Collar agreement (cap at 11.31%; floor at 8.81%; front-end fee of 3.2%).

The results are presented in Exhibit 2.4 below.

Exhibit 2.4   All-in borrowing cost per annum

| | Market rate: 6-month Libor (%) | | | | | |
	6	8	10	12	14	20
No hedge (%)	6.00	8.00	10.00	12.00	14.00	20.00
Interest rate swap (%)	11.68	11.68	11.68	11.68	11.68	11.68
Ceiling rate agreement						
Market rate (%)	6.00	8.00	10.00	12.00	14.00	20.00
Ceiling rate refund (%)	–	–	–	(0.69)	(2.69)	(8.69)
Fee amortisation (%)	1.37	1.37	1.37	1.37	1.37	1.37
Total (%)	7.37	9.37	11.37	12.68	12.68	12.68
Floor–Ceiling rate agreement						
Market rate (%)	6.00	8.00	10.00	12.00	14.00	20.00
Ceiling rate refund (%)	–	–	–	(0.69)	(2.69)	(8.69)
Floor rate payment (%)	2.81	0.81	–	–	–	–
Fee amortisation (%)	0.87	0.87	0.87	0.87	0.87	0.87
Total (%)	9.68	9.68	10.87	12.18	12.18	12.18

Exhibit 2.4 presents a summary of the results of the four selected hedging alternatives at various levels. What is apparent in this analysis is that there is no single answer for all rate levels. For example, at the 6% Libor level the 'no hedge' strategy is the most economical; at the 12% level or above, fixing the rates via an interest rate swap is the cheapest. The results under the cap or under the collar are

rather ambiguous. Indeed, to obtain more meaningful data for making a sound hedging decision, this framework should be further refined by making various interest rate forecasts for the entire period, as in the example used in connection with Exhibit 2.2 above, and then comparing the individual strategies, given each specific forecast. Decisions should then be made given the borrower's objectives and attitude towards risk.

Other methodologies and frameworks for making the hedging decision are discussed extensively in other parts of this book.

3 Forecasting interest rates

W.P. Ridley

Introduction

I sometimes think it is appropriate to paraphrase Mark Twain on giving up smoking: 'Forecasting interest rates is easy: I produce a new forecast every day.' The reason that interest rate projections have to be considered each day is because markets adjust daily to give the forward view of rates of money market managers as a whole.

Exhibits 3.1 and 3.2 show the yield curves for short and long rates in the UK and US at end-September 1987. Three points should be considered.

Exhibit 3.1   US and UK yield curves, September 1987

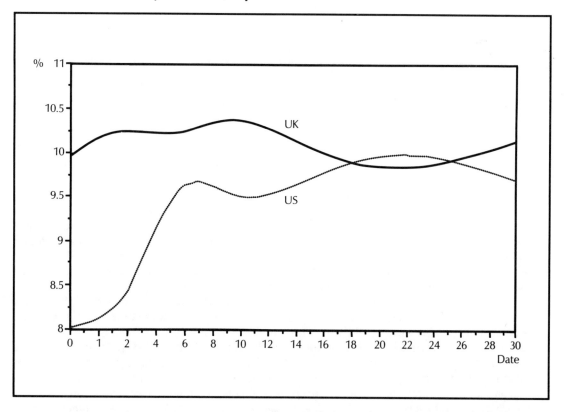

1   The short and long rates are shown separately because there are clear distinctions between the two. Typically, in the first market, the banks and discount houses are the dominant players with the central bank a major participant in either direction; in the second, the central bank is normally

Exhibit 3.2 FT 5- and 25-year high coupon yields (UK gilts), end-September 1987

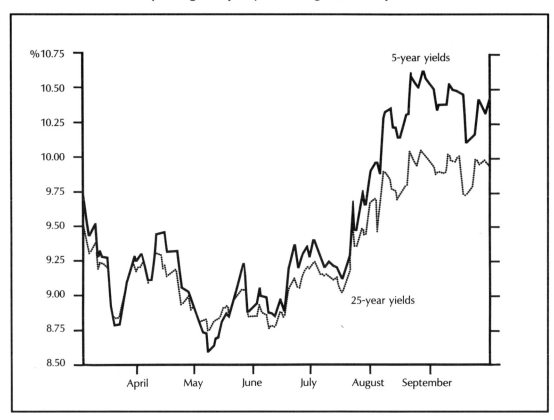

a seller of debt as government deficits have to be funded while the purchases are those with longer liabilities as insurance and pension funds. Commercial banks are likely to be small players and to concentrate on short bonds.

2   The yield curve may be upward sloping, but not necessarily so. It is sometimes thought that longer dated instruments should give higher yields than shorter dated instruments because they are less liquid and more volatile. In practice, most market instruments are highly liquid regardless of their maturity, with 30-year bonds saleable at a moment's notice and payment being made in two days or so. Volatility – long bonds are clearly more volatile than money market instruments; a 1% change in yield can lead to a variation of over 10% in the price of a bond but only a $\frac{1}{4}$% variation in the price of a three-month instrument. However, this makes bonds attractive if rates are falling – or thought to be falling – so it does not mean that investors necessarily get higher yields by buying longer bonds.

3   International comparisons need to be treated with caution. At the end-September 1987, short rates in the US were much lower than the UK. This could perhaps be explained by the more rapid growth in money supply in the UK even if the dollar was clearly the weaker currency. In the long term, however, the supply of government bonds, running at over US$150bn a year for the US and US$3bn a year in the UK, might have been expected to lead to much higher yields in the US than in the UK, particularly as domestic savings in the US were so much lower than the UK and the inflation prospects were similar. International flows, in this case purchases by Japanese institutions, held down US yields.

Bearing these factors in mind, it is worth reviewing the interest rate forecasts implicit in these yield curves. In the UK, the market was looking for minimal changes in rates. A one-year instrument was yielding only 0.2% more than a three-month instrument; and a 30-year bond much the same as a five-year bond. In the US, the market was expecting higher rates and by measuring the difference between, say, three-month, six-month and one-year yields, it was possible to calculate not only the extent of the expected movement in rates but also the timing. These market forecasts are not academic projections; they are backed by very large funds that swing between the various maturities and between fixed and floating rate instruments and therefore provide the base for any forecast.

Using this base, the forecaster can draw up his own forecasts. Interest rate projections begin by reviewing a range of possible outcomes, attaching probabilities to them and drawing up a probability curve which will provide the most likely outcome. Then by taking one standard deviation on the best estimate, one can draw up a projected band of interest rates. This provides both the range of likely outcomes (within which the eventual rate should fall two-thirds of the time) and indicates the scale of risk in the best estimate. This can be displayed as shown in the diagram where (1) represents the best estimate and (2–3) the band covered by the range of likely outcomes. From this band it is possible to measure the degree of risk in the forecast.

Projection of interest rates

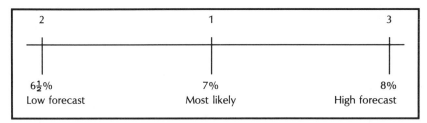

It must be stressed that this measure of risk is a statistical one, not a business one. Business risk takes account of the impact on profitability of errors in projections. As soon as assets and liabilities are not matched, e.g. in terms of maturity of money borrowed and money lent, a business risk is being taken. It is then necessary to take account, not only of the likely outcomes, but also the consequence of an outcome with a serious impact on profitability even if it is accorded only a small probability. A recent example of a trader in the Japanese bond futures market provides a chilling reminder of this risk. Bond yields in Japan rose from $2\frac{1}{2}$% to $6\frac{1}{4}$% within six months – a most improbable occurrence. The losses incurred were larger than the equity base of the trader's employer – a chemical company. He was reported as saying, 'it was not the policy that was wrong, it was just a question of timing'. The trader does not start from a calculation of the maximum amount the company should put at risk. For the businessman, it is of overriding concern.

With this proviso, the guides to interest rate projections are discussed under two headings: the objectives of the authorities and monetary analysis.

Objectives of the authorities

- A satisfactory rate of economic growth, taking account of the long-term potential and short-term unused capacity.
- An exchange rate target, whether set by international undertakings or by national interest.
- Holding down the level of inflation, both in the short and long term.
- Control of the growth of monetary aggregates.

When these objectives produce contradictory pressures, it is necessary to judge which objective has priority.

The way money markets switch their attention from one aggregate to another invites much criticism: one moment they are concerned with the balance of payments figures; the next the money supply figures, even including weekly figures that are known to be erratic. However, this is not irrational provided these figures are a determinant of monetary policy. Those who are forecasting interest rates may or may not believe in the importance of these indicators; but they are concerned with the reaction of central banks. If central banks pay more attention to the growth in monetary aggregates than the exchange rate – as in the UK in 1979-80 and the US in 1982-83 – then that has to be the forecaster's focus of attention.

It is therefore easy to claim that forecasts tend to be merely judgemental rather than supported by economic fundamentals. In part, this is true but there are two important elements to remember. The broad parameters of official policy are likely to be known and it should be possible to allow for the factors that will influence official action. Some examples are given in Exhibit 3.3.

Exhibit 3.3 Guidelines to official policy

UK: Medium-term financial strategy
Steady reduction in growth of M3/£M3 planned in 1979 – hiatus in 1981 lost favour in 1985; moves to abandon the objective in 1986. Little use as an indicator of interest rates after 1981.

France: Coordinate economic policy with Germany
Following the short-lived burst of economic growth in 1982, price controls, pressure on wage increases and exchange controls were introduced. High interest rates were reduced as policy was effective.

  The long awaited re-alignment of the French franc within the European Monetary System following the elections in 1986 allowed interest rates to fall further.

US: Targetted monetary growth
The arrival of Volcker at the Federal Reserve led to greater commitment to targets for growth in M1 (and to a lesser extent, M2 and M3). By 1985, the pressure on the banks, savings and loans institutions, and the Lesser Developed Countries (whose borrowing was largely in US dollars with interest rates related to those of the US), led to a relaxed commitment to targets. Greater concern was paid to the pace of growth in the US economy which, post-1984, remained sluggish.

Central Banks: Coordinated approach to exchange rates and interest rates
In September 1985, there was a coordinated move to lower the dollar and the whole structure of interest rates worldwide. Aided by the collapse of the oil price, this move held together until spring 1986. It was quickly resuscitated in October 1986 but by mid-1987, central banks switched to independent action until the fall in the dollar in October 1987 made them switch their priorities back to cooperation on interest rates. This was a good indicator that US interest rates would fall regardless of the weakness in currency in 1986-87.

The broad direction of interest rates is therefore only understood by having regard to official policy even if official policy not only changes over time but can be sharply reversed. Yet these reversals are often predictable. For instance, as long as officials think that:

- monetary growth reflects in advance the nominal growth in the economy,
- or that exchange rates indicate the tightness or laxity of economic policy,
- or an internationally coordinated policy can be implemented to rectify imbalances.

One should expect a switch of emphasis as the limitations of these approaches become more evident. For instance, the widespread adoption of monetary targets reflected a political belief that growth in money governed the growth in demand for goods and services. To many observers, this was a simplistic approach which would be reversed. The following is a quote from the 1959 Radcliffe Report.

Though we do not regard the supply of money as an unimportant quantity, we view it as only part of the wider structure of liquidity in the economy. We cannot find any reason for supposing or any experience in monetary history indicating, that there is any limit to the velocity of circulation; it is a statistical concept that tells us nothing directly of the motivation that influences the level of total demand. An analysis of liquidity, on the other hand, directs attention to the behaviour and decisions that do directly influence the level of total demand.

These words ring with fuller force after the experiments with monetary targets. The key to forecasting interest rates in recent years has been the ability to analyse liquidity and its impact on demand. Growth worldwide between 1984–87 has been low despite loose monetary policies. To forecast a continued downturn in interest rates, it has been necessary to predict that the looser monetary policy would not of itself revive demand. The key to such a prediction has been the strains on liquidity in the US evident in three key respects:

1 The personal sector was heavily indebted by the end of 1984. The sector was therefore insufficiently liquid to respond to monetary stimulus or lower interest rates by increasing purchases, e.g. for cars on credit (whereas if, as normally happens, a looser monetary policy follows a period of retrenchment, the personal sector would have started the period with a higher level of savings).
2 The corporate sector was affected by the high dollar which led to subdued profits and spare capacity. This discouraged investment despite the fall in interest rates.
3 The banking sector and savings and loans industry remained under heavy pressure with certain organisations having what is politely called 'negative net worth'. It was important therefore to restore margins and liquidity rather than encourage growth in long-term lending.

Even against that background, the successive cuts in the discount rate through 1985 and 1986 could only have been safely predicted when it was clear that the US administration and the Federal Reserve were prepared to countenance – and indeed encourage – devaluation of the dollar (in marked contrast to the UK, which tried to prop up sterling after each devaluation by a rise in interest rates).

This highlights the importance of official policy. Where monetary control or exchange rate stability is the prime objective, forecasters have a ready touchstone for their projections. In the early days of monetarism moreover, some governments believed that growth in the economy and movements in the exchange rates flowed from changes in the money supply aggregates. As this naive belief has died, governments – and forecasters – have had to pay more attention to monetary analysis.

Monetary analysis

Together with official policy, the forecaster has to take account of key monetary indicators. These include:

- Real interest rates.
- The overall level of savings.
- The sectoral balances within the economy.

Real interest rates

One measure of the tightness of interest rates is the difference between nominal interest rates and inflation. A rule of thumb is that real rates of 3 points or above are high and will therefore be restricting growth; real interest rates of 1 point or below will be aiding growth.

Exhibit 3.4   Real rates of return, end-1986

Country	3 months interest rate	Long Bond yields	Inflation Current (a)	Inflation Underlying (b)	Real rates based on (a)	Real rates based on (b)
UK	11	$10\frac{1}{2}$	3	$4\frac{1}{2}$	$7\frac{1}{2}$–8	6–$6\frac{1}{2}$
Germany	$4\frac{1}{2}$	6	0	2	$4\frac{1}{2}$–6	$2\frac{1}{2}$–4
Japan	3	5	0	2	3–5	1–3
US	5	$7\frac{1}{2}$	2	4	3–$5\frac{1}{2}$	1–$3\frac{1}{2}$

Exhibit 3.4 highlights the problems with the calculation of real rates. What figure for inflation should we use? The latest figure, whether a deflator used for the whole economy, or, more commonly, a consumer index measurement, is of no direct relevance; it is the impact of the cost of borrowing on the prospective growth of the economy that is material, not the historic cost. The underlying inflation is therefore normally the measurement that is relevant; and although there is no way of identifying that figure precisely, there is often a broad consensus – led by government forecasts – on the scale of inflationary pressures in an economy.

The next question is which interest rate should one be examining. Long rates are likely to be set by market forces as the government is normally the seller of bonds whereas short rates are usually determined in large measure by the central bank. Both need to be considered.

Exhibit 3.4, which broadly represents the position at the end of 1986, has some intriguing features:

- The 3% rule of thumb figure for real rates based on underlying inflation appears to have some significance for Germany, Japan and the US. Japan has clearly the lowest rate but this reflects the highest level of savings. After Japan, the US shows the lowest figures (rather surprisingly given its debt position). The German real rates reflect considerable caution by the Bundesbank as far as short rates are concerned; the long rates indicate the concern of German domestic financial institutions who are more concerned with protecting capital than investing in volatile bonds (let alone equities).
- By contrast, real rates in the UK are extraordinarily high, particularly at the short end of the spectrum. The support required for sterling is a part explanation but, as we shall see later, it is not entirely satisfactory. In the short term an apparent real rate some 3 points higher than the norm may not compensate for a 3–5% fall in currency; but a long bond that is offering real rates 3 points above the average offers a long-term protection against devaluation – particularly if the underlying rate of inflation is taken into account in the calculation. In the case of the UK, the $4\frac{1}{2}$% inflation figure shown in Exhibit 3.4 already allows for some $2\frac{1}{2}$ points excess inflation compared with Japan and Germany.
- The spread of rates on short- to long-term instruments varied between $1\frac{1}{2}$–$2\frac{1}{2}$ points in the case of Germany, Japan and the US, but in the case of the UK, was only half a point. We will return to this point below.

The broad conclusion from an examination of real rates is that at the end of 1986, UK rates – and to a lesser extent, German rates – were out of line and were set to fall whereas US rates were set to rise. But these rates must be seen in the context of domestic saving.

Overall level of savings

The overall level of saving in an economy is easily identified. The current account of the balance of payments represents the converse of domestic savings. If the outcome of the public, corporate and personal sectors taken together is in surplus, the current account will show an equivalent surplus. An estimate of domestic savings (or the current account outcome) of the same four economies is shown in Exhibit 3.5.

Exhibit 3.5 Estimated domestic savings (or current account outcome 1986, 1987 in US$bn)

Country	1986	1987
UK	$(1\frac{1}{2})$	$(2\frac{1}{2}\text{--}5)$
Germany	38	40–45
Japan	86	80–90
US	(141)	(150–160)

The extraordinary excess of US borrowing is evident; the Federal Reserve deficit of some US$150–200bn swamps the modest level of savings in the personal and corporate sectors leading to an overall excess of spending over income of over US$140bn per year. The level of borrowing flowing from such a pattern of expenditure is likely to hold up the level of rates. German and Japanese rates by contrast could be expected to be below normal given their excess of savings. The UK falls between the two extremes with expenditure only marginally above income. High rates in the UK do not therefore derive from the overall level of saving and borrowing in the economy.

Sectoral balances

The overall level of saving or of borrowing within the economy does not therefore reflect the pressures within the economy. For that purpose it is necessary to go at least to a sectoral basis and, possibly, further, for example:

- A large government deficit in relation to long-term savings is likely to lead to high bond rates to attract investors.
- A corporate sector deficit can be funded either long or short but it often starts by being funded short and even longer funding may be related to movement in short rates.
- The personal sector outcome is perhaps the most complex; it represents the balance from long-term savings (such as pension fund and insurance flows), long-term borrowing (largely mortgage finance), short-term borrowing (bank loans, credit card debt and three to five year instalment finance) and short-term savings (banks, building societies, short-term government debt). It is therefore appropriate to dissect the personal sector outcome to identify the pressures on interest rates. Where housing finance is on a floating rate basis, as in the UK, it puts pressure on short rates. If there are insufficient personal sector deposits – with banks and building societies – to finance calls on short-term loans and floating rate mortgages, there will be upward pressure on short rates. An excess of long-term savings is likely to lead to lower yields on government debt and equities; but in the absence of exchange controls, the fall in yields will be restricted by the opportunities overseas.
- A current account deficit has to be matched by capital inflows – these may be long term (e.g. purchase of equities or bonds) or short term (e.g. bills, banking deposits).

It must be stressed, however, that it is not just new flows that need to be considered. Existing holders of financial assets are continuously adjusting their portfolios depending on their view of interest rates; and there are movements between fixed and floating rate debt aided by swaps between currencies. These flows can swamp new flows.

Conclusion

The approach outlined above allows for a forecast of interest rates and on the yield curve depending on government and monetary policy. Many can refine this structure; but it is more important, first to identify the major influences on the direction of rates, then to consider the short-term pressures. It is these short-term pressures that have to be continually re-examined. For instance, at the time of writing, the question is whether Central Banks outside the US will lower their interest rates and intervene to protect the dollar. If they do intervene, will they neutralise the excess liquidity by selling bonds and therefore hold back the bond market? If the dollar stabilises, will the central banks then revert to concern about money supply? It is like being at the North Pole – the ice cracks and the path changes every day.

4 Measurement of exposure

Brian Leach

Introduction

The past decade of structural changes in the finance world has increased the importance of managing interest rate exposure. Two of the most significant changes are greater interest rate volatility and the proliferation of complex financial products. Volatility subjects corporations to unacceptable swings in financing costs; complex products increase the difficulty of precisely measuring interest rate exposure. These two structural changes have forced corporations to institute comprehensive risk management programmes and become increasingly sophisticated about interest rate measurement techniques.

This chapter is intended as a 'road map' for risk managers. It should make managers more comfortable with measurement systems and, therefore, more effective in instituting policy. The chapter will address the first three of six critical steps necessary in establishing a risk management programme: defining interest rate exposure, measuring risk and building data systems. The remaining three steps are included in Exhibit 4.1 and are discussed in other chapters.

Exhibit 4.1 Establishing a risk management programme

```
1   Define interest rate exposure by setting objectives
2   Select interest rate risk measurement methodology
3   Build data systems
4   Review measurement results
5   Analyse possible actions
6   Take action
```

Defining interest rate exposure by setting objectives

There is no universal definition of exposure. What is highly speculative for one firm may be perceived as relatively risk free by another. Corporations must each arrive at their own definition. Once exposure is defined, its components can be measured and corrective actions can be evaluated and taken.

One very effective method of defining exposure is for senior management to set a series of risk objectives. Setting these objectives is a very difficult task. Each department involved in the discussions may have objectives that are unique to their own area of responsibility and are, therefore, inconsistent with other departmental objectives within the firm. For example, a credit department may be more concerned with the credit worthiness of a transaction than with profit potential. Not only will objectives differ among departments within the same firm but also among firms within the same industry. Some finance companies, for example, often have the objective of being interest rate neutral, i.e. the value of the firm's assets will equal the liabilities regardless of changes in interest rates. Alternatively, other finance companies aggressively seek out risk. These firms, although seeking substantially different risk objectives, need measurement systems to achieve the desired results.

There are a variety of primary, secondary and tertiary risk objectives (see Exhibit 4.2). The primary risk objective for every firm is to control an account designated as the main indicator of exposure. The type of account designated depends on the composition of the assets and liabilities of the corporation, how critical they are to the firm's profitability and to what extent they are exposed to interest rates. At one end of the spectrum is simply the measurement of net interest income, composed of interest income less interest expense. This is generally the most revealing exposure measurement for pure financial accounts. At the other end of the spectrum is the measurement of the firm's equity exposure, composed of the market value of assets less liabilities. Measuring the firm's equity exposure may require the risk manager to convert non-financial assets into financial assets – a potentially tedious and costly endeavour. There is nothing, of course, to preclude a firm from monitoring both accounts or a relevant subgrouping of these accounts. In general, an industrial concern is better served by focusing on net interest income since it has relatively few financial assets. Alternatively, a financial institution with predominantly financial assets and liabilities, would best be served by monitoring equity exposure in addition to other interest-sensitive accounts.

Secondary risk objectives may include credit exposure, basis risk and liquidity needs. Credit exposure should aggregate the firm's total credit exposure to any one individual, firm or industry. This exposure should measure the change in market value of each credit exposed account for a given change in credit quality. Basis risk is important to the risk manager that uses one instrument to offset the risk of another. Basis risk is present to the extent that changes in interest rates are not constant across all instruments. If a commercial paper exposure, for example, is hedged with Eurodollar futures, then there is basis risk. This exposure can be determined by measuring the change in market value of one instrument (e.g. commercial paper) for a given change in rates, assuming that there has been no change in the market value of the hedging instrument (e.g. Eurodollars). To monitor liquidity needs requires measuring the size of the potential mismatch between cash inflows and outflows over some specified time period. This type of determination will alert the risk manager to any imminent financing or investment needs.

A tertiary objective for a risk management programme is to study historical behaviour patterns. Monitoring these patterns will better prepare a corporation to make risk decisions. For example, a firm might study how fast loans, with no prepayment penalties, prepay given an increasingly favourable economic environment. Tracking this pace of prepayment leads to a better understanding of customers' behaviour patterns and substantially increases the effectiveness of a risk manager.

Exhibit 4.2   Risk objectives

Primary objective	**Secondary objectives**	**Tertiary objective**
– Main indicator of exposure	– Credit exposure	– Historical behaviour patterns
• net interest income	– Basis risk	
• net equity exposure	– Liquidity needs	

For every risk objective selected, a firm must determine the target accounts most critical for accomplishing the objective and the relevant measurement time period. The appropriate target accounts are unique for each firm, and the appropriate time period over which the objective should be accomplished is dependent upon the risk-taking attitude of the firm. Risk managers should set acceptable exposure boundaries and concomitant response times. The exposure boundaries may be absolute dollar amounts or percentage figures and may vary from quarter to quarter depending on the seasonality of the business involved. The response time should be dictated by the extent to which an exposure boundary is exceeded; the more it is exceeded, the faster the required response time (see Exhibit 4.3). As with most things in life, an exposure manager pays for speed of service. Waiting for an exposure to self-correct has a low initial cost but may take a long time, substantially increasing the firm's risk exposure during the self-correction period.

Exhibit 4.3   Response time

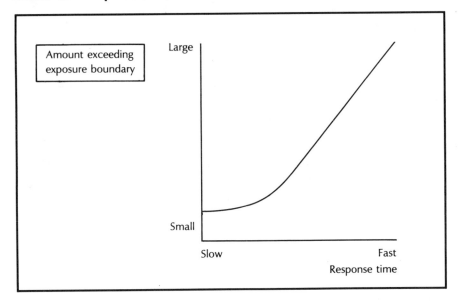

Selecting interest rate risk measurement methodology

A firm should select a measurement methodology which provides the data necessary to take actions that satisfy risk objectives. The three primary methods for measuring interest rate risk are gap analysis, duration analysis and simulation analysis. These methods are not mutually exclusive but do have distinct strengths and weaknesses. Gap analysis is best used to analyse liquidity needs; it can quickly tell a risk manager the par value of assets or liabilities that are maturing or repricing in a given time period. This information is invaluable in evaluating cash flow needs. Gap analysis is, however, a very limited interest rate exposure management tool, in that it cannot adequately account for the time value of money nor measure the exposure of option embedded securities. Duration analysis, on the other hand, is a very flexible tool which measures accurately a firm's interest rate exposure. It requires a little more quantitative skill to develop than some of the other management tools, but in return generates extremely useful information. Duration, however, is not a good cash management tool, because it provides only limited information about the timing of specific cash flows. Simulation is an excellent exposure forecasting tool, but is time consuming and is only as accurate as the accuracy of its assumptions. In addition, the time consuming nature of this method limits its usefulness as a day-to-day management tool. The next three subsections discuss these measurement methodologies in greater detail.

Gap analysis

Gap analysis, also referred to as gap management or cash matching, is frequently used by banks and it is one of the more established tools available to risk managers. The concept is to monitor the net difference in the total par value of assets less the total par value of liabilities repricing or maturing during a specified time period. For each time period, if the par value of assets exceeds the par value of liabilities, then a positive gap exists; if assets equal liabilities, then the period is gap neutral; if assets are less than liabilities, then a negative gap exists. By way of illustration, the firm shown in Exhibit 4.4 is gap neutral for the first three periods, has a positive gap in period four and a negative gap in period five. To be gap neutral in period four, assets should be sold or liabilities added that mature or reprice in this period. Similarly, in period five, the risk manager would add assets or sell liabilities to attain gap neutrality.

Exhibit 4.4   Gap analysis: Example 1

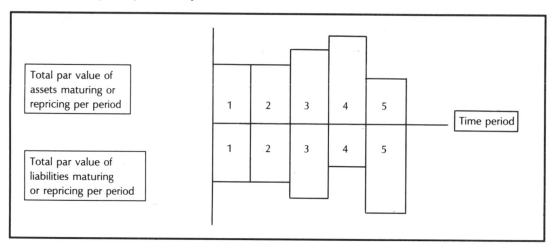

Gap analysis was originally designed to monitor cash flow needs and to identify interest rate exposure. It is fairly successful at the former and not entirely effective at the latter. Its effectiveness in monitoring cash flow needs is limited to the near term. This is due to the usual practice of using shorter gap periods in the near term and longer periods in the far term (see Exhibit 4.5).

Exhibit 4.5   Gap analysis: Example 2

Gap period	1	2	3	4	5	6	7	8
Time	0–30 dys	1–3 mos	3–6 mos	6–12 mos	1–2 yrs	2–5 yrs	5–10 yrs	10–30 yrs

This set of periodicities forces managers to focus on near term problems and can mask longer term problems with potentially serious consequences. These consequences are best illustrated by examining three cases (see Exhibit 4.6).

Exhibit 4.6   Gap analysis: Example 3

	Case A (maturity)	Case B (maturity)	Case C (maturity)
Assets of US$100m	2 years	3 years	2 years
Liabilities of US$100m	4 years	5 years	2 years + 1 day

All three cases in Exhibit 4.6 would be considered gap neutral for a gap period extending from two to five years (i.e. gap period 6 in Exhibit 4.5), and these positions have substantially different cash flow risks. Case A is the only situation in which gap analysis will, in one more day, identify a legitimate cash flow mismatch. This will occur because the assets will move forward to the 1–2 year gap period, while the liabilities remain within the 2–5 year gap. Case B, with a maturity mismatch of two years, will not be considered a gap problem until another year passes. Case C, which does not really have a maturity mismatch will, in one more day, move from gap neutral to a positive gap in period 5 and on to a negative gap in period 6 and then, in two days, will return to gap neutral. This is simply a situation where a one day timing mismatch, with generally no substantive consequences, has been highlighted by the gap methodology.

One way to improve gap analysis' ability to monitor cash flows is to subdivide each gap period into smaller and smaller periods. If this logic were extended to the absurd, the appropriate gap periods would each be one day, forcing the risk manager to perfectly match all cash inflows and outflows. A risk manager forced to match cash flows perfectly will jeopardise the competitive standing of the firm. Selling assets in a positive gap period or liabilities in a negative gap period to attain gap neutrality indicates a total disregard for relative value. The gap manager is reacting to par values not market values, and thus is making decisions based upon cash flow needs and not upon interest rate exposure. The risk manager, intent on filling gaps, loses flexibility in neutralising interest rate risk. Focusing on the maturity of assets or liabilities which the manager intends to buy or sell prevents the firm from participating in undervalued sectors of the market and may eliminate some very profitable asset/liability spreads. This type of response best illustrates the three main weaknesses in gap analysis' potential to control effectively interest rate exposure.

The first of gap analysis' weaknesses is that it monitors the timing of cash flows but ignores the relative price sensitivities of various instruments. In other words, gap analysis does not account for the time value of money. For example, gap analysis assumes a 30-year asset is neutralised by a 30-year liability even if one is a zero coupon security and the other is a high coupon security. As long as rates are stable and, thus, prices do not change, relative price sensitivities can be ignored. They cannot, however, be ignored in an unstable rate environment. An effective exposure measurement system must identify the relative price sensitivities of various instruments.

Gap technology's second weakness is that it precludes a risk manager from taking discrete incremental steps to control exposure, introducing instead an exposure management process with a domino effect. This domino effect is caused by the risk manager's attempts to plug gaps. The process of plugging gaps creates a series of subsequent cash flows which cause new gaps to appear in later periods. These new gaps must then be plugged, perpetuating the problem.

Finally, gap management cannot effectively measure the interest rate exposure of futures or options. These instruments, which have cash flows that are contingent upon rate movements, cannot simply be slotted into one gap period. A gap manager must decide, for example, if a 3-month call option on a 10-year security should be included in the 10-year gap, the 3-month gap, both, or neither.

In summary, gap analysis is effective as a short-term cash management tool, is marginally effective as a longer-term cash management tool and is ineffective as an exposure management tool.

Duration analysis

Duration analysis, although relatively recent in the interest rate exposure management field, has rapidly become the standard risk measurement tool. This pace of acceptance is due to several factors. Primarily, it is easy to use and, unlike other 'quick 'n easy' analytical tools, provides extremely relevant output. An effective risk manager should have a conceptual understanding of duration analysis, knowledge of its additivity properties, and an awareness of its one shortcoming, referred to as 'duration drift'.

Concept The purpose of duration is to identify the magnitude of a firm's interest rate exposure. Investment portfolio managers have done this for years by measuring the price movement of a bond for a given change in yields or, in other words, the dollar value of a basis point. For example, if a portfolio manager owned a 30-year bond with a 10% coupon, the manager could use a bond calculator to determine that the bond's price would fall from 100.000% to 99.905% for a 1 basis point change in yield to maturity from 10.00% to 10.01%. Therefore, the portfolio manager would know that for every US$1m of par value investment in bonds, a basis point change in yields would change the portfolio's value by US$950 (e.g. US$950 = (100.000%–99.905%) × US$1,000,000). The portfolio manager uncomfortable with this magnitude of interest rate/price exposure, could sell the 30-year bond and buy a 10-year note. A 10-year note with a 10% coupon has a price exposure of US$620 for a 1 basis point change in yields from 10.00% to 10.01%. The portfolio manager, by switching from 30-year assets to 10-year assets, has effectively cut the portfolio's interest rate exposure by one-third.

This methodology of the dollar value of a basis point, as used by investment portfolio managers, is the conceptual foundation of duration. Duration, rather than expressing the dollar value of a basis point, expresses the maturity of a zero coupon bond that would result in the same percentage price exposure as the instrument being measured. Duration is a price exposure scale against which all interest sensitive instruments can be measured. The more price sensitive an instrument, the longer its duration.

The exact definition of duration is not nearly as essential as attaining a conceptual understanding. Below are a few descriptions meant solely to be an intuitive approach to this understanding. As with most intuitive approaches, what is intuition for one reader will be incomprehensible for the next. So,

Exhibit 4.7 The duration concept: Example 1

| | | | Duration: Weighted by market price | | | Average life: Weighted by par | |
| | | | Present value | | | Cash flow | |
Year	Cash flow	Discount factor	Amount	%	Weighted yrs	as % of total par	Weighted yrs
(a)	(b)	(c)	(d)	(e)	(f)	(g)	(h)
0.5	3.25	1.0338	3.14	0.0317	0.02	0.0272	0.01
1.0	3.25	1.0686	3.04	0.0306	0.03	0.0272	0.03
1.5	3.25	1.1047	2.94	0.0296	0.04	0.0272	0.04
2.0	3.25	1.1420	2.85	0.0287	0.06	0.0272	0.05
2.5	3.25	1.1805	2.75	0.0277	0.07	0.0272	0.07
3.0	103.25	1.2204	84.61	0.8517	2.56	0.8640	2.59
Totals	119.50		99.33	100.00	2.77	100.00	2.80

Notes
(a) Time period
(b) Semi-annual coupons and principal
(c) Discount factor $= (1 + (\frac{6.75}{200}))^{(2 \times (a))}$
(d) Present value of cash flows $= (b) \div (c)$
(e) Present value of cash flows as a percentage of total present value $= (d)/$sum of $(d) = (d)/99.33$
(f) Duration weighted years $= (e) \times (a)$
(g) Par value of cash flows as a percentage of total par value of cash flows $= (b)/$sum of $(b) = (b)/119.5$
(h) Par value weighted years $= (g) \times (a)$

rather than belabour each description, the reader should choose one that seems most logical and continue on. These descriptions are meant as a framework for a more thorough understanding of duration. Although generally correct, the descriptions are not intended to be a precise definition of duration, which is provided later in this section.

One method of conceptualising duration is to think of it as an instrument's percentage price change, given a 100 basis point change in yield. A bond calculator would show that the price of a 3-year note with a 6.50% coupon would, for example, fall from 99.331% to 96.710% for a 100 basis point increase in yield from 6.75% to 7.75%. This price decrease from 99.331% to 96.710% is a 2.64% change in price. Thus, for conceptual purposes, it can be said that this note has a duration of 2.64 years.

A second method of conceptualising duration is to consider it as the weighted average number of years over which a security's total cash flows occur. The essential element of this approach is selecting the appropriate weighting. Duration uses a weighting based on the market price of the security. An alternative approach, used in calculating the average life of a security, is a weighting based on the security's par value. This latter method, however, is not recommended for risk managers because it does not account for the time value of money.

For purposes of illustration, the calculations used in both of these methods, assuming a 3-year note with a 6.50% semi-annual coupon and a yield to maturity of 6.75%, are shown in Exhibit 4.7. Using a market priced weighting, this security has a duration of 2.77 years. A par value weighting results in an average life of 2.80 years. The disparity between the duration and average life does not appear large in this example, because the security's market price is close to par (e.g. 99.33%) and the maturity of the underlying issue is relatively short (e.g. three years). If this was a 30-year security with a market price of 75%, its duration would be 11 years, while its average life would be 20 years.

Exhibit 4.8 is a visual representation of the results in Exhibit 4.7. It is a see-saw of the percentage cash flows, balanced such that 50% of the cash flows occur before and after a point in time.

Exhibit 4.8   The duration concept: Example 1

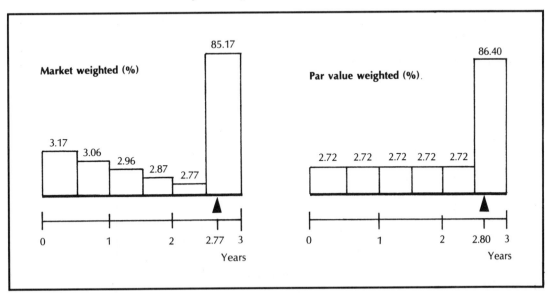

Another way of thinking about the balancing concept discussed above is to recognise that monetary assets and liabilities are subject to reinvestment risk on coupon cash flows and to market price risk on principal value. Thus, during rising interest rates, reinvestment of coupons at higher rates will offset losses on principal value; during lower rates, the gains on principal value will be offset by reduced reinvestment opportunities. Duration can be thought of as the time period over which these two risks neutralise each other (see Exhibit 4.9). For example, given a 6.5% 3-year note in a 6.75% yield environment the value of reinvested coupons would offset the principal loss after 2.78 years. The duration of this note is, therefore, 2.78 years. If this note were held longer than 2.78 years, the value of the reinvested coupons would outweigh the principal loss and if held shorter than 2.78 years would be less than the principal loss.

Exhibit 4.9   The duration concept: Example 2

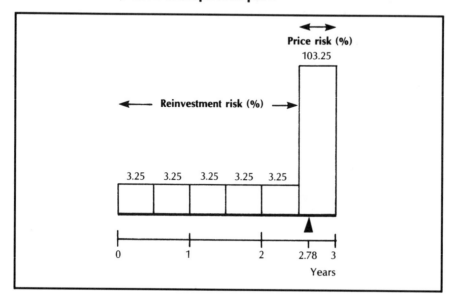

A third method of visualising duration is as the slope of a line tangent to a graph of price versus yield (see Exhibit 4.10). Those readers comfortable with calculus will recognise this as the first

Exhibit 4.10   The duration concept: Example 3

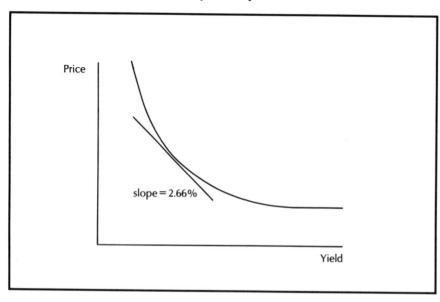

derivative of price as a function of yield. This approach, again, indicates that duration can be thought of as the change in price for a given change in yield. For example, a line tangent to a graph of price versus yield for a 3-year note with a 6.50% coupon would have a slope of 2.66% at a 6.75% yield to maturity level. This security, therefore, has a duration of 2.66 years.

A formal definition of duration is shown in equation (1).

$$\text{Duration } I = \frac{\displaystyle\sum_{t=0}^{n} CF_{It} \times PZ_t \times t}{\displaystyle\sum_{t=0}^{n} CF_{It} \times PZ_t} \tag{1}$$

Where

I = Financial instrument (e.g. 3-year note with 6.5% coupon)
t = Time
n = Final cash flow period
CF_{It} = Cash flow of instrument I occurring at time t
PZ_t = Market determined price of a zero coupon bond maturing at time t. Calculated based on the zero coupon yield curve.

Referring to equation (1), the product of CF_{It}, PZ_t and t, is the market value of a zero coupon bond with a par value sufficient to match the future cash flows of instrument I, weighted by the appropriate number of years. The sum of this product divided by the sum of the product of CF_{It} and PZ_t results in the average number of years that the present value of each cash flow remains outstanding. As an example, the duration of a 3-year note with a 6.5% coupon is 2.69 years as calculated below (see Exhibit 4.11).

Exhibit 4.11 Duration of a 3-year note with a 6.5% coupon

Time (t)	Cash Flow (CFIt)	0% coupon price* (PZt)	Required market value (CFIt × PZt)	Weighted market value (CFIt × PZt × t)
0.5	3.25	97.23%	0.0316	0.02
1.0	3.25	93.85	0.0305	0.03
1.5	3.25	90.46	0.0294	0.04
2.0	3.25	87.38	0.0284	0.06
2.5	3.25	83.99	0.0273	0.07
3.0	103.25	79.37	0.8195	2.46
Totals			99.33	2.67

Duration (2.67/99.33) = 2.69 years

*Based on the zero coupon spot curve of 5.70%, 6.45%, 6.80%, 6.86%, 7.10% and 7.85%.

The major difference between this formal definition and the previous intuitive approaches is the concept of using time-specific zero coupon rates versus a constant yield to maturity. In other words, the discount factor, rather than being a constant 6.75%, varies from a low of 5.70% in year 0.5 to a high of 7.85% in year 3. All of the techniques, described above, resulted in durations ranging from

2.64 years to 2.78 years. This slight variation is generally unimportant from an overall risk management perspective. However, accuracy should be pursued to the extent that the benefits outweigh the costs.

Duration can be used not only to measure the interest rate exposure of standard interest-sensitive instruments, but also to measure the exposure in leveraged contracts, such as options. The duration of these instruments is the product of:

1   Du: the duration of the underlying instrument;
2   $(P\triangle o/P\triangle u)$: the price change of the option relative to the price change of the underlying instrument; and
3   (Pu/Po): the price of the underlying instrument relative to the price of the option.

$$\text{Option Duration} = (Du) \times (P\triangle o/P\triangle u) \times (Pu/Po)$$

For example, as concluded earlier, the duration of a 3-year note with a coupon of 6.5% and a price of 99.33% is 2.69 years. An option pricing model can be used to show that the price of a 1-month at-the-money call option will change by approximately 45% of that of the aforementioned 3-year note (e.g. a US$1.00 increase in the price of the 3-year note will generate a US$0.45 increase in the option's price). Finally, assuming an option cost of 0.15%, this option has a duration of 802 years.

$$802 \text{ years} = (2.69) \times (0.45/1.00) \times (99.33/0.15)$$

The duration of an option is conceptually the same as the duration of other interest-sensitive instruments; that is, the price change of the instrument as a percentage of the original price. Referencing the example above, the 3-year note was determined to have a price change of 2.69% for a given change in yields and the option was determined to have a price change of 45% of the change in the underlying security's price. Thus, the option price will change by 1.21% (0.45 × 2.69%) for a given change in yields. This 1.21% price change as a percentage of the 0.15% original price of the option is approximately 802%, which equates to a duration of 802 years. This large duration is due to the highly leveraged nature of options. Once the duration of the option is calculated it becomes just another input into the total duration of the portfolio. Because leveraged contracts typically have very large durations they can be used to rapidly reposition a portfolios's total exposure.

Additivity property   The most useful aspect of duration is its additivity property. This property enables the risk manager to take incremental steps in controlling exposure and the search for relative value among all maturities of assets or liabilities. The additivity property of duration states that the price times the duration of one instrument plus the price times the duration of a second instrument divided by the combined price of both instruments equals the total portfolio's duration, see equation (2).

$$\text{Portfolio duration} = [(P1 \times D1) + (P2 \times D2)]/(P1 + P2) \qquad (2)$$

Where:
$P1$ = Market price of instrument 1
D = Duration of instrument 1
$P2$ = Market price of instrument 2
$D2$ = Duration of instrument 2

For example, US$56m of a five year duration can be added to US$20m of a 10 year duration to form a combined portfolio of US$76m of 6.3 year duration. Alternatively, algebra can be used to show these same positions in security, 1 and 2 are equal to a US$60m portfolio with an eight year duration, a US$48m portfolio with a 10 year duration, or a US$96m portfolio with a five year duration as demonstrated on the next page.

Portfolio duration	Portfolio composition
6.3 years	= [(56 × 5) + (20 × 10)]/76
8.0 years	= [(56 × 5) + (20 × 10)]/60
10.0 years	= [(56 × 5) + (20 × 10)]/48
5.0 years	= [(56 × 5) + (20 × 10)]/96

Assuming a constant yield curve shape, these positions each have an equivalent exposure of a 4.5% change in market value for a 100 basis point change in yields.

This additivity principle enables an exposure manager to take incremental actions in adjusting the risk profile of the firm's assets and liabilities. To adjust duration, the manager chooses the most advantageous spot on the yield curve to buy or sell the appropriate market value of assets or liabilities.

Duration drift   Duration is not a static analysis. As interest rates change, duration will also change. A portfolio which is duration neutral when rates are at one level will not necessarily be duration neutral at another level. This phenomenon is called duration drift or convexity. Essentially this drift occurs due to the fact that prices and yields do not change linearly (see Exhibit 4.12a) but rather have varying rates of change (see Exhibit 4.12b).

Exhibit 4.12   Establishing a risk management programme

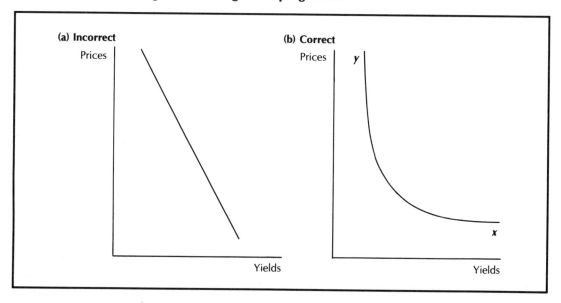

As Exhibit 4.12 demonstrates, a small change in yields at point x will have a small effect on prices, while a small change in yields at point y will dramatically effect prices. A risk manager that does not adjust the composition of the firm's portfolio as rates change from point x to point y will be passively changing the firm's interest rate exposure. Duration drift is a relatively minor problem requiring the risk manager to recalculate a portfolio's duration as rates change and then to adjust accordingly.

Simulation analysis

Simulation analysis is the process of taking a plan, generally a budget, and testing its integrity against a variety of assumptions about future market conditions. This type of analysis, because it incorporates so many elements of a firm's business, is an excellent method of identifying potential problems, profit opportunities and prospective interest rate risk exposure. These attributes help make simulation analysis one of the most popular budget planning tools.

Risk managers usually subject a budget to a best, worst and most likely interest rate scenario; others use a Monte Carlo simulation technique (i.e. a multitude of randomly generated rate forecasts). Simulation analysis, in whatever form, familiarises the risk manager with the consequences of the market's actions. It helps identify the critical components that impact the interest rate risk of the firm. It gives the risk manager a better sense of the magnitude of the firm's exposure for a given rate movement. It generates ideas on how to position the business to take advantage of plausible rate movements, and forces a prospective look at exposure rather than simply a historical review.

An exhaustive simulation analysis incorporates countless interest rate forecasts as well as the secondary and tertiary consequences of these forecasts. It is an extensive exercise that, if done properly, can produce some very important results. Unfortunately, the extensive nature of simulation analysis precludes its frequent use. The constant probing of managers' expectations about future business trends, the continuous reprogramming necessary to account for these expectations, and the computer time necessary to run the various simulations, makes this analysis a very time-consuming analytical tool. Additionally, the data requirements are enormous. It should include not only current statistics but also information about the future, whether planned or possible. Finally, there is the risk that even after all of the inputs are established, the simulation results may lack relevance. This can often happen when a firm tries to incorporate too many inputs. The time and data constraints imposed by simulation analysis force most risk managers to use sporadically a complete simulation analysis and otherwise more frequently run less exhaustive simulations.

Data systems

An effective interest rate measurement system is composed of four basic elements: data inputs, assumptions, calculations and outputs. A weakness in any one of these four elements can seriously impair the risk manager's ability to control interest rate exposure.

Data inputs and assumptions should be as extensive as is necessary to support the selected risk measurement methodology. Simulation analysis will, obviously, require more inputs and assumptions than gap analysis. These inputs may include managerial judgements, consumer preferences, macro-economic forecasts, industry specific forecasts, interest rate forecasts, potential business opportunities, etc. It is important that inconsistent assumptions within the firm be reviewed (e.g. one department has a budget based on rising rates and another on falling rates).

It goes without saying that the calculations, logic and programming underlying the data system must be accurate.

Finally, the output should be in a form that allows risk managers to make decisions, take actions and see the results of their actions. This report may include several of the items shown in Exhibit 4.13.

Exhibit 4.13   Presentation of data output

	Assets	Liabilities	Net
Market value	US$m	US$m	US$m
Par value	US$m	US$m	US$m
Weighted average credit quality	AAA	AAA	AAA
Weighted average maturity	n yrs	n yrs	n yrs
Weighted average call date	n yrs	n yrs	n yrs
Duration without options	n yrs	n yrs	n yrs
Duration with options	n yrs	n yrs	n yrs
Duration drift without options	n yrs	n yrs	n yrs
Duration drift with options	n yrs	n yrs	n yrs
Weighted average yield to maturity without options	%	%	%
Weighted average yield to maturity with options	%	%	%

Conclusion

This chapter is intended to introduce interest rate risk managers to the various topics that must be addressed in establishing an exposure measurement system. It intentionally does not recommend one system at the expense of others because each system has strengths and weaknesses. Rather, it lays the groundwork for enabling risk managers to review the unique needs of their businesses and to determine the steps necessary to meet those needs. In assessing those needs it is critical that risk managers begin by defining exposure. Once a definition of exposure is determined, an appropriate measurement system can be selected.

5 Management of interest rate risk

Victor J. Farhi and Tony Thurston

Introduction

There is no such thing, in a complex and competitive world, as a simple hedging decision. This is especially true of decisions involving hedging interest rates. An approach should however be developed to distinguish between exposure and risk. Once this distinction has been made, it is essential to use an effective framework for decision making to define and arrive at the most appropriate hedging strategy. This approach is described below.

With increased volatility in recent years, more corporate treasurers are focusing attention on ways to minimise interest rate risk, as opposed to merely trying to stabilise interest cost. Treasurers have learned the hard lessons of foreign exchange fluctuations and their impact on their profit and loss accounts; but failure to hedge against interest rate fluctuations has probably been easily written off as an opportunity cost without further penetrating examination.

The business environment has changed; not only have corporate treasurers been faced with unprecedented volatility in interest rates, but at the same time their role has changed. Corporate treasurers have become far more performance oriented as treasury functions have become centralised. Financial technology has taken a quantum leap and fostered the development of new financial products, instruments and techniques, giving treasurers far greater flexibility in managing their cash flows by allowing them to transfer interest rate risk to those better able or more willing to bear it. After all, should a major manufacturing company run the unnecessary risk that an inappropriate financing decision could wipe out the otherwise healthy profitability of its core business?

Just as foreign exchange risk management has developed from simple forward transactions into futures and options, so too has interest risk management given rise to the proliferation of new techniques such as forward rate agreements, swaps, caps, floors and collars, interest rate guarantees and swaptions. In spite of their increasing availability and the growing imperatives for using them, we have found that even the traditional hedging decision:

1 to do nothing,
2 to eliminate the risk fully, or
3 to manage the risk,

is generally, for a variety of reasons, taken incorrectly.

The accounting profession too, seems to have taken a 'black box' approach to interest rate risk management, emphasising the reporting and accounting impact of the use of risk management instruments rather than their risk transfer, evaluation and application aspects.

To hedge or not to hedge

We can begin by asking why we believe interest rate risk should be managed. First, the uncertainty created by interest rate fluctuation has often made corporate financial decisions extremely difficult. This is particularly so in the UK, where interest rates have traditionally been used by the authorities as a means of stabilising exchange rate fluctuations. The extent of uncertainty grows in significance in line with the extent of a firm's gearing structure. In the case of a new firm, or in a leveraged buyout situation, interest rate volatility may put at risk the company's very survival.

Secondly, the increased volatility of interest rates in all the major currencies has created uncertainty as to both the timing of borrowing decisions and the size of such borrowings.

Exhibit 5.1 illustrates US dollar 6-month Libor every month since 1977. The random pattern and extensive changes in direction clearly highlight the difficulties faced by corporate treasurers. Indeed, most corporate treasurers fail to appreciate fully the greater volatility of interest rates compared to currencies and, moreover, the greater impact this volatility has on the company's profitability (see Exhibit 5.2).

Exhibit 5.1   US dollar 6-month Libor, 1977-87

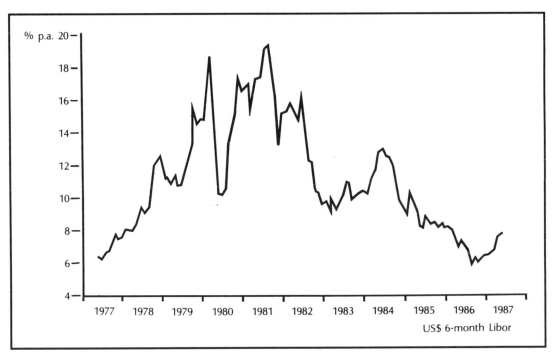

The third major reason for attempting to manage the interest rate risk is essentially a passive one: risk management may allow the firm to benefit from the opportunities it otherwise would miss through the inability to negate or control interest rate risk. If these risks are clear to all treasurers or if there is a universally agreed need to control such risks, why do treasurers seem not to attribute much importance to controlling them?

Our experience suggests that there are several reasons. First, the risk is not always apparent. Consider a corporate treasurer reviewing some of the fixed interest assets and liabilities on his balance sheet. He is naturally concerned with a possible move in rates. Should he be concerned with:

- a change in the value of the assets due to a change in interest rates,
- hedging the cost of funding these assets, or alternatively,
- looking at both sides of his balance sheet and hedging the duration gap between similar assets and liabilities?

Recognition of risks which are not readily apparent is clearly critical to formulating the appropriate strategy, yet this process is sometimes missed.

Exhibit 5.2   US dollar 6-month Libor, 1984-88. Annualised volatility

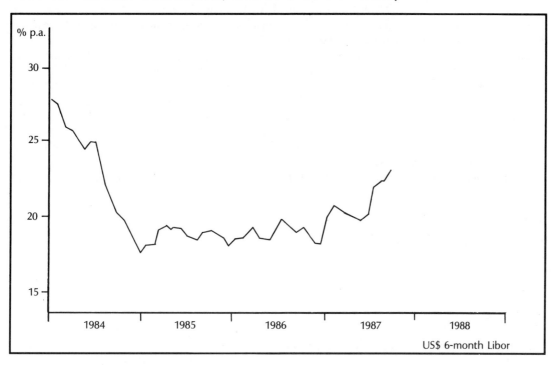

An example of failure to recognise a risk can be seen in the recent experience of some firms which have issued bonds with debt warrants. Some initially focused on the apparent savings generated by issuing this type of paper. They may not have attached similar importance to the call option which had in effect been sold and the asymmetric risk which had thereby been undertaken: if term rates fall, the debt warrants will be exercised and the firm will be required to issue new paper above the level of current market rates. If term rates rise, the warrants will not be exercised and no new debt will need to be issued. However, the firm which subsequently needs new funds would of course have to issue more debt at the new, higher market rates.

The call option arises because the firm which issues bonds with debt warrants gives the investor the right to take advantage of future interest rate movements in his favour (assuming the quality of the bonds remains largely unchanged).

Another reason why treasurers seem not to act to control risks can be the legal environment. It will quite often dictate the availability and liquidity of the necessary hedging instruments. In Germany, for example, it is not possible to sell Schuldschein bonds 'short' and this has restricted the growth of the swap, cap and collar markets denominated in Deutschmarks.

A third reason is that the tax and accounting treatment of these hedging instruments has often been unclear and understandably has tended to lag behind innovation in the financial markets. Doubt as to whether cap premium may be treated as a trading expense and hence tax deductible, and the lack of an agreed policy on accounting for swaps, create problems to such an extent that the decision to do nothing has been easier to live with.

Even in the UK it was only very recently decided that cap premiums may be a deductible expense for a trading company. The economic viability of such a hedge may be called into question if the after-tax cost of it is greater than the anticipated risk. The policies of the firm itself may hinder its ability to make effective hedging decisions. Quite often no policy exists for managing interest rates. The treasurer is often put in the conflicting situation of being made responsible for ensuring that the firm is hedged against rising rates but is at the same time criticised if he fails to take advantage of falling rates.

We can see that hedging decisions often have an internal 'political' cost in the firm. If the treasurer incurs a significant cost by hedging, but in hindsight the hedge is found unnecessary, he may be criticised for a 'wrong' decision. Frequently, the financial risk to the firm may be perceived to be lower than the corporate or political risk to the individual.

Finally, it seems that there is no real framework offered to treasurers within which they may quantify exposure and evaluate risk, and as a result select an appropriate hedging strategy in the light of their needs.

Breakeven analysis is usually the basis on which corporate treasurers are asked to make decisions. We believe, however, that this simplistic view is not acceptable. It assumes, for example, that average rates apply throughout the period of review. But average rates are not always relevant. Rates may average 12% per annum but they may equally well have risen to 20% per annum at some point. This may indeed jeopardise the survival of the firm.

The framework which we have developed deals with some of these factors and follows a series of steps:

- Exposure analysis
- Quantification of risk
- Strategy evaluation
- Decision monitoring

Exposure analysis

Exposure analysis requires the following action:

1 Preparation of cash flow estimates of current and anticipated assets and liabilities, broken down by quarter or semi-annual period, extending well into the future to cover the current stage of the firm's operations and risk.
2 Incorporation of these flows into a full economic exposure analysis recognising the internal matching of assets and liabilities denominated in the same currency or across currency blocks. This may be more important than considering the merits of a liability management reporting system.
3 For interest rate exposure, preparation of a 3- or 6-month disaggregation of the cash flows in order to analyse the underlying floating rate Libor risk. This is consistent with the structure of most interest rate hedging instruments.
4 A breakdown of the portfolio in terms of the ratio of fixed to floating liabilities and assets by currency. On the basis of current interest rate structure the distribution of interest payable (present valued) can be calculated. This will allow the treasurer to concentrate on the largest mismatches and hence the areas of greatest risk.

Quantification of risk

As a background let us assume that the net exposure is identified as a US$10m loan over a 5-year period, with a single repayment, attracting a floating rate of interest reset every 3 months.

At this stage there is unlimited exposure to rising interest rates. In examining the possibilities the treasurer considers some of the usual hedging instruments. He requests quotations for swap rates and cap prices. He is offered a 5-year fixed rate swap at 9.16% per annum. Premium rates for caps at between 9 and 10½% strike rates are quoted at from 4.74% to 3.32% up front. He now searches for a framework within which he can make a sensible comparison of these alternatives and determine with which instrument, and at what target rate, to hedge his net exposure.

He knows that in undertaking a swap transaction he will no longer be exposed to unlimited profits and losses as interest rates change in the future. His only consolation might be that he will have fixed his funding cost. If he purchases a cap he will set a limit on his maximum future borrowing cost at a rate which equals the cap rate plus the cost of the cap premium amortised over the life of the loan. With a cap rate of 9% he would be able to limit his maximum borrowing cost to approximately 10.11% per annum.

A decision to enter into a swap will immediately increase his cost of funds compared with the current 3-month Libor rate (which, assuming a normal positive yield curve, will invariably be lower than the swap rate). He will endure an opportunity loss during every subsequent interest period that short-term rates remain below the fixed swap rate. To justify entering into the swap he will need to be confident that, over the life of the loan, the short-term rate will, on average, exceed the fixed swap rate. In the absence of a formal structure for decision making he may well postpone the hedging decision due to his inability to evaluate the alternatives.

The approach we take offers the necessary decision making framework. This involves a comparison of the fixed swap rate with the current or assumed 3-month Libor rate. The first step therefore is to adjust the current or assumed 3-month Libor rate by a measure of interest rate volatility. Here, the treasurer can choose to use either historical volatility, market-implied volatilities or his own view. Each approach is valid. In the first two cases, a perspective can be drawn by considering the pattern of volatility, particularly the highest and lowest levels actually reached or implied by the market. As the treasurer is concerned with adverse movements in interest rates the 3-month Libor rate must be projected over the 5-year period of the exposure.

Exhibit 5.3 is built up from the most pessimistic of each successive 3-month Libor high/low projections. This upward adjustment will reflect the assumed volatility at a given statistical confidence level. (An adjustment of one standard deviation of volatility will provide a confidence level of about 68%, and two standard deviations will provide in excess of 95%.)

Exhibit 5.3   A volatility adjusted curve

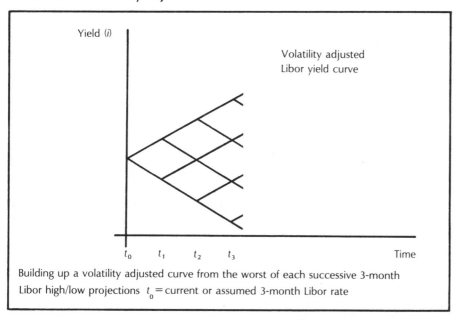

For a bullet loan the periodic interest payments (projected by the volatility adjusted Libor yield curve) are then discounted to a present value at the zero coupon rate on the curve for each period (PV_1). This is a measure of the exposure to interest rate risk given the anticipated Libor yield curve.

It represents the estimated cost of funding on a floating rate basis (see Exhibit 5.4). This is not, however, a quantification of risk. The risk is quantified by the negative impact of changes in interest rates in the future, given an assumed level of volatility and the timing of the cash flows. The concept of volatility is used in preference to reliance on a forecast which implies some measure of certainty of the forecast's correctness. The emphasis is on managing risk and not crystal ball gazing.

Exhibit 5.4   Analysis of exposure: 1

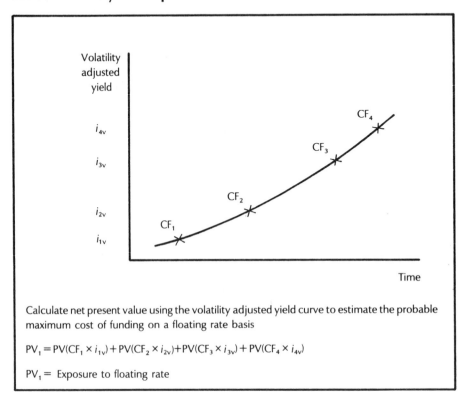

Calculate net present value using the volatility adjusted yield curve to estimate the probable maximum cost of funding on a floating rate basis

$$PV_1 = PV(CF_1 \times i_{1v}) + PV(CF_2 \times i_{2v}) + PV(CF_3 \times i_{3v}) + PV(CF_4 \times i_{4v})$$

$PV_1 =$ Exposure to floating rate

The next stage is to calculate the fixed swap rate cost attributable to the principal at each interest payment between now and the maturity of the next exposure. If the cash flows are now discounted at the zero coupon rates a new present value will be derived (PV_2) which represents the estimated cost of funding on a fixed rate basis. This can be compared with the previous exposure value (PV_1). The difference between them is a reasonable measure of the risk, in terms of profit and loss, of an adverse movement in interest rates given the volatility assumptions just made. This provides a rational basis on which to evaluate different strategies (see Exhibit 5.5).

Strategy evaluation

The treasurer can now compare this present value (PV_2) with that derived from the volatility adjusted yield curve (PV_1). If PV_2 exceeds PV_1 it is clear from the foregoing that the implied cost of fixing his cost of funds through a swap exceeds the estimated cost of funding on a floating rate basis. He is thus able to determine whether, given the assumptions, a swap is likely to be preferable to retaining his exposure on a floating rate basis.

Exhibit 5.5 Analysis of exposure: 2

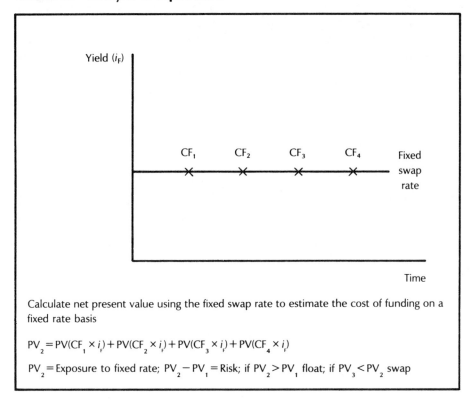

Calculate net present value using the fixed swap rate to estimate the cost of funding on a fixed rate basis

$PV_2 = PV(CF_1 \times i_F) + PV(CF_2 \times i_F) + PV(CF_3 \times i_F) + PV(CF_4 \times i_F)$

PV_2 = Exposure to fixed rate; $PV_2 - PV_1$ = Risk; if $PV_2 > PV_1$ float; if $PV_3 < PV_2$ swap

But, as we can recall, the treasurer has also considered the alternative of purchasing a cap. We can therefore 'cap' the volatility adjusted Libor curve and recalculate a new present value (PV_3). If the cost of the cap is less than the value of PV_1 minus PV_3 the cap should be purchased (see Exhibit 5.6).

Decision monitoring

Having made the initial decision, it is nevertheless essential that the treasurer continues to assume responsibility for managing his exposure. If the comparison of present values shows that a decision not to hedge is appropriate, this is only valid whilst the yield curve remains unchanged. As soon as the yield curve changes, the appropriate strategy must be re-evaluated and the procedure above must be repeated, since this will impact his perception of risk and hence his volatility assumption. Whatever course the treasurer takes, he must continue to monitor market conditions. Hedging is a continuous process.

The process of re-evaluation and marking to market the exposure and risk, will provide a degree of comfort for a harried treasurer. The analysis does not, however, relieve him of the problem of when to transact a swap when the model suggests this to be the most appropriate strategy. The framework does not comment on whether today is the best day to transact. Moreover, the analysis depends crucially upon the volatility assumptions which will incorporate explicitly or implicitly the risk aversion of the treasurer. Perceptions of risk and hence volatility change quickly and often for short-term considerations which do not apply in the corporate environment, where often there is only one opportunity to choose the 'right' hedge.

Nevertheless, a decision to purchase a cap or to enter into a swap can be changed to the treasurer's advantage at some point in the light of changes in market conditions and/or his exposure profile. The cap may be resold, or the swap unwound and either a new cap purchased, a new swap entered into, or the treasurer may revert to floating rate funding.

Exhibit 5.6   Analysis of exposure: 3

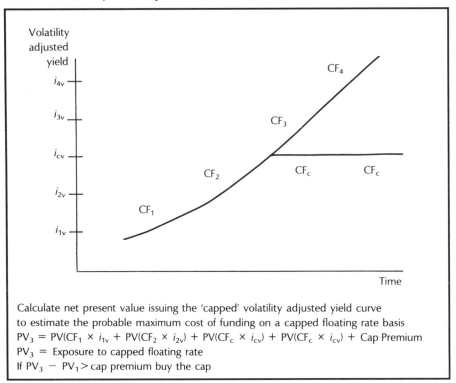

Calculate net present value issuing the 'capped' volatility adjusted yield curve
to estimate the probable maximum cost of funding on a capped floating rate basis
$PV_3 = PV(CF_1 \times i_{1v} + PV(CF_2 \times i_{2v}) + PV(CF_c \times i_{cv}) + PV(CF_c \times i_{cv}) + \text{Cap Premium}$
$PV_3 = $ Exposure to capped floating rate
If $PV_3 - PV_1 > $ cap premium buy the cap

Summary

In this chapter we have demonstrated that interest rate exposure is not a total unknown – it can be quantified in terms of risk. Interest rate volatility can be applied to the decision making process, to enable a comparison of likely outcomes, using various hedging strategies.

Once a treasurer has made an initial hedging decision he is not 'off the hook' – he has a continuing responsibility for interest rate management. However, he is not unaided in this jungle of doubt and uncertainty. A rational approach to risk management is possible, using the framework we have outlined to make a sensible choice from the competing array of hedging opportunities.

PART II
Elements of interest rate risk management

1 Accounting framework: United States

Benjamin S. Neuhausen

Introduction

The authoritative accounting literature in the US as of the beginning of 1988 contains relatively few specific requirements dealing with interest rate protection products other than futures contracts. Financial Accounting Standards Board (FASB) Statement No. 80, *Accounting for futures contracts*, governs the accounting for futures contracts. The accounting framework for other interest rate protection products has been influenced by Statement 80 but does not comply in every respect. This chapter describes the framework that is broadly applicable to interest rate protection products. Individual chapters later in the book describe in more detail the accounting applicable to specific interest rate protection products.

The FASB currently has a major project underway dealing with financial instruments and 'off balance sheet financing' issues. Interest rate protection products are included in the scope of that project. Accordingly, practices in this area may change if the FASB or the Securities and Exchange Commission promulgate new standards. Readers should be aware that this is an evolving area of accounting.

Hedge versus speculation

The first major issue in accounting for interest rate protection products is whether they are entered into for hedging purposes or whether they are entered into for speculation. Those that are entered into for speculation ordinarily are accounted for on either a market value basis (recognise all gains and losses in income currently) or on a lower-of-cost-or-market basis (recognise all losses in income currently but defer gains until the position is closed out). Those that are entered into for hedging purposes are accounted for symmetrically with the underlying hedged item, that is, the gains and losses on the interest rate protection product are deferred initially and are included in income at the same time that the loss or gain on the hedged item created by the interest rate movement is included in income (hedge accounting is discussed further below).

The accounting standards and conventions include criteria for determining when interest rate protection products are hedges for accounting purposes. Those that do not qualify as hedges for accounting purposes are deemed to be speculative for accounting purposes. In certain cases, interest rate protection products may represent economic hedges but fail to meet the criteria to be accounted for as hedges. In this case, the gains or losses on the interest rate protection product may be included in income in a period different from the period when the loss or gain on the underlying hedged item is included in income. Assuming the hedge is effective, the cumulative gain or loss on the interest rate protection product will equal and offset the cumulative loss or gain on the underlying hedged position, but the offset may be imperfect in particular quarters or years.

Hedging criteria

Generally, three criteria must be satisfied for any interest rate protection product to be considered a hedge for accounting purposes:

1 *The underlying transaction that is being hedged exposes the company to interest rate risk.* This means that the company's income will be increased or decreased by the effect of changing interest rates on the transaction. For example, if the company owns a variable-rate security or has borrowed under variable-rate debt, income will be directly affected by changes in interest rates. If the company owns fixed-rate investments that it intends to sell prior to maturity, changing interest rates will change the value of the investment and, hence, the gain or loss on sale. FASB Statement No. 80, requires that the risk exposure be assessed on a total enterprise basis, taking into account other assets, liabilities, firm commitments, and anticipated transactions. Thus, if a company has funded variable-rate investment securities with variable-rate debt that reprices over the same interval, it has no interest rate risk on an enterprise basis and, therefore, would not consider any futures contracts that hedge either the investments or the debt to be accounting hedges. For other interest rate protection products, risk may be assessed either on a total enterprise basis or on an individual transaction basis.

2 *The enterprise designates the product as a hedge.* This means that the enterprise must document in its records the purpose of the interest rate protection product and the underlying item or items that are being hedged. Some enterprises use interest rate protection products to hedge asset/liability mismatches (sometimes referred to as gap or duration hedges). While these may represent good economic hedges, it is not sufficient for accounting purposes to designate the products as a hedge of a mismatch or gap; to be considered a hedge for accounting purposes, the products must be designated as a hedge of specific assets, liabilities, commitments, or anticipated transactions.

3 *The interest rate protection product is effective as a hedge.* This means that there must be high correlation between the gains or losses on the interest rate protection product and the losses or gains caused by changing interest rates on the underlying hedged item(s). If high correlation is not achieved, the product would cease to be regarded as a hedge for accounting purposes and would begin to be accounted for as a speculative position. For options and futures contracts, this criterion to be considered a hedge for accounting purposes requires not only that high correlation be achieved but also that the enterprise demonstrate at the inception of the hedge that high correlation is probable. An interest rate protection product may be based on a financial instrument or an interest rate different from the item intended to be hedged (a cross-hedge). This may qualify to be considered a hedge for accounting purposes provided there is a clear economic relationship between the two interest rates or the two financial instruments and the correlation between them is high.

Types of transactions that may be hedged

Interest rate protection products may be hedges for accounting purposes of existing assets, existing liabilities, firm commitments, or anticipated transactions, as follows:

Hedge of existing asset or existing liability Examples of uses of interest rate protection products that might qualify as hedges include the following:

1 Using interest rate protection products to protect against a market value decline on an existing fixed rate investment security.
2 Using interest rate protection products to protect against the risk of falling interest rates for fixed rate borrowings used to fund floating rate assets.

Hedge of a firm commitment to buy or sell interest-bearing assets or to issue or retire debt instruments A firm commitment is an agreement, usually legally enforceable, under which performance is probable because of sufficiently large disincentives for nonperformance. One example of a transaction that might qualify as a hedge of a firm commitment for accounting purposes is the use of an interest rate protection product to protect against the risk of rising interest rates on a fixed price contract to purchase fixed rate investment securities when issued.

Hedge of an anticipated transaction An anticipated transaction is a transaction that an enterprise expects, but is not obligated, to carry out in the normal course of business. An interest rate protection product might qualify as a hedge of an anticipated transaction (an anticipatory hedge) for accounting purposes if the criteria above and the following two additional criteria are satisfied:

1   The significant characteristics and expected terms of the anticipated transaction are identified. The significant characteristics and expected terms include the expected date of the anticipated transaction, the type of financial instrument involved, the expected maturity of the instrument, and the quantity to be purchased, sold, issued, or redeemed.
2   It is probable that the anticipated transaction will occur. Considerations in assessing the likelihood that a transaction will occur include the frequency of similar transactions in the past, the financial and operational capability of the enterprise to carry out the transaction, the length of time to the anticipated transaction date, the extent of loss or disruption of operations that could result if the transaction does not occur, and the likelihood that transactions with substantially different characteristics might be used to achieve the same business purpose (for example, an enterprise that intends to raise cash may have several ways of doing so ranging from short-term loans to common share offerings). If an enterprise contemplates two or more similar alternative transactions, an interest rate protection product may qualify as a hedge of the anticipated transaction if all hedge requirements are met regardless of which alternative is consummated.

Examples of transactions that may qualify as hedges of anticipated transactions include:

1   Use of an interest rate protection product to protect against the risk of rising interest rates on a floating-rate debt obligation or to protect against the risk of falling interest rates on a floating rate investment security. The repricing of the interest rate is an anticipated transaction. (The repricing is not a firm commitment because the company can sell the investment or retire the borrowing.) This transaction differs from a hedge of an existing fixed rate asset or liability because the value of a floating rate asset or liability tends not to change as interest rates change. Accordingly, what is being hedged is the anticipated repricing of the interest rate, not the value of the security.
2   The use of an interest rate protection product to protect against the risk of rising interest rates on the anticipated rollover of short-term borrowings, such as rollover of commercial paper or repurchase agreements. The rollover is the anticipated transaction.
3   The use of an interest rate protection product to protect against the risk of rising interest rates on the anticipated issuance of fixed rate debt at a future date.

Accounting treatment for hedges

As noted in the introductory section of this chapter, interest rate protection products that qualify to be treated as hedges for accounting purposes are accounted for symmetrically with the underlying hedged item. If the underlying hedged item is accounted for (or, for a firm commitment or anticipated transaction, will be accounted for) at market value, then any interest rate protection product hedging that item also will be accounted for on a market value basis. Market value accounting for interest-bearing financial instruments is relatively rare in the United States, restricted for the most part to broker-dealers and to the trading accounts of financial institutions.

Most interest-bearing investments are carried at amortised cost (original cost plus cumulative amortisation of discount or less cumulative amortisation of premium) and most borrowings are carried at amortised proceeds (original proceeds plus cumulative amortisation of discount or less cumulative amortisation of premium). The effect of interest rate changes on the value of the investment or the borrowing is not recognised immediately in income. Accordingly, the effect of interest rate changes on an interest rate protection product used to hedge an asset carried at amortised cost or a liability carried at amortised proceeds should be deferred rather than recognised in income immediately, to match the timing of the gain or loss on the underlying hedged item. This is accomplished as follows:

Hedge of existing asset or existing liability   If an interest rate protection product qualifies to be treated as a hedge of an existing fixed rate asset or liability, the gain or loss on the product created by changing interest rates should be deferred and treated as an adjustment of the carrying amount of the underlying hedged asset or liability. That adjustment is like discount or premium and should be amortised as an adjustment of interest over the remaining life of the underlying hedged item. For example, a company may hedge an existing fixed rate investment. If interest rates rise, the company is exposed to risk because the value of the investment will drop. That drop in value will be recognised in income over the remaining life of the investment in the form of a reduced spread between the yield from the investment and the cost of borrowed funds. An interest rate protection product that hedges the investment will generate a gain when interest rates rise. That gain should be deferred as an adjustment to the carrying amount of the investment and amortised as a yield adjustment over the remaining life of the investment. The amortisation of the gain from the protection product will offset the reduced spread that would have been encountered had the company not hedged.

Hedge of a firm commitment   If an interest rate protection product qualifies to be treated as a hedge of a firm commitment, the gain or loss on the product created by changing interest rates should be deferred and treated as an adjustment to the transaction that satisfies the commitment. For example, a company may hedge a fixed price commitment to buy fixed rate investment securities when issued. If the company does not hedge and interest rates rise, the company will have a loss on the commitment that will be recognised when it becomes probable. When issued, the investment security would be recorded at its market value rather than at the committed purchase price. If the company hedges the commitment, the gain on the product will offset the loss on the commitment, eliminating the need to recognise a loss during the commitment period. When issued, the investment security will be recorded at its committed purchase price less the gain from the protection product which, if the hedge was effective, will equal the security's market value.

Hedge of an anticipated transaction   If an interest rate protection product qualifies to be treated as a hedge of an anticipated transaction, the gain or loss on the product created by changing interest rates should be deferred and treated as an adjustment to the transaction when it occurs. For example, a company may use an interest rate protection product to protect against the risk of rising interest rates over the remaining life of a floating-rate debt obligation. If the company does not hedge and rates rise, interest expense will be higher over the remaining term of the debt. If the company does hedge and interest rates rise, the interest rate protection product will generate a gain. The gain should be deferred and taken into income as an adjustment to the higher interest expense on the debt.

Early termination of hedges

If an interest rate protection product qualifies as an accounting hedge of a firm commitment or an anticipated transaction and the product is closed out before the committed/anticipated transaction occurs, the cumulative gain or loss on the product should continue to be deferred. The company hedged itself against the effects of changing interest rates during the period that the product was held, and the resulting gain or loss should continue to be deferred as an adjustment to the transaction when it occurs. The fact that the company has chosen to become exposed to additional changes in interest rates does not change the nature of the protection product during the period it was held. Of course, if interest rates move adversely after the protection product is closed out and create losses on the committed/anticipated transaction, those losses must be recognised as they occur.

If an interest rate protection product qualifies as an accounting hedge of a firm commitment or an anticipated transaction and it becomes evident that the committed/anticipated transaction will not occur, the interest rate protection product becomes speculative for accounting purposes at that point and accumulated gains and losses should be accounted for as though the product had always been considered speculative. If it becomes evident that the committed/anticipated transaction will occur, but in a smaller amount than expected, a *pro rata* portion of the interest rate protection product becomes speculative for accounting purposes at that point while the remainder continues to be accounted for as a hedge.

2 Accounting framework: United Kingdom

Mark Davis

Introduction

Before discussing the accounting treatment of interest rate instruments in detail, it will be useful to consider the broad framework in the UK, particularly as, in the absence of detailed accounting rules for many of the instruments, one must generally resort to basic accounting principles in order to determine the most appropriate accounting treatment.

For the purposes of preparing statutory accounts, UK companies must comply with generally accepted accounting principles in the UK (UK GAAP). This is embodied in the accounting provisions of the Companies Act 1985, statements of standard accounting practice (SSAPs) and statements of recommended practice (SORPs), issued by the Consultative Committee of Accountancy Bodies in the UK. These are supported by occasional technical releases on various matters.

The majority of the Companies Act provisions are contained in schedules to the Act, the application of which depends on the status of the company. Most companies fall under Schedule 4 of the Act, which reflects the requirements of the EC (European Community) 4th Directive on Company Law. Such companies are referred to as 'corporates' in the text. Banks which are authorised by the Bank of England and insurance companies fall under Schedule 9 of the Act, a temporary remnant of older UK law, which applies pending the adoption of the EC directives on the financial statements of banks and insurance companies. A limited number of UK merchant banks are exempted from a number of the requirements of Schedule 9. These, however, only concern disclosure and thus those banks should comply with GAAP in terms of income recognition and valuation.

Neither the Companies Act nor any SSAP or SORP provides any specific guidance on interest rate protection instruments. SORPS are being developed for the banking sector which will address such instruments. Currently, SSAP2 sets out four fundamental accounting concepts from which some accounting principles can be derived.

1 *Going concern:* this requires valuation of assets and liabilities on the presumption that the company is continuing in business as a going concern.
2 *Consistency:* this requires that a company applies accounting policies consistently from one year to the next.
3 *Prudence:* only profits which have been earned and ascertained with reasonable certainty should be recognised. Account should be taken of all liabilities or losses that have arisen or are likely to arise in respect of the accounting period or prior periods.
4 *Accruals:* this is also referred to as the matching concept and requires that income and expense are accrued and recognised as they are incurred (not as cash is received and paid), and matched with one another as far as possible.

Schedule 4 adds a fifth concept for corporates – that assets and liabilities be valued individually. Consequently, a corporate must value a portfolio of interest rate sensitive assets individually and not as a whole. Nevertheless, when valuing an asset, account should be taken of the treatment of the liability funding it.

A sixth concept that might be added is that of substance over form. In certain circumstances the substance rather than the legal form of a transaction should be reflected in the financial statements. It also implies that the circumstances of a particular transaction, its intention and its economic reality, should be considered in determining the most appropriate accounting treatment.

In applying these principles to interest protection instruments, some recognition is generally given to the treatment adopted in the US which is discussed in Part II, Chapter 1.

Applying the principles

The concepts of prudence and accruals may give rise to an apparent conflict when accounting for interest rate instruments. SSAP2 states that in such cases, the concept of prudence should prevail. Care should be taken in the application of this rule. It does not, for example, justify the recognition of losses and the deferral of profits when marking to market. The matching concept should be followed and any provision for counterparty risk or market illiquidity made as necessary. Most interest rate instruments are dealt with through established interbank markets or recognised exchanges and thus such risks are normally so low as to require no provision.

The concepts of matching and of economic substance suggest that one must consider whether a particular transaction or instrument is for hedging purposes or not. As in the US, if the product is a hedge then it should be matched with the item being hedged. The effect of any change of interest rates on the hedging instrument and the hedged item should generally be accounted for in the same period.

Hedging criteria

The previous chapter discussed the criteria which must be satisfied for an interest rate protection instrument to be treated as a hedge. Despite the lack of a UK equivalent to FASB80, the same principles usually apply in the UK.

1 *The underlying transaction that is being hedged must expose the company to interest rate risk.* Substance over form would suggest that the economic reality of the situation is recognised and, therefore, that the risk exposure of the total enterprise should be considered to the extent that it can be readily ascertained. If an interest rate sensitive asset is match funded, no interest rate exposure exists. Any 'hedge' taken out against the asset will increase the company's exposure to interest rates movements, rather than reduce it, and thus would not qualify as a hedge for accounting purposes. If fellow subsidiaries have opposing interest rate exposures which net out in aggregate, either subsidiary may enter a hedging transaction and account for it as a hedge in their individual accounts. If only one subsidiary enters a hedge, on consolidation an adjustment should be made in order to account for the instrument as a speculative transaction, if the accounting treatment adopted is material to the financial statements.

2 *The enterprise should designate the product as a hedge.* Given the different accounting treatment of hedges and speculative transactions, it is necessary to determine when undertaking a transaction what its purpose is, in order to maintain adequate books and records and in order to ensure that the company complies with the concept of consistency. The records should also indicate what is being hedged. This may be an individual asset, liability or commitment or a group of such items. The concept of substance over form would suggest that if an instrument is effective as a hedge against an interest rate exposure which arises as a result of repricing mismatches within a portfolio of assets and liabilities, then the product may be accounted for as a hedge, even if it is not identified with a

particular asset, liability or commitment. Such a policy of specifying 'macro hedges' should only be adopted if there is consistency of accounting treatment of items within the portfolio. If different accounting treatments are adopted, it will not be possible to ensure that the hedging transaction is accounted for on a symmetrical basis with the position being hedged.

3 *The interest rate protection instrument must be effective as a hedge.* The concepts of both matching and substance over form suggest that it is likely that a reasonable degree of correlation will exist between the effect of interest rate changes on the hedging transaction and their effect on the item being hedged. The degree of correlation required is a matter of debate.

4 *There must be reasonable certainty that the transaction will act as a hedge.* There must be a genuine intention to use the instrument as a hedge. If the hedged item is an anticipated transaction then it must be probable that the transaction will actually occur.

Types of transactions that may be hedged

Any interest rate sensitive asset or liability can be hedged including for example:

- An existing liability which is subject to floating interest rates, so that the company is at risk of interest rates rising.
- An existing liability which is subject to a fixed rate of interest, so that the company will be locked into a relatively expensive source of funds if interest rates fall.
- An existing security, the price of which fluctuates according to interest rate levels.
- An existing asset bearing a fixed rate of interest (whether or not it is intended to hold the asset to maturity), so that the company is at risk of receiving a relatively low earnings stream if interest rates rise.
- A firm commitment to borrow or invest funds in the future (whether or not the rate is predetermined).
- An anticipated transaction involving the borrowing or investing of funds.

Where a fixed rate security is funded by a floating rate liability, one may wonder whether any hedge which is taken out, should be considered a hedge against the asset or as a hedge against the liability. In reality it is the interest rate position or mismatch created by the differing repricing characteristics of the asset and liability which is being hedged. As most companies will not identify a particular source of funds for each asset, it is usually necessary to allocate the hedge arbitrarily to either the asset or the liability.

Banks may arbitrage between two instruments, such as a futures and an FRA, or between an instrument and a cash market transaction such as a deposit. Where a deposit is involved, the bank may designate the instrument as a hedge, if it satisfies the criteria discussed above. If two instruments are involved, both may be marked to market and the distinction between hedging and speculating becomes less relevant.

In conclusion, it appears that, given the lack of authoritative guidance in the UK, companies have greater scope than their US counterparts in determining whether a particular transaction is a hedge.

Accounting treatment for hedges

If a transaction qualifies as a hedge, any profit arising on the hedge as a result of interest rate movements should be recognised in the same accounting period as the related loss on the item being hedged, and vice versa. The life-span of a hedge is shown in Exhibit 2.1.

Assume that at t_0, a company decides to hedge an anticipated borrowing, or an existing borrowing, the interest rate on which is determined at t_1. The hedge can be ignored for accounting purposes until t_1, any margin payments being held in suspense. Alternatively, at any time between t_0 and t_1 the hedge can be marked to market and any profit or loss deferred. This simply gives rise to balance sheet entries with no effect on the profit and loss (P&L) account. At t_1 the hedge is realised, giving rise to a profit or loss which is then deferred and amortised over the interest rate period which the hedge was designed to cover $(t_1 - t_2)$. The deferred profit or loss on the hedge is accounted for separately and, not usually, as an adjustment to the carrying value of the liability.

Exhibit 2.1   Life-span of a hedge

t_0	t_1	t_2
Hedge transaction date	Start of hedging period	End of hedging period

A company might also enter a transaction at t_0 to hedge against the effects of interest rate movements on the price of an investment held by the company. Corporates normally account for fixed asset investments at cost less permanent diminution in value and for current asset investments at the lower of cost and market value. Either type of investment may be revalued to current cost (market value). If, prior to t_1, the corporate maintains the investment at cost, then the hedge may be ignored for accounting purposes. If provision is made to reflect a fall in the value of the investment, due to interest rate movements, then the provision should be reduced by the increase in the market value of the hedge. In such cases the existence of the hedge is effectively reflected in the carrying value of the investment. Where an investment is revalued to market value and gives rise to a profit which is credited to revaluation reserve, then any loss on the qualifying hedge should be debited directly to the same reserve, in order to preserve the symmetry of accounting.

In summary, one must consider both the accounting treatment of the hedged item and the period to which the hedge relates. If interest on the hedged item is accounted for on an accruals basis, profit or loss on the hedge should be accrued or amortised over the interest period to which the hedge relates. If the hedged item is accounted for at market value, then the hedge should be marked to market.

Termination of hedges

In some cases a hedge will not exactly match the timing of the hedged transaction. For instance, a futures taken out to hedge against anticipated borrowings, may be closed out a few days before the borrowings are drawn down. Generally, such timing differences can be ignored and the profit or loss on the futures will be deferred and amortised in accordance with the rules previously discussed.

In other cases, a hedge may be realised and replaced with another hedge or covered in the cash market. Again any profit or loss on the original hedge should be deferred. Where, however, a company decides to terminate a hedge and accept the resulting interest rate risk, a different treatment may be appropriate. If the hedge is showing a profit, then it should be deferred, since that implies that a loss is likely to be incurred on the item previously hedged. If, however, the hedge is showing a loss, prudence dictates that it is recognised immediately, since it is not certain that the item previously hedged will show a corresponding profit, given potential fluctuations in interest rates before the commencement of the original hedging period.

If the hedged item is disposed of prematurely, the hedging instrument ceases to be an effective hedge and should be accounted for as a speculative transaction.

Speculative transactions

Where a particular transaction fails to qualify as a hedge it should be treated as a speculative transaction. In Chapter 1, concerning the US, it is suggested that the instrument should be accounted for on a lower of cost or market basis or at market value.

Corporates in the UK are subject to the Schedule 4 requirements that only realised profits are reflected in the profit and loss account. The term 'realised profits' is not defined in the Companies Act. Schedule 4 makes it clear, however, that any profits arising on marking securities to market should be treated as unrealised and credited directly to a revaluation reserve. It would seem, therefore, that any profits arising on the revaluation of interest rate instruments should be treated in the same way. Technically, corporates should therefore value speculative contracts at the lower of cost or market, or at market with profits credited directly to revaluation reserve. Losses, on the other hand, should be treated as realised and charged against income in accordance with the concept of prudence.

The position is slightly different for banks. A technical release of the CCAB (TR556) concluded that, having regard to the special nature of banking transactions and operations, profits arising from the revaluation of trading instruments to market value ought to be treated as realised in a bank. Consequently, banks normally mark to market their trading instruments and take both profits and losses to the P&L account.

The rationale for such a treatment is that a bank has the choice at any time to close out the interest rate exposure created by the instrument and realise the profit or loss to date. There is some debate as to which rate should be used when assessing market value, where there is a spread between bid and offer prices. Those who argue that the real purpose is to fair value the instrument, suggest a mid-market price is most appropriate. Others argue that the purpose of revaluing is to calculate the profit or loss which would arise if the position is closed, and that a more conservative 'buy-back' approach should be adopted. Either method appears acceptable providing it is used consistently.

A problem also arises where the market for a particular instrument is thin, or where it is difficult to obtain appropriate interest rates with which to value non-marketable instruments. Usually, a counterparty can be found if the rate offered is sufficiently attractive. Alternatively, a matching position can be constructed using other financial instruments. Generally, therefore, where markets are thin, or instruments cannot be traded, a conservative approach to valuation may be necessary, but profits arising may nevertheless be treated as realised.

Some corporates, such as dealing companies or those with large treasury departments which effectively operate as in-house banks, may argue that TR556 is as relevant to them as it is to a bank. In such circumstances corporates may take revaluation profits to the P&L account by utilising the provision in Schedule 4 which allows departure from normal accounting rules where the directors believe there are special reasons for doing so. They may consider, for instance, that profits arising on the revaluation of dealing securities should be credited to the P&L account in order for the financial statements to show a true and fair view. A corporate would have to disclose, however, particulars of the departure, the reasons for it and its effect, in a note to the accounts.

Alternative accounting

Whilst the distinction between speculative and hedging transactions outlined above may appear to be an effective framework for accounting, in reality it has a number of drawbacks. Interest rate exposure is inherent to the business of banking. Banks seek to create profits through the management of repricing mismatches or gaps in their asset and liability portfolios. They will create or reduce exposures to interest rate fluctuations, according to their perceptions of future rate movements. Individual transactions are generally not designated as hedges or speculative transactions. A particular transaction may serve to close an interest rate exposure in one time period and simultaneously increase the interest rate exposure in another. Historical cost accounting has a number of deficiencies as a basis for performance measurement in these circumstances. A simple example will illustrate the problem.

Assume that on 1 January 1988 a bank purchases a US$10m CD (certificate of deposit) with a coupon rate of $10\frac{1}{2}\%$ which matures with interest on 31 December 1988. The bank funds the purchase with a 6-month deposit at 10%. At the same time it contracts to take a US$10.5m 6-month deposit on 1 July 1988 at $10\frac{3}{8}\%$. The forward deposit provides the funds to repay the principal and interest on the earlier deposit. (In practice an FRA would normally be used.) If one accounted for these transactions on a accruals basis and accounted for the two deposits individually, the results would be as shown in Exhibit 2.2.

Exhibit 2.2   Timing of cash flows

Date	Accrued interest (US$)		Margin (US$)
	CD	Deposits	Profit/(loss)
January – June	525,000	(500,000)	25,000
July – December	525,000	(544,687)	(19,687)
Total	1,050,000	(1,044,687)	5,313

The example is interesting because it demonstrates the importance of the timing of cash flows. Interest on the first deposit falls due on 30 June 1988, whilst interest on the asset it is funding is not received until 31 December. Funding the intermediate interest payment results in a loss in the second six months, despite the apparent positive margin indicated by the rates.

The forward deposit in this example acts as a hedge against rising interest rates. Yet even if it is accounted for as a hedge, the results appear to be distorted. In a fully matched transaction such as this, one would expect the overall profit of US$5,313 to be allocated equally between the two six month periods. If the CD is sold, the position becomes even more distorted. A fall in interest rates will result in the CD increasing in value and thus an apparent profit. In reality this profit is offset by the fact that the bank is locked into a new, rather expensive source of funds. Whilst the profit on the CD is taken to the profit and loss account immediately, the 'loss' on the funding flows through over time on an accruals basis. Clearly it is not necessary for the bank to sell the CD. A policy of marking to market would have the same effect.

One might argue that the CD should be accounted for at cost, and if sold, any profit should be amortised and matched against the interest cost on the forward deposit which was acting as a hedge. In a bank, however, which considers its interest rate gaps in total, it may be impossible to identify what if anything was designed to act as a hedge against the CD.

What happens if the bank does not take out the forward deposit and after three months interest rates rise? At that stage the bank will clearly be facing a funding loss. If the CD is marked to market, the loss will be recognised immediately. If, in order to avoid the distortion discussed in the last paragraph, it is not marked to market the loss will be deferred. Whichever accounting policy is adopted for the CD, therefore, it appears likely that there will be some distortion in the allocation of profit and losses between accounting periods.

These distortions will seldom be material to corporates and thus a simple distinction between hedging and speculative transactions will provide a satisfactory basis for accounting. Banks, however, which deal in large volumes of interest rate instruments will require a reasonably accurate indication of the profits and losses arising on a daily basis from decisions to hedge or to run particular positions.

The only satisfactory solution is to 'fair value' both assets and liabilities. Liabilities are generally not marketable, but a net present value can be computed by discounting the cash flows arising from the liabilities, using the yield curve for that instrument to determine the relevant discount rate. A variety of technical problems have to be solved in adopting such an approach, but none of these appear to be insurmountable. The acceptability of net present value accounting for statutory reporting purposes is unclear. In the example above net present value accounting would result in the UK$5,313 being recognised as a profit (at its discounted value) on day one. Nevertheless, if adequate provision is made for any counterparty risk and ongoing administrative costs, such a policy does not appear to contravene the concept of prudence or that of accruals. Having locked into a profit of US$5,313, the bank has earned that profit. Following the logic of TR556, such a profit would fall to be treated as realised by a bank. However, it must be said that the application of NPV accounting to statutory financial statements would be innovative and banks would be well advised to consult their auditors before considering adopting such a policy.

In subsequent chapters we have considered more traditional UK accounting approaches to a number of interest rate protection instruments. One area however, where NPV accounting is of immediate relevance, is in the treatment of swaps which are discussed in Part IV, Chapter 3.

Disclosure

Corporates are required by SSAP2 and Schedule 4 of the Companies Act to state the significant accounting policies adopted. The best practice is to indicate for each instrument the policy of income recognition adopted, distinguishing between hedging and speculative transactions.

Schedule 4 requires disclosure of financial commitments that have not been provided for and that are relevant to an assessment of the company's state of affairs. Together with SSAP18 it also requires disclosure of material contingent liabilities except where the possibility of loss is remote. Consequently, where an instrument hedges an anticipated commitment, the existence of the hedge and the amount of any profit or loss which has not been recognised should be disclosed if material. If corporates defer profits on speculative transactions because of the 'realised' profit restrictions in Schedule 4, they may require disclosure as contingent gains in accordance with SSAP18.

Even where profits and losses to date have been recognised in income, future interest rate fluctuations may give rise to a loss. Consequently, it is normal practice for corporates to indicate the nature and extent of all 'off balance sheet' financial instruments, where they are material, in a contingent liability note.

Where an instrument hedges a particular asset or liability, it will normally be appropriate to disclose the hedge in any note to the accounts concerning the asset or liability. An interest rate swap in respect of a company's borrowings, for example, would be disclosed in the note which deals with the company's borrowings.

Banks are not subject to the requirements of Schedule 4, but must comply with SSAP2 and SSAP18. Because the volume of business in interest rate instruments is generally significant in a bank, disclosure of the accounting policies adopted will be required. In their contingent liabilities note, however, most banks currrently only disclose the nature of interest rate instruments which have been undertaken in the normal course of business. Few give any indication of the extent of their involvement. Greater disclosure in this respect will be required on implementation of the EC directive on bank accounts.

The SORPs currently being developed by the British Bankers Association will also address disclosure. Banks will probably be required to provide more information in respect of counterparty and interest rate risk. It is unlikely, however, that the disclosure will be as comprehensive as that suggested by the FASB exposure draft on disclosures about financial instruments.

3 Taxation framework

Robert Henrey, Rick Solway, Mike Mason,
Randy Vivona, R. Emerson and Charles Kolstad

UNITED STATES (Robert Henrey, Rick Solway, Mike Mason and Randy Vivona)

Assumptions

In analysing the US tax treatment of the transactions discussed below, we have made the simplifying assumptions that the transactions discussed below are denominated in US dollars and entered into by a US entity. Also, our analysis discusses the tax treatment only from the perspective of the *corporation* looking to obtain protection from interest rate fluctuations.

THE INSTRUMENTS

Interest rate futures contract

Description of transactions

An interest rate futures contract is a contract to buy or sell (make delivery) a specific amount of a specified financial instrument, such as a note or bond issued by a government or instrumentality at a future date for a specified price (the price is established at the time of the contract). The value of the contract changes as the interest rate market changes. The contract is traded on various US exchanges regulated by the Commodity Futures Trading Commission and represents an irrevocable commitment of the contract holder to buy or sell a debt instrument. It is used for both hedging and speculative purposes. Interest rate futures which are currently traded on US exchanges include contracts related to US Treasury bills, US Treasury notes, US Treasury bonds, and certificates of deposit.

US tax treatment

Character of gain or loss

Generally, any gain or loss recognised on an interest rate futures contract was treated as capital gain or loss, 60% of which was long term and 40% of which was short term. The Tax Reform Act of 1986 eliminated the tax rate differential for long-term capital gains, and amounts recognised after 31 December 1986 are taxed at the full corporate rate. Nevertheless, the tax law still requires the taxpayer to distinguish between capital and ordinary income transactions because capital losses can only offset capital gains and cannot be deducted from ordinary income.

In the event that the contract is used for hedging purposes (see discussion below regarding 'Timing'), gain or loss on the contract will generally be treated as ordinary.

Interest income expense

Not applicable.

Timing

Generally, gain or loss on an interest rate futures contract is recognised in the year in which the contract is closed. Any open position is marked to market on the last day of the taxable year as if it were terminated on that day. Gain or loss is measured by the increase or decrease in the value of the contract from the date it was entered into (or the end of the preceding taxable year, if later).

If a contract qualifies as a hedging transaction, mark to market treatment does not apply. A contract will be considered a hedge if:

- it is entered into in the normal course of the entity's trade or business;
- it reduces the risk of price or interest rate risk;
- the position is identified as a hedge at inception; and
- the hedged item gives rise to ordinary income or loss.

Gain or loss on a contract that qualifies as a hedge is recognised only at the close of the contract.

If the contract constitutes one leg of a straddle (one position substantially diminishes the taxpayer's risk from holding another position), then any loss on the contract may not be recognised to the extent that there is unrealised gain on the offsetting position at the end of the taxable year. Rather, recognition of such loss must be deferred until the time when the gain is recognised.

Also, in the case where a contract constitutes one leg of a straddle, any interest or carrying charges incurred in order to purchase and hold that contract are generally not deductible; rather, they are capitalised as part of the cost of the contract.

Finally, as held by the Supreme Court in *Corn Products Refining Co.* v. *Commissioner of Internal Revenue*, a contract entered into in a context which clearly relates to the taxpayer's trade or business will generate ordinary income or loss, even if the contract is not identified as a hedge. The contract will, however, be marked to market on the last day of the taxable year.

Source

Subject to Regulations, gain on an interest rate futures contract is generally sourced in the country of residence of the taxpayer. Thus, if a US entity (as opposed, for example, to a foreign branch of a US corporation) enters into a contract, gain on the contract will be US source. Losses are generally allocated to the geographical area (i.e. foreign or domestic) to which gains are sourced.

Interest rate swap agreement

Description of transaction

An interest rate swap is an agreement between two parties to exchange payments (i.e. cash flows). Typically, one party is obliged to make payments based on a fixed interest rate while the other party agrees to make payments based on a floating rate (e.g. Libor, commercial paper or Treasury bills). The respective interest rates are applied as a minimal principal amount. There is generally no exchange of principal. Actual payments may be made on a net basis.

Interest rate swaps are transacted directly between two parties. An intermediary such as a commercial or investment bank may act either as agent or principal.

US tax treatment

The tax law does not specifically address the tax treatment of interest rate swaps. We have, however, developed the following understanding of the US tax treatment of interest rate swaps.

Character of income or expense

Generally, a swap payment is treated as ordinary income to the recipient and generates an ordinary deduction for the payer.

Interest income expense

The issue of whether swap payments could be treated as interest (or other fixed or determinable annual or periodic income) for some purposes rermains unsettled and controversial, even under the new tax law. The significance of the issue stems from:

1 The question of whether withholding should be imposed on cross-border swap payments (Revenue Ruling 87–5 and Notice 87–4, issued by the Inland Revenue Service mid-1987, both indicate that withholding shall not be imposed on swap payments);
2 The question of whether cross-border swap payments should be included in or deducted from income gross or net of withholding;
3 The need to allocate and apportion interest expense on a US consolidated basis for purposes of determining a US entity's foreign tax credit limitation. In Notice 87–4, the IRS indicated that it would not rule on the issue of whether swap payments constitute interest for this or any other purpose.

Timing

Swap receipts should be recognised no later than when received and swap payments should be deducted when paid. There is question as to the ability to accrue swap payments similarly to the way in which interest is accrued. There is a strong argument in favour of accrual as the amount to be accrued can be accurately determined and is evidenced by a legally enforceable agreement. The theoretical problem with swap payment accruals lies in the fact that indebtedness is not created between the swap parties.

Source

In mid-1987 the IRS determined that all swap income attributable to a US entity will be considered US source even though such income is paid by a foreign entity. Similarly, the related swap expenses would be allocated to US source income for purposes of computing the foreign tax credit limitation.

Interest rate option contract

Description of transaction

An interest rate option is a contract which gives the holder the right but not the obligation to fix the interest rate for a specified future date on a loan or interest rate swap (i.e. swaption). Interest rate options of this type are negotiated between parties 'over the counter' or in the interbank market; they are not currently traded on a government regulated board or exchange. The buyer purchases the contract for a fee determined by reference to the difference between the spot interest rate on the contract date and a specified rate on a specified future date and to time value.

US tax treatment

Character of gain or loss

A contract relating to a borrowing or swap agreement that is considered an integral part of the option purchaser's day-to-day business operations or that is necessary to protect or generate ordinary operating income should produce an ordinary loss in the amount of fee paid. If the contract was held for speculative purposes and subsequently sold in the market, capital gain or loss would arise. If a speculative option is allowed to expire, a capital loss would occur in the amount of the fee paid.

Interest income/expense

Upon exercise of the option, the question arises as to the appropriateness of deducting the fee paid to acquire the option as additional interest expense on an underlying borrowing. IRS code provisions are somewhat narrow in the treatment of deductions as interest. It would not appear that the fee paid would be integrated with the borrowing and thereby reduce the proceeds received upon issuance and create bond discount. By analogy, gain or loss on an interest rate futures that was entered into in anticipation of future borrowings would not be treated as an adjustment to interest expense.

Timing

In the event that the option expires without being exercised, the fee paid to acquire the option premium will be deducted in the period in which the option expires.

In the event that the option is exercised, the fee paid to acquire the option premium should probably be amortised over the life of the underlying loan or interest rate swap.

Source

Subject to regulations, the gain or loss on the interest rate option will be sourced by reference to the taxpayer's country of residence.

Forward rate agreement

Description of transaction

An agreement where a buyer (seller) seeks to protect against a rise (fall) in interest rates on agreed principal amount as of a specified future date. On the settlement date, the counterparties will compare the then current interest rate with the rate specified in the agreement. If the current rate is greater than the agreement rate, the buyer will receive, up front, the interest differential determined over the life of the loan. Conversely, if the current rate is below the agreement rate, the seller will receive the differential from the buyer.

US tax treatment

The tax law does not cover forward rate agreements, but we have developed the following understanding of the treatment based on general tax principles.

Character of income or expense

Generally, the character of the interest differential income or expense is ordinary.

Interest income/expense

The interest differential income or expense is most likely not treated as interest as there is no principal exchange involved.

Timing

The interest differential income or expense is recognised when received or paid.

Source

The source of any interest differential income is determined by reference to the taxpayer's country of residence.

Interest rate cap, floor and collar agreements

Description of transaction

An interest rate cap is an agreement in which the seller (i.e. provider) of the cap agrees to make payments to the purchaser (typically a borrower looking to limit exposure to floating rate liabilities) if interest rates rise above a certain level. The cap places a ceiling on the level to which a floating interest rate may rise during the period covered by the agreement. The provider of the cap need not be the lender of the floating rate debt which the borrower wishes to hedge. The provider may have issued debt on a floating rate basis but which is subject to a maximum or ceiling.

The purchaser enters into the cap agreement by paying the provider an up-front fee. The amount of this fee is based in part on the length of time for which the purchaser requires the cap protection as well as the interest rate ceiling on which the agreement is based.

If, during the term of the agreement, market interest rates rise above the ceiling specified in the agreement, then the cap provider is required to make payments to the purchaser which are sufficient to bring the purchaser's interest rate cost down to the ceiling rate. When market rates are below the ceiling, the purchaser pays market rates to the lender without receiving any payments from the cap provider. The cap agreement thus provides the purchaser with fixed rate liabilities when market rates exceed the agreement's ceiling rate and floating rate liabilities when market rates are below the ceiling level.

An interest rate floor is similar to a cap agreement, except that it is entered into or purchased by a floating rate lender who wishes to hedge against decreases in market interest rates, as such decreases will reduce the lender's earnings on floating rate assets. In this case, the cap provider assures the purchaser, for an up-front fee, that the interest rate on the purchaser's floating rate assets will not fall below a specified floor level during the term of the agreement.

An interest rate collar is an agreement which provides the purchaser with a hedge against increases and decreases in market interest rates. The agreement integrates a cap and a floor concept to offer floating rate asset *and* liability management potential in a single instrument.

US tax treatment

Again, the tax law provides no specific guidance on caps, floors and collars. Our comments are thus based on general US tax principles.

Character of income or expense

The up-front and subsequent payments (receipts) made for a cap, floor, or collar agreement will be treated as an ordinary deduction (or as ordinary income).

Interest income or expense

Although the up-front payments and subsequent payments at each settlement date are in essence indexed to interest rates, the payments themselves would most likely not be considered interest as debt is not created between the seller and purchaser of the cap, floor or collar.

Timing

There is a strong likelihood that the proceeds from the sale of the cap, floor or collar agreement must be treated as current taxable income upon receipt. Any amounts subsequently paid to the purchaser of the cap would be deductible when paid. The possibility also exists that the transaction will be held 'open' until payments are subsequently made or the contract expires (similar to the tax treatment afforded the writer of a stock option).

The purchaser of a cap may be forced to amortise the up-front fee paid over the life of the cap while picking up any income received at a particular settlement date in the year in which it is received. As is the case with the seller of a cap, floor or collar, the purchaser may have to wait until it is determined whether any amount is payable before deducting the up-front payment (again similar to purchasing a stock option, the premium of which is not immediately deductible).

The uncertainty with respect to the timing of income and deductions has lead to various mechanisms to achieve a more equitable result. Writing a series of agreements or contracting for annual payments with the total amount held in escrow are ways in which the timing issues may be resolved.

Source

The source of income relating the agreements will most likely be determined according to the taxpayer's country of residence.

UNITED KINGDOM (R. Emerson)

General

Describing the UK tax treatment of hedging transactions is fraught with difficulty for a number of reasons. Most of these arise from the fact that the basic framework of UK tax law is derived from early Victorian times, when a treasurer's life was somewhat simpler than it is today. Subsequent legislation has only served to complicate matters and there is little or no statutory guidance on the tax treatment of any financial instrument. Equally, there is little or no guidance to be derived from case law, and a review of the few relevant cases leaves one with the feeling that the courts may not have fully understood what they were dealing with. This is particularly so in cases involving the relevance of accountancy principles, although to be fair to the legal profession there is little consensus between accountants on some of the major issues. It is therefore comforting to know that many theoretical uncertainties can be ignored in practice because of guidance given by the Inland Revenue of their treatment of particular transactions. The Inland Revenue's views are, of course, capable of being challenged but a taxpayer ignores them at his peril.

The main danger that a UK taxpayer faces in entering into hedging transactions is 'tax fragmentation', caused by the tax treatment of the hedge being different from that of the underlying risk. A pre-tax hedged position therefore may not be truly hedged on an after-tax basis.

The uncoordinated approach of UK tax legislation to the financial sector makes it difficult to adopt any straightforward method of reviewing whether a particular instrument creates a true after-tax hedge, but the following comments may be helpful.

First, it is necessary to determine whether the hedge and the risk will both be regarded as revenue or capital items. This will usually involve an analysis of the nature of borrowings and the use to which funds are put. As a general rule borrowings will only be regarded as revenue items if they are short term and used for the purposes of the borrower's trade. The categorisation of a hedge as a revenue or capital item will usually follow from the nature of the underlying risk, but this general rule can be modified by specific legislation.

If the revenue or capital nature of the hedge differs from that of the underlying risk, there is a clear mismatch, because although an income loss may be capable of offsetting capital gains, capital losses cannot be offset against income. However, even if the nature of the hedge corresponds to that of the underlying risk there may be problems. For instance, losses of a capital nature will only be allowable capital losses if they arise on the disposal of an asset as opposed to the settlement of a liability. Revenue losses will generally only qualify for tax relief if they arise in the conduct of a trade as opposed to the business of managing investments. Finally, even if the profit (or loss) on a hedge and the loss (or profit) on the underlying risk are both taxed in the same way, they may need to be recognised for tax purposes in different periods.

With these obstacles, a taxpayer may wonder whether UK tax law provides the opportunity for any effective after-tax hedging. In practice, as Exhibit 3.1 shows, many of these obstacles only arise if the hedge and the underlying risk are not related to trading activities. Exhibit 3.1 attempts to simplify a complex area into a series of straightforward questions, and it should therefore not be regarded as an infallible guide. The reader should refer to the following pages for the detailed reasoning behind the exhibit.

Exhibit 3.1 Hedging: tax flowchart

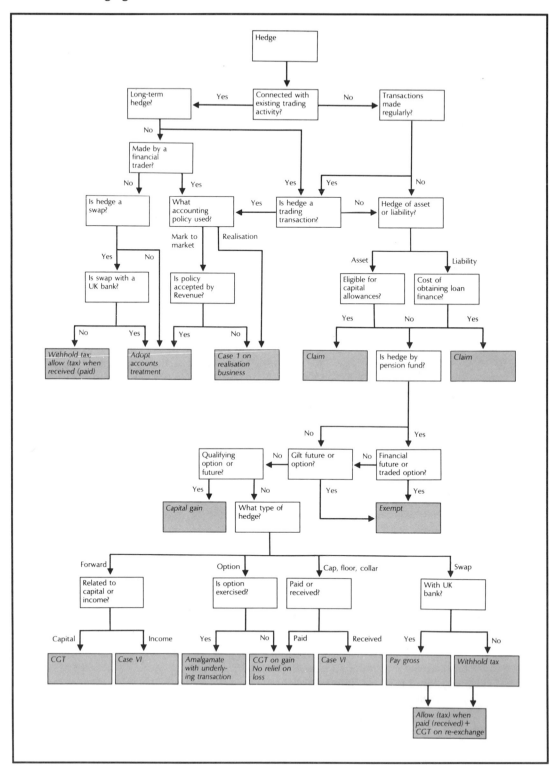

Interest rate swaps

The starting point of any consideration of the tax treatment of swaps, in common with that of many other financial instruments, is to review the accounting treatment. It is well established that the recognition of profit and loss is first a matter to be determined by the principles of current commercial accounting practice. So far as those principles accord with tax law, they are conclusive, but where they conflict with tax law, the law will prevail (see, for instance, *Willingale* v. *International Commercial Bank Limited* 52 TC 243 and *BSC Footwear Limited* v. *Ridgway* 47 TC 495).

The difficulty with an approach leaving the primary treatment to be determined by current commercial accounting principles is that those principles are still in a state of flux. Therefore, an approach adopted in this chapter is to consider the tax treatment of the payments involved in swap transactions, taking account both of the strict position under UK tax law, and the effective concessions allowed by the Inland Revenue. As a preliminary comment, a number of problems under strict UK tax rules are eliminated involving swap arrangements by Inland Revenue practice, but this applies only to swap transactions involving recognised banks and financial traders.

Nature and treatment of periodic payments

Most swap arrangements contain provision for periodic payments to be made, which reflect (and are usually calculated by reference to) the differential between the interest rates underlying the swap transaction. In each case, it will be necessary to review the swap contract, but as a general rule the following tax issues arise.

Periodic payments as 'annual payments'

It is clear that the standard International Swap Dealers Association (ISDA) terms and the British Bankers Association Interest Rate Swaps (BBAIRS) terms do not create any indebtedness, so periodic payments cannot be treated as interest. Under UK tax rules, periodic payments will only qualify as interest if they represent 'payment by time for the use of money' (*Bennet* v. *Ogston* 15 TC 374), and are paid in respect of a debt (re: *Euro Hotel (Belgravia) Limited* 51 TC 293).

Nevertheless, as the periodic payments are clearly contractual, may prove to be recurrent, and are of an income nature, they will be 'annual payments'. From this classification, two further issues arise:

1   Will a UK resident counterparty have to deduct basic rate income tax at 25% from annual payments made under the swap?
2   How will tax relief be given to a UK resident counterparty for those annual payments?

Deduction of basic rate income tax from periodic payments

A distinction has to be drawn between the strict legal position, and the Inland Revenue view, which does not accord with the law. Payments may be made in three situations:

1   Between parties who are not banks or financial traders; or
2   between counterparties and a bank or financial trader acting as an intermediary, although dealing as principal; or
3   on the interbank market, between banks and other financial institutions directly.

Under UK rules, periodic payments qualifying as 'annual payments' will only be subject to deduction of tax by the payer where those payments are 'pure income profit'. Payments will only be 'pure income profit' where they are received as passive investment income and the recipient cannot properly set related expenses incurred in earning that income against the payments to calculate any profit (see re: *Hanbury* 38 TC 588 and *CIR* v. *Campbell* 45 TC 427).

A summary of the strict legal position is as follows:

1   Periodic payments under swap agreements between parties who are *not* banks or financial services traders are subject to deduction of basic rate tax by the payer.
2   Periodic payments under swap transactions involving an intermediary bank or financial services traders are not subject to deduction of tax. Periodic payments made *by* the intermediary bank or financial services trader dealing as principal to the counterparties will be subject to deduction of tax, unless:
    –   the periodic payments have a source outside the UK (this is extremely unlikely where the swap agreement involves a paying party or counterparty in the UK);
    –   the recipient of the periodic payments can claim exemption under the 'other income' article of a double tax agreement (see Article 21 of OECD Model Agreement).
3   Periodic payments under swap agreements made on the interbank market between banks or financial services traders acting as principal parties will not be subject to deduction of tax.

The Inland Revenue's analysis is that all periodic payments under swap arrangements are 'annual payments', payable under deduction of 25% income tax. However, Inland Revenue practice is to allow a more liberal tax treatment for banks carrying on a bona fide banking business in the UK, and other financial services traders. The practice confirms these effective concessions:

●   Periodic payments under swap agreements may be made *to* a bank acting as principal in the ordinary course of its business without deduction of tax.
●   Periodic payments under swap agreements may be made *by* a bank or financial trader without deduction of tax, where the bank or financial trader acts as principal in the ordinary course of its business.

UK tax relief for periodic payments under swap transactions

The strict position is that an 'annual payment' (even if not subject to deduction of tax), cannot be a trading expense (Section 74(m), Taxes Act 1988). However, any periodic payments under swap agreements by a UK corporate taxpayer will qualify as charges on income, whether or not they are subject to deduction of tax. This is specifically provided in Section 338(3)(a), Taxes Act 1988, under which the only requirement is that the payments should be 'annual payments'. As a result, there is no need to deduct basic rate tax to establish a claim to a tax deduction for payments made by a UK entity. Periodic payments to non-residents will only be deductible if the payer:

●   withholds basic rate tax from the payment; or
●   makes the payments out of offshore UK Case IV or V income; or
●   the payer has advance clearance to pay without withholding from the Inspector of Foreign Dividends, because of applicable double tax relief.

Strictly speaking, tax relief will only be available when the annual payment is made. However, Inland Revenue practice modifies the strict position. The treatment accepted may be summarised as follows:

1   Periodic payments to recognised UK banks under swap agreements made by UK *trading companies* are deductible as trade expenses, and therefore on an accruals basis.
2   Periodic payments by a UK *trading company* other than to a UK bank are deductible when paid.

3   Periodic payments under swap agreements made by UK *investment companies* are deductible as charges on income, on a paid basis.

UK tax treatment of initial arrangement or facility fees

Because almost all swaps are relatively long-term arrangements, initial fees will not qualify as trading expenses. Neither will they be charges on income, as they will not be recurrent. No relief can be obtained under the relief for loan finance costs (Section 77, Taxes Act 1988), because a swap does not involve any loan, advance or indebtedness.

The practical solution is to ensure that the periodic payments under the swap are increased to cover these fees, or that the fee is annualised over the swap term. As a result, the payments should be deductible as periodic payments, subject to the commentary above.

Early termination of swaps

Any payment made by a trading company to a UK bank should, on the Inland Revenue's analysis, be an allowable trading deduction when paid on the grounds that it is a payment made to get rid of an onerous trading liability (*Anglo-Persian Oil* v. *Dale* 16 TC 253). Any payment in other circumstances is unlikely to qualify for any form of tax relief.

The receipt of a lump sum on early termination should be taxable as a chargeable gain arising on the disposal of contractual rights (*Marren* v. *Ingles* 54 TC 76).

Interest rate futures contracts

Banks, financial trading companies and insurance companies with the exception of their life funds, will generally be regarded as entering into futures transactions as part of a trade, so their profits and losses will be taxed accordingly. Equally, other trading companies which enter into a futures contract to hedge a trading liability should treat any profits or losses on such contracts as part of their overall trading profits, following *Imperial Tobacco Limited* v. *Kelly* 25 TC 292.

For accounting purposes, the hedge will normally be treated in the same way as the underlying risk and so may be recognised on an accruals basis. The normal tax rule, however, is that profits and losses may not be anticipated and should only be recognised when 'realised'. The Inland Revenue have stated that: 'a profit or loss could be treated as realised either when matched contracts are acquired, which is perhaps technically more correct or when the clearing house is notified of set-off. Either approach, if consistently applied, should be acceptable unless the time of set-off were manipulated for tax reasons'. In practice, the Inland Revenue often accept that the taxation treatment can follow the accounting treatment, especially in the case of a non-financial trader.

The treatment of a taxpayer who enters into a futures contract otherwise than in the course of a trade depends upon the nature of the contract. Profits and losses on gilt futures will not give rise to any capital gain or loss by specific exemption (Section 67, Capital Gains Tax Act 1979). This exemption works well for profits, but there seems little prospect of any alternative relief for losses. The only hope would be to claim the loss as an 'incidental expense of obtaining loan finance' (Section 77, Taxes Act 1988) but the Inland Revenue would certainly dispute any such claim. As regards any contract quoted on a futures exchange recognised by the Inland Revenue (which includes LIFFE and the major US exchanges), profits and losses will be treated as capital gains and losses (Section 72, Finance Act 1985). Profits and losses made from contracts on other exchanges are likely to give rise to profits under Schedule D Case VI (taxable as income) or to losses under the same case which may only be offset against current or future Case VI income.

UK pension funds have a blanket exemption from taxation in respect of transactions in financial futures, however regularly they enter into such deals (Section 659, Taxes Act 1988 and Section

149B(1)(g), Capital Gains Tax Act 1979). In contrast to the legislation providing capital gains treatment for non-traders, the pension funds legislation gives no definition of a financial futures, so pension funds can enter into any such contract quoted on any exchange without tax liability.

Forward rate agreements

A forward rate agreement (FRA) is essentially an over the counter (OTC) interest rate future. As such, it is a short life wasting asset on which any profits and losses will be regarded as being of a revenue nature.

Any trading company entering into a forward rate agreement to hedge a trading risk (i.e. an actual or expected interest expense which would be allowed as a trade deduction) should treat profits and losses on the FRA as part of its normal trading results for tax purposes. Such profits and losses will be realised when payment is received or made.

Any profit or loss made in other circumstances should be treated by the taxpayer as taxable under Schedule D Case VI, following the Inland Revenue's 1982 ruling on LIFFE transactions. The alternative capital gains treatment would result in profits still being subject to tax, at the same rates as income, without any relief for losses. The only alternative prospect of relief for a loss would be again as 'incidental cost of obtaining loan finance', if one can prove to the satisfaction of the Inland Revenue that the expenditure was incurred 'wholly and exclusively for the purposes of obtaining the finance'.

Interest rate options

The UK taxation treatment of options follows, to a great extent, that of futures. Profits and losses arising from options contracts entered into by a financial trader, or by an ordinary trader to hedge a trading liability, are treated as part of trading income when realised. On a strict theoretical basis this would be only when the option expires, is sold or otherwise closed out. In practice, the Inland Revenue will often allow the tax treatment to follow that of the accounts, provided the accounting treatment is consistent from year to year.

Profits and losses on gilt options transactions for non-trading purposes are exempt from tax (Section 67, Capital Gains Tax Act 1979). The treatment of other options depends on their nature.

A traded option is defined as an option which, at the time of its abandonment or disposal, is quoted on a recognised stock exchange or recognised futures exchange. A financial option is defined to include:

1   an interest rate option granted by a member of a recognised stock exchange or an authorised person or listed institution within the meaning of the Financial Services Act 1986; and
2   an interest rate option granted to an authorised person or listed institution concurrently and in association with an option granted by the authorised person or listed institution to the grantor of the first mentioned option.

'Listed institution' is defined by the Financial Services Act 1986 as a listed money market institution. The definition of an 'authorised person' includes a member of a Self Regulatory Organisation or Recognised Professional Body.

The effect of the above definitions is that virtually every interest rate option taken by a taxpayer in the UK will be a financial option. Any profit on the disposal of such an option will be taxed as a capital gain, and any loss on sale or abandonment will be an allowable capital loss.

A gain on the disposal of an option which does not qualify as a traded or financial option is likely to arise as a result of a transaction with a foreign counterparty, so profits should be taxed as income under Schedule D Case V. On the other hand, there will be no relief for losses because UK tax law allows only the carry forward of foreign *trading* losses (Section 393, Taxes Act 1988).

The tax exemption for authorised UK pension funds (Section 659, Taxes Act 1988) applies only to dealings in traded options. Profits and losses accruing to funds as a result of OTC interest rate option contracts are therefore subject to income tax at 15% under Schedule D Case VI because they are not income from investments (Section 592(2), Taxes Act 1988).

Caps, floors and collars

Initial premiums and periodic payments are not regarded as interest for the same reasons as apply to swap payments. Furthermore, the Inland Revenue do not regard such payments as 'annual payments'. This is surprising, in the light of the Revenue's stated view that periodic swap payments are 'annual payments', as periodic cap payments are made under a binding obligation and are capable of recurring by reference to a predetermined formula (*Moss Empires Limited* v. *IRC* 21 TC 264).

Caps as 'annual payments'

Categorisation of periodic cap payments as annual payments would result in their being treated in exactly the same manner as periodic exchange fees under a swap. Any initial premium paid by a trading company would be an allowable deduction only if the underlying borrowing was short term. No relief could be obtained in any other circumstances, by either a trading or an investment company, because financing costs are not an allowable management expense (*Bennet* v. *Underground Electric Railways* 8 TC 475). Periodic receipts would, however, be taxable either as trading income or under Schedule D Case III.

Periodic annual payments by a non-financial concern would be allowed either as a trading expense or as a charge on income. Arguably, any initial premium received by a non-financial trader for writing a cap lasting for more than two or three years should be a tax-free capital receipt not related to the sale of any asset. The danger of such an argument is that it would result in disallowance of periodic payments under specific anti-avoidance legislation (Section 125, Taxes Act 1988).

The Inland Revenue view

For not wholly convincing reasons, the Inland Revenue differentiate caps from swaps and regard cap payments as neither interest nor annual payments. This has the advantage that all cap payments may be made without withholding tax, but it places significant obstacles in the way of obtaining tax relief for payments. The Inland Revenue's view is understood to be as follows.

The receipt of an initial premium by a bank or financial trader is regarded as taxable in full upon receipt without deduction for any provision for future periodic payments. This is on the grounds that the quantity of such payments cannot be assessed with reasonable certainty (*Owen* v. *Southern Railway of Peru* 36 TC 602). The alternative view would be that the receipt does not of itself represent a realised profit, because it relates to future obligations. Accordingly, the receipt should be spread over the life of the contract (see *BD Cowen* v. *CIR* 19 TC 155).

The receipt of an initial premium from a cap related to the hedging of borrowing for the purposes of a trade should be taxable as part of the trading profits of a trading company. Equally, cap payments made on such a hedge should be allowable as a trading deduction.

The receipt of an initial premium on a cap related to the hedging of short-term borrowing by an investment company should be taxable as income under Schedule D Case VI. The receipt of a premium in relation to a long-term cap may escape tax altogether because there is no disposal of any asset. There is, correspondingly, no relief available to an investment company for periodic cap payments because they are neither charges on income nor expenses of management.

The payment of an initial premium by a trading company is an allowable expense when paid if the underlying borrowing is taken out for trading purposes. Receipts of periodic cap payments by the trading company will be part of the company's trading profits (*Imperial Tobacco* v. *Kelly* 25 TC 292). The payment of an initial premium in any other circumstances by a non-financial concern will not qualify for tax relief, although any subsequent receipts will be taxable as income under Schedule D Case VI.

Composite transactions

It is possible, by using a combination of instruments, to create the effect of something entirely different. For instance, cross-options can effectively create a future or a loan and a purchase of stock combined with a high-priced long-dated option can effectively create a zero coupon bond in the hands of the option holder. Often the UK tax treatment of the constituent parts of such 'synthetic securities' will be radically different from the treatment of the real security which the synthetic emulates. If such synthetic security arrangements are entered into otherwise than in connection with a trade, the normal taxation treatment would be to deal separately with each constituent part. However, if tax motives play too great a part in the creation of the synthetic, the Inland Revenue may be able to tax the synthetic itself as a composite transaction under the Ramsay principle.

Summary

The current UK tax climate is so complex that only companies wishing to hedge trading risks can do so without potentially grave tax problems. There seems little prospect of any solution to these problems in the short term, and the likelihood of any solution begin forced on the UK as a result of EEC harmonisation is equally remote. Taxpayers, therefore, need to exercise great care when contemplating hedging arrangements.

JAPAN (Charles Kolstad)

Interest rate futures contract

Description of transaction

In Japan, the only interest rate futures contract available in the market is a contract (hereinafter JGB futures contract) to buy or sell (make delivery) a specific amount of 10-year Japanese Government bonds at a future date for a specified price (the price is established at the time of the contract). The value of the contract changes as the interest rates change. The contract is traded on the Tokyo Stock Exchange, and is used for both hedging and speculative purposes.

At the end of 1987, certain Japanese financial institutions were allowed by the Ministry of Finance to trade interest rate futures contracts listed on foreign exchanges.

Japanese tax treatment

Character of gain or loss

For corporation tax purposes, any gain or loss recognised on an interest rate futures contract or bond futures contract is treated as ordinary income or loss. Thus, gain on an interest rate futures contract or bond futures contract is taxed at the same rate applicable to all other income, and losses can be offset against other income.

For individual tax purposes, generally, any gain or loss from buying or selling a JGB futures contract is classified as 'miscellaneous income'. Such income is taxed at the regular tax rates. If there is a loss on a JGB futures contract, the loss can only be offset against other 'miscellaneous income'; it cannot be offset against other income. Any gain derived from a 'delivery' of bonds is treated as gain from the transfer of securities and is, in general, exempted from individual tax. Any loss on a delivery of bonds cannot be generally offset against any other income. The transfer of securities is subject to the securities transfer tax.

If individuals buy or sell JGB futures contracts as part of their business, any gain or loss on such transactions is classified as 'business income'. Gains will be taxed at the regular progressive individual tax rates, while loss can be deducted from other income, or carried forward three years (if there is a net operation loss during the tax year).

Transactions involving JGB futures contracts are subject to bourse transaction tax of 1/100,000.

Interest income expense

Not applicable.

Timing

Gain or loss on an interest rate futures contract or bond futures contract is recognised in the year in which the contract is closed. Such contracts are accounted for on a cost basis, not a lower-of-cost-or-market, or mark to market basis in Japan. Thus, unrealised gains or losses on any open positions should not be recognised at the end of the taxable year. Realised gain or loss is measured by the increase, or decrease, in the value of the contract from the date it was entered into to the date of the sale.

The tax treatment of an interest futures contract or bonds future contract does not depend upon whether the transaction is a hedging transaction.

Source

Any gain or loss derived from buying or selling JGB futures contracts listed on the Tokyo Stock Exchange would be sourced in Japan. Gain or loss on an interest rate futures contract or bond futures contract traded on a foreign exchange would currently be sourced in the country in which the exchange is located.

Interest rate swap agreement

Japanese tax treatment

Japanese tax law does not specifically address the tax treatment of interest rate swaps. However, we have developed the following understanding of the Japanese tax treatment of interest rate swaps.

Character of income or expense

Generally, an up-front swap payment is treated as ordinary income to the recipient and generates an ordinary deduction for the payer. A strong argument can be made that termination or swap assignment payments are deductible in the year the payment is made. However, the tax authorities may require the payer to amortise the payment over the term of the swap if the payment relates to replacement with a new swap rather than a termination or assignment of an existing swap.

Interest income expense

Under Japanese tax law, the types of payments that are classified as interest payments are well defined. Because payments made to a person who is not a lender of funds is not considered interest, the swap payments would not be treated as interest. As a result, any swap payment to a non-resident would not be subject to Japanese withholding tax.

Timing

Provided swap payments and receipts are matched in terms of timing, swap receipts should be recognised when received and swap payments should be deducted when paid.

In the case where the timing of swap payments and receipts are not matched, there is a question as to the ability of the payer to accrue and deduct swap payments. Although there is no reliable authority, the tax authorities are likely to allow recognition of swap payments and receipts on an accrual basis.

Source

Generally, any income derived from business in Japan is deemed to constitute Japan source income. Thus, swap receipts under a swap contract with a Japanese resident, or a Japanese permanent establishment of a non-resident, would be sourced in Japan.

Interest rate option contract

Description of transaction

Although interest rate option contracts are not popular in Japan so far, they are available on an individually negotiated basis. The buyer purchases the contract for a fee determined by reference to the difference between the spot interest rate on the contract date, and a specified rate on a specified future date and to time value.

Japanese tax treatment

Japanese tax law does not specifically address the tax treatment of an interest rate option contract.

Character of gain or loss

Fees paid by the option holder would be treated as an ordinary expense regardless of whether the interest rate option is held for speculation or hedging purposes.

Interest income/expense

As there is no principal exchange involved, a fee paid by the holder of an interest rate option contract would not be treated as interest. As a result, the fee would not be subject to Japanese withholding tax if paid to a non-resident.

Timing

The treatment of the interest rate option fee is not specifically addressed under Japanese tax law. Because direct trading in this type of instrument by Japanese companies only began at the end of 1987, the Tax Authorities have not yet ruled on this issue. In the case of short-term foreign currency options, the option fee is typically deducted in the year of the payment, rather than being amortised over the life of the option or included in the cost of the currency when the option is exercised. Until the Tax Authorities address this issue, it would be reasonable to apply the same treatment to an interest rate option fee.

Source

Generally, any income derived from business in Japan is deemed to constitute Japan source income. Thus, the fee paid by the holder of an interest rate option contract who is a Japanese resident, or a Japanese permanent establishment of a non-resident, would be sourced in Japan.

Forward rate agreement

Forward rate agreements, where a buyer (seller) seeks to protect against a rise (fall) in interest rates on an agreed principal amount as of a specified date, are available on an individually negotiated basis.

Japanese tax treatment

Japanese tax law does not specifically address the tax treatment of a forward rate agreement. However, we have developed the following understanding of the Japanese tax treatment of a forward rate agreement.

Character of income or expense

Any income (or expense) received (or paid) in connection with a forward rate agreement would be treated as ordinary income or expense.

Interest income/expense

As there is no principal exchange involved, the interest differential would not be treated as interest. As a result, any payments to a non-resident in connection with a forward rate agreement would not be subject to Japanese withholding tax.

Timing

The payment or receipt would be recognised at the time of settlement.

Source

Generally, any income derived from business in Japan is deemed to be Japan source income. Thus, any amounts received with respect to a forward rate agreement from a Japanese resident or a Japanese permanent establishment of a non-resident, would be sourced in Japan.

Interest rate cap, floor and collar agreements

Japanese tax law does not specifically address the tax treatment of interest rate cap, floor or collar agreements. However, we have developed the following understanding of the Japanese tax treatment of caps, floors or collars.

Character of income or expense

The up-front and subsequent payments (receipts) made for a cap, floor or collar agreement would be treated as an ordinary expense (or as income).

Interest income or expense

As the principal amount in interest rate cap, collar or floor agreements is nominal, and principal amounts are not exchanged by the parties of the agreement, the interest differential income or expense would not be treated as interest. As a result, payments made to non-residents in connection with the agreement would not be subject to Japanese withholding tax provided the interest rate is determined independently from the cap, floor or collar agreement.

Timing

It is not clear how the payments should be treated for Japanese tax purposes. The purchaser of the cap, floor or collar may be required to capitalise the fee and amortise it over the life of the agreement. It is likely that the seller of a cap, floor or collar will be required to include the fee in income in the year of the sale. Until specific guidelines are issued by the Tax Authorities, it would be reasonable for any payments under the agreement to be deducted by the seller in the year paid, and included in income by the buyer in the year received.

Source

Generally, income derived from business in Japan is deemed to be Japan source income. Thus, an amount received from a Japanese resident or a Japanese permanent establishment of a non-resident with respect to the cap, floor or collar agreement would be sourced in Japan.

PART III

Interest rate futures

1 The mechanics of interest rate futures

Richard A. Hutchison

Introduction

A futures contract is a form of forward contract in that it conveys the right to purchase or sell a specified quantity of an asset at a fixed price on a fixed future date. Although *financial* futures are a relatively recent development, the concept of futures markets is well developed with commodity future markets having been in existence since the early 19th century.

Commodity futures markets first developed out of a need for producers and merchants to limit their price risks between the production of their product and the sale of the product at some time in the future. The uncertainties of weather, political instability and the risks associated with transportation could result in very large fluctuations in prices over comparatively short periods of time.

Historically, although faced with relatively high volatility in commodity prices, companies could expect reasonable stability in foreign exchange and interest rate prices. In the 1950s and 1960s, international and national monetary policies provided insurance against financial risks, in part through fixed exchange rate systems and through interest rate targeting. In recent years, however, there has been a general breakdown in government supplied economic stability. This has resulted in corporations with a sense of survival searching out ways of transferring this new-found financial risk to other parties.

In response to this demand for a vehicle to transfer financial risk from one party to another, the International Monetary Market at the Chicago Mercantile Exchange introduced financial futures in 1972. Since their initial introduction financial futures have developed rapidly with increases in both the volumes traded and the instruments available. Today there are financial futures exchanges in Chicago, New York, London, Sydney, Hong Kong, Bermuda, Kansas City, Peru, Philadelphia, Singapore, Tokyo, Vancouver and São Paulo.

The London International Financial Futures Exchange (LIFFE) which opened in September 1982 now trades in a wide range of financial future contracts including: long and short gilts, Japanese government bonds, US Treasury bonds, 3-month Eurodollar interest rates, 3-month sterling interest rates and the major currencies. In the first seven months of 1987 the volume traded in the long gilt contract on LIFFE was approximately four million contracts representing a nominal value of some £200bn.

The interest rate financial futures markets perform four important functions, they:

1   Provide facilities for the transfer, and hence management, of interest rate risk.
2   Perform a forward pricing function and thus facilitate the intertemporal allocation of resources.
3   Collect and disseminate information.
4   Facilitate the holding of inventories in private hands.

Given the above functions of the futures markets, especially point (3), it is obviously important that any corporate or financial institution which is in any way affected by interest rate fluctuations should at least understand the operations of the futures markets and be aware of the opportunities available.

Futures contracts

A futures contract is a form of forward contract in that it provides the ability to fix a price today for delivery of a financial instrument at some time in the future. Specifically, a financial futures contract is a commitment to make or take delivery, at a designated time in the future, of a specified quantity and quality of a financial instrument, at a price agreed through open outcry in a centrally regulated market place. The essential features of the futures contract are:

- Standard quantity.
- Specific financial instrument.
- Future date.
- Open outcry.
- Daily resettlement.

Each of these features is discussed in further detail below.

Standard quantity Each contract for a given type of financial instrument is for the same standard quantity, e.g. £50,000.

Specific financial instrument The contract specification lays down not only the type of financial instrument but also its quality. For example, the long gilt future specifies a notional gilt with a 12% coupon and the following contract standard:

- Delivery may be made of any gilt with 15–25 years to maturity, as listed by LIFFE. Stocks with an optional redemption date will be considered to have an outstanding term to the first redemption date.
- No variable rate, index-linked, convertible or partly paid gilt may be delivered.
- Gilts are not deliverable within the period of three weeks and one day before the ex-dividend date.
- Interest must be payable half yearly.

Future date The delivery of the amounts specified in the contract must take place during a specified month in the future. For example, the long gilt future is deliverable only in March, June, September and December.

Open outcry All transactions must be executed on the floor of the exchange and prices are instantly available to all participants.

Daily resettlement An important characteristic of financial futures is that although each contract obviously must have a buyer and seller in order to be executed, the contract obligation is not between the buyer and seller but to the clearing house. After a transaction has been recorded, the clearing house substitutes itself for the other party and becomes the seller to every buyer and the buyer to every seller. In this way it achieves its primary role which is to guarantee the performance of every transaction done on the floor.

The clearing house willingness and ability to undertake this role rests upon the financial discipline it imposes on members to put up margin. Both buyers and sellers are required to put up initial margin to the clearing house, either cash or acceptable collateral, to provide a cushion against adverse price movements.

The minimum level of this initial margin is set by the clearing house and reflects the volatility of the underlying cash instrument. Typical margins may range from 0.2% to 3% of the face value of the contract. In the case of the long gilt, the initial margin is currently £1,500 on a notional value of £50,000.

In addition to the initial margin, the parties to a future contract are required to settle daily margins based on daily price movements of the underlying futures contracts.

Pricing

In any contract it is important to understand the method of quotation and the relationship of the futures quotation to the underlying cash price. For example, the 3-month sterling and Eurodollar interest rate contracts are quoted on an index basis. If the annual interest rate on one of these time deposits was, for example, 10%, the price would be quoted as:

$$\text{Price} = 100 - 10 = 90.00$$

If the interest rate then rose to 12%, the new price would be quoted as:

$$\text{Price} = 100 - 12 = 88.00$$

One tick on these contracts is one-hundredth of one per cent, e.g. a change from a price of 95.01 to 95.02. The value of one tick is therefore:

$$\left\{ \begin{array}{l} \text{one-hundredth of} \\ \text{one per cent} \end{array} \right\} \times \left\{ \begin{array}{l} \text{one-quarter of} \\ \text{a year} \end{array} \right\} \times \left\{ \begin{array}{l} \text{face value} \\ \text{of contract} \end{array} \right\}$$

Sterling $= 0.0001 \times 0.25 \times £250,000 = £6.25$
Eurodollar $= 0.0001 \times 0.25 \times \text{US\$1m} = \text{US\$25.00}$

The 20-year gilt contract is quoted, as in the cash market, on a discount basis (with 100 as par). For example, if the current yield on this 12% instrument is 14%, then the price will be $96 - \frac{21}{32}$. If the yield falls to 13%, the price will rise to $92 - \frac{30}{32}$. One tick for this instrument (which is one thirty-second) is worth:

$$\left\{ \begin{array}{l} \text{one thirty-second} \\ \text{of one per cent} \end{array} \right\} \times \left\{ \begin{array}{l} \text{face value} \\ \text{of contract} \end{array} \right\} = (0.03125 \times 0.01) \times £50,000 = £15.625$$

As has already been stated, the futures contract is a form of forward contract and has a number of properties very similar to both forward rate agreements (FRAs) and interest rate swaps.

A futures contract has zero initial value. At maturity, unlike a forward contract, the futures contract should approach the underlying cash price and thus again has zero value. The futures contract is in effect rewritten every day so that value is accumulated in the daily margin account over the life of the contract.

In some respects the futures contract may be considered as being the equivalent of a series of forward rate agreements. This is an important concept to grasp both from the point of view of understanding how future contracts are priced and identifying specific opportunities where it may be cheaper or simpler to hedge interest rate risk with futures contracts as opposed to other hedging instruments. The realisation that a futures contract may be considered as being a series of forward rate agreements can also significantly simplify the accounting and internal control treatment of futures contracts.

Pricing a 3-month sterling futures contract

The usual method for the pricing of a LIFFE 3-month sterling futures contract is the determination of whether an arbitrage opportunity exists between the futures market and the cash or forward market.

Consider a 3-month sterling contract with a delivery date of 20 December. In theory the 3-month interest rate for a 3-month period commencing on 20 December should be identical to that implied for the same period by the cash market, for example:

	125 days		90 days	
20 August		20 December		20 March

125-day sterling interest rate 20 August mid-point $= 10.3125\%$
215-day sterling interest rate 20 August mid-point $= 10.5625\%$

This information allows the calculation of the forward rate for the period 20 December–20 March.
90-day implied forward rate

$$= \left\{ \left[\frac{1 + (0.105625 \times 215/360)}{1 + (0.103125 \times 125/360)} \right] - 1 \right\} \times 360/90 = 0.1053257 \ (10.53\%)$$

Because this is a mid-point rate, the Libor rate is obtained by adding $\frac{1}{16}\%$ (half the usual $\frac{1}{8}\%$ bid-offer spread).

$$\text{Equivalent Libor rate} = 10.53\% + 0.0625\% = 10.5925\%$$

Because the 3-month sterling futures price is $(100 - \text{Libor})$ the equivalent futures price for delivery 20 December is:

$$(100 - 10.5925) = 89.41$$

The difference between this theoretical futures price and the actual December futures price is termed the value basis and measures how undervalued or overvalued the futures contract is relative to the cash market.

The choice of which instrument to deliver against an interest rate futures contract generally lies with the seller of the contract. In order to establish a fair price for the contract, the buyer should assume that he will receive that instrument which optimises the profit or loss for the seller.

The decision when to deliver against a futures contract, at the beginning or end of a delivery month, depends basically upon the relationship between the running yield on the underlying financial instrument and the financing cost of the position. If the seller can earn more on the underlying instrument in accrued interest than he pays in financing costs, then the seller is likely to maintain the position as long as possible by delivering at the end of the delivery month.

Advantages of a futures contract

The futures contract has a number of advantages which may distinguish it from alternative hedging instruments:

- Off-balance sheet.
- Liquidity.
- Low, or nil, use of credit lines.
- Open market.

When financial futures were first introduced, their main advantages were that they were off-balance sheet and because of the standard contract were relatively liquid. This allowed risk adverse companies to manage their risk without blowing up the balance sheet. Recent developments in the swap and FRA markets have to some extent reduced this advantage.

Futures still have a significant advantage over other hedging instruments in that the credit risk is very low or non-existent and that the market is truly open in that all participants are located in the one geographical location and all prices are made public.

Disadvantages of a futures contract

The major disadvantages normally associated with financial futures contracts include:

- Daily margin calls.
- Basis risk.
- Inflexibility associated with standard contracts.
- Internal control requirements.
- Tax and accounting treatment.

The first three points are discussed in greater detail below.

Daily margin calls   For large banks and financial institutions with well developed back offices used to daily transfers and mark to market revaluations, the daily margin call is unlikely to represent a significant disadvantage. For corporate treasuries and private individuals, however, the requirement to settle margin on a daily basis can prove to be a significant administrative disadvantage.

The daily requirement for margin does, however, force a discipline upon management to ensure that an appropriate hedging strategy is implemented and fully understood by senior management, especially non-financial management, and also that the hedge is closely monitored during its life.

On the assumption that the hedge is executed in order to protect against adverse movements in the underlying asset or liability, then because of the daily margin settlement, a futures hedge might produce favourable cash flows as compared to alternative hedging instruments.

Basis risk   Basis is defined as the cash price minus the futures price and normally relates to the near date futures contract although, of course, basis exists for each outstanding contract. The more dissimilar the cash instrument to be hedged and the futures contract being used, the greater the basis risk.

$$\text{Basis} = \text{Current cash price} - \text{Future price}$$

As has already been stated, at delivery the futures price should be very close to the underlying cash price, hence over the life of the contract the basis approaches zero. This behaviour of the basis over time is known as convergence. As time progresses and the futures contract approaches maturity the basis should narrow as it tends towards zero.

Generally, the variability of the basis is much less than the variability of the spot price or the futures price. Although spot and futures prices may be extremely volatile the difference between them may be more constant. This relatively low variability of the basis can be used to reduce the cost of a hedge by corporate and individual hedgers.

Although the basis may remain relatively stable, convergence ensures that it will vary over time. If it is the intention of the hedger to take delivery, convergence is of course desirable. Under the conditions of a positive yield curve, future prices are at a discount to spot, so convergence should operate in favour of buyers of futures and obviously in a negative yield curve environment future prices are at a premium to spot and convergence operates in favour of sellers. Thus, a long hedger in a normal market and a short hedger in an inverted cash market can benefit from convergence and hence reduce the cost of the hedge.

It should be noted, however, that it may be difficult to close-out a futures contract in the last few days before delivery because of declining liquidity.

Inflexibility of standard contracts   The inflexibility of standard contracts both from the limitation of delivery dates and of contract types can place constraints on the ability of futures to hedge an underlying commercial transaction.

With increased volatility in interest rates in general, the corporate treasurer should consider the applicability of macro interest rate hedges to protect the company from unfavourable interest rate movements. Obviously, basis rate risk is less important in a macro hedge than in a micro hedge.

As the sophistication of financial markets improves and the demand for new financial products increases, the cash instruments available in the futures markets are likely to increase significantly.

Hedging interest rate risk with futures

Interest rate futures contracts can be used to hedge against interest rate fluctuations. Buying a futures contract provides protection from falling interest rates for investors who anticipate investing at some future date. Selling financial futures protects against rising rates for holders of fixed-income securities. The ability of a futures contract to hedge a given interest rate exposure depends upon the relationship between the risk being hedged and the individual futures contract. A measure of the relationship between the two is given by the 'regression coefficient', although it should be emphasised that a regression coefficient based on historical data is not necessarily an accurate indication of how prices will move in the future. The following is an example of a long hedge by a Eurodollar lender.

A company is going to realise US$2m in five months time from the sale of assets. The company's treasurer wants to keep the US$2m in 6-month Eurodollar deposits in anticipation of an eventual dollar fixed investment. His risk is that rates will fall before he can make his first deposit in five months from now. One alternative available is to hedge with futures.

The first calculation the treasurer must make is how many contracts are required. LIFFE's 3-month Eurodollar contract is for US$1m and, therefore, the number of contracts required is:

$$\text{Face value} \times \text{Maturity mismatch} \times \text{Regression coefficient}$$
$$= \frac{2}{1} \times \frac{180}{90} \times 0.94 = 3.76, \text{ when rounded is 4 contracts.}$$

The hedge works out as follows:

Cash market	Futures market
30 May	
Anticipate inflow of US$2m in October. Six-month Euro's now at 7.5%, giving potential interest of US$15,000	Buy four December 3-month futures at 93.00 (7% yield)
Basis = − 50 ticks	
31 October	
Place US$2m in 6-month Eurodollar deposits at 6.75%	Sell four December futures at 93.70 (6.3% yield)
Basis = − 45 ticks	
Loss	Gain
Interest income is now only US$67,500, a reduction of US$7,500	70 ticks on four contracts at US$25 per tick equals US$7,000

Hedge evaluation

The hedge was imperfect – the gain on futures did not completely offset the loss on cash: it was only $(7000/7500) \times 100 = 93\%$ effective. There are several possible reasons for this:

1 The number of contracts had to be rounded to 4 from 3.76.
2 There was a change in basis. The opening basis was − 50 ticks whereas the closing basis was − 45 ticks. Such a change in basis is possible because:

- This is a cross-hedge and thus more risky than a simple hedge.
- The hedge was placed in a rather distant contract – December, a full seven months away. It might have been better to use June and September contracts which could then be rolled into December.
- There was a twist in the whole yield curve. Note that the curve was negatively sloped in May. Let the set of prices at that time and in October be:

	Spot (6-month Euro)	December (futures)	March (futures)
30 May	85.5 (7.5%)	86 (7.0%)	86.5 (6.5%)
	(basis = −50)	(spread = −50)	
31 October	86.25 (6.75%)	86.70 (6.3%)	87.15 (5.85%)
	(basis = −45)	(spread = −45)	

The futures yield curve became flatter, although this is still an 'inverted' market. By buying a December/March spread (i.e. buy one December and sell one March contract), the hedger would have gained back the five ticks which he lost on the simple hedge.

Summary

Given its function in the financial markets, corporate treasurers cannot now afford to ignore the futures markets even if they do not actively use the market to hedge. For the hedger, the futures contract, like all other hedging instruments, offers a number of advantages and disadvantages. It is up to the individual company to ascertain which particular instrument is best suited to its needs.

Generally, from the corporate point of view the futures contract will be the cheapest and simplest hedge when:

- Entering into a macro hedge.
- The company is convinced that the cash market will move against them (resulting in a positive cash flow from daily margins).
- The basis risk acts in their favour.

2 Accounting treatment: United States

Benjamin S. Neuhausen

Introduction

The accounting for interest rate futures contracts in the United States is governed by Financial Accounting Standards Board (FASB) Statement No. 80, *Accounting for futures contracts*, which was issued in 1984. Interest rate futures contracts are the only interest rate protection products whose accounting is governed by an authoritative accounting pronouncement. As a result, the rules governing the accounting are more specific and, in some respects, more stringent than the accounting requirements for other products. Because of the similarities between futures contracts and other interest rate protection products, however, the accounting for other products has been developed in part by analogy to Statement No. 80.

As noted in Part II, Chapter 1, 'Accounting framework: United States', the accounting for futures, together with other interest rate protection products, is the subject of a major FASB project and could change.

Overall basis of accounting

Transactions in futures contracts involve a deposit of funds or the pledging of an acceptable security, representing a margin deposit. Funds deposited as margin should be recorded simply as a 'deposit'. Consistent with the accounting treatment for forward-type activities (e.g. foreign exchange forward contracts), the gross amount of securities deliverable under futures contracts should not be reported in the balance sheet.

Generally, unrealised gains and losses resulting from a change in quoted market values of futures contracts, as well as realised gains and losses, should be recognised currently in the income statement. This basis of accounting (commonly referred to as 'mark-to-market') should be followed when (1) futures contracts are entered into for speculation; (2) futures contracts represent hedges of asset positions, contemplated asset purchases or short positions, all of which are, or will be, carried at market value; or (3) the criteria for 'hedge accounting' for specific hedging transactions, discussed below, are not met.

Accounting treatment for hedges

FASB Statement No. 80 provides for different accounting treatment of certain futures contracts that are hedges. Futures contracts may be (1) hedges of existing assets, liabilities, or firm, fixed-price commitments to buy or sell financial instruments, or (2) hedges of probable future financial transactions that an enterprise expects but may not be legally obligated to enter into (commonly referred to as 'anticipatory hedges').

Hedge accounting treatment applies only if the criteria discussed in this section are met and if the related assets or liabilities are or will be accounted for on an historical cost or a lower-of-cost-or-market basis.

Hedge accounting is based on a concept of symmetry between the accounting for the futures contracts and the assets or liabilities being hedged. As explained in more detail later in this section, gains or losses on futures contracts entered into as hedges generally are deferred, rather than being recognised currently in income. Hedge accounting requires the designation of specific assets or liabilities to determine the appropriate time to recognise deferred gains and losses and/or the amortisation period of such gains and losses. In addition, hedge accounting is appropriate if the enterprise can designate groups of like items (e.g. loans that have similar terms) to be hedged.

Criteria for hedges of existing assets, liabilities or firm commitments

Futures contracts qualify as hedges of existing assets, liabilities or firm, fixed price commitments for accounting purposes if both the following conditions are met:

- The assets, liabilities or firm, fixed price commitments expose the company to interest rate risk. The nature of the company's business and its other assets, liabilities and commitments need to be considered to decide whether there is risk exposure. For example, a company that owns fixed interest rate financial instruments would not be exposed to interest rate risk if the instruments are funded by fixed interest rate debt of similar maturity.

   Some companies conduct their risk management on a decentralised basis and cannot assess their interest rate risk on a company-wide basis. They can satisfy this criterion if the item to be hedged exposes the business unit that enters into the futures contract to interest rate risk.
- The futures contracts reduce the interest rate exposure and are designated as hedges. There must be a probable high correlation between changes in (a) the fair value of the hedged assets, liabilities, or firm commitments, and (b) the market value of the futures contracts.

   The hedger needs to consider the correlation during relevant past periods and also the correlation that could be expected at higher or lower interest rates. The futures contract may be for a financial instrument different from the item to be hedged, if there is a clear economic relationship between their prices and high correlation is probable.

Criteria for anticipatory hedges

Futures contracts qualify as a hedge of anticipated transactions if both the criteria for hedges of existing assets, liabilities or firm commitments and both of the following conditions are met:

- The significant terms of the anticipated transaction are identified, including the expected date, the type of financial instrument, the expected maturity and the quantity.
- The expected transaction is likely to occur. To determine that an anticipated transaction is likely, a company should consider the frequency of similar transactions in the past, the company's ability to carry out the transaction, the length of time until the anticipated transaction date, the loss or disruption of operations that could occur if the transaction is not consummated, and the likelihood that the same business purpose could be satisfied by a substantially different transaction (e.g. a company planning to issue long-term bonds could also raise funds by selling common or preferred stock). Sometimes a company may have a choice among similar transactions to satisfy a business purpose (e.g. issuing commercial paper, borrowing under a revolving credit agreement or selling short-term receivables with recourse). In such cases, futures contracts may qualify as hedges if all the other hedge criteria are satisfied for each of the possible transactions and the company is likely to enter into one of the possible transactions.

Discussion of hedge accounting

Gains and losses on futures contracts that meet *all* the conditions described above are deferred as an adjustment to the carrying amount of the hedged item. If futures contracts hedge existing assets or liabilities, at each reporting date the deferred gains or losses are classified as an adjustment of the carrying amount of the hedged assets or liabilities. If the futures contracts hedge firm, fixed price commitments, the deferred gains or losses are included in the measurement of the transactions that satisfy the commitments. Similarly, if futures contracts hedge expected transactions, the deferred gains or losses are included in the measurement of the transactions when they occur.

The deferred gains or losses on futures contracts are applied to adjust the carrying amount of an existing asset or liability, or will be applied to adjust the carrying amount of a future asset or liability. Those adjustments become an integral part of the carrying amount of the asset or liability and are accounted for as such. Thus, deferred gains or losses that adjust the carrying amounts of interest bearing assets and liabilities are like discounts or premiums and are amortised to interest income or expense over the remaining lives of the instruments.

For hedges of firm commitments and anticipated transactions, the amortisation starts when the anticipated transaction is entered into. For hedges of existing assets and liabilities, amortisation must start no later than the date that a particular contract is closed out, regardless of whether the contract is replaced by a similar contract for later delivery ('rolled over').

If deferred gains or losses become part of the carrying amount of an asset carried at the lower of cost or market, they become part of cost in the cost versus market comparison.

A company must regularly assess the results of futures contracts designated as hedges to determine whether they continue to be highly correlated with changes in the values of the hedged items. If the expected high correlation has not occurred, the company stops accounting for the futures contract as a hedge and begins marking to market. The deferred gain or loss on the futures contract through that date continues to be treated as an adjustment to the carrying amount of the hedged item only to the extent the futures results have been offset by changes in the price of the hedged item. Any accumulated gain or loss on the futures contract in excess of the accumulated unrecognised loss or gain on the hedged item since the time the hedge transaction was entered is recognised in income.

If the financial instrument being hedged is deliverable under the futures contract and if it is likely that the company will hold both the hedged instrument and the futures contract until the contract's delivery date, Statement No. 80 allows, but does not require, separate accounting for the 'premium' or 'discount' on the futures contract (the difference between the spot price and the futures price of the instrument). The 'premium' or 'discount' on the futures contract may be amortised to income over the life of the contract rather than being included in the result of the cash transaction. The FASB concluded that this 'premium' or 'discount' on the futures contract could be viewed as an adjustment to the yield of the hedged instrument during the life of the contract rather than during the period after the contract is closed.

If a company hedges an anticipated transaction and learns that the amount of the transaction is likely to be less than originally expected, a *pro rata* portion of the futures gain or loss is recognised currently in income. If the hedge contract is closed before the anticipated transaction occurs, the futures gain or loss should continue to be deferred until the anticipated transaction takes place.

Disclosure

FASB Statement No. 80 requires disclosure of (1) the nature of the items that are hedged with futures contracts, and (2) the method of accounting for the futures contracts (including a description of the events that result in recognising the changes in value of futures contracts in income).

3 Accounting treatment: United Kingdom

Mark Davis

Overall basis of accounting

There is no UK equivalent of Financial Accounting Standards Board (FASB) Statement No. 80. The principles outlined in Part II, Chapter 2 should therefore be followed in accounting for futures. The accounting treatment is primarily determined by whether the futures qualifies to be treated as a hedge or is to be treated as a speculative transaction.

Hedging criteria

Futures will generally not provide a perfect hedge. Some basis risk will generally exist between a futures and the item that it is hedging. The more dissimilar the item being hedged and the instrument underlying the futures contract, the greater the basis risk. There is no rule as to the degree of correlation between rate changes in the two instruments concerned, although a correlation coefficient of 0.6 or more is generally considered adequate to justify designating the futures as a hedge.

Where cross hedging, weighted hedges may be used, based on the regression coefficient between changes in the rates of the item hedged and changes in the rate of the instrument underlying the future. Consequently, there will be a difference between the amount of the futures contracts and the amount of the item being hedged. Such differences do not preclude the futures being treated as hedges. However, where it is clear that the company is 'over hedged' and the number of futures is in excess of that reasonably required to cover the hedged item, it will be necessary to pro rate the futures, the excess being treated as speculative transactions.

Where a company uses a strip of futures to hedge a number of interest periods, the profit or loss on each future within the sequence should be deferred and amortised over the interest period it was designed to hedge. Similarly, where a rolling hedge is used and futures for one month are realised and simultaneously replaced by futures of a longer maturity, any gain or loss on the first future should be deferred and amortised over the interest rate period which the roll is ultimately designed to hedge. Clearly it is important that the company not only designates the futures as a hedge, but also identifies which interest period each futures contract is designed to hedge.

Accounting treatment for hedges

Where an interest rate future is used to hedge the interest cost of obligations, profits or losses on the future should initially be taken to a suspense account and be amortised over the period of the loan that the futures contract was intended to cover.

Where interest rate futures are used to hedge anticipated transactions, profits or losses on such contracts should be held in suspense until the transaction occurs, and amortised as described above. If it becomes known that the transaction will not occur, the recognition of either profit or loss should take place immediately.

If interest rate futures are used to hedge assets, the treatment of the future will depend on the accounting treatment adopted for the asset. Where the asset is carried at cost, profits or losses should be amortised over the interest period being hedged. If the asset is carried at the lower of cost or market, any provision for diminution in the value of the asset should be reduced by any profit on the futures contract.

Initial or deposit margins are a form of collateral and are thus recorded on the balance sheet. Variation margins have to be met daily and reflect profits or losses on the market value of the future. If any profit or loss on the future is taken to income, the corresponding entry may be netted against the margin accounts. With LIFFE futures, the margin paid or received each day represents the net movement in deposit and variation margins for the previous day, on all the company's open futures. It is usual, therefore, to post the margin entry to a suspense account, analyse its constituent parts, and account for each in the relevant manner.

Accounting for speculative transactions

Where futures are speculative, they are normally recorded at market value with profits and losses being recognised immediately. As discussed in Part II, Chapter 2, corporates are restricted from taking unrealised profits to the P&L account. They should therefore value futures at the lower of cost or market or provide the additional disclosure required if they choose to include unrealised profits in income.

Banks normally mark to market all speculative contracts and include the resulting profits and losses in the P&L account. The corresponding entry will normally be to the margin account in the balance sheet, to the extent that variation margin has been paid or received in respect of changes in the market value of the futures. Any initial or deposit margin on the future does not affect profit or loss and thus remains in the balance sheet until the future matures.

Disclosure

Disclosure of accounting policies and contingent liabilities should accord with the principles discussed in Part II, Chapter 2.

Corporates must adopt the formats for balance sheet and P&L account laid down by Schedule 4. Profits and losses on futures should normally be included within the captions 'interest receivable and similar income' or 'interest payable and similar charges'. Deferred profits and losses and margin payments should be shown under 'deferred income' or 'prepayments'. Technically, deferred profits and losses should be split between those due within one year and those due after one year, according to the timing of their release to P&L account. This implies that margins in respect of individual futures should be shown gross, notwithstanding the fact that there is a net settlement with the exchange.

Banks are not subject to the requirements of Schedule 4 to account separately for each asset and liability. Consequently, they normally simply include deposit and variation margins on a net basis within the accrued interest figures in the balance sheet.

4 Documentation of interest rate futures

Patrick Daniels and David J. Gilberg

United Kingdom

Introduction

In considering the documentation affecting an interest rate futures contract, the following aspects require analysis:

(a) the relationship between broker and client; and
(b) the relationship between the broker and the market in which the relevant contract is traded.

This last mentioned aspect may be subdivided into:

(i) the standard form of contract traded on the relevant exchange;
(ii) the rules of the relevant exchange;
(iii) the procedure and rules adopted by the clearing house responsible for the orderly implement ation of trades in a given standard form of contract on the relevant exchange; and
(iv) the provisions of any national law or local law governing futures trading within its particular jurisdiction.

Of particular importance in connection with the relationship between client and broker will be:

(i) the account opening forms;
(ii) the terms of trading adopted by the broker; and
(iii) the various notices which a customer may expect to receive from his broker from time to time such as confirmation of trades, settlement statements, positions held, margin calls, delivery warnings and delivery invoices.

This section is primarily concerned with the practice adopted in England, particularly with reference to contracts traded on the London International Financial Futures Exchange (LIFFE); the following section deals with US practices.

Broker and client

In the rules of LIFFE, it is provided that members shall be deemed to act as principals in all contracts made with one another in the pit and in all parallel and related contracts which arise when a non-clearing member is involved. Furthermore, a member is prohibited from making any contract similar in terms to a class of contract permitted to be made by members of LIFFE in the pit, unless that member has made or arranges for a matching contract to be made. By adopting these rules, LIFFE has sought to eliminate the possibility of a member's purporting to act in market transactions as the agent of his client and not as principal. By doing so it has avoided a matter of controversy which has featured frequently in disputes falling to be decided by the English Courts.

If an agent is known to be an agent and names his principal in contracting with a third party, 'the contract is the contract of the principal, not that of the agent, and *prima facie* at common law the only person who can sue is the principal and the only person who can be sued is the principal' (*Montgomerie* v. *United Kingdom Steamship Association*, 1891, 1QB370).

In the case of transactions on futures markets, it would be highly impractical if members trading with another insisted on doing so only as agents because of the risk that either of the principals involved might be unable to perform his part of the contract. There must be confidence in the ability of parties transacting on a futures market to fulfil their obligations. Many members therefore adopt the stance that they are trading as principals not only with their fellow members but also with their clients.

This view of dealings between brokers and clients helps to overcome the obvious difficulty that many features of those dealings are more consistent with a relationship of agency between broker and client. For example, brokers should keep clients' funds in segregated bank accounts and will be obliged to do so when the Financial Services (Clients' Money) Regulations 1987 come into force. In this respect, it is clearly acting as an agent and, in the event of its insolvency, clients would reasonably expect their money to be protected from the claims of the broker's general creditors. It would also seem odd for a broker to charge commission to the client in relation to dealings which were purportedly conducted exclusively on a principal-to-principal basis. From the client's viewpoint, it is therefore important to ascertain whether a broker is trading with him on a principal-to-principal basis and, if so, what steps have been taken by that broker to protect client moneys.

In order to open an account with a broker, a client will normally be asked to sign account opening forms. In the case of corporate clients, this will normally involve the passing of appropriate resolutions by the company concerned and the supply to the broker of a copy of the company's constitutional documents. If a third party is to give instructions to the broker on the client's behalf, a suitable Power of Attorney will also have to be furnished to the broker to enable him to act on those instructions. In cases where the client is introduced by an introducing broker to the broker with whom the account is to be opened, instructions would have to be given as to any arrangements for the sharing of commission between clearing broker and introducing broker.

The broker will also expect the client to sign a risk disclosure statement similar in form to that required by Rule 1.55 of the Commodity Futures Trading Commission in the United States of America. In addition to obtaining such a statement, the broker will also wish to ensure that the client is fully aware of the basis on which futures or option trading is to be conducted. This will normally take the form of standard terms and conditions covering such matters as:

(a) the method of giving instructions and the right of the broker to refuse to act on a particular transaction if he does not wish to;

(b) notice to the client that transactions entered into by the broker shall be governed by the regulations and customs of the particular market on which a given transaction is conducted;

(c) an exclusion of liability for failure by the broker to prevent losses incurred through changes in relevant market regulations, government restrictions, closure of markets and other events not within the broker's control;

(d) in the case of financial futures and options, an indication that the parties contemplate delivery of the underlying subject matter.

   This was of particular importance before Section 63 of the Financial Services Act 1986 provided that certain futures contracts in which no delivery was contemplated would no longer be unenforceable at law as gaming contracts;

(e) the conclusion by the broker, in relation to contracts with the client, of an equivalent contract on the floor of the relevant market and the supply to the client of a contract note setting out the price at which the equivalent contract was executed;

(f) limitations on the authority of the broker's employees or agents to advise the client and disclaimers of responsibility for losses other than losses directly resulting from the negligence, wilful default or fraud of the broker;

(g) a statement of the risk which the client should consider before entering into futures transactions, such as the risk of unlimited potential loss in relation to such transactions;

(h) an acknowledgement from the client that services furnished by the broker are not exclusive and that the broker may deal on his own account or for other clients;

(i) arrangements for joint accounts;

(j) authority for the broker to disclose particulars of clients' dealings with the broker to appropriate authorities or associations by whose rules the broker may be bound;

(k) arrangements with regard to the payment by the client to the broker of amounts by way of margin as security for transactions entered into by the broker as a result of instructions received from the client and for the liquidation of the clients' positions in event of the clients' failure to meet margin calls;

(l) the arbitration of disputes between client and broker. Normally such disputes are settled by arbitration in accordance with the by-laws, rules and regulations of the exchange, clearing house, association or market subject to which the relevant transaction was effected; and

(m) the law which shall govern the contract between broker and client.

In addition to the rules and regulations of the relevant exchange on which transactions are effected, the Financial Services Act 1986 provides for recognition of self-regulatory organisations which will be responsible, among other things, for the conduct of their members. The Association of Futures Brokers and Dealers Limited will be responsible for those firms requiring authorisation in order to carry on investment business comprising dealing and broking in financial and commodity futures and options. Its current draft rules include comprehensive conduct of business rules covering not only customer relations but also the keeping of proper records in relation to client transactions, customer agreements and the provision of risk disclosure statements. The draft rules also cover calling clients and issuing advertisements and the proper practice in relation to clients' money.

Broker and the clearing house

In the case of dealings on LIFFE, it is a requirement that members of LIFFE should require margin payments from their clients at least equal in value to that required by the clearing house, which in the case of LIFFE is the International Commodity Clearing House (ICCH). Dealings in LIFFE are registered with ICCH and full members only can deal directly in the market. ICCH, as the clearing house, guarantees that the transactions registered with it will be fulfilled in accordance with the rules of LIFFE.

In consideration of that guarantee and of the registration of the transaction by ICCH, the buyer and seller agree to accept by way of novation such other buyers and sellers as ICCH may from time to time appoint for the sale or purchase of the contract to which the transaction relates. ICCH is able to back its guarantees in two ways. It can substitute itself as seller in the case of cash buyers on the market and as buyer in the case of each seller. Thus it is in a position to offset sales against purchases provided that LIFFE members perform their obligations. In addition, it requires members to pay an initial margin when a contract is registered with ICCH and it debits members with a variation margin where losses on contracts transacted by them justify it. It may also meet emergencies by requiring payment of additional margins.

Having regard to these precautions, and to the ICCH guarantee, it is therefore unlikely that the default of a member in respect of his obligations to the market would result in loss to other members or their clients.

However, if a loss did occur, the question whether the member was acting as principal towards his client or simply as agent of the client in concluding the transaction giving rise to loss would be critical in determining who would bear that loss. As an agent, the member would be entitled to look to his client for an indemnity. As a principal, he would have to bear the loss himself because failure of his counterparty in the market would not discharge his responsibility to fulfil his own obligations to his client. It would be recalled from the earlier paragraph covering the broker and his client that the rules of LIFFE require its members to act solely as principals.

Standard form contracts

LIFFE has six interest rate contracts and three option contracts on interest rate futures. The interest rate contracts are the long gilt, short gilt, Japanese Government bond, US Treasury bond, 3-month Eurodollar and 3-month sterling contracts. Each contract follows a standard form (see the Appendices at the end of Parts III and V), in which the first section sets out the definitions of specific words or phrases used in the contract. Further sections deal with the contract specification, price, last trading day, Exchange Delivery Settlement Price, payment, emergency provisions, default, Force Majeure, arbitration, the choice of English law as the governing law and the application of the terms of the contract to contracts which are not registered by the clearing house. Provision is also made to subject each contract to the rules of LIFFE and to the provisions of its Articles of Association. In particular, it is the Rules which prevail in the event of any conflict between the terms of the contract and the Rules. Under the Rules, provision is made for the board of directors of LIFFE to implement procedures for such matters as:

(a) determining the opening and closing ranges of contract prices;
(b) to display on the market the prices at which bids and offers have been made and at which contracts have been made;
(c) to secure the registration of contracts;
(d) to establish a limit on the maximum price fluctuations on the market for a particular contract and to restrict or suspend dealings in a contract;
(e) the conduct of business on the floor of LIFFE; and
(f) to require the clearing house to disclose to LIFFE particulars of contracts concluded by members.

The Rules also contain detailed rules for the arbitration of disputes. Such arbitrations are conducted by three members of the Business Conduct Committee of LIFFE of whom not more than one is to be a director of LIFFE. In addition to providing arbitrators, the Business Conduct Committee of LIFFE supervises the conduct of members of LIFFE and business transacted on LIFFE. It also investigates any alleged violation of the Rules. The award of the arbitrators is expressed to be final and binding in all cases, subject to Section 1 of the Arbitration Act, 1979 which provides that leave of the court is required to revoke the arbitrators' authority and, as a matter of practice, leave will only be obtained to such a revocation in exceptional circumstances. A summary of each contract issued by LIFFE has been prepared by it as a guide to dealers and investors and it provides a summary of the essential features of each contract.

United States

Introduction

The documentation of interest rate futures transactions in the US is similar to the manner in which such transactions are documented in the UK. Under US law, however, futures trading is governed by a separate federal statute, the Commodity Exchange Act (CEA), which grants exclusive jurisdiction over such trading to an independent Federal agency, the Commodity Futures Trading Commission (CFTC). As a result, the regulation of interest rate futures contracts, including the documentation requirements, is centralised to a much greater degree in a single regulatory authority.

Moreover, the scope of the CEA and the CFTC's exclusive jurisdiction is extremely broad, pre-empting all other Federal and state laws and encompassing every type of futures trading conducted in the US. For example, the CFTC has jurisdiction over the offer and sale in the United States of futures contracts traded on non-US exchanges. Pursuant to this authority, the CFTC has recently adopted regulations which require registration on the part of any person making offers or sales of such instruments into the US. Accordingly, a UK broker offering LIFFE interest rate futures to US persons may be subject to CFTC registration and to the documentation considerations outlined herein.

Further, the CEA prohibits all off-exchange futures trading within the US. Interest rate futures contracts may therefore be entered into only on a regulated exchange in accordance with exchange rules, which are themselves subject to CFTC approval. In this regard, the principal interest rate futures contracts presently available in the US are traded on the Chicago Board of Trade (CBT) and the International Monetary Market of the Chicago Mercantile Exchange (IMM), and are based on US Treasury securities (i.e. Treasury bills, notes and bonds) and Eurodollar deposits.

In addition, under the CEA, an exchange seeking to offer a particular futures contract must apply to the CFTC for approval by submitting a formal application setting forth the substantive terms and conditions of the contract as well as the manner in which it will be traded, including margining and price and position limits. In order to approve the contract, the CFTC must ensure that it serves a legitimate economic purpose and that the contract and trading specifications are consistent with the requirements of the CEA. The form and content of interest rate futures contracts, therefore, as well as their trading, are subject to extensive CFTC oversight.

Broker and client

Transactions in exchange-traded futures contracts may be effected in the US only by a brokerage firm which is registered with CFTC as a 'futures commission merchant' (FCM), and is a member of the relevant exchange and its clearing house. As in the UK, therefore, each broker trading or clearing transactions through an exchange must act as principal in establishing, maintaining or liquidating positions, regardless of whether such transactions are for the broker's own account or on behalf of clients.

Nevertheless, a US broker is regarded as an agent in so far as the client is concerned. For this reason, under the form of account agreement most commonly used in the US, a broker does not purport to enter into separate 'back-to-back' contracts – one with the client and another with the clearing house – acting as principal in each case. To the contrary, the agreement states that the broker is acting as agent for the client in connection with all transactions executed and cleared on an exchange, despite the fact that the exchange and its clearing house continue to view the broker as the principal.

With respect to the documentation of account relationships, CFTC regulations and exchange rules require that a grant of trading discretion to a broker be made through a written power of attorney, executed by the client and identifying the scope of the broker's authority. Although it is customary for brokers and clients to enter into written agreements in other instances as well, they are not specifically required to do so, and the content of such agreements therefore varies widely. Nevertheless, the approach most commonly used in the US generally differs from the standard UK agreement, as described above, in the following respects:

(a) The agreement, as noted, typically states that the broker will act as agent for the client in entering into all transactions;

(b) the agreement generally grants the broker the right to liquidate all or a part of the client's account upon the occurrence of one or more events of default, or, in many instances, whenever the broker deems it necessary to do so for its protection. In addition, the broker is often granted the right to establish margin levels higher than those imposed by the relevant exchanges;

(c) the broker is ordinarily granted the right to establish position limits lower than those imposed by the relevant exchange, whenever the broker believes it necessary to do so for its protection;

(d) the agreement may grant the broker a security interest in all property of the client held by the broker or its affiliates;

(e) the agreement may specify the actions which must be taken by the client in order to make or accept delivery under a futures contract, or to close out open positions prior to delivery; and

(f) the agreement generally requires the client to indemnify the broker against losses incurred through the client's trading.

CFTC regulations also require that brokers provide their futures clients with a number of risk disclosure statements and related documents, and that each client acknowledge receipt of the documents in writing. The principal such documents are: (i) the basic Risk Disclosure Statement referred to above; (ii) a Bankruptcy Disclosure Statement, indicating the client's general understanding of its rights in the event of the broker's bankruptcy; (iii) a Foreign Futures Disclosure Statement, if futures are to be traded on non-US exchanges; and (iv) an Arbitration Agreement, if the broker wishes to require all disputes to be submitted to arbitration. Finally, CFTC regulations require brokers to furnish their clients with written confirmations of each transaction and with monthly statements of the status of the clients' accounts.

Broker and the clearing house

The legal relationship between a broker and a clearing house in the US is not materially different from that which exists in the UK.[1] In terms of documentation, a broker seeking to become a member of an exchange and/or its clearing house must submit an application and make a number of undertakings, including an agreement to be bound by exchange or clearing house rules, to file periodic reports of financial condition and trading activity and to make its books and records available for inspections and audits.

In addition, as a self-regulatory organisation, the exchange retains broad jurisdiction to regulate virtually every aspect of a member firm's activities, including its account opening and maintenance procedures, registration of employees, establishment and enforcement of margin requirements and financial condition. Moreover, each exchange has the authority to discipline its members and to require changes in their organisational structures or operations.

Standard form contracts

Most interest rate futures contracts traded in the US do not actually exist in written form. As a result, there is no formal documentation and each contract entered into is in effect a verbal agreement to make or receive delivery of the underlying instrument in accordance with the rules of the exchange on which the contract is traded. Nevertheless, these rules establish specific terms and conditions, which are automatically incorporated by reference into each contract traded, such as specifications for deliverable instruments, permissible methods of delivery and payment for instruments delivered. The exchanges also regulate certain related activities, such as the use of 'exchanges of futures for physicals' (EFPs), although the physical transaction forming a part of an EFP is subject to private negotiation. In addition, exchange rules in the US cover many of the points noted above in connection with LIFFE rules, including price and position limits.

---

[1] It should be noted that most futures exchanges in the US have their own clearing houses, each of which is responsible only for the clearance of transactions executed on the particular exchange. The relevant clearing house interposes itself between the buyer and seller of each contract, in the same manner as the ICCH, and thereby guarantees the performance of each clearing member which is a party to the contract.

5   Case study: Interest rate futures*

M. Desmond Fitzgerald

Introduction

This case study gives illustrations of hedging with futures by a commercial bank and a portfolio manager.

Hedging for a commercial bank

The essence of commercial banking is to borrow at one rate from customers and lend either to the government, through purchases of public sector fixed interest securities, or to other customers at a higher rate of interest. The difference between the cost of borrowing and the average lending rate, less any operating expenses, represents the profitability of the bank. The presence of interest rate risk is obvious: if the cost of borrowing increases while the lending rate remains fixed for a period, the profitability of the bank will decline. The profitability of the bank will also decline if the average lending rate falls while the cost of borrowing remains unchanged. The use of financial futures may allow the banker, if he so desires, to lock in borrowing or lending rates to preserve a particularly attractive spread.

Most bank balance sheets contain a large number of natural hedges: for instance, loans with 3-month rollovers are often matched against 3-month maturity certificates of deposit and/or interbank deposits. These natural hedges must be eliminated by netting out the maturities of the assets and liabilities sides of the balance sheet to arrive at the mismatched position which may need to be hedged. Consider the following net exposed balances of a bank.

Maturity (days)	Net exposed balance (US$m)	Category
0–90	1,500	Liability
91–180	1,000	Asset
181–270	1,000	Asset
271–365	1,500	Asset
No maturity or non-interest sensitive	2,000	Liability

Step 1

1 February Determine exact rollover dates for assets and liabilities.
US$1,500m of liabilities (90-day certificates of deposit) 1 April
US$1,000m of assets (6-month interbank loans) 1 July
US$1,000m of assets (9-month loans) 1 October
US$1,500m of assets (12-month loans) 1 January
Current rate on 90-day CDs = 13.5%.

---

*This chapter is reprinted, with some revisions, from *Financial futures* by M. Desmond Fitzgerald. Published by Euromoney Publications, 1983.

Step 2

Determine hedge structure

        Lock in 13.5% CD rate on US$1.5bn 1 April–1 July
        Lock in 13.5% CD rate on US$500m 1 July–1 October
        Hedge with IMM domestic CD futures–Liquid contract: correlation = 0.97
        Regression coefficient = 1.05.

Strip hedge

	Cash CD market	*CD futures market*
1 Feb.	CD rate = 13.5%	Sell 1,575 June CDs 87.00
		Sell 525 September CDs 86.50
1 April	Re-issue US$1.5bn CDs at rate of 14.25%	Buy 1,575 June CDs 86.30
	Additional cost = 1,500,000,000 × $(0.1425\text{–}0.135) \times \frac{1}{4}$ = US$2.8125m	Futures profit = 1,575 × US$25 × 70 ticks = US$2.75625m
1 July	Re-issue US$500m CDs at 14.5%	Buy 525 September CDs 85.80
	Additional cost = 500,000,000 × $(0.145\text{–}0.135) \times \frac{1}{4}$ = US$1.25m	Futures profit = 525 × 70 ticks × US$25 = US$918,750
	Total additional cost = US$4.0625m	Total futures gain = US$3.675m

Step 3

Hedge evaluation

$$\text{Hedge efficiency} = \frac{3.675}{4.0625} \times 100 = 90.5\%$$

	1 February–1 April	*1 February–1 July*
Change in cash rate	75 bp	100 bp
Implied futures price change from regression coefficient	71 bp	95 bp
Actual futures price change	70 bp	70 bp

Hence an adverse basis change between the cash CD and the September T-bill contract accounts for most of the hedge efficiency. The appropriateness of using the same regression coefficient to relate the cash CD rate to both the June and September T-bill contracts should be investigated.

This example illustrates most of the practical points of hedging the liabilities side of a bank's balance sheet to lock in a suitable spread in the period before assets are rolled over. However, an alternative method of locking in borrowing rates for three-month money on 1 April and 1 July would be to use the forward-forward interbank market. For example, suppose on 1 February, the following set of interbank borrowing and lending rates was observed:

Interbank rates 1 February

59-day money	$13\frac{5}{8}$ – $13\frac{3}{4}$
150-day money	$13\frac{3}{4}$ – $13\frac{7}{8}$
242-day money	$13\frac{1}{8}$ – 14

We can work out the implied borrowing costs for the three-month periods beginning 1 April and 1 July.

$$\text{Borrowing rate 1 April–1 July} = \left\{ \frac{1 + (0.1375 \times [150/360]) - 1}{1 + (0.1375 \times [59/360])} \right\} \times \frac{360}{91}$$
$$= 13.45\% \ (0.1345)$$

$$\text{Borrowing rate 1 July–1 October} = \left[\frac{1+(0.13875\times[242/360])}{1+(0.13875\times[150/360])}\right]-1 \quad \times\frac{360}{92}$$
$$= 13.12\% \ (0.1312)$$

In this case, the implied borrowing rates in the so-called strip yield curve are lower than the current cash CD rate, which the bank hoped to lock in by putting on a strip hedge in CD futures. Given that the futures hedge is subject both to basis risk, and to the possibility of adverse variation margin payments, it is likely that the bank would prefer to hedge this exposure in the forward-forward market rather than the futures. Forward-forward hedges are frequently preferred to futures for short hedges for banks, because the bank is able to operate on the advantageous side of the bid-ask spread in the interbank market.

Hedging by portfolio managers

The financial futures market provides virtually unlimited opportunities for portfolio managers to tailor the returns on existing portfolios, or to lock in rates on anticipated sales or purchases of assets.

A classic simple hedge for a portfolio manager is to lock in an interest rate or yield on an anticipated purchase of securities. For instance, consider a portfolio manager in the UK who is intending to purchase a particular gilt-edged stock at a later date. If he is worried that gilt interest rates will rise prior to the purchase date, he can lock in the effective price of the gilt by hedging the anticipated purchase with gilt futures contracts on LIFFE.

Example

It is 30 March. The manager of a gilt portfolio intends to purchase £1,000,000 nominal of Treasury 15.5% 1998 gilt stock at the end of July. The price of this gilt is 108-14 giving a currrent yield to maturity of 13.94%. Being worried about falling interest rates he decides to hedge the prospective purchase in the futures market.

The number of contracts for full hedge is found by:

$$\text{Face value} \times \text{Money equivalency} \times \text{Conversion factor}$$
$$\frac{£1,000,000}{£50,000} \times 1 \times 1.242 = 24.84$$

The conversion table of LIFFE indicates that 1.242 times as many standardised 20-year 12% gilt futures are required as actual Treasury 15.5% 1998s. To simplify this example further, the gilt cash market prices exclude accrued interest.

Cash market	Futures market
30 March	30 March
Expect to purchase £1,000,000 nominal of Treasury 15.5% 1998 on 30 July	Buy 25 September gilt futures at 87-02
Current market price is 108-14. Yield to maturity 13.94%	
Market value of gilt = £1,084,375	
Price is equivalent to 87-10 for LIFFE standard gilt	

$$\text{Basis} = +8 \text{ ticks}$$

Cash market

30 July

Buy £1,000,000 nominal of Treasury 15.5% 1998 at 114-20

Yield to maturity = 13%

Market value of gilt = £1,146,250

Price is equivalent to 92-09 for LIFFE standard gilt

Gilt purchase costs an additional £61,875

Futures market

30 July

Sell 25 September gilt futures at 92-18

Basis = −9 ticks

Futures profit = 25 contracts × 176 ticks
(92-18 − 87-02)
× £15.625 = £68,750

The effectiveness of this hedge was as high as 111%. The change in basis from a positive 8 ticks to a negative 9 ticks favoured the long hedger. If the hedger has reason to believe the basis will move in a favourable direction, this fact can be used in hedge design. For example, in the above case the investor will realise that the basis of 8 ticks will be eliminated by the end of August, assuming the futures market is pricing itself off the cheapest deliverable gilt, which is almost certainly the Treasury 15.5% 1998 described in the example. Transactions costs would lead one to expect the standard gilt in the delivery month to trade at a premium over the equivalent parity price (obtained from the conversion table) for the cheapest deliverable gilt.

Assume, however, that the investor believed the basis would move from +8 ticks to zero by the end of July as the process of convergence occurred. The investor knows that convergence during the life of the hedge is forecast to produce a cash gain per contract of £125. A neutral hedger would put on the hedge for a lesser amount than the 25 contract shown above. To determine the optimal hedge *ex post* it is necessary to see how many contracts would have been required to produce the equivalent profit on the futures position to that loss on the cash position, assuming the basis only moved from +8 to zero.

Futures gain per contract = £15,625 × 167 ticks (92-09 − 87-02)
= £2,609.38
Ex post perfect hedge = £61,875/£2,609.38 = 23.71

Depending upon the maximum level of adverse interest rate change the investor was forecasting, the hedger could have afforded to purchase only 24 rather than 25 contracts to produce a good hedge.

There is always an alternative strategy available to a portfolio manager in these hedges of prospective asset purchases. In the above case, the manager could simply have purchased the asset immediately by borrowing short-term funds. The current price of the gilt is locked in with certainty, but there is a cost of borrowing between 30 March and 30 July. On the other hand, accrued interest on the Treasury 15.5% 1998 will be gained by the investor over the same period. Careful comparison of the respective costs of hedging in the futures market and/or borrowing funds and purchasing assets immediately need to be made by the prospective hedger. In most cases, it is quite likely to be the case that simple direct purchase of the asset may be the favoured strategy.

Appendix: US Treasury bond future Summary of contract

Unit of trading	US$100,000 par value notional US Treasury bond with 8% coupon
Delivery months	March, June, September, December
Delivery day/Exercise day/Expiry day	Any business day in delivery month (at seller's choice)
Last trading day	Seven Chicago Board of Trade working days prior to last business day in delivery month
Quotation	Per US$100 par value
Minimum price movement	US$1/32
(Tick size and value)	(US$31.25)
Initial margin	US$3,000
(straddle margin)	(zero)
Trading hours	08.15–16.10

Contract standard

1 Delivery may be made of any US treasury bond maturing at least 15 years from the first day of the contract month if not callable; if callable, the earliest call date must be at least 15 years from the first day of the contract month.
2 Bonds must be delivered in multiples of US$100,000 par value.
3 Interest must be payable half-yearly.
4 Bonds must be capable of transfer by means of the US Federal Reserve wire transfer system.

For the US Treasury bond contract, a business day in the delivery process is defined as a day when banks in New York and Chicago are open for business as well as LIFFE. The last trading day is defined to coincide with the last trading day for the Chicago Board of Trade US Treasury bond futures contract, where there is a LIFFE trading day.

Exchange delivery settlement price (EDSP)

The LIFFE EDSP shall be that settlement price established on the same day on the Chicago Board of Trade for deliveries into the Chicago Board of Trade US Treasury bond futures contract.

PART IV

Interest rate swaps

1 The mechanics of interest rate swaps

Cory N. Strupp

Introduction

An interest rate swap is a transaction in which two parties agree to make periodic payments to each other, calculated on the basis of specified interest rates and a specified principal amount. Typically, the payment to be made by one party is calculated using a floating rate of interest (such as Libor, the prime rate or a commercial paper rate), while the payment to be made by the other party is determined on the basis of a fixed rate of interest or a different floating rate. An interest rate swap can be used to transform one type of asset or interest obligation into another and thereby enable a swap participant to tailor its assets and interest obligations to meet its needs in a given rate environment, to reduce its cost of borrowing, or to hedge against future changes in rates.

The market

The interest rate swap market had its inception in 1981. Initially, swaps were viewed as one-off transactions, but that perception was quickly dispelled as their widespread usefulness became apparent and their popularity spread. By the end of 1987, the notional principal amount of interest rate swaps outstanding was believed by knowledgeable observers to be in excess of US$600bn.

Participants in the swap market are many and varied: any substantial borrower or investor is a potential interest rate swap participant. Commercial banks and investment banking firms often act as intermediaries, bringing together swap counterparties with complementary needs, frequently in complex chains of matching transactions. Commercial banks also enter into swaps as end users, to cover their own funding needs and to establish fixed returns on floating rate investments. Together, acting as intermediaries and end users, commercial banks and investment banking firms constitute the primary swap market.

In addition to the primary market, a secondary swap market has also begun to develop. In this market, existing swap positions are traded. For example, an intermediary which is unable to match a particular swap may go into the secondary market and purchase a matching swap from another intermediary. Although this market is growing, its development has been impeded by several factors. First, interest rate swap agreements ordinarily require that a party obtain the consent of its counterparty for any assignment. Secondly, differences in documentation often make it difficult to match swaps. This latter problem has been addressed, in part, by the *Code of standard wording, assumptions and provisions for swaps* (the *'Swaps code'*), which was developed by the International Swap Dealers Association and which provides certain standard definitions and terms relating to the basic elements of interest rate swaps. The *Swaps code* not only enables parties to communicate more quickly and accurately, but also facilitates the matching of swaps and its use has contributed to the development of a secondary market.

Basic swap structures

In its simplest form, an interest rate swap can be undertaken by two parties. For example, a borrower seeking to pay interest at a fixed rate, but which has already borrowed at floating rate or for some reason is able to borrow more favourably at a floating rate, can enter into an interest swap to accomplish its desired result. In order to do so, it needs to locate another borrower that wants to pay interest at a floating rate but which has already borrowed at a fixed rate or has available to it a lower fixed rate than is available to the first borrower. The borrower wanting to pay a fixed rate borrows the principal amount that it needs, but at its more favourable floating rate. The borrower wanting to pay a floating rate borrows an identical amount at the favourable fixed rate available to it. (Of course, if a borrower were entering into the swap with respect to existing debt, it would not undertake a new borrowing. Moreover, the amounts borrowed do not have to be identical if one party or the other is willing to leave a portion of its borrowing uncovered by the swap.) The two then enter into an agreement in which each undertakes to make periodic payments to the other in amounts equal to, or determined on the same basis as, the other's interest cost. Only payments corresponding to interest are made; payments relating to principal amounts are not made by either party. The net result of the exchange is that each party is able to obtain the type of interest rate, fixed or floating, that it wants and on acceptable terms.

Neither lender is a party to the swap; each borrower continues to be obligated to its own lender for the payment of both principal and interest. In fact, the lenders would not necessarily even know that the swap had been undertaken. Each swap party takes the risk that the other may not make its swap payments, which would leave the non-defaulting party with the interest cost of its own borrowing uncovered by the swap.

A simple interest rate swap is illustrated in Exhibit 1.1 using assumed amounts. Suppose that one borrower is an industrial company that can obtain funds with a 10-year maturity at a floating rate of 1% above Libor, but that it would be compelled to pay a fixed rate of 12% on its bonds for the same

Exhibit 1.1   Interest rate swap with assumed amounts

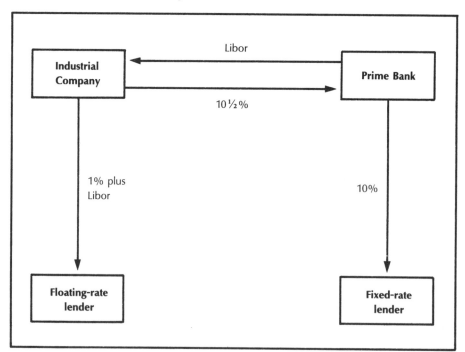

term. Also, assume that the other borrower is a prime bank that has access to floating rate funds at Libor and 10-year funds at a fixed rate of 10%. The fixed interest rate differential between the borrowers is 2% and the floating rate differential is 1%. To establish the interest rate swap, the industrial company borrows at 1% plus Libor, and the prime bank borrows at 10%, with the drawdown, interest payment and maturity dates for the two separate borrowings being identical. The industrial company and the prime bank then enter into a swap agreement in which each agrees to make payments to the other in amounts based on the interest cost of the other's financing, and in which the industrial company agrees to pay an additional $\frac{1}{2}$% premium to the prime bank.

These terms will produce a total fixed interest cost to the industrial company of $11\frac{1}{2}$% (10% plus the $\frac{1}{2}$% premium plus the 1% above Libor). Because the industrial company's cost to borrow fixed rate funds directly would be 12%, it obtains a $\frac{1}{2}$% saving through the swap. The bank also benefits because its effective cost of floating rate funds is reduced by $\frac{1}{2}$%, i.e. it becomes Libor minus $\frac{1}{2}$%. In addition, the bank may benefit by using its fixed rate borrowing (converted to a floating rate through the swap) to replace existing interbank borrowings undertaken to fund its loan portfolio. To the extent that its fixed rate borrowing has a longer maturity than the interbank funds being replaced, the bank will have improved the liability maturity structure of its balance sheet.

Although it is possible for the principals in a swap transaction to negotiate the swap directly with each other, in fact most interest rate swaps take place through an intermediary. The intermediary links the two principals by entering into separate, but parallel, interest rate swap transactions with each of them. Often the intermediary will be the originator or organiser of the transaction, and the intermediary may also serve to provide credit support for either of the parties. Exhibit 1.2 illustrates a swap transaction using an intermediary.

Exhibit 1.2   Matched swaps

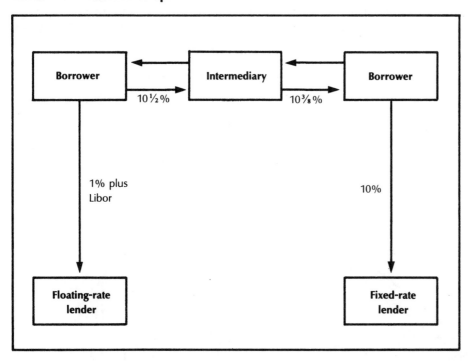

While the intermediary in most matched swaps is a commercial bank, investment banking firm or other professional participant in the market, a commercial, industrial or financial company which has entered into a swap transaction as principal may, in effect, become an intermediary by entering into a parallel swap. For example, an industrial company may wish to terminate an existing swap exposure, but for various reasons be reluctant to notify its counterparty of that intention. The same economic result can be achieved by entering into a parallel or matching swap transaction, which may entail either paying an amount to, or receiving an amount from, the new counterparty to reflect changes in market interest rates that have occurred since the original transaction.

The risk being assumed by an intermediary is limited. The payments being made by the intermediary in each swap are covered by the payments it receives from the other swap. If its counterparty in one of the swaps fails to make a payment, then the intermediary will be relieved of its obligation to make payments to that party but it will continue to be obligated to make payments to the other counterparty. The risk being assumed by the intermediary in respect of the defaulting party is limited to the risk that prevailing rates will have risen or fallen (depending on whether the defaulting party is the fixed rate payer or the floating rate payer) since the transaction began and that the intermediary, if it must replace the defaulting party in order to cover its continuing obligation in the other swap, will receive less from a new fixed rate payer or be required to pay more to a new floating rate payer/fixed rate receiver.

Interest rate swaps do not necessarily have to be entered into between borrowers. For example, an interest rate swap can be structured so that payments are made between a lender and a borrower. In the transaction shown in Exhibit 1.1, the industrial company which prefers to be a fixed rate borrower could have obtained fixed rate funds from a lender that prefers to lend at a floating rate. The lender could convert its fixed rate return to a floating rate return by entering into a swap. The net result, shown in Exhibit 1.3, is the same as in the transaction illustrated in Exhibit 1.1 – the industrial company pays $11\frac{1}{2}\%$ and the prime bank pays Libor minus $\frac{1}{2}\%$; only the payment flows and related risks and costs have changed.

With this latter structure the industrial company might well be justified in viewing the transaction as nothing more than a conventional fixed rate loan, ignoring the existence of the interest rate swap to which it is not a party. However, it might find itself drawn into the swap arrangements in several

Exhibit 1.3   Interest rate swap with a lender

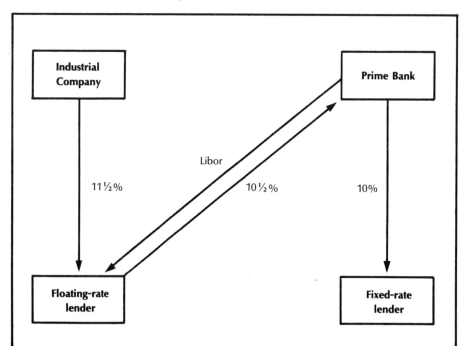

ways. Most importantly, it might have to pay fees to induce the other parties to participate in the transaction. In addition, since the industrial company benefits from the swap, its lender (the floating rate lender) might require indemnification against any failure by the counterparty in the lender's swap to make a payment. Similarly, the swap counterparty (the prime bank) might want to look to the industrial company for indemnification against the failure of the floating rate lender to make its swap payments. These would all be points for negotiation among the parties.

Variations of the basic structure

Although a typical interest rate swap follows the basic structure outlined above, with one party making payments calculated on the basis of a fixed rate of interest in return for payments based on a floating rate, and both payments to be made over a predetermined period of time, variations of this basic structure are numerous. These variations include zero coupon swaps, floating for floating swaps, callable and putable swaps, extendable swaps, forward swaps and delayed rate settings. In order to deal with different credit risks, swap obligations may be secured by collateral or be supported by a guarantee or a standby letter of credit. In addition, payments may or may not be made with the same frequency; for example, it is not uncommon for floating payments to be made semi-annually in return for an annual fixed payment.

Zero coupon swaps

A zero coupon swap is similar to a fixed for floating swap in that one party's payment obligation is determined on the basis of a floating rate of interest while the other's payment obligation is determined on the basis of a fixed rate. However, unlike the usual swap in which each party makes periodic payments to the other, in a zero coupon swap the floating rate payments are made

Exhibit 1.4   Zero coupon swap

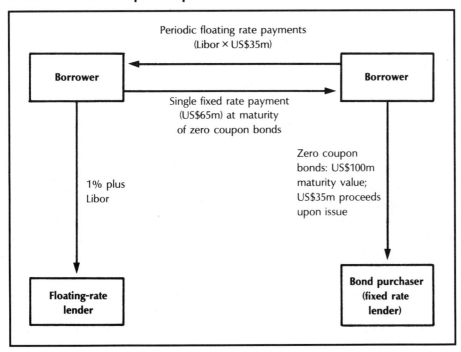

periodically throughout the life of the transaction but only one fixed rate payment is made, on the scheduled termination of the agreement. The fixed payment is structured in this manner to reflect the underlying obligation on zero coupon bonds issued by the party to whom that payment is made. While that party may wish to borrow at a floating rate, it may find that it can obtain a more favourable rate by issuing zero coupon bonds. Consequently, it would issue the bonds and enter into an interest rate swap, agreeing to make floating rate payments periodically in return for a single payment equal to the difference between the issue price and the redemption value of the bonds at maturity. In so doing, it would realise its objective of paying a floating rate while covering the redemption cost of its bonds. A zero coupon swap, with assumed amounts, is shown in Exhibit 1.4.

Floating for floating swaps

In a floating for floating interest rate swap each party makes floating payments to the other. Rather than taking advantage of pricing disparities between the fixed rate and floating rate markets, as in the case of a fixed for floating interest rate swap, this form of swap is often used to take advantage of differentials between different floating rate markets or to cover floating rate obligations undertaken in other interest rate swap transactions. The payments in a floating for floating swap may be calculated on the same pricing basis but with different pricing periods (such as a swap of payments based on 6-month Libor in return for payments based on 1-month Libor) or different pricing bases (such as 6-month Libor for a 1-month commercial paper rate). These swaps are also referred to as 'basis swaps', as the effect of the swap is to change the basis on which a variable interest cost is calculated.

Callable, putable, extendable and forward swaps

Although the usual interest rate swap runs for a fixed period of time (commonly 1 to 10 years into the future), borrowers can also structure swaps with variable lives. A callable or putable swap allows a borrower to enter into an interest rate swap for a fixed period, but with an option to terminate the swap prior to its scheduled maturity date. A swap with this option is either callable or putable, depending on which party has the right to terminate – a fixed rate payer that has the right to terminate a swap has bought a 'call', whereas a fixed rate receiver that has the right to terminate has bought a 'put'. The party with the right to terminate the swap usually may do so at any time during its life and pays for the privilege by an adjustment in the periodic payments – for example, a fixed rate payer would pay a slightly higher fixed rate in return for the right to call – and by making a payment (ordinarily calculated as a percentage of the notional principal amount) upon exercise of the call. Callable and putable swaps are used by borrowers whose underlying borrowings or investments allow a corresponding early retirement or are otherwise subject to a change in maturity and by intermediaries who are counterparties to callable and putable swaps.

Extendable swaps, which give one party the option to extend the life of the swap beyond its scheduled maturity date, are economically equivalent to callable and putable swaps. For example, a borrower who has a 3-year swap that it may extend to seven years is in the same position as a borrower with a 7-year swap that it may call after three years.

Forward swaps enable a borrower to set the rates for calculating swap payments at a time when market interest rates appear to be favourable (such as, in the case of a fixed rate payer, when the spread between US Treasury bills and fixed rates is small), even though the borrower does not have an immediate borrowing need. A borrower may know that it will need to raise funds at a given time in the future and that it will do so by borrowing fixed rate funds and swapping them into a floating rate. If rates presently available in the swap market are favourable, the borrower can eliminate any uncertainty over the future availability of those rates by entering into a forward swap, which establishes the fixed and floating rates at the time it is entered into but does not begin until a stated future date.

A similar option, delayed rate setting, can be used by borrowers who have immediate financing needs, but who are faced with unfavourable rates. Delayed rate setting allows a borrower to enter into a swap immediately, but with an option to set the swap rates at any time within a given period on the basis of an agreed formula.

Asset-based swaps

In an asset-based swap, one or both of the parties enters into the transaction to alter the form of return it is receiving on an investment, rather than to convert the cost of a borrowing. For example, an investor receiving a fixed rate of return might wish, instead, to receive a floating rate but be unable for any of a variety of reasons to sell its fixed rate asset. By entering into a swap, the investor can obtain the floating rate it desires while retaining its original investment. Alternatively, an investor that is prohibited from holding a particular type of asset can use an asset-based swap to obtain a return equal to, or based on, the asset's return while holding a different, permitted investment.

Pricing

When interest rate swaps were first developed, substantial front-end fees were often paid by one party to the other, in addition to the spread built into the payment streams. Today, front-end fees have all but disappeared and spreads have narrowed considerably.

The pricing of fixed for floating swaps is driven by several factors, including the relationship between the rates on Eurodollar futures and US Treasury securities (the 'TED spread') in case of short-term swaps and the relationship between the rates for corporate borrowing and US Treasury securities in the case of longer-term swaps. At the end of 1986 good quality fixed rate payers were paying rates equal to 90 to 110 basis points (depending on maturity) over the rate on US Treasuries of comparable maturities in return for floating rate payments calculated at a specified rate, such as Libor, without an additional spread. At that time lesser quality fixed rate payers faced spreads of up to 10 to 15 basis points above those paid by good quality payers.

The pricing of floating swaps is based on the historical and forecast relationship between the respective floating rate indices in the cash and futures markets. At the end of 1986, good quality counterparties in a typical commercial paper-for-Libor swap paid between 30 and 35 basis points over the commercial paper rate in return for payments equal to Libor.

2 Accounting treatment: United States

Benjamin S. Neuhausen

Introduction

The authoritative accounting literature in the US contains no rules specifically applicable to accounting for interest rate swaps. Accordingly, practice has evolved based on analogies to similar areas in accounting, such as accounting for interest rate futures contracts. However, practice is not uniform in all respects. This chapter describes the accounting practices that are most supportable based on generally accepted accounting principles. The reader should be aware that other, less supportable practices, may be followed by some companies.

As noted in Part II, Chapter 1, 'Accounting framework: United States', the accounting for swaps, along with other interest rate protection products is the subject of a major Financial Accounting Standards Board (FASB) project and could change.

This chapter is divided into two sections. The first describes the accounting by end-users of interest rate swaps, that is, companies who enter into swaps either as hedges or to speculate on interest rate movements. The second section describes the accounting by swap intermediaries – the commercial and investment banks who enter into interest rate swaps as a line of business.

ACCOUNTING BY END-USERS

Balance sheet treatment

A company that enters an interest rate swap has a right to receive a stream of cash payments and is obligated to make a stream of cash payments. The right to receive payments could be recorded as a receivable at the discounted present value of the estimated payments to be received and the obligation to make payments could be recorded as a liability at the discounted present value of the estimated payments to be made. In practice, however, this is not done for two reasons. First, most swap agreements provide for right of offset; the parties settle their cash payments on a net basis. Where right of offset exists, receivables and payables can be offset on the balance sheet. Secondly, under current accounting practice, executory contracts (contracts in which both parties have future performance obligations) generally are not recorded on balance sheets as assets and liabilities. Accordingly, under current practice, swaps are not recorded on the balance sheet at inception.

Ordinarily, the parties to an interest rate swap never exchange the notional principal amount of a swap. Accordingly, no basis exists for recording the notional principal amount on the balance sheet.

Hedging criteria

As with other interest rate protection products, the first major issue in accounting for interest rate swaps is whether they are entered into for hedging purposes or for speculation. As noted in Part II,

Chapter 1, three criteria generally must be satisfied for an interest rate protection product to be considered a hedge for accounting purposes:

1   The underlying transaction that is being hedged exposes the company to interest rate risk.
2   The company designates the interest rate swap as a hedge.
3   The interest rate swap is effective as a hedge.

In addition, to be considered a hedge of an anticipated transaction (such as the resetting of interest rates on variable-rate assets or debt or the rollover of short-term investments or debt), two additional criteria must be satisfied:

1   The significant characteristics and expected terms of the anticipated transaction are identified.
2   It is probable that the anticipated transaction will occur.

In practice, interest rate swaps are generally accounted for as hedges if the second and third criteria (designation and effectiveness) are satisfied; the other criteria are not necessarily applied. Often, of course, all of the criteria would be satisfied. For example, if a company issues long-term variable rate debt and enters an interest rate swap to fix the rate, all three basic criteria are satisfied if the variable rate side of the swap correlates well with the variable rate on the debt. In addition, the two additional criteria for hedges of anticipated transactions are satisfied. In other cases, however, such as the use of an interest rate swap to unfix the interest rate on a fixed rate borrowing, the first criterion (underlying hedged item exposes the company to interest rate risk) may not be satisfied.

Accounting treatment for hedges

The hedge accounting described in this section applies to companies that follow the usual practice of accounting for interest-bearing financial instruments at amortised cost (for assets) or amortised proceeds (for liabilities). The accounting for an interest rate swap that hedges an asset or liability accounted for on a market value basis would be the same as the accounting described below for speculative interest rate swaps.

If a swap is used to hedge an existing asset or liability, including fixing the interest rate on a variable rate asset or liability, the accounting is quite simple. Any fee paid or received and any costs incurred to execute the swap should be deferred and amortised by the interest method over the life of the swap. Settlement payments should be accrued each period as a net adjustment to interest income/expense for the underlying transaction. Under this approach, it is not necessary to determine the changing market value of the swap from period to period; as long as both the underlying transaction and the interest rate swap remain in effect, the income effect is solely a function of initial costs and fees and the settlement payments. This approach is sometimes described as 'synthetic instrument' accounting, because it results in the accounting for the underlying asset/liability (instrument) as though its nature had been changed from variable to fixed rate or vice versa.

Sometimes an interest rate swap contract might be used to hedge a commitment to buy an interest-bearing instrument or to issue debt. (A firm commitment is defined in Part II, Chapter 1 as an agreement, usually legally enforceable, under which performance is probable because of sufficiently large disincentives for non-performance.) Any fee paid or received and any costs to execute a swap that hedges a firm commitment should be deferred and amortised by the interest method over the life of the resulting asset or liability to which the commitment relates. Settlement payments during the commitment period should be deferred and reported as an adjustment to interest income or expense over the life of the resulting asset or liability to which the commitment relates. If it is anticipated at any time that the firm commitment will not be fulfilled, the swap should be accounted for as a speculative position as described below, unless the swap can then be designated as a hedge of another transaction.

An interest rate swap also may be used to hedge a transaction that the company expects, but is not obligated, to enter, such as an anticipated issuance of debt. To follow hedge accounting in this particular situation, the swap should satisfy at least the second and third general criteria (designation and effectiveness) *and* the two special criteria for hedges of anticipated transactions (identification and probability). The accounting is identical to the accounting for a swap that hedges a firm commitment – defer fees, costs, and settlement payments during the period before the anticipated transaction is consummated and amortise them by the interest method over the life of the consummated transaction. If it is expected at any time that the anticipated transaction will be less than the amount originally hedged, a *pro rata* portion of the swap should be accounted for as a speculative position as described below, unless that portion can then be designated as a hedge of another transaction.

Speculative swaps

If a swap does not satisfy the conditions to be accounted for as a hedge or if a swap hedged a firm commitment or anticipated transaction that will not occur, the swap should be accounted for as a speculative position. In industries with specialised accounting principles that require market value accounting, these swaps should be accounted for on a market value basis, with gains and losses included in income currently. For other industries, speculative swap positions should be accounted for on a lower-of-cost-or-market/higher-of-proceeds-or-market basis (i.e. defer gains but recognise losses currently).

Because prices of interest rate swaps are not quoted publicly, determining their fair value will require either mathematical models or quotations from knowledgeable third party intermediaries. Regardless of what means is used to estimate market value, it is important that the estimate consider the effect of credit considerations on the valuation. Significant factors include collateralisation of the transaction and the current credit standing of the swap counterparty.

Swap terminations

Sometimes a company will decide to terminate an interest rate swap before the expiration of its term. This may be accomplished in two ways. One is to directly terminate the swap and pay or receive the cash payment specified in the swap agreement for early termination. The other method is to enter a reverse swap for a period equal to the remaining term of the original swap. For example, a company that issued 10-year variable rate debt in 1982 and entered a 10-year swap to receive variable rate and pay 12% fixed may wish to terminate that swap in 1987 to take advantage of lower interest rates. One method is to pay off the counterparty to terminate the swap. The other method is to enter a 5-year reverse swap under which the company will pay variable rate and receive a fixed rate of, say 8%. No up-front cash payment is required in the latter case, but the company has locked in a 4% loss (12% minus 8%) for five years. The termination loss under the second method is the discounted present value of the locked in 4% loss.

A gain or loss on early termination of an interest rate swap that qualified as a hedge generally should be deferred and amortised over the term of the original swap. However, if the underlying transaction being hedged also is closed out, the gain or loss from terminating the swap should be recognised currently in income. A gain or loss on early termination of a speculative interest rate swap should be included in income currently.

The conclusion to defer and amortise the gain or loss from early termination of a swap that qualified as a hedge is based on the treatment required by FASB Statement No. 80 when a futures contract is closed out but the underlying hedged transaction continues in effect. The FASB Emerging Issues Task Force has discussed the accounting for terminations of interest rate swaps, and the discussion in this section is consistent with the consensus reached by that body.

Swap extensions

In this transaction, a swap is extended beyond its original term and the fixed interest rate side of the swap is adjusted. For example, assume that the original swap calls for fixed payments at 12% for a remaining 5-year term at a time when interest rates have dropped to 8%. The parties might agree to extend the swap to 10 years in exchange for a decrease in the fixed rate side to 10%.

For accounting purposes, a swap extension should be viewed as a termination of the original interest rate swap and the acquisition of a replacement swap. These two elements are accounted for separately, using current market values and interest rates. In the example above, the loss on terminating the original swap is embedded in the above-market fixed rate on the replacement swap. The loss is equal to the discounted present value of the 2% above-market rate for the 10-year term of the replacement swap. The loss should be accounted for as described in the section on swap terminations above. The other side of the accounting journal entry recording the loss is to record a deferred income account that will be amortised back to income over the life of the replacement swap to reduce its fixed rate from 10% to the 8% market rate. Failing to follow the accounting specified would spread part of the loss on terminating the original swap over years 6 to 10.

Forward swaps

A forward interest rate swap is an agreement to enter into an interest rate swap with defined terms at an agreed date in the future. For example, a company may enter into a forward swap that calls for a 7-year swap beginning three years in the future under which the company will receive a variable rate and pay a fixed rate of 8%. A company might enter such an arrangement as a hedge of debt that it expects to issue three years in the future. Perhaps the company has existing high interest rate debt outstanding that can first be called three years from today. The company plans to call the existing debt and issue new 7-year notes. The forward swap 'locks in' the cost of the refinancing notes. The forward swap clearly locks in a cost if the new notes are variable rate notes matching the variable rate in the forward swap, but it also does so if the new 7-year notes are fixed rate notes. If interest rates rise in the intervening three years, the forward swap can be terminated at a gain; the gain on the swap will economically offset the higher interest rate on the new notes and result in a financing cost based on today's interest rates. Conversely, if interest rates fall in the intervening three years, the forward swap can be terminated at a loss; the loss will effectively raise the financing cost on the new notes to today's interest rates.

Another form of the forward swap is a double swap. Rather than entering a forward 7-year swap beginning three years from today, the company in our example could enter two swaps:

1 A 10-year swap beginning today under which it will receive a variable rate and pay 8% fixed, and
2 A 3-year swap beginning today under which it will pay the same variable rate and receive 7% fixed.

Effectively, this double swap creates a seven-year forward swap beginning three years from today. The company pays a 1% fee (8% rate paid less 7% rate received) for each of the next three years.

For a forward swap to qualify as a hedge for accounting purposes, it must satisfy at least the second and third general criteria (designation and effectiveness) and the two criteria for hedges of anticipated transactions (identification and probability). If these conditions are satisfied, any fees paid for the forward swap (including the net amounts paid or received during the double swap period) are deferred. Using our example above, if variable rate debt is issued at the end of three years and the swap is left intact, the deferred fees would be amortised as an adjustment of interest on the debt. The settlement payments on the swap would be accounted for as adjustments of interest expense each period. If fixed rate debt is issued at the end of three years, the swap will presumably be terminated. If the term of the fixed rate debt is similar to the 7-year term of the swap, the gain or loss upon swap termination, including the deferred fees, would be recorded as premium or discount on the new debt and amortised as an adjustment of interest expense over the life of the debt.

Disclosure

Although no specific disclosure requirements exist, it is desirable to disclose the following information with respect to use of interest rate swaps:

- How and why they are used.
- Their effect on interest expense and interest rate risk. For example, a company might disclose that one-third of its short-term debt has effectively been changed to a weighted average fixed rate of 8% by use of interest rate swaps.

ACCOUNTING BY INTERMEDIARIES

This section of the chapter discusses the following topics:

1 How to present swaps on the balance sheet.
2 When to record swap fees in income.
3 How to account for changes in the value of swaps and when to recognise those changes in income.
4 How to account for settlement payments on swaps.
5 How to account for terminations of interest rate swaps.
6 Footnote disclosures.

Balance sheet presentation

An intermediary may be a principal to a swap transaction or may serve solely as an agent bringing the two counterparties together.

If the intermediary is solely an agent, he clearly need not record any swap commitment on his balance sheet. His only right is to collect a fee for bringing the parties together, and he has no obligation under the swap.

If the intermediary is a principal to a swap transaction, he has a right to receive a stream of cash payments and is obligated to make a stream of cash payments. The right to receive payments could be recorded as a receivable at the discounted present value of the estimated payments to be received and the obligation to make payments could be recorded as a liability at the discounted present value of the estimated payments to be made. In practice, however, this is not done for the same reasons that end-users do not record swaps on their balance sheets. As will be discussed later, the intermediary will record assets and liabilities on his balance sheet during the term of the swap if he recognises gains or losses caused by changing interest rates.

Ordinarily, the parties to an interest rate swap never exchange the notional principal amount of a swap. Accordingly, no basis exists for recording the notional principal amount on the intermediary's balance sheet.

Intermediary as agent: income recognition

If the intermediary acts solely as an agent in arranging the swap and bringing the two swap counterparties together, the intermediary's sole service is rendered at inception and the intermediary bears no risks. Therefore, the intermediary should recognise all fees in income upon completion of his services. If the intermediary's fee is not paid immediately, the fee income should be recorded at the discounted present value of amounts to be received. The receivable for fees to be collected is subject to the normal requirement to provide an allowance for uncollectible amounts.

If the intermediary is solely an agent, he is unaffected by the effect of changing interest rates on the value of the swap and, accordingly, is not affected by any of the issues discussed in the remainder of this chapter.

This situation of the intermediary acting solely as agent is becoming rarer as the swaps market matures.

Intermediary as principal: overall accounting principles

If the intermediary is a principal in a swap transaction, his accounting should be guided by the following two broad accounting principles:

1   Since the intermediary retains risks as a principal, he should record income only for services performed or as he is released from risk, and the amount of income recognised should be commensurate with the services performed or risks eliminated in relation to risks retained.
2   Losses should be recognised as soon as they become probable.

These two principles do not, by any means, answer all of the questions about accounting for swaps or allow us to clearly choose the best alternative from the diverse accounting methods followed in practice. They do provide useful guidelines, however, in evaluating the reasonableness of various accounting approaches.

The intermediary's accounting may differ depending on whether he is in a matched or unmatched position. In a matched position, the intermediary locates two parties, arranges the swap, remains in the transaction as a principal for each party (the two parties may not even know one another's identity), and collects the payment from one party and pays the other party on each settlement date. The intermediary in a matched swap position does not assume interest rate risk, however, because his rights and obligations under the matched swaps economically offset. The intermediary assumes default (credit) risk, because he must perform his obligations with each party even if the other party defaults. A matched position may involve more than two parties in more complex situations, and may not always be perfectly matched. In an unmatched position, the intermediary enters into a swap with a customer before locating a counterparty. In this situation, the intermediary is exposed to interest rate risk unless he is otherwise hedged.

Matched and unmatched positions are dynamic rather than fixed. Unmatched positions become matched when a counterparty is located. Matched positions become unmatched if the intermediary terminates the swap with one party while continuing the swap with the other party. Accordingly, the intermediary's accounting for a swap may vary over its life as it changes from matched to unmatched or vice versa.

Accounting during the term of a swap

Unmatched swap positions

Because an unmatched swap position exposes an intermediary to significant interest rate risk (unless he is otherwise hedged), no fee income should be recognised at the inception of an unmatched swap position. Two methods may be used to account for unmatched swap positions:

1   The mark-to-market method, under which each unmatched swap is revalued at each reporting date. Gains and losses are included in income currently. Up-front fees are viewed as part of the original cost/proceeds of the swap. Under this method, a liability would be recorded on the intermediary's balance sheet, equal to the cumulative net losses on swaps creating losses, and an asset would be recorded equal to the cumulative net gains on swaps creating gains.
2   The aggregate lower-of-cost-or-market (higher-of-proceeds-or-market) method, under which the entire portfolio of unmatched swaps is revalued at each reporting date. Aggregate net losses are recognised immediately; aggregate net gains are deferred. Up-front fees are viewed as part of the original cost/proceeds of the swap. Under this method, a liability would be recorded on the intermediary's balance sheet to the extent of cumulative net losses on the portfolio.

In deciding which alternative to use, an intermediary should consider its accounting policies for other related items. For example, an intermediary that accounts for other trading positions at market value should account for unmatched swap positions at market value.

Under either method, the determination of market value creates measurement problems. The ideal way to determine market value for any asset or liability is to look to the price for a similar item in a free market. Although swaps are becoming more standardised and the secondary market in swaps is becoming more active, it still is often difficult to find the market price for a comparable swap in the secondary market. When market prices are unavailable, the intermediary must use a surrogate for market. Most often, that surrogate is to discount the fixed leg of a swap at a current market interest rate. Different methods and rates may be used. For example, the fixed leg of a 7-year swap could be discounted using the current market interest rate for 7-year debt. Because a swap effectively represents interest payments only, it may be more meaningful to use the current market interest rate for stripped coupons on 7-year debt. Still another approach, which is becoming more common, is to view the fixed leg as a series of zero coupon bonds and to discount the settlement payments using the yield curve for stripped securities. This applies a one-year rate to the settlement payment one year in the future, a two-year rate to the settlement payment two years in the future, etc. Regardless of which method is used to estimate the market value of a swap position, the estimate should include the effect of credit considerations, such as the current credit standing of the counterparty and the collateral for the swap.

Under either method, net settlement payments are not included in income. Instead, net settlement payments made reduce the liability (or increase the asset) recorded for a swap or swap portfolio, and net settlement payments received increase the liability (or decrease the asset) recorded for a swap or swap portfolio. The reason for this is that the settlement payment represents partial realisation of the gain or loss already recorded on the swap.

If an unmatched swap position becomes a matched swap position, it should be transferred from the unmatched swap portfolio to the matched portfolio at its then current market value (or at the lower of cost or market if that is the accounting method used).

If the intermediary enters into transactions to hedge the interest rate risk exposure on unmatched swap positions, the hedging transaction should be accounted for similarly to the swaps, that is, on a lower-of-cost-or-market or mark-to-market basis.

Matched swap positions

In practice, four methods are used to account for matched swap positions.

One method is to follow the mark-to-market method, the same as if the swap positions were unmatched. Gain positions are valued at bid prices and loss positions are valued at ask prices. No income is recognised at swap inception. This method may be chosen for several reasons:

- If swaps move frequently from matched to unmatched and back, it is simpler to account for all the swaps the same, because no special accounting is required when a swap transfers from one position to the other.
- The market value of a swap is the best measure of the intermediary's credit risk (the loss he is exposed to if his counterparty defaults) at any point in time. Basing the accounting on this meaningful amount makes it easy to assess credit risk directly from the accounting records. If one of the other methods is used to account for matched swap positions, a separate system must be developed and used to monitor credit risk.
- Matched swap positions may not be perfectly matched. Marking both sides to market automaticallly accounts for any risks retained from imperfect matching.

In spite of those advantages, many intermediaries prefer to follow a different approach for matched positions. The other three approaches basically ignore the changes in the swap's value caused by changing interest rates on the grounds that the gain on one leg of a matched position will be offset by an equal (or almost equal) loss on the other leg. Therefore, these approaches focus on when to recognise fee income, which may be received in the form of explicit up-front fees, in the form of a locked in spread between the payments on the two legs of the matched swap, or both. The three approaches are as follows:

1   Recognise no fee income at the inception of the swap. Instead, recognise the income ratably over the life of the swap. This approach views the intermediary's major function as the bearing of default (credit) risk and, therefore, recognises income as the intermediary collects payments and is released from that risk.
2   Some intermediaries recognise fee income at the inception of the swap to the extent of the direct costs of arranging the swap. The remainder of the income is recognised ratably over the life of the swap. Intermediaries who follow this approach agree that their major function is bearing default risk. However, they believe that they should recognise enough income at inception to offset their direct costs, so as not to show a loss at the inception of what is expected to be a profitable transaction.
3   Finally, some intermediaries calculate a fair price (up-front fee) for assuming credit risk and servicing the swap and record that income over the life of the swap. The remainder of the income is recognised at inception. This approach ordinarily generates a profit at inception and is based on a philosophy that arranging the swap is a separate function that should generate a profit. The income recognised at inception should not exceed the fee that would be charged for an agency-only swap.

The FASB recently released Statement No. 91, *Accounting for nonrefundable fees and costs associated with originating or acquiring loans and initial direct costs of lessors*. That Statement concludes that originating loans is not a separate function and that direct costs incurred in and fees received from originating loans should be deferred and included in income over the life of the loan. Although the FASB project does not address the accounting for arranging interest rate swaps and no lending of funds occurs in a swap, some analogies exist. Therefore, the second and third approaches described above may need to be reconsidered.

Accounting for terminations of interest rate swaps

If a swap is terminated voluntarily, the intermediary will receive or pay a termination settlement. The FASB Emerging Issues Task Force has discussed the accounting for terminations of interest rate swaps, and the discussion in this section is consistent with the consensus reached by that body.

If the swap was unmatched or if the swap was half a matched position accounted for at market value, the difference between the swap settlement payment and the carrying amount of the swap should be recognised as an immediate gain or loss.

If the swap was half of a matched position that was not being marked to market, the swap settlement payment and any unamortised fees should be recognised as an immediate gain or loss. The continuing half of the swap position now becomes an unmatched position and should be accounted for in accordance with the intermediary's normal accounting policy for unmatched swaps (i.e. market value or lower-of-cost-or-market value). If the continuing unmatched half is 'underwater', an immediate loss is recognised.

If the termination is involuntary, because a counterparty defaults, the intermediary must record a loss for any uncollectible receivables from the defaulting party. In addition, if the defaulted swap was half of a matched position, the continuing half becomes an unmatched position that should be accounted for as described in the preceding paragraph.

Footnote disclosure

There are no specific requirements regarding the disclosure of interest rate swaps.

APB Opinion No. 22, *Disclosure of accounting policies*, requires disclosure of accounting policies that involve any of the following:

a. A selection from existing acceptable alternatives;
b. Principles and methods peculiar to the industry in which the reporting entity operates, even if such principles and methods are predominantly followed in that industry;
c. Unusual or innovative applications of generally accepted accounting principles.

Accounting by intermediaries for interest rate swaps fulfils all three conditions and, accordingly, disclosure of the accounting policies used is required. In addition to that required disclosure, the following additional disclosures are desirable:

- A description of why swaps are being entered into, for example, to earn income, to manage the intermediary's own interest rate exposure, etc.
- The magnitude of the intermediary's swap activity, perhaps measured by the notional principal amounts of swaps outstanding.
- The amount at risk from outstanding swaps. The best measure of risk is the cost the intermediary would incur if its swap counterparties defaulted on all swaps in which the intermediary is in a gain position leaving the intermediary obligated to fulfil its obligation on all swaps in which the intermediary is in a loss position. In other words, it is the cost the intermediary would incur to replace at current market rates all those outstanding swaps for which such cost exists. More intermediaries are making this disclosure in recent years.

3 Accounting treatment: United Kingdom

Mark Davis

Overall basis of accounting

There is no authoritative guidance in the UK on accounting for interest rate swaps. Consequently, the treatment adopted should be based on the principles outlined in Part II, Chapter 2, 'Accounting framework: United Kingdom'. Many swaps are tailored to suit the needs of a particular corporate and a large number of variations exist on the plain vanilla swap. The accounting treatment in each case should reflect the economic reality of the transaction. This chapter outlines the application of the basic principles to a simple swap and considers the accounting treatment of corporates and banks.

CORPORATES

Hedges of liabilities

Corporates are normally end-users of swaps, generally in order to reduce their exposure to interest rate fluctuations or in order to achieve a lower interest cost of borrowings. If a swap satisfies the hedge criteria outlined in Part II, Chapter 2, it will normally be accounted for as a hedge. The corporate continues to disclose its liabilities at the amount payable on maturity. However, it accrues the net amount of interest, that is the amount of interest payable on its borrowing plus or minus an accrual in respect of the swap payment. Technically, under the rules of Schedule 4, these accruals should be shown separately in the balance sheet. The swap payment receivable from the counterparty should not be netted off against the interest payable on the borrowing.

A corporate will normally pay arrangement fees at the outset of the swap. These are generally written off immediately. In return for paying a larger up-front fee, the corporate may pay lower fixed rate payments or be allowed a lower margin over floating rates. In such cases the up-front fee may be considered to be part of the overall cost of the swap and amortised to the P&L account over the life of the swap. Where the swap is connected with the issue of securities, however, care should be taken with the accounting treatment. Schedule 4 precludes corporates from capitalising the expenses on any issue of debentures. If the swap arrangement fee is considered to be an issue expense, it must be written off immediately either to the P&L account or to the share premium account.

Hedges of assets

Swaps are normally used as medium- or long-term hedges. Any asset being hedged will therefore normally be carried at cost less provision for permanent diminution in value or revalued to market value with the surplus being carried to revaluation reserve. In either case, the existence of the hedge should be recognised in determining the amount of any provision required or of the revaluation surplus.

Accounting for speculative transactions

Where a swap does not meet the hedging criteria, it should be accounted for as a speculative transaction. A corporate cannot normally trade swaps and there is no readily apparent market value for the instrument. Prudence, however, suggests that the existence of a swap should not be ignored. If interest rates have moved adversely it is probable that the corporate will have to make future net payments under the swap agreement. Provision for such payments should be made immediately. A variety of valuation methods may be adopted in order to determine whether provision is necessary. The corporate might ascertain the profit or loss which would arise if it closed down the swap, either by entering a second matching swap or by terminating the swap by agreement with the counterparty.

In practice, neither method is satisfactory. Termination of the swap generally involves some penalty. The cost of a matching swap would reflect the credit risk attaching to the corporate. A more appropriate method would appear to be to fair value the swap by reference to current market rates of interest. This involves discounting the future cash flows under the swap to give a net present value. If as a result of fair valuing the swap, a loss arises, provision should be made immediately. As discussed in Part II, Chapter 2, corporates may only recognise realised profits. Consequently, if a profit arises on the swap it should normally be ignored, any net receipts under the swap being recognised on an accruals basis.

Disclosure

The corporate should disclose the accounting policy adopted in respect of interest rate swaps. Where the swap is hedging the corporate's borrowings, the notes to the accounts should give details of the swap and its impact on the corporate's effective interest costs. Technical release TR677, *Accounting for complex capital issues*, suggests that the commercial effect, including any counterparty risk, is clearly explained. The net interest cost will normally be disclosed in the P&L account. Similar disclosure will be made where a swap hedges an asset.

If a speculative swap is material, the notional principal amount should be disclosed in a contingent liability note. If a profit arises on valuation of the swap and this is deferred, that profit may require disclosure as a contingent gain.

BANKS

A bank may play a number of roles in the swaps market. It can be an end-user of a swap, in the same way as a corporate, or it may act as an intermediary. As an intermediary, a bank may simply act as an agent, finding counterparties with opposing swap requirements, or it may act as a matched principal and transact a swap with each of the counterparties. Other banks will take unmatched positions in swaps, transacting a swap with one counterparty and 'warehousing' it until another counterparty can be found with opposing requirements. This will result in the bank holding a portfolio of swaps, which although not matching, will hedge each other to a certain extent.

Banks as end-users

Where a bank uses a swap to hedge an asset or liability, it will account for the swap in the same way as a corporate, as discussed in the previous section.

Intermediary as agent

If the intermediary acts solely as an agent in bringing two counterparties together and assumes no risk, then the arrangement fee may be taken straight to the P&L account. An agent which both channels funds between the counterparties and acts as a guarantor, is effectively a matched principal and should account for the swap transactions as such.

Intermediary as matched principal

If the bank has a perfectly matched swap position it will simply collect a payment from one counterparty and pass it on to the other counterparty on each settlement date, retaining a proportion representing the bank's margin. The interest payments and receipts should be accrued normally so that the margin is recognised over the life of the swap. Interest received and paid are normally netted and the margin shown as fee income in the P&L account. Frequently, the majority of the bank's income from such swaps is in the form of an up-front fee, part of which represents a reward for the bank's ongoing counterparty risk in respect of the matched swaps. Prudence would suggest that in such circumstances, a bank should recognise a proportion of the fee on origination of the swaps to cover the costs incurred, but defer the remainder of the fee and recognise it in income over the life of the swap.

Bank as unmatched principal

Where a bank has an unmatched swap it is exposed to both interest rate risk and credit risk. Frequently, a bank will maintain a portfolio of swaps which partially match, but because of the differences in the timing of payments or in the rates on which the swaps are based, it will be exposed to repricing or basis risk. The bank may use securities such as US Treasuries to hedge swap positions on a macro or individual basis. In such cases it may be possible to identify the swaps as hedges of the security positions or vice versa. It is generally preferable, however, to ascertain the fair value of each swap on an individual basis. This provides a better measure of performance and avoids the need for arbitrary allocations of swaps as speculative or hedging transactions. If the swap is recorded at fair value, any Treasuries position hedging a swap will be marked to market and there is no need to defer any profit or loss arising on termination on a Treasuries hedge which is replaced by a matched swap.

The fair value or market value of a swap can be calculated by revaluing each leg of the swap. If the bank is receiving a fixed rate from the counterparty it values that leg as if it were a fixed rate investment. The redemption yield used for valuation purposes is based on the current risk-free rate plus a margin for the credit risk attaching to the counterparty (which should be determined at the outset of the swap). If the counterparty's credit rating worsens during the life of the swap it may be appropriate to widen the margin for revaluation purposes. The floating rate leg of the swap should also be revalued as if it were an investment, although this will change in value only to a limited extent as a result of short-term interest rate changes during each interest period. The change in value of the fixed rate 'investment' indicates the profit or loss on the swap since its previous valuation date. Alternatively, the notional principal can be ignored and each interest payment and receipt discounted at rates obtained from a risk-free yield curve (adjusted by the counterparty risk margin). If material, the discounted cost of future administrative expenses can be thrown into the calculation for good measure.

The excess of the present value of the income stream over the payment stream will represent the fair value of the swap. Both profits and losses arising on revaluation should be taken to the P&L account. Whilst the bank may not be able to assign a profitable swap easily, it will usually be able to close its position and lock into the profit by using a second swap or a combination of other financial instruments. Consequently, it would seem appropriate for a bank to treat any profits arising on the revaluation as realised.

If the interest payments on the swaps are accrued in the normal manner, then revaluation profits and losses must be reversed daily in order to avoid double counting. The margins above the risk-free rate, received by the bank to cover counterparty risk, will then be recognised in income on an accruals basis over the period of the swap.

A bank will normally treat swap income as a dealing profit or loss rather than as interest received or paid. The latter treatment tends to distort the P&L account, since there are no corresponding interest bearing assets and liabilities on the balance sheet.

Disclosure

Banks should disclose the accounting policy adopted in respect of swaps. Currently, most banks indicate only the existence of swap transactions in the contingent liabilities note with no mention of the amounts involved. Better practice would be to disclose the nature of the bank's involvement with swaps (e.g. whether it acts as a matched principal or actively speculates on interest rate movements) together with some indication of the amounts of swaps outstanding.

4 Documentation of interest rate swaps

Anthony C. Gooch and Linda B. Klein

Introduction

When the market was in its infancy, there was a certain amount of controversy concerning the need for formal documentation for swaps, as the basic concepts are fairly simple, and the agreement is usually made over the telephone, with the papers to come later. Under these circumstances, some asked why swaps could not be documented on tickets, like currency trades. The view which has prevailed in the market is that something more elaborate is needed, at least for medium- and long-term transactions, particularly because of the desirability of dealing precisely with events of default, the appropriate measure of damages if a swap is terminated prematurely and other credit-related matters.

There have been several efforts to simplify the process of documenting swaps through the publication of standard terms. A major attempt has been made under the auspices of the International Swap Dealers Association, Inc, known as ISDA. In 1985, ISDA published the first edition of a *Code of standard wording, assumptions and provisions for swaps* (the *'Swaps code'*), which was revised to include additional terms in the current, 1986 edition. The *Swaps code* is a compendium of defined terms and conventions frequently used by participants in the US dollar interest rate exchange market. The parties to a swap agreement are free to incorporate some or all of those terms into their contract, and to incorporate them subject to any variations they may specify. By so doing, they are often able to avoid setting forth in full complex provisions describing, e.g. the floating rate or rates involved in a transaction, and the method to be used to calculate the payments to be made in the event of early termination of the parties' obligations.

In August 1985, the British Bankers' Association released its *Recommended terms and conditions for London interbank interest rate swaps – single currency fixed/floating swaps, cross currency swaps and cross currency floating-rate swaps*. Referred to as the BBAIRS terms, they are designed for use in transactions with maturities of two years or less among banks in that market. The parties may vary the BBAIRS terms for a particular transaction, but to the extent they do not, documentation of their transactions with each other may consist of a simple confirmation (for which the terms provide a sample form) setting forth the details necessary to determine the payments to be made in connection with the swap. However, the BBAIRS terms may not be suitable for some parties and some swap transactions. For instance, the BBAIRS terms contemplate a series of separate agreements between the parties but, for reasons described later in this chapter, institutions in today's market often prefer a single master agreement approach to documenting all their swaps with a given counterparty. In addition, the BBAIRS terms do not include some important provisions (e.g. certain events of default, and the right to withhold payments to a party that is in default), they lack some of the precision that many institutions customarily seek in their agreements, at least for longer-term transactions, and they are not designed for use in agreements with non-bank counterparties or with bank counterparties outside the London interbank market (which are not subject to the same scheme of regulatory oversight).

There have also been useful attempts at standardisation elsewhere. For instance, the Australian market has produced swaps terms modelled on those published by the British Bankers' Association. In addition, and independently of these organised efforts, many participants in the swap market found another way to simplify documentation: the master agreement format. It enables two parties that expect to engage in a course of swap dealings with each other to set out in one agreement the basic terms and conditions of their arrangements and then to amend them to add the specific terms of each swap as it is done. The supplemental amendment in each case can be memorialised in a very brief document, often called a confirmation, and many master agreements permit the parties to deliver the supplement by telex.

In March 1987, ISDA published two standard master agreements for swaps. The first incorporates terms from the 1986 *Swaps code* and is designed to document only US dollar interest rate swaps. The second contains substantially similar and additional terms so that the agreement can be used for currency exchange transactions and single currency swaps involving any currency; it does not expressly incorporate terms from the *Swaps code* because, as noted, it is designed only to deal with US dollar rate swaps. These standard agreements permit the parties to select among some terms and to add others on a schedule. A *User's guide* to the two forms and a lexicon of defined terms for use with the master currency and interest rate standard agreement have been prepared by ISDA. Undoubtedly, experience with these forms will lead to their further refinement, as market participants discover the kinds of changes required to customise the forms to reflect their particular policies and practices.

Appendices A and B at the end of this chapter are examples of an interest rate swap agreement for a single transaction and a master interest rate swap agreement. Appendix A illustrates the sort of documentation that would be required if one of the parties were a US banking institution and the other were a corporation from another jurisdiction. It therefore contains provisions to address issues that arise in cross-border swaps and also includes some terms applicable only to the corporation that generally would not be included, or would be made reciprocal, in an agreement between two financial institutions that regularly participate in the swap market as part of their business. Appendix A assumes that the parties have chosen to document their transaction without incorporating terms from the *Swaps code*; the swap contemplated in that sample provides for payments calculated at a fixed rate to be made annually by the corporation in exchange for payments calculated on the basis of Libor to be made semi-annually by the bank.

Appendix B illustrates a master agreement approach for two US bank parties that have agreed to incorporate *Swaps code* terms, and Appendix C includes two sample confirmations under that master agreement – one illustrating *Swaps code* terminology for documenting a fixed/Libor swap with payment dates scheduled to occur semi-annually on the Libor side and annually on the fixed-rate side, the other illustrating terms for quarterly matched payment dates in a fixed/prime rate swap.

This chapter deals only with the issues raised under New York law by conventional single currency rate swap documentation. Part I deals with single swap agreements; Part II with special features for cross-border rate swaps and Part III with the master agreement approach and the *Swaps code*. Our aim has been to give an overview of problems peculiar to contracts for swaps and not to deal with broader issues of documentation that arise in commercial contracts generally as well as swap agreements.

Variants of the samples included in Appendices A, B and C, together with a sample currency swap agreement, appear as fully annotated documents in our book on *Swap agreement documentation* published by Euromoney Publications PLC in February 1987. The reader who would like a more extensive analysis of some of the questions addressed in this chapter may find that book a helpful companion. Later references to it in this chapter will simply note the title and the relevant pages. (A second edition of that book, enlarged to include a sample interest rate and currency swap agreement prepared on an ISDA form, is scheduled to appear in 1988.)

I Documentation for single interest rate swaps between US counterparties

Although parties that expect to do a series of swaps with each other are likely to negotiate a master agreement for the reasons summarised in Part III, the single swap agreement is still the vehicle used for many interest rate exchange transactions. Many companies (sometimes referred to by market-makers as 'end users') may have their first exposure to the swap market when they use a rate swap to hedge against the risks of rising interest rates by 'converting' their liabilities incurred in connection with a floating rate note (FRN) issue, or a Libor borrowing, to a fixed rate. In those instances a single swap agreement may well be used. Others may choose the single swap agreement to document the creation of a 'synthetic security'. For example, an investor in fixed rate Eurobonds may engage in a rate swap in which the investor pays to its counterparty amounts equal to the stream of interest payments generated by the bond in exchange for receipt of a stream of Libor-based payments like those that a floating rate note might produce but at a rate higher than the yield that might be available at the time on a publicly issued FRN. The resulting package is sometimes referred to in the market as a 'synthetic FRN'.

Documentation of these transactions can require special attention to questions relating to the synchronisation of swap payments with the payments to be made under the underlying debt instruments or assets, and to ensuring that the method adopted to determine the floating rate used for the swap follows the provisions in the bond, note or loan documents precisely, or almost precisely. In most other respects, however, the issues raised by documentation of these transactions are the same as those raised by preparation of other swap agreements. The main areas covered in swap agreements are outlined below.

Definitions

The details on calculation of the rates being swapped are perhaps the most important of the definitions.

On the floating rate side, the great majority of swaps involve a Libo rate. Other floating rates that are swapped with some frequency in the US dollar market are the federal funds rate and the prime rate, as well as bankers acceptance rates, certificate of deposit (CD) rates, commercial paper rates and Treasury bill rates for obligations of various maturities. Commonly used definitions of each of these rates are available in the *Swaps code*. The floating rate base most frequently used in fixed/floating rate swaps in the Canadian and Australian dollar markets are bankers acceptance or bank 'bill' rates. The *1987 interest rate and currency exchange definitions* published by ISDA for use in connection with the ISDA standard *Interest rate and currency exchange agreement* include definitions of rates used in swaps involving 15 currencies.

The swap agreement will identify the source for the rate quotations, which might be a published source or reference banks or dealers, the frequency with which the rate is to be reset, whether there is to be compounding, and the day count fraction (such as 'actual days over 360') to be used to compute the floating rate swap amounts. If obligations of the type involved are offered in various maturities, the agreement will specify the appropriate maturity (e.g. 3-month Libor deposits) which, in *Swaps code* terms, would be referred to as the 'Designated Maturity'. If the amount of the deposit or instrument used as the basis for the rate is relevant in determining the rate, the amount will have to be stated in the agreement. This may, for example, be appropriate in a Libor definition based on rate quotations to be supplied by reference banks. Finally, some rates may be quoted or published on a bank discount basis. If they are to be converted to a bond equivalent yield or money-market basis for purposes of the swap, the swap agreement will also have to specify how the conversion is to be done.

On the fixed rate side, the principal features to be set forth in the definitions are the fixed rate (or fixed rate payment amounts) and the day-count fraction to be used where a rate, as opposed to a specified amount, is applicable. That fraction will often be the 'bond basis' of a year of 12 months of 30 days each.

The parties' fixed and floating payment obligations, determined on the bases set out in the definitions, are generally computed by one of the parties designated in the agreement as the agent of the other for the purpose. The calculation agent may have other functions as well, such as determination of an interest rate applicable to any amount not paid when due, or selection of alternative rate sources when the primary source chosen is unavailable.

Payments

These sections set forth the basic payment obligations and the settlement mechanics. Whenever possible, the payment obligations in a swap should be structured so that the two parties' payments can be netted against each other. This is desirable for several reasons. First, netting ensures that a party will not have to make its payment without receiving the corresponding payment from the other party. The parties' worries about payment risks in the context of a bankruptcy are thus reduced. Second, in a cross-border swap any concern about withholding taxes is greatly reduced because, if a tax were applicable, it would probably apply only to the relatively small net payment, and only if the party making the payment were located in the jurisdiction imposing the tax. When netting is not possible, if a party fails to make a payment the other party is left to such remedies as it may have at law to compel the other party to pay and to its contractual and other rights to suspend its own further performance pending payment or to call for early termination.

Netting is simple in a single currency interest rate swap when the parties' payment obligations have the same frequency (for example, both are quarterly or both are semi-annual) and the precise payment dates can be made to coincide. Full netting is not possible, however, when the frequencies of the parties' payments do not match, as is the case in the swap illustrated in Appendix A, where the corporation's fixed rate payments are due annually but the bank is required to make floating rate payments semi-annually. Only the second semi-annual payment can be netted against the annual fixed rate obligation.

Even when the frequencies do coincide, the exact payment dates may not. This happens, for example, when each party wants to receive payment on dates that will coincide precisely with the dates on which it will have to make payment on an underlying obligation and different countries' holidays are taken into account in the papers for the parties' respective underlying obligations or different market conventions are followed with respect to the timing of payments that fall due on weekends or holidays. Although this is a recurrent problem in currency swaps – which can also involve other timing concerns – this kind of situation does not often arise in rate swaps.

When there is a mismatch in rate swap payment dates, the swap agreement sometimes affords the party required to make payments more frequently, a right to adjust its payment dates so that payments can be netted in circumstances in which it becomes apparent that the other party may be unable to make its next payment. Section 2(c) of Appendix A illustrates one adjustment mechanism that is sometimes used for the purpose.

If there are conditions to a party's payment obligations, they will often be set forth in the portion of the swap agreement that deals with payments. Many agreements permit each party to defer or suspend its payments at any time (1) when the other party is in default under the swap agreement or (2) when there is some event or circumstance with respect to the other party that would ripen into an event of default if notice were given or a grace period elapsed. This is the position taken in Section 10.2 of the *Swaps code* and in both of the ISDA standard master agreements. This approach can be viewed as a contractual extension of a party's common law right under New York law to suspend its performance if there is a material failure by the other party to render performance due at an earlier time. This approach may, however, operate too harshly if the event relied upon to justify the suspension or deferral of payments is relatively unimportant, so there may be doubts as to the enforceability of that approach in some circumstances.

Under any approach, in agreements that provide for suspension or deferral of payments, the agreement should also deal with the end of the suspension or deferral period and payment of the amount deferred. Section 2(b) of Appendix A illustrates a method for ensuring that the suspension of payments will not result in a forfeiture of the suspended payments.

Representations and warranties

This portion of the agreement records the statements that each of the parties has made to the other regarding its financial condition and the like. The prevailing practice in the market has been to keep these provisions to a minimum and to make them largely reciprocal, as is generally appropriate since the payment obligations are reciprocal. Specially tailored representations and warranties from only one party are, however, often appropriate where governmental and other authorisations may be required (e.g. in swaps with companies in regulated industries and in cross-border swaps).

For parties that are new to swaps, counsel should be asked to examine carefully the correctness of what otherwise might seem run-of-the-mill representations, such as the statement that the agreement has been duly executed by a person authorised for the purpose, or that the party has the power and authority to enter into the agreement. The source of authority in each case may be clear for other kinds of commercial transactions, including a loan or bond issue in connection with which the swap is done; however, as swaps are a relatively new phenomenon, the same enabling laws, by-laws or other external or internal authorisations may not clearly apply to swaps. In addition, the basic representation that the agreement constitutes a legal, valid and binding obligation of each of the parties must be examined in the light of applicable bankruptcy or insolvency and gaming laws, among others. Further discussion of these subjects may be found in *Swap agreement documentation*, pp. 18–21.

Covenants

This part of the agreement sets forth the promises each party has made to the other about future actions that are ancillary to the basic obligation to make payments when and as they are due, including any affirmative or negative financial covenants to which either party has agreed. Such financial covenants are rare in swaps between market-makers but are sometimes found in swaps with end users, especially when the swap is related to a loan agremeent which itself contains financial covenants.

Closing documents

This section, sometimes referred to as 'conditions precedent', establishes which documents, such as certificates and opinions of counsel, are to be delivered, and by whom, in connection with the transaction. It is desirable to have these matters dealt with as covenants rather than conditions precedent whenever the swap agreement is reached before the contract is signed. In such cases, the parties are likely to act in reliance on the existence of the agreement (e.g. by entering into hedging arrangements) before the conditions are fulfilled; to treat document delivery as a condition precedent inappropriately suggests otherwise. Moreover, it seems that treatment of document delivery obligations as a covenant has the necessary compulsory effect. Assuming that the swap agreement includes a failure to perform covenants as an event of default, the covenant provides a contractual basis for terminating the swap and claiming damages if the counterparty fails to comply with an important closing requirement like the obligation to deliver evidence of a necessary governmental or regulatory agency authorisation.

Defaults, termination events and remedies

Another important part of the swap agreement will deal with events of default, termination events and related remedies.

The events of default in swap agreements should be drafted with particular sensitivity to the special nature of swap transactions and the ways in which swaps are different from other kinds of transactions involving credit risk. In particular, the default provisions from term loan agreements are often too stringent for swaps.

After a loan is made, all the remaining obligations of any significance are the borrower's, so the events of default are there only to protect the lender. From the lender's point of view, it is desirable to have highly rigorous events of default that will permit the lender to judge whether to call its loan at the first sign of financial difficulties of the borrower. The lender can always waive an unintentional default or one that it decides is not material, if it wishes to keep the loan in place.

A swap is quite different. First, it is likely that one party will develop a strong desire to terminate the swap because of changed economic conditions, in which case the other party will have an equally strong desire to keep the swap in place. Secondly, the events of default in a swap (or most of them) are normally reciprocal; both parties have the benefit (and the burden) of the events of default. Although neither party will want to sacrifice necessary protections, neither should want to include provisions that would make termination too easy.

It is desirable, therefore, for the documentation to include grace periods for payment defaults and materiality tests for defaults relating to untrue representations and warranties, as well as notice requirements and opportunities to cure failures to perform ancillary covenants. The desirability of cross-default clauses should be carefully considered in each case, and there should be protection against *de minimis* situations when cross-default clauses are included.

Where default remedies are concerned, the swap agreement will provide that the non-defaulting party may give notice of termination and that, if it elects to do so, it will be entitled to damages, including the costs to it of the lost bargain. Several drafting pitfalls to be avoided in this area are as follows.

First, care should be taken that only the non-defaulting party has the right to give a notice of termination and that only the basic payment obligations of the parties are stated to be terminated; other provisions of the agreement will have to survive, such as the provisions relating to damages and interest on overdue amounts. Secondly, special consideration should be given to payment obligations that accrued before, but were not yet payable by, the early termination date, or that would be payable on that date but for the early termination. The main issue is whether they are to be paid in accordance with the provisions of the agreement relating to payments in the absence of default or are to be covered under the damages provision. Thirdly, the agreement should provide for the handling of amounts that were scheduled to be paid (as opposed to merely accrued) by each of the parties on or before the date as of which damages for loss of bargain are determined. If any such amount is payable by the non-defaulting party, but that party is not required to pay it to the defaulting party, the non-payment may be a forfeiture that is contrary to applicable law. See *Swap agreement documentation*, p. 32.

A mistake that occurs all too often in swap agreements is to overlook the need to specify when settlement upon early termination will occur. The approach illustrated in Appendixes A and B calls for settlement on the early termination date, and has the parties' basic swap payment obligations terminate as of that date, which is the same date as of which damages for loss of bargain are determined, as described in the next part of this chapter. The great advantage of this approach is its simplicity. A more complex approach, found, e.g. in the ISDA standard master swap agreements, provides for a sequence of events beginning with the effectiveness of a notice of termination and ending with payment of settlement amounts, which may or may not be due on the early termination date.

Finally, termination should not be the exclusive remedy of the non-defaulting party; that party should also have the options of leaving the agreement in place and suing for damages and of seeking specific performance of the counterparty's obligations. It should be noted that the contractual right to terminate and provisions for automatic termination in the event of a party's insolvency or bankruptcy may be unenforceable in some circumstances. *Swap agreement documentation*, pp. 20–1, 28–9, 71–2 deals at length with this problem as it arises under certain bankruptcy and insolvency laws.

There is agreement that, in the case of early termination of a swap because of a default, the defaulting party should pay the non-defaulting party damages to compensate it for any loss it suffers as a result; there is, however, no consensus beyond that fairly simple proposition. There is a substantial majority view, but one which is not unanimous, that the non-defaulting party should never have to make a termination payment to the defaulting party; the minority view is that the non-defaulting party should not be allowed to reap a windfall from the default.

There is greater controversy regarding termination payments if early termination occurs because of supervening illegality or to avoid a 'gross-up' obligation arising from the imposition of withholding tax. Some drafters treat these situations – which are neither party's fault and are often called 'termination events' – as if they were cases of default, and as if the party affected by the illegality or taxation were the defaulting party. Under that approach, the affected party must make a payment if the other party is damaged, but the other party does not have to pay over any windfall that it may realise by virtue of termination. The prevailing approach is to require the party that benefits from the termination to make a payment to the other.

Even those who agree that windfalls should not occur in no-fault situations may disagree on how the appropriate termination payment should be calculated. Some agreements provide that, when only one of the parties is affected by the termination event, the amount of the damages to be paid or the benefit to be shared should be computed by looking only to the other party's situation. However, if both parties are affected by the termination event, each determines the amount of its own damages or benefit from the early termination and half the difference between the two must be paid by the party with the lesser damages or greater benefit. Another approach, illustrated in Appendix A, would take both parties' loss or gain into account even if only one party were affected by the termination event.

The first approach seems especially appealing in connection with termination events that are within the control of one of the parties. For example, many swap agreements now include a termination event similar to the one illustrated in Section 13 of Appendix A, which would be triggered by certain mergers, consolidations and sales of assets by a party. A variant included in the ISDA standard agreements would permit early termination on a no-fault basis in such circumstances if the entity produced by the merger or consolidation, or the transferee that assumes the swap in the transfer of assets, were of materially weaker credit standing than the original party to the agreement that engaged in the merger, consolidation or asset sale immediately before the event. Some market participants believe that under such circumstances it is appropriate for the value of the swap agreement to be calculated only with reference to the other party, although they would take the value to each of the parties into account if early termination occurred in connection with other termination events, such as supervening illegality.

Calculation of payments upon early termination

There has been substantial evolution in the thinking of major market participants and their counsel regarding the proper method for calculating damages in the event of early termination. At one time swap papers usually provided simply that the defaulting party would pay damages to the non-defaulting party and made clear that those damages would include the cost of the lost bargain. They did not, however, spell out the mechanics for computing damages. This approach has come to be known as the 'indemnification' approach. Then a number of efforts were made to develop formulas for computing damages. One such approach is embodied in the Formula provisions of the *Swaps code*.

As the swap market moved away from perfectly matched swaps between two end users and gained in depth, it became possible to provide for measuring damages upon early termination of a swap by looking at the cost of entering into a replacement swap. Appendix A illustrates this market-oriented 'agreement value' approach and provides for a fall-back to the indemnification method if it is not possible to find agreement value. Further discussion of these three approaches is included in *Swap agreement documentation*, pp. 31–7.

Miscellaneous

Sections 17–26 of Appendix A illustrate other matters usually dealt with in the documentation for medium- and long-term swaps. One that deserves special mention is the conventional prohibition against assignment or transfer of a party's rights or obligations without the consent of the other party. This stricture is the major obstacle to the development of a secondary market in rate exchange agreements, in the sense in which that term is used in connection with investment instruments such as bonds. It is, however, a logical consequence of the mutuality of the parties' obligations in swaps: because, as rates may move up and down, each party may have to look to the other for payments over the entire term, the credit concerns of both the parties lead them to seek a veto over any potential substitute counterparty. The issuer of a bond, of course, does not have that kind of concern with respect to the holder, because only the issuer has obligations after it has received the proceeds of initial sale of the instrument. As illustrated in Appendix A, the prohibition is usually somewhat attenuated when assignment or transfer may be the only way to avoid early termination because of supervening illegality or because a party's obligation to make 'gross-up' payments to the other in connection with withholding taxes has made the swap transaction economically impracticable.

II Special features of cross-border swaps

Supervening illegality and taxation

Swap agreements between counterparties from different countries generally provide for termination in the event of supervening illegality. Most cross-border swaps also include a 'gross-up' provision that obligates a party required to make withholding for taxes in respect of swap payments to pay the recipient the additional amount necessary to make that party whole. Those or related provisions usually entitle the party required to pay the additional amount to terminate the swap. Sections 7 and 8 of Appendix A are examples of both kinds of provisions. Both are discussed further in *Swap agreement documentation*, pp. 49–52, as are common exceptions to these provisions.

Judgment currency provisions

These clauses are included in cross-border swap agreements to protect each party against any foreign exchange loss that it suffers if it receives a payment (pursuant to a court judgment or otherwise) in a currency other than the currency which it was entitled to receive under the contract. For an example, see Section 24 of the sample agreement in Appendix A, and for further discussion of these clauses, see *Swap agreement documentation*, pp. 62–3.

III Master swap agreements

As noted, when parties expect to enter into a course of swap dealing with each other, they tend to adopt the master format so as to facilitate and expedite documentation of their various swaps. They may also do so because their intention is that all the swaps be treated as a single agreement, so that the risk involved in them all can be viewed in the aggregate. This single agreement approach is discussed further below.

Once the parties have agreed on basic rate definitions, payment provisions, allocation of costs and expenses and risks, and other fundamental issues, it would be wasteful not to preserve that agreement and apply it to future dealings, to the extent appropriate. The master format makes this possible and enables the parties to document a swap in a short confirmation or supplement to the master agreement. As illustrated in the samples in Appendix C, the confirmation or supplement merely spells out the financial terms of the particular transaction and, if required by the peculiar features of that transaction, modifies or adds to the previously agreed upon standard terms.

Appendix B is a sample of a master agreement that uses the *Swaps code*. The sample confirmations in Appendix C illustrate how the drafting of provisions on floating rates has been greatly facilitated by the *Swaps code*. Each of them makes use of one of the *Swaps code* definitions for a floating rate. Choice of the appropriate defined term from the *Swaps code* (e.g. 'Prime' or 'Prime-Reference Banks') is all that is required to incorporate into the swap agreement a complex and carefully prepared rate definition. In most cases, the *Swaps code* permits a choice between obtaining a floating rate from published sources and computing it on the basis of quotations obtained from reference banks or dealers. Similar choices are available for swaps involving currencies other than US dollars in the *1987 interest rate and currency exchange definitions* published by ISDA for use in connection with the ISDA standard *Interest rate and currency exchange agreement*.

Other definitions can be drafted by completing *Swaps code* provisions. For example, the *Swaps code* calls for default interest on late payments if the parties specify 'Default Rate' in their agreement, but, as shown in Appendix C, they must also specify the rate at which default interest is to accrue.

The *Swaps code* does not deal with some subjects the parties may wish covered in their agreements, and in some instances the *Swaps code* offers a variety of approaches to a particular subject. If the parties incorporate a provision that embodies this 'menu' approach, they must therefore choose among the options either by expressly selecting one of them or by remaining silent and thereby selecting the 'default choice' prescribed by the *Swaps code*. For example, if the first of the sample confirmations were silent on the appropriate Floating Rate Day Count Fraction, the silence would be interpreted to mean that the parties had chosen the same calculation basis as is specified in that confirmation, because that is a presumption built into the *Swaps code*; however, if the parties had remained silent about the Fixed Rate Day Count Fraction, their silence would have been tantamount to a choice of Actual/365 – which was not what the parties agreed. Familiarity with *Swaps code* presumptions is, therefore, critical for those that incorporate its terms.

Drafters use a variety of approaches to adoption of the *Swaps code*. The practice illustrated in Appendix B is to spell out which of the *Swaps code* sections are to be incorporated by reference in the swap agreement. Other agreements incorporate all the operative provisions of the *Swaps code*, sometimes by saying that the *Swaps code* is to 'govern' the swap in all relevant respects. We believe that the approach of designating which *Swaps code* sections are to apply is less likely to produce an unintended result and more likely to produce an agreement that would be easily explained in court proceedings.

As illustrated in Section 1 of Appendix B, a common practice is to incorporate provisions from the current edition of the *Swaps code*, without reference to subsequent changes. This is a natural consequence of regarding the *Swaps code* as a source for particular definitions and provisions selected by the parties, and not a complete body of law for swaps adopted by a governmental body with power to legislate.

Two issues stand out as particularly important when parties decide to adopt a master format with a set of standard terms and conditions for swaps between them. The first is how, if at all, to reflect in the master documentation the procedure to be followed by them in entering into each swap to be covered by the standard terms. The second is whether, or to what extent, the several swaps will be treated as inseparable parts of the same agreement or as unrelated, individual agreements that simply have in common the fact that they incorporate provisions set forth in the standard terms.

Provisions for bringing swaps under the master agreement

As previously mentioned, in many cases the parties strike their deal over the telephone. Each of them may then send the other a telex confirming what it believes to be the basic terms of the swap. This practice may bring to light a misunderstanding during the telephone conversation. In the meantime, one or both of the parties may have entered into another swap or other transaction to hedge the risk of the deal it believes it struck. Because rates can be volatile, the parties often cannot wait to sign a written contract before they act in reliance on their telephone dealings. If there is no master agreement in place between the parties when they reach their agreement, they cannot avoid the somewhat troublesome gap between the making of the oral contract and the execution of a written agreement. The master format, however, can address the problem.

Some major market participants include in their master documentation a provision that spells out how and at what stage of their dealings the parties will be bound with respect to a swap, how they will handle mutual mistake, and what will happen if one of them does not comply with the agreed upon method for confirming the terms of a transaction in a timely fashion. Section 2 of Appendix B illustrates such a provision.

Whether or not they include such provisions in their contract (the ISDA standard agreements do not), the parties should lessen the risk involved in an oral agreement through an immediate exchange of confirmations by telex or facsimile transmission. Inconsistencies in confirmations are not infrequent, and the parties generally resolve them amicably upon discovering that they exist – which is the practical reason why the confirmation process is so necessary. At a technical level, the use of confirmations may satisfy an applicable statute of frauds – a requirement that the oral agreement, at least in its essence, be evidenced in writing. Failure to satisfy that requirement could make it impossible for a party to enforce the oral contract. For further discussion, see *Swap agreement documentation*, pp. 72–4.

The relationship among swaps under a master document

The master approach used by some major participants in the swap market at one time treated each swap between the parties as a wholly separate contract that simply incorporated previously agreed upon standard terms and conditions to the extent specified in the individual 'take down' agreement. The prevailing approach today is to treat the various swaps under the master as part of the same agreement, which may be separable for certain purposes, if necessary, but not others. This approach is preferable for parties especially concerned with aggregating the swaps for purposes of credit analysis or with seeking to ensure unitary treatment of the master and all swaps under it in the event of the counterparty's insolvency.

Commercial banks, in particular, may wish to be able to aggregate all swaps with a single counterparty. Swaps may be only a portion of their business with the counterparty, and they may quickly reach the limit of transactions permissible with the same party under their internal credit policies if each individual swap is analysed separately as using part of that available credit allocation. At any time some swaps with a counterparty may constitute assets and, to the extent of the flow of payments to be made by the counterparty, will involve credit risk; however, other swaps with the same party may constitute liabilities of the commercial bank at the time if it is the party required to make payments. To the extent that the various swaps are tied to each other under the same agreement, it may be possible to offset the assets and liabilities for purposes of credit limits and other purposes.

In this vein, important considerations in documenting the swaps under the master will be whether a party may withhold payment under the swaps that are unfavourable to it if the counterparty fails to make a payment under the favourable ones, and whether all may be terminated if one is in default. Under the bankruptcy laws of some jurisdictions – including the United States – this may not be possible once proceedings have commenced. (See pp. 19–21 of *Swap agreement documentation*.) Nevertheless, linkage of the swaps may prove important in the context of the bankruptcy of a counterparty subject to the US Bankruptcy Code. If such a counterparty were to become a debtor in a bankruptcy case, and if swaps were determined to be executory contracts of the kind that the debtor or its trustee in bankruptcy was entitled to assume or reject, the parties' course of treating all swaps under the master document, to the extent practicable, as inseparable parts of the same agreement could be important in an attempt to compel the debtor, or the trustee, to assume or reject all the swaps together, and thus to prevent it from 'cherry picking', that is, from keeping in place only the swaps that are favourable to the insolvent counterparty.

In the light of such concerns, some market participants have increased the ways in which the swaps done under their master agreements are integrated. For example, some provide that payments due to and payable by a party on any given day under all swaps under the master (or all swaps done out of the same office or branch) will be netted. In *Swaps code* terminology, this is referred to as the convention involving 'Net payments – Corresponding payment dates'. In addition, many master agreements (including the ISDA standard forms) provide for aggregation of amounts calculated in respect of the swaps in the case of early termination, so that any value of a swap to the defaulting party is netted against the value of other swaps to the non-defaulting party. If the net result is in favour of the non-defaulting party, it is entitled to damages to that extent; however, if the net result is that the non-defaulting party will benefit from the early termination, it is not required to turn the net benefit over to the defaulting party. Section 12 of Appendix B illustrates this approach using *Swaps code* terminology.

Master agreements should address each substantive area on its own merits where the issue of separability of swaps under the master is concerned. So, for example, in cross-border swap masters or masters that contemplate both currency and interest rate swaps, the documentation should take into account the possibility that some swaps but not others might become subject to supervening illegality or become taxable. Thus, illegality or withholding taxes might affect currency swaps but not interest rate swaps, and a withholding tax might affect only swaps of certain maturities or swaps with mismatched payment dates.

Conclusion

Medium- and long-term interest rate swaps are transactions involving extensions of credit which often are, or can be, very substantial in amount. The nature of the risks involved is of growing concern to market participants and the regulatory agencies that exercise oversight authority with respect to some of them. The parties' understanding regarding the calculation of rates and the mechanics of payments (particularly their understanding on the question of conditionality) should therefore be spelled out with precision. The *Swaps code* considerably facilitates this task for US dollar rate swaps. Provisions with credit impact, such as representations and warranties, covenants and events of default, should also continue to be dealt with as matters of great importance, and it can be expected that they will sometimes be broader in swaps with end users than they are in swaps between major financial institutions. Although some swaps will undoubtedly continue to be documented singly, most swaps now are, and will continue to be, handled with simple confirmations, once the necessary network of master swap agreements has been put in place.

Appendix A: Interest rate exchange agreement

This agreement is a sample of the kind of documentation that might be used for a single US dollar interest rate swap in which a bank organised under the laws of the United States is the floating rate payer and a corporation organised under the laws of Switzerland is the fixed rate payer.

This sample is merely an illustration and should not be used for an actual transaction; each transaction will have its own special features, and the agreement drafted to document it should be carefully tailored to address the legal and business problems that it presents.

INTEREST RATE EXCHANGE AGREEMENT dated as of July 1, 1987 between BIG BANK, N.A. (the 'Bank') and HEDGED CORPORATION (the 'Company'), whereby the parties agree as follows.

1.   *Definitions.* For purposes of this Agreement, the following terms shall have the meanings indicated.

'Affiliate', with respect to either party, means any entity that is controlled by that party, any entity that controls that party or any entity under common control with that party. For purposes of this definition, 'control' of an entity means direct or indirect ownership of a majority in voting power of the shares or other ownership interests in that entity.

'Agreement Value', with respect to a party, means an amount determined as provided in Section 16.

'Banking Day' means a day on which banks are not required or authorized by law to close in New York City that is also a London Banking Day.

'Calculation Period' means the period commencing on July 1, 1987 and ending on January 4, 1988 and thereafter each period beginning on the last day of the preceding Calculation Period and ending on the first day of the sixth month thereafter, subject to the following exceptions: (i) if a Calculation Period would otherwise end on a day that is not a Banking Day, it shall be extended to the following Banking Day, unless that Calculation Period would, as a result, extend into the following calendar month, in which case the Calculation Period shall end on the preceding Banking Day, and (ii) the final Calculation Period shall end on July 1, 1994, whether or not it is a Banking Day.

'Damages', with respect to a party, means an amount determined as provided in Section 15(c).

'Defaulting Party' has the meaning given to that term in Section 12.

'Dollars' or *'$'* means lawful money of the United States.

'Early Termination Date' has the meaning given to that term in Section 14(b).

'Event of Default' has the meaning given to that term in Section 12.

'Fixed Amount', for each Fixed Amount Payment Date, means $6,400,000.

'Fixed Amount Payment Date' means the Floating Amount Payment Date scheduled to occur in July of each year.

'Floating Amount', for each Calculation Period, means the amount that would accrue during that Calculation Period on the Notional Principal Amount at LIBOR for that Calculation Period, computed as provided in Section 3(a).

'Floating Amount Payment Date', for each Calculation Period, means the last day of that Calculation Period.

'Indebtedness', with respect to either party, means any present or future indebtedness of that party, as debtor, borrower or guarantor, in respect of money borrowed (other than indebtedness in respect of deposits received), including interest or any Indebtedness.

'LIBOR', for each Calculation Period, means the rate (expressed as an annual rate) equal to the arithmetic mean (rounded up, if necesary, to the nearest 1/100,000 of 1%) of the rates shown on the 'LIBO' page display (or any substitute display) of the Reuter Monitor Money Rates Service as the London interbank offered rates of the banks named on that display at approximately 11.00 a.m. (London time) on the second London Banking Day before the first day of that Calculation Period for deposits in Dollars for a period of six months, subject to Section 3(c).

'London Banking Day' means a day on which dealings in deposits in Dollars are carried on in the London interbank market.

'Merger Event' has the meaning given to that term in Section 13.

'Notional Principal Amount' means $80,000,000.

'Reference Market-maker' has the meaning given to that term in Section 16(a).

'Taxes', with respect to payments hereunder by either party, means any present or future taxes, levies, imposts, duties or charges of any nature whatsoever that are collectible by withholding except for any such tax, levy, impost, duty or charge that would not have been imposed but for the existence of a connection between the party receiving the payment and the jurisdiction where it is imposed.

'United States' means the United States of America.

2. *'Exchanges.* (a) On the terms and subject to the conditions set forth herein, on the Floating Amount Payment Date for each Calculation Period, the Bank shall pay the Company the Floating Amount for that Calculation Period, and, on each Fixed Amount Payment Date, the Company shall pay the Bank the Fixed Amount for that Fixed Amount Payment Date; *provided, however*, that the payments to be made in accordance with this Section on any day that is both a Fixed Amount Payment Date and a Floating Amount Payment Date shall be made on a net basis; and *provided further, however*, that if any payment due hereunder is scheduled to be made on a day that is not a Banking Day, that payment shall be made on the following Banking Day.

(b) The obligation of each party to make each payment to be made by it pursuant to Section 2(a) is subject to the condition that no event or condition that constitutes (or that with the giving of notice or the lapse of time or both would constitute) an Event or Default with respect to the other party shall be continuing. This condition shall, however, be deemed to have been satisfied for purposes of Section 15 and shall no longer apply when that other party has performed all its payment obligations hereunder.

(c) Notwithstanding the definition of 'Floating Amount' and the provisions of Section 2(a), if the Bank in its reasonable judgment determines at any time that there has been a material adverse change in the Company's condition that is likely to affect the Company's ability to perform its payment obligations hereunder, the Bank may, by notice to the Company, elect to defer the due date for any Floating Amount scheduled to be paid by it thereafter on a Floating Amount Payment Date that is not also a Fixed Amount Payment Date to the next Fixed Amount Payment Date after that Floating Amount Payment Date. If such a notice is given, the Bank shall pay the Company on that Fixed Amount Payment Date both the deferred Floating Amount payment and interest thereon at LIBOR for the Calculation Period that is coextensive with the period of the deferral, together with any other amounts scheduled to be paid by it on that date.

(d) Any amount of interest payable in accordance with Section 2(c) shall be treated as if it were an amount payable pursuant to Section 2(a) for all purposes of Section 2, Section 3(a) and Section 3(b).

3. *Computations and Determinations.* (a) Each Floating Amount and any interest payable pursuant to Section 2(c) or Section 5 shall be computed on the basis of a 360-day year and actual days elapsed from and including the first day of the relevant period to but excluding the last day thereof.

(b) The Bank shall determine LIBOR for each Calculation Period and the amount of each payment to be made pursuant to Section 2(a) and, no later than the second Banking Day before such a payment is due, shall give notice to the Company specifying the amount of the payment and the party required to make it and indicating how the amount was computed. If a change in the number of days in a Calculation Period occurs after the Bank has given a notice relating to that period under this Section, as soon as practicable thereafter the Bank shall give the Company notice of the change and of any resulting change in an amount payable pursuant to Section 2(a).

(c) For purposes of determining LIBOR for each Calculation Period, the rules set forth below shall apply if the 'LIBO' page (or a substitute) is not being displayed by the Reuter Monitor Money Rates Service at the time for the determination.

(i) LIBOR for that Calculation Period shall be the rate (expressed as an annual rate) equal to the arithmetic mean (rounded up, if necessary, to the nearest 1/100,000 of 1%) of the rates at which deposits in Dollars in an amount substantially equal to the Notional Principal Amount would be offered at that time by the principal London offices of Barclays Bank PLC, The Bank of Tokyo, Ltd., Bankers Trust Company and National Westminster Bank PLC to major banks in the London interbank market for a period of six months, as quoted to the Bank; or

(ii) if at least one but not all of the London offices of those institutions supplies the Bank with the necessary quotation at the time, the Bank shall determine LIBOR for that Calculation Period on the basis of the quotation or quotations supplied to it; or

(iii) if none of those offices supplies the Bank with the necessary quotation, LIBOR for that Calculation Period shall be the arithmetic mean (rounded as provided above) of the rates quoted to the Bank by the principal lending offices of four major banks in New York City selected by the Bank as their respective lowest lending rates for loans in Dollars to leading European banks for that period and in that amount at approximately 11.00 a.m. (New York City time) on the first day of that Calculation Period.

4. *Making of Payments.* All payments hereunder shall be made to the account specified for the intended recipient in Exhibit 4A.1, or to such other account in New York City as that party may have last specified by notice to the other party, and shall be made in funds settled through the New York Clearing House Interbank Payments System or such other same-day funds as are customary at the time for the settlement in New York City of banking transactions denominated in Dollars.

5. *Default Interest.* If any amount due hereunder is not paid when due, interest shall accrue on that amount to the extent permitted by applicable law at a rate per annum equal for each day that amount remains unpaid to the sum of 1% and the rate quoted by the principal London office of the Bank at 11.00 a.m. (London time) for overnight deposits in Dollars, in an amount substantially equal to the overdue amount, for value on that day or, if that day is not a London Banking Day, on the preceding London Banking Day. Interest hereunder shall be payable from time to time on demand.

6. *Arrangement Fee.* The Company shall pay the Bank an arrangement fee of $100,000 on July 1, 1987.

7. *Supervening Illegality.* If it becomes unlawful for either party to make any payment to be made by it hereunder, or to receive any amount to be received by it hereunder, as a result of the adoption of, or any change in, or change in the interpretation of, any law, regulation or treaty, that party shall give notice to that effect to the other party and shall use reasonable efforts (a) to assign or transfer its rights and obligations under this Agreement, subject to Section 18, to another of its branches, offices or Affiliates, or to any leading participant in the interest rate exchange market, that may make those payments and receive those amounts lawfully and without withholding for or on account of Taxes or (b) to agree with the other party to modify this Agreement or change the method of payment hereunder so that the payment or receipt will not be unlawful. If an assignment or agreement is not made as provided herein on or before the tenth day after that notice becomes effective, either party may give notice of termination as provided in Section 14.

8. *Taxes.* (a) Except as otherwise required by law, each payment hereunder shall be made without withholding for or on account of Taxes. If either party is required to make any withholding from any payment under this Agreement for or on account of Taxes, it shall (i) make that withholding, (ii) make timely payment of the amount withheld to the appropriate governmental authority, (iii) forthwith pay the other party such additional amount as may be necessary to ensure that the net amount actually received by it free and clear of Taxes (including any Taxes on the additional amount) is equal to the amount that it would have received had no Taxes been withheld and (iv) on or before the thirtieth day after payment, send that other party the original or a certified copy of an official tax receipt evidencing that payment; *provided, however*, that if a party fails to perform or observe its covenant set forth in Section 10(b), the other party shall be under no obligation to pay any additional amount hereunder to the extent that the withholding would not have been required if the failure had not occurred.

(b) If either party would be required to make any withholding for or on account of Taxes and pay any additional amount as provided in Section 8(a) with respect to any payment to be made by it in accordance with Section 2(a), that party shall give notice to that effect to the other party and shall use reasonable efforts (i) to assign or transfer its rights and obligations under this Agreement, subject to Section 18, to another of its branches, offices or Affiliates, or to any leading participant in the interest rate exchange market, that may make the payments to be made by it hereunder and receive the amounts to be received by it hereunder lawfully and without withholding for or on account of Taxes or (ii) to agree with the other party to modify this Agreement or change the method of payment hereunder so that those payments will not be subject to the withholding. If an assignment or agreement is not made as provided herein on or before the tenth day after that notice becomes effective, the party required to make the withholding may give notice of termination as provided in Section 14.

9. *Representations and Warranties.* Each of the parties makes the representations and warranties set forth below to the other as of the date hereof.

(a) It is duly organized and validly existing and has the corporate power and authority to execute and deliver this Agreement and to perform its obligations hereunder.

(b) It has taken all necessary action to authorize its execution and delivery of this Agreement and the performance of its obligations hereunder.

(c) All governmental authorizations and actions necessary in connection with its execution and delivery of this Agreement and the performance of its obligations hereunder have been obtained or performed and remain valid and in full force and effect.

(d) This Agreement has been duly executed and delivered by it and constitutes its legal, valid and binding obligation, enforceable against it in accordance with the terms of this Agreement, subject to all applicable bankruptcy, insolvency, moratorium and similar laws affecting creditors' rights generally.

(e) No event or condition that constitutes (or that with the giving of notice or the lapse of time or both would constitute) an Event of Default with respect to it has occurred and is continuing or will occur by reason of its entering into or performing its obligations under this Agreement.

(f) There are no actions, proceedings or claims pending or, to its knowledge, threatened the adverse determination of which might have a materially adverse effect on its ability to perform its obligations under, or affect the validity or enforceability against it of, this Agreement.

(g) It is not required by applicable law to make any deduction or withholding for or on account of Taxes from any payment (other than interest payable pursuant to Section 2(b), Section 2(c) or Section 5) that it is required to make under this Agreement.

(h) It has delivered to the other party its financial statements specified below:

(i) the Bank: the Bank's annual report for the fiscal year ended December 31, 1986, containing the Bank's financial statements as at that date and for that fiscal year prepared in accordance with generally accepted accounting principles in the United States, consistently applied (except insofar as any change in the application thereof is disclosed in those financial statements and is concurred in by the accountants that certified those financial statements), and certified by independent public accountants as fairly presenting the Bank's financial condition as at that date and the results of its operations for that fiscal year; and

(ii) the Company: the Company's financial statements as at December 31, 1986 and for the fiscal year ended December 31, 1986, prepared in accordance with generally accepted accounting principles in Switzerland, consistently applied (except insofar as any change in the application thereof is disclosed in those financial statements and is concurred in by the accountants that certified those financial statements), and certified by independent public accountants as fairly presenting the Company's financial condition as at that date and the results of its operations for that fiscal year.

10. *Covenants.* (a) Each of the parties shall give the other notice of any event or condition that constitutes (or that with the giving of notice or the lapse of time or both would constitute) an Event of Default with respect to it, other than one referred to in Section 12(a), not later than the third Banking Day after learning of that event or condition.

(b) If either party is required at any time to execute any form or document in order for payments to it hereunder to qualify for exemption from withholding for or on account of Taxes or to qualify for such withholding at a reduced rate, that party shall, on demand, execute the required form or document and deliver it to the party required to make those payments.

(c) So long as it has any obligations under Section 2, the Company shall deliver to the Bank, as soon as available and in any event on or before the ninetieth day after the end of each of the Company's fiscal years, its financial statements for that fiscal year, prepared in accordance with generally accepted accounting principles in Switzerland, consistently applied (except insofar as any change in the application thereof is disclosed in those financial statements and is concurred in by the accountants that certified those financial statements), and certified by independent public accountants as fairly presenting the Company's financial condition at the close of that fiscal year and the results of its operations for that fiscal year.

11. *Closing Documents.* On or before July 15, 1987, each party shall deliver to the other a duly executed certificate substantially in the form set forth in Exhibit 4A.2, together with the attachments referred to therein, and the Company shall deliver to the Bank an opinion of counsel for the Company with respect to the matters addressed in subsections (a) through (f) of the Company's representations and warranties set forth in Section 9. The opinion may be to the best of counsel's knowledge insofar as it relates to the matters addressed in subsections (e) and (f) of Section 9. The documents required hereunder shall be in form and substance satisfactory to the recipient.

12. *Events of Default.* For purposes of this Agreement, the term 'Event of Default' shall mean any of the events listed below in respect of a party (the 'Defaulting Party').

(a) That party (i) fails to pay any amount payable by it hereunder as and when that amount becomes payable and does not remedy that failure on or before the third Banking Day after notice from the other party of the failure or (ii) fails duly to give any notice to be given by it pursuant to Section 10(a), or to cure the event or condition that should have been reported in that notice, on or before the fifth day after that notice should have been given.

(b) That party fails duly to perform any covenant to be performed by it hereunder, other than those set forth or referred to in Section 10(b) or Section 12(a), and does not remedy that failure on or before the thirtieth day after notice from the other party of the failure.

(c) Any representation or warranty made by that party in this Agreement, other than in Section 9(g), proves to have been incorrect, incomplete or misleading in any material respect at the time it was made.

(d) That party (i) is dissolved, (ii) fails or is unable to pay its debts generally as they become due, (iii) makes a general assignment for the benefit of its creditors, (iv) commences, or consents to the commencement against it of, any action or proceeding for relief under any bankruptcy or insolvency law or any law affecting creditors' rights that is similar to a bankruptcy or insolvency law, (v) is the subject of an order for relief or a decree in any such action or proceeding, (vi) has commenced against it without its consent any action or proceeding described above, if that action or proceeding is not dismissed on or before the sixtieth day after it is commenced or if any dismissal thereof ceases to remain in effect, or (vii) seeks or becomes subject to the appointment of a receiver, custodian or similar official for it or any of its property.

(e) That party or any of its Affiliates fails to pay when due any amount owing in connection with any other interest rate or currency exchange transaction or any other interest rate protection transaction, however described, between that party or that Affiliate, on the one hand, and the other party to this Agreement or any of its Affiliates, on the other, if the failure is not remedied during any applicable grace period.

(f) An event of default (however described) takes place that has the effect (or that, with the giving of notice or the lapse of time or both, would have the effect) of causing or permitting Indebtedness of that party in an aggregate amount exceeding 2% of that party's stockholders' equity to become due before the scheduled maturity date of that Indebtedness, or that party fails to pay when due Indebtedness in an aggregate amount exceeding 2% of its stockholders' equity.

13. *Mergers and Transfers of Assets.* For purposes of this Agreement, a 'Merger Event' shall be deemed to have occurred with respect to the Company (a) if the Company merges or consolidates with another entity and the Bank's policies in effect at the time would not permit it to enter into an interest rate exchange transaction with the entity that is produced by or survives the merger or consolidation or (b) the Company sells or otherwise transfers all or substantially all its assets.

14. *Early Termination.* (a) At any time while an Event of Default with respect to a Defaulting Party is continuing, the other party may, in its absolute discretion, give notice of termination in accordance with this Section. If a party gives notice of supervening illegality, in the circumstances described in Section 7 either party may give notice of termination in accordance with this Section. If a party is required to pay any additional amount pursuant to Section 8, it may give notice of termination in accordance with this Section in the circumstances described in Section 8. If a Merger Event occurs with respect to the Company, the Bank may give notice of termination in accordance with this Section.

(b) Any notice of termination hereunder (i) shall state the grounds for termination, (ii) shall specify a date that is not before, nor more than ten days after, the date the notice of early termination is given on which the payments required by Section 15 shall be made as provided therein (the 'Early Termination Date') and (iii) shall declare the obligations of the parties to make the payments required by Section 2 that are scheduled to be made after the Early Termination Date to be terminated as of that date, and those obligations shall so terminate and be replaced by the parties' obligations to make the payments specified in Section 15.

15. *Payments upon Early Termination.* (a) If notice of termination is given hereunder on the ground of an Event of Default, the Defaulting Party shall pay the other party that other party's Damages if they exceed zero.

(b) If either party gives notice of termination on the ground of supervening illegality, because it is required to pay an additional amount pursuant to Section 8 or because of the occurrence of a Merger Event, each party shall pay the other one half the other's Damages (if they exceed zero) and, if a party would realize any gain or benefit as a result of the termination, it shall also pay to the other party one half of that gain or benefit.

(c) A party's Damages in the event of early termination shall be its Agreement Value, if that party's Agreement Value can be determined. If a party's Agreement Value cannot be determined, its Damages shall be an amount of Dollars equal to the sum of the losses (including loss of bargain), if any, that it may incur as a result of the early termination or as a result of the event that served as the ground for early termination.

(d) Payments to be made in accordance with this Section shall be made on the Early Termination Date, together with all other amounts then due hereunder, and shall be payable on a net basis. A party entitled to be paid any amount in respect of its Damages in accordance with this Section shall submit to the other party a statement in reasonable detail of those Damages. A party required under Section 15(b) to pay any amount in respect of its gain or benefit as a result of early termination shall submit to the other party a statement in reasonable detail of that gain or benefit.

16. *Agreement Value.* (a) For the purpose of determining a party's Agreement Value, that party shall select four leading participants in the interest rate exchange market (each a 'Reference Market-maker'), in its sole discretion and in good faith, with a view to minimizing that Agreement Value; *provided, however*, that in doing so the party shall be entitled to select market participants that are of the highest credit standing and that otherwise satisfy all the criteria that party applies generally at the time in deciding whether to enter into an interest rate exchange transaction.

(b) A party that is seeking to determine its Agreement Value shall request from each of the Reference Market-makers it has selected a quotation of the amount in Dollars which that Reference Market-maker would charge or pay that party on the Early Termination Date as a flat fee for entering into an agreement, effective on the Early Termination Date, pursuant to which that party would make all the payments scheduled to be made by it under Section 2 of this Agreement after the Early Termination Date and that Reference Market-maker would make all the payments the other party to this Agreement is scheduled to make under Section 2 of this Agreement after the Early Termination Date. If a Reference Market-maker would pay a flat fee to enter into such an agreement, the quotation obtained from that Reference Market-maker shall be expressed as a negative number for the purpose of determining Agreement Value, and if it would charge a flat fee, the quotation shall be expressed as a positive number for that purpose.

(c) A party's Agreement Value shall be the arithmetic mean (rounded up, if necessary, to the nearest cent) of the fees described in Section 16(b) that are quoted to that party by the Reference Market-makers it has selected or, if only one Reference Market-maker will quote such a fee to that party, that party's Agreement Value shall be the amount of the fee quoted by that Reference Market-maker.

17. *Costs and Expenses.* (a) Each of the parties shall pay, or reimburse the other on demand for, all stamp, registration, documentation or similar taxes or duties, and any penalties or interest that may be due with respect thereto, that may be imposed by any jurisdiction in respect of its execution or delivery of this Agreement. If any such tax or duty is imposed by any jurisdiction as the result of the conduct or status of both parties, each party shall pay one half the amount of the tax or duty.

(b) A party that fails to perform any of its obligations hereunder shall pay, or reimburse the other on demand for, all reasonable costs and expenses incurred by the other in connection with the enforcement of its rights under this Agreement, including, without limitation, fees and expenses of legal counsel.

18. *Non-Assignment.* Neither party shall be entitled to assign or transfer its rights or obligations hereunder or any interest herein to any other person or any of its other branches or offices without the written consent of the other party to this Agreement, and any purported assignment or transfer in violation of this Section shall be void. The parties are acting for purposes of this Agreement through their respective branches or offices specified in Exhibit 4A.1. Neither party shall withhold its consent to an assignment or transfer proposed pursuant to Section 7 or Section 8 if (a) the proposed assignee or transferee meets the criteria set forth in Section 7(a) or Section 8(b) (as the case may be), and (b) the policies of the party whose consent has been sought, as then in effect, would permit it to enter into an interest rate exchange transaction with the proposed assignee or transferee without credit support.

19. *Waivers; Rights Not Exclusive.* No failure or delay by a party in exercising any right hereunder shall operate as a waiver of, or impair, any such right. No single or partial exercise of any such right shall preclude any other or further exercise thereof or the exercise of any other right. No waiver of any such right shall be effective unless given in writing. No waiver of any such right shall be deemed a waiver of any other right hereunder. The right to terminate provided for herein is in addition to, and not exclusive of, any other rights, powers, privileges or remedies provided by law.

20. *Interpretation.* The section headings in this Agreement are for convenience of reference only and shall not affect the meaning or construction of any provision hereof.

21. *Notices.* All notices in connection with this Agreement shall be given by telex or cable or by notice in writing hand-delivered or sent by facsimile transmission or by airmail, postage prepaid. All such notices shall be sent to the telex or telecopier number or address (as the case may be) specified for the intended recipient in Exhibit 4A.1 (or to such other number or address as that recipient may have last specified by notice to the other party) and shall be sent with copies as indicated therein. All such notices shall be effective upon receipt, and confirmation by answerback of any notice sent by telex as provided herein shall be sufficient evidence of receipt thereof.

22. *Amendments.* This Agreement may be amended only by an instrument in writing executed by the parties hereto.

23. *Survival.* The obligations of the parties under Section 8, Section 15 and Section 17 shall survive payment of the obligations of the parties under Section 2 and Section 5 and the termination of their other obligations hereunder.

24. *Currency.* Each reference in this Agreement to Dollars is of the essence. The obligation of each of the parties in respect of any amount due under this Agreement shall, notwithstanding any payment in any other currency (whether pursuant to a judgment or otherwise), be discharged only to the extent of the amount in Dollars that the party entitled to receive that payment may, in accordance with normal banking procedures, purchase with the sum paid in such other currency (after any premium and costs of exchange) on the Banking Day immediately following the day on which that party receives that payment. If the amount in Dollars that may be so purchased for any reason falls short of the amount originally due, the party required to make that payment shall pay such additional amounts, in Dollars, as may be necessary to compensate for that shortfall. Any obligation of that party not discharged by that payment shall, to the fullest extent permitted by applicable law, be due as a separate and independent obligation and, until discharged as provided herein, shall continue in full force and effect.

25. *Jurisdiction; Governing Law; Immunity.* (a) Any action or proceeding relating in any way to this Agreement may be brought and enforced in the courts of the State of New York or of the United States for the Southern District of New York, and the Company irrevocably submits to the nonexclusive jurisdiction of each such court in connection with any such action or proceeding.

(b) The Company hereby irrevocably appoints Eternal Mail Box, which maintains an office in New York City on the date hereof at Broad and Narrow Streets, New York, New York 00000, as its agent to receive service of process or other legal summons in connection with any such action or proceeding. So long as the Company has any obligation under this Agreement, it shall maintain a duly appointed agent in New York City for service of such process or other summons, and if it fails to maintain such an agent, any such process or other summons may be served by mailing a copy thereof by certified or registered mail, or any substantially similar form of mail, addressed to the Company as provided for notices hereunder. Any such process or other summons may be served on the Bank by mailing a copy thereof by certified or registered mail, or any substantially similar form of mail, addressed to the Bank as provided for notices hereunder.

(c) The Company irrevocably waives to the fullest extent permitted by applicable law all immunity (whether on the basis of sovereignty or otherwise) from jurisdiction, attachment (both before and after judgment) and execution to which it might otherwise be entitled in any action or proceeding related in any way to this Agreement.

(d) This Agreement shall be governed by, and construed in accordance with, the law of the State of New York.

26. *Counterparts; Integration of Terms.* This Agreement may be executed in counterparts, and the conterparts taken together shall be deemed to constitute one and the same agreement. This Agreement contains the entire agreement between the parties relating to the subject matter hereof and supersedes all oral statements and prior writings with respect thereto.

IN WITNESS WHEREOF the parties have caused this Agreement to be duly executed and delivered as of the day and year first written above.

BIG BANK, N.A.   HEDGED CORPORATION

By: _____   By: _____

Title: _____   Title: _____

Exhibit 4A.1   Addresses for Notices and Accounts for Payments

BIG BANK, N.A.

Address:	One Financial Center
	New York, NY 00000
Attention:	Swaps Group leader
Telex No.:	00000 BB
Telecopier No.:	(000) 000–0000

Account for Payments

Account No.:	00–000
Depositary:	Big Bank
	One Financial Center
	New York, NY 00000

HEDGED CORPORATION

Address:	1, Gnomestrasse
	Zurich, Switzerland
Attention:	Corporate Treasury Group Officer
Telex No.:	00000 HC
Telecopier No.:	(000) 000–00000

Account for Payments

Account No.:	00–000
Depositary:	Other Big Bank
	Big Bank Plaza
	New York, NY 00000

Exhibit 4A.2   Certificate

Pursuant to Section 11 of the Interest Rate Exchange Agreement dated as of July 1, 1987 between Big Bank, N.A. and Hedged Corporation (the 'Agreement'), _____ _____[a] hereby certifies to _____[b] as follows:

(1) _____[c] is a _____ _____[d] of _____[a] duly appointed, and a specimen or facsimile of [his] [her] genuine signature is set forth on Exhibit A hereto.

(2)   [He] [She] was in office on the date of [his] [her] execution of the Agreement and at that time was authorized to execute the Agreement and all documents to be delivered thereunder on behalf of _____ .[a]

(3)   Also attached, as Exhibit B hereto, are certified copies of all documents evidencing all necessary corporate and other authorizations and approvals required for the execution and delivery by _____[a] of the Agreement and the performance of its obligations thereunder.

IN WITNESS WHEREOF, this certificate has been executed on and as of _____ , 1987.

[NAME OF PARTY]

By: _____

Title: _____

Notes: [a] Name of party delivering certificate; [b] Name of party receiving certificate; [c] Name of officer; [d] Title of officer.

Appendix B: Master interest rate exchange agreement

This agreement is a sample of the kind of documentation that might be used for a master US dollar interest rate swap agreement between two banks organised under the laws of the United States. The sample illustrates an agreement that incorporates by reference selected provisions of the 1986 edition of the Code of Standard Wording, Assumptions and Provisions for Swaps *published by the International Swap Dealers Association, Inc.*

This sample is merely an illustration and should not be used for an actual transaction; each transaction will have its own special features, and the agreement drafted to document it should be carefully tailored to address the legal and business problems that it presents.

MASTER INTEREST RATE EXCHANGE AGREEMENT dated as of July 1, 1987 between BIG BANK, N.A. ('Big Bank') and BIGGER BANK, N.A. ('Bigger Bank'), whereby the parties agree as follows.

1. *Definitions.* For purposes of this Agreement and each Rate Swap Transaction hereunder, the following terms have the meanings indicated, and each capitalized term that is used but not defined in this Agreement or in the Confirmation of a Rate Swap Transaction hereunder is incorporated herein by reference from, and has the meaning given to it in, the Code of Standard Wording, Assumptions and Provisions for Swaps, 1986 Edition, as published by the International Swap Dealers Association, Inc. (the 'Swaps Code'), without regard to any revision or subsequent edition thereof, as completed or supplemented herein or in that Confirmation.

'Big Bank Amount', for each Big Bank Calculation Period for any Rate Swap Transaction, means (i) the Fixed Amount for that Calculation Period, if Big Bank is the Fixed Rate Payor for that Rate Swap Transaction, (ii) the Floating Amount for that Calculation Period, if Big Bank is the only Floating Rate Payor for that Rate Swap Transaction, or (iii) the Big Bank Floating Amount for that Calculation Period, if both parties are Floating Rate Payors for that Rate Swap Transaction.

'Bigger Bank Amount', for each Bigger Bank Calculation Period for any Rate Swap Transaction, means (i) the Fixed Amount for that Calculation Period, if Bigger Bank is the Fixed Rate Payor for that Rate Swap Transaction, (ii) the Floating Amount for that Calculation Period, if Bigger Bank is the only Floating Rate Payor for that Rate Swap Transaction, or (iii) the Bigger Bank Floating Amount for that Calculation Period, if both parties are Floating Rate Payors for that Rate Swap Transaction.

'Confirmation', for each Rate Swap Transaction, means the written communication, substantially in the form set forth in Exhibit 4B.1, sent by Bigger Bank to Big Bank in connection with that Rate Swap Transaction in accordance with Section 2.

'Default Rate' means Prime, reset daily, plus 1%.

'Indebtedness', with respect to either party, means any present or future indebtedness of that party, as debtor, borrower or guarantor, in respect of money borrowed (other than indebtedness in respect of deposits received), including interest on any Indebtedness.

2. *Transactions.* (a) The parties intend to enter into Rate Swap Transactions under this Agreement from time to time on the understanding that each such Rate Swap Transaction will constitute an integral part of this Agreement, and it is an essential part of the parties' bargain that all Rate Swap Transactions hereunder be treated as a single agreement for all purposes. The terms of each such Rate Swap Transaction shall be those set forth in this Agreement as modified or supplemented for purposes of the relevant transaction by the Confirmation relating to it.

(b) The parties anticipate that their Rate Swap Transactions with each other will usually be concluded over the telephone. Bigger Bank shall promptly send Big Bank a Confirmation of each Rate Swap Transaction between them, and Big Bank shall promptly confirm the accuracy of that Confirmation by signing a copy and returning it to Bigger Bank by hand or by facsimile transmission. Any request for correction of error in a Confirmation shall be made immediately upon receipt thereof. In the absence of an immediate request for correction of error, a Confirmation shall be deemed correct as sent, and Big Bank shall be bound by the terms of the Rate Swap Transaction set forth therein as fully as if Big Bank had signed the Confirmation and returned it to Bigger Bank as provided herein. If a correction of an essential term is immediately requested and the parties are unable to agree on the correction, the attempted transaction shall be void, inasmuch as there will not have been a meeting of the minds on the essential terms of that transaction.

3. *Payments.* (a) On the terms and subject to the conditions set forth herein, Bigger Bank shall pay Big Bank the applicable Bigger Bank Amount on each Bigger Bank Payment Date and Big Bank shall pay Bigger Bank the applicable Big Bank Amount on each Big Bank Payment Date. Those payments shall be made on a Net Payments – Corresponding Payment Dates basis and, unless the parties otherwise agree, the following conventions shall apply with respect to the adjustment of Period End Dates and Payment Dates (other than the final such dates): (i) the Modified Following Banking Day payments convention shall apply to the payments to be made hereunder by each party in connection with each Rate Swap Transaction involving a 'LIBOR' Floating Rate Option unless the rule set forth in the next clause applies to that Rate Swap Transaction; and (ii) the Delayed Payment convention shall apply to each Rate Swap Transaction involving Reset Dates scheduled to occur during the last week of any Calculation Period.

(b) Each payment hereunder shall be made in accordance with the procedures set forth in Section 10.1 of the Swaps Code. All payments hereunder shall be made to the account specified for the intended recipient on the signature page hereof, or to such other account in the same city as that party may have last specified by notice to the other party.

(c) The obligation of each party to make payments pursuant to this Section is subject to the conditions set forth in Section 10.2(a) of the Swaps Code. However, these conditions shall be deemed to have been satisfied for purposes of Section 12 and shall no longer apply when all payments to that party that are required hereunder have been made.

4. *Calculation Agent; Rounding.* Bigger Bank shall be the Calculation Agent for purposes of each Rate Swap Transaction between the parties and, as such, shall have the responsibilities set forth in Section 4.8 of the Swaps Code. The rounding convention set forth in Article 8 of the Swaps Code is incorporated herein by reference.

5. *Default Rate.* Amounts payable hereunder that are not paid when due shall bear interest as provided in Section 10.3 of the Swaps Code.

6. *Arrangement Fee.* In connection with each Rate Swap Transaction, the arrangement fee (if any) agreed upon by the parties shall be paid by Big Bank to Bigger Bank or by Bigger Bank to Big Bank (as agreed) on or before the seventh day after the Effective Date of that Rate Swap Transaction or such other date as may be agreed upon by the parties.

7. *Representations and Warranties.* Section 15.1 of the Swaps Code is incorporated herein by reference. Each of the parties makes to the other the representations and warranties set forth in subsections (a) through (c) of Section 15.1 of the Swaps Code (Basic Representations, Absence of Certain Events and Absence of Litigation).

8. *Covenants.* Section 16.1 of the Swaps Code is incorporated herein by reference. Each of Big Bank and Bigger Bank shall observe and perform each of the agreements set forth in subsections (e) and (f) of Section 16.1 of the Swaps Code (Give Notice of Default and Certain Events and Maintain Authorizations and Comply with Laws).

9. *Closing Documents.* (a) On or before July 15, 1987, each party shall deliver to the other a duly executed certificate substantially in the form set forth in Exhibit 4B.2, together with the attachment referred to therein. The certificate and the attachment shall each be in form and substance satisfactory to the recipient.

(b) Each party shall, as soon as practicable, deliver to the other party such documents as that party has agreed to deliver in connection with each Rate Swap Transaction.

10. *Events of Default.* Section 11.10 of the Swaps Code is incorporated herein by reference. For purposes of this Agreement, the term 'Event of Default' means, with respect to a party, any of the events listed below which occurs or relates to that party, subject to the notice requirements and Cure Periods, if any, indicated below, or immediately, if none is so indicated.

(a) Failure To Pay (Swaps Code Section 11.7(e)). Cure Period: 5 days After Notice.

(b) Breach of Covenant (Swaps Code Section 11.7(a)). Cure Period for breach of the covenant to Maintain Authorizations and Comply with Laws: 10 days After Notice.

(c) Misrepresentation (Swaps Code Section 11.7(g)).

(d) Failure to Pay Under Specified Swaps (Swaps Code Section 11.7(f)). Specified Swaps: all rate swaps, rate caps, currency exchange and similar transactions, however described, between Big Bank or any of its Affiliates, on the one hand, and Bigger Bank or any of its Affiliates, on the other.

(e) Any event or occurrence takes place that has the effect (or that, with the giving of notice or the lapse of time or both, would have the effect) of causing or permitting Indebtedness of that party in an aggregate amount exceeding $25,000,000 (or the equivalent thereof in any currency or currencies) to become due before the scheduled maturity date of that Indebtedness, or that party fails to pay when due Indebtedness in an aggregate amount exceeding $5,000,000 (or such equivalent).

(f) That party (i) is dissolved, (ii) fails or is unable to pay its debts generally as they become due, (iii) makes a general assignment for the benefit of its creditors, (iv) commences, or consents to the commencement against it of, an action or proceeding seeking relief under any bankruptcy or insolvency law or any law affecting creditors' rights that is similar to a bankruptcy or insolvency law, (v) is the subject of an order for relief or a decree in any such action or proceeding, (vi) has commenced against it without its consent any action or proceeding described above, if that action or proceeding is not dismissed on or before the sixtieth day after it is commenced or if any dismissal thereof ceases to remain in effect, or (vii) seeks or becomes subject to the appointment of a receiver, trustee, custodian or other similar official for it or any of its property.

(g) That party sells or otherwise transfers all or substantially all its assets without the consent of the other party to this Agreement or merges or consolidates with or into another entity without such consent, if the purchaser or transferee of the assets or the entity produced by or surviving the merger or consolidation fails to assume the party's obligations under this Agreement through operation of law or pursuant to arrangements reasonably satisfactory to the other party to this Agreement.

11. *Termination Pursuant to Notice.* (a) Section 11.1 and Section 11.6 of the Swaps Code are incorporated herein by reference with respect to the right to give notice of termination in connection with any Event of Default. The day designated in a notice of termination as the Early Termination Date shall be a date that is not before, nor more than ten days after, the date the notice of termination becomes effective hereunder.

(b) Any notice of termination given hereunder shall declare the obligations of the parties in connection with all Rate Swap Transactions to make the payments required by Section 3 that are scheduled to be made after the Early Termination Date specified in the notice to be terminated as of that date, and those obligations (but not any other payment obligations hereunder) shall so terminate and be replaced by the parties' obligations to make the payments required by Section 12.

12. *Payments upon Early Termination.* (a) In the event of termination as provided in Section 11, the parties shall settle on an Agreement Value – Limited Two Way Payments basis their payment obligations in respect of each Calculation Period that, but for the early termination, would end after the Early Termination Date; *provided, however*, that if a relevant Market Quotation with respect to any Rate Swap Transaction cannot be determined, Indemnification – Limited Two Way Payments shall be the alternative measure of damages for purposes of settlement of the parties' payment obligations in respect of each such Calculation Period for that Rate Swap Transaction.

(b) Aggregation is specified by the parties in respect of each measure of damages specified in this Section 12.

(c) At the time for the settlements referred to in Section 12(a), the parties shall pay all amounts they would have been required to pay pursuant to Section 3 on or before the Early Termination Date but for the conditions specified in Section 3(c), together with all other amounts then due hereunder.

13. *Cancellation.* At any time when there are no Rate Swap Transactions hereunder, either party may give notice of the cancellation of this Agreement effective immediately.

14. *Costs and Expenses.* (a) The parties shall indemnify each other for expenses as provided in Section 12.7 of the Swaps Code.

(b) Each of the parties shall pay or reimburse the other on demand for, all stamp, registration, documentation or similar taxes or duties, and any penalties or interest that may be due with respect thereto, that may be imposed by any jurisdiction in respect of its execution or delivery of this Agreement. If any such tax or duty is imposed by any jurisdiction as the result of the conduct or status of both parties, each party shall pay one half the amount of the tax or duty.

15. *Non-Assignment.* Neither party shall be entitled to assign or transfer its rights or obligations hereunder or any interest herein in connection with any Rate Swap Transaction to any other person, or to any of its branches or offices located outside the United States, without the prior written consent of the other party, and any purported assignment or transfer in violation of this Section shall be void.

16. *Waivers; Rights Not Exclusive.* Section 20.1 of the Swaps Code is incorporated herein by reference. The right to terminate provided for herein is in addition to, and not exclusive of, any other rights, powers, privileges or remedies provided by law.

17. *Interpretation.* Section 20.4 of the Swaps Code is incorporated herein by reference.

18. *Notices.* Article 14 of the Swaps Code is incorporated herein by reference. The addresses and telex numbers of the parties for notices are initially as specified on the signature page of this Agreement.

19. *Amendments.* This Agreement may be amended only by an instrument in writing executed by the parties hereto or, in connection with a Rate Swap Transaction, by the parties' agreement hereunder with respect to that Rate Swap Transaction.

20. *Survival.* The obligations of the parties under Section 6, Section 12 and Section 14 shall survive payment of the obligations of the parties under Section 3 and Section 5 and the termination of their other obligations hereunder.

21. *Jurisdiction; Governing Law; Service of Process.* Article 13 and Section 20.3 of the Swaps Code are incorporated herein by reference. Any process or other legal summons in connection with any action or proceeding relating in any way to this Agreement may be served by mailing a copy thereof by certified or

registered mail, or any substantially similar form of mail, addressed to the intended recipient as provided for notices hereunder.

22. *Counterparts; Integration of Terms.* Section 20.2 of the Swaps Code is incorporated herein by reference. This Agreement (as supplemented with respect to each Rate Swap Transaction by the agreement of the parties hereunder as recorded in the Confirmation thereof) contains the entire agreement between the parties relating to the subject matter hereof and supersedes all oral statements and prior writings with respect thereto.

IN WITNESS WHEREOF, the parties hereto have caused this Agreement to be duly executed and delivered as of the day and year first written above.

BIG BANK, N.A.   BIGGER BANK, N.A.

By: _____   By: _____

Title: _____   Title: _____

Address: One Financial Center   Address: One Money Center
           New York, NY 00000   New York, NY 00000

Attention: Swaps Group Leader   Attention: Swap Administrator
Telex No.: 00000 BB   Telex No.: 00000 BGBK
Telecopier No.: (000) 000–0000   Telecopier No.: (000) 000–0000

Account for Payments   *Account for Payments*

Account No.: 00–000   Account No.: 00–000
Depositary: Other Big Bank   Depositary: Biggest Bank, N.A.
           Big Bank Plaza   Money Plaza
           New York, NY 00000   New York, NY 00000

Exhibit 4B.1   Confirmation

Date: _____
To: Big Bank, N.A.
Telex No.: 00000 BB
Attention: Swaps Group Leader
From: Bigger Bank, N.A.
Telex No.: 00000 BGBK

We are pleased to confirm our mutually binding agreement to enter into a Rate Swap Transaction with you in accordance with our telephone agreement with [name] on _____ , 19____ , pursuant to the Master Interest Rate Exchange Agreement between us dated as of July 1, 1987.

Bigger Bank Rate Swap Transaction Reference Number: _____

Effective Date: _____

Termination Date: _____

Notional Amount: _____

[Fixed Rate Payor: _____
Floating Rate Payor: _____]
[Both parties are Floating Rate Payors]

[Bigger Bank] Calculation Periods for Payments:
    [First Period: Effective Date to but excluding _____
    Later Period End Dates: _____ after the first Period End Date and finally the
        Termination Date]

[Big Bank] Calculation Periods for Payments:
    [First Period: Effective Date to but excluding _____
    Later Period End Dates: _____ after the first Period End Date and finally the
        Termination Date]

Payment Dates: Each party pays on ____ [its own] Period End Dates
                                   ____ Delayed Payment basis

[Fixed Rate: _____ percent per annum
    Fixed Rate Day Count Fraction: _____]

[Bigger Bank's] Floating Rate Option: _____
    [Designated Maturity: _____ months]
    [Spread: (plus) (minus) ____ percent]
    Floating Rate Day Count Fraction: _____
    [Rate for first Calculation Period: _____ percent]
    Reset Dates: _____
    [First compounding period: Effective Date to but excluding _____]
    [Compounding: _____]

[Big Bank's] Floating Rate Option: _____
    [Designated Maturity: _____ months]
    [Spread: (plus) (minus) _____ percent]
    Floating Rate Day Count Fraction: _____
    [Rate for first Calculation Period: ____ percent]
    Reset Dates: _____
    [First compounding period: Effective date to but excluding _____]
    [Compounding: _____]

Office or branch through which we are acting: _____

Office or branch through which you are acting: _____

Arrangement Fee: _____
Payable by: _____
Due date: _____

[Closing documents: _____]

Documentation: The Master Interest Rate Exchange Agreement dated as of July 1, 1987 between Big
        Bank and Bigger Bank as modified by this Confirmation.

    Please confirm to us that the terms set forth herein accurately reflect our Rate Swap
Transaction with you by signing a copy of this Confirmation and sending it back to us promptly by
hand or by facsimile transmission. Please notify us immediately if you believe there is an error in this
Confirmation.

Confirmed:

BIGGER BANK, N.A.   BIG BANK, N.A.

By: _____   By: _____

Title: _____   Title: _____

Exhibit 4B.2   Certificate

Pursuant to Section 9 of the Master Interest Rate Exchange Agreement dated as of July 1, 1987 between Big Bank, N.A. and Bigger Bank, N.A. (the 'Agreement'), _____ _____[a] hereby certifies to _____[b] as follows:

(1) _____[c] is a _____ _____[d] of _____[a] duly appointed, and a specimen or facsimile of [his] [her] genuine signature is set forth on Exhibit A hereto.

(2)   [He] [She] was in office on the date of [his] [her] execution of the Agreement and at that time was authorized to execute the Agreement and all documents to be delivered thereunder on behalf of _____ .[a]

IN WITNESS WHEREOF, this certificate has been executed on and as of _____ , 1987.

[NAME OF PARTY]

By: _____

Title: _____

Notes: [a] Name of party delivering certificate; [b] Name of party receiving certificate; [c] Name of officer; [d] Title of officer.

Appendix C: Sample confirmations

Annual fixed/semi-annual Libor payments

Confirmation

Date: July 1, 1987
To: Big Bank, N.A.
Telex No.: 00000 BB
Attention: Swaps Group Leader
From: Bigger Bank, N.A.
Telex No.: 00000 BGBK

We are pleased to confirm our mutually binding agreement to enter into a Rate Swap Transaction with you in accordance with our telephone agreement with Mr. Swapper on July 1, 1987, pursuant to the Master Interest Rate Exchange Agreement between us dated as of July 1, 1987.

Bigger Bank Rate Swap Transaction Reference Number: 00000

Effective Date: July 1, 1987
Termination Date: July 1, 1992

Notional Amount: $45,000,000

Fixed Rate Payor: Big Bank, N.A.
Floating Rate Payor: Bigger Bank, N.A.

Bigger Bank Calculation Periods for Payments:
  First Period: Effective Date to but excluding January 4, 1988.
  Later Period End Dates: Each July 1 and January 1 after the first Period End Date, subject to the Modified Following Banking Day convention, and finally the Termination Date

Big Bank Calculation Periods for Payments:
  First Period: Effective Date to but excluding July 1, 1988
  Later Period End Dates: Each July 1 after the first Period End Date, subject to the Modified Following Banking Day convention, and finally the Termination Date

Payment Dates: Each party pays on its own Period End Dates
Fixed Rate: _____ percent per annum
  Fixed Rate Day Count Fraction: 30/360

Floating Rate Option: LIBOR
  Designated Maturity: six months
  Floating Rate Day Count Fraction: Actual/360
  Reset Dates: First day of each Bigger Bank Calculation Period

Office or branch through which we are acting: Principal Office in New York City

Office or branch through which you are acting: Principal Office in New York City

Arrangement Fee: None

Documentation: The Master Interest Rate Exchange Agreement dated as of July 1, 1987 between Big Bank and Bigger Bank as modified by this Confirmation.

Please confirm to us that the terms set forth herein accurately reflect our Rate Swap Transaction with you by signing a copy of this Confirmation and sending it back to us promptly by hand or by facsimile transmission. Please notify us immediately if you believe there is an error in this Confirmation.

Confirmed:

BIGGER BANK, N.A.   BIG BANK, N.A.

By: _____   By: _____

Title: _____   Title: _____

Prime/Libor transaction, net quarterly payments

Confirmation

Date: July 1, 1987
To: Big Bank, N.A.
Telex No.: 00000 BB
Attention: Swaps Group Leader
From: Bigger Bank, N.A.
Telex No.: 00000 BGBK

We are pleased to confirm our mutually binding agreement to enter into a Rate Swap Transaction with you in accordance with our telephone agreement with Ms. Trader on July 1, 1987, pursuant to the Master Interest Rate Exchange Agreement between us dated as of July 1, 1987.

Bigger Bank Rate Swap Transaction Reference Number: 0000

Effective Date: July 1, 1987

Termination Date: July 1, 1992

Notional Amount: $50,000,000

Both parties are Floating Rate Payors

Calculation Periods for Payments:
First Period: Effective Date to but excluding October 1, 1987
Later Period End Dates: Each January 1, April 1, July 1, and October 1, after the first Period End Date and finally the Termination Date

Payment Dates: Each party pays on Delayed Payment basis

Bigger Bank's Floating Rate Option: Prime
    Floating Rate Day Count Fraction: Actual/365
    Reset Dates: Each day in the Term

Big Bank's Floating Rate Option: LIBOR
    Designated Maturity: Three months
    Spread: plus x/100 of 1 percent
    Floating Rate Day Count Fraction: Actual/360
    Reset Dates: First day of each Calculation Period

Office or branch through which we are acting: Principal office in New York City

Office or branch through which you are acting: Principal office in New York City

Arrangement Fee: None

Documentation: The Master Interest Rate Exchange Agreement dated as of July 1, 1987 between Big Bank and Bigger Bank as modified by this Confirmation.

    Please confirm to us that the terms set forth herein accurately reflect our Rate Swap Transaction with you by signing a copy of this Confirmation and sending it back to us promptly by hand or by facsimile transmission. Please notify us immediately if you believe there is an error in this Confirmation.

Confirmed:

BIGGER BANK, N.A.   BIG BANK, N.A.

By: _____   By: _____

Title: _____   Title: _____

5 Case study: Structuring of swaps

Irene S. Leibowitz

Introduction

This chapter is a case study which discusses the structuring of swaps, building from plain vanilla swaps to more sophisticated structures.

To most end users in the swaps market, a swap appears to be a rather simple transaction. Clients approaching any major financial institution would find that swaps can be made, fitting exactly and perfectly with their objectives. However, what most clients do not realise is the 'tailoring process' behind the scenes, where dealers work constantly to respond to clients' requests. This results in dealers laying off risk on each other. Generally, dealers service clients by trading in order to provide a workable, liquid swaps market.

Exhibit 5.1　Interest rate swap: 1

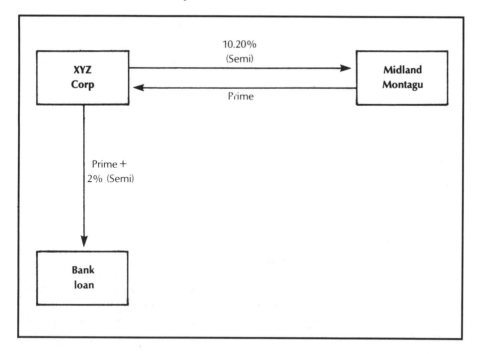

Interest rate swap

Each example in this chapter builds from a plain vanilla swap structure by adding more variations. Exhibit 5.1 shows the type of simple problem which instigated the swap market. XYZ Corporation wants to hedge their interest rate risk on a prime-based bank loan. They approach a dealer (we) and ask for a quote. We quote the prime/fixed market at a 235/245 level, i.e. Treasury bonds plus 235 on the bid side; Treasuries plus 245 on the offered side. The Treasury rate is 7.75% (this example uses a 5-year Treasury, because XYZ wants a 5-year swap maturity). Thus, by adding 245 basis points to 7.75% we quote XYZ Corporation a 10.20% semi-annual rate versus prime. This prime flow will be used to service XYZ's bank loan. Now, they are locked, with an all-in cost of 12.20% resulting from the 10.20% fixed rate, plus the 2% loan margin.

We, however, are not locked, because we need to find a prime flow to pass along to XYZ Corporation and a way of laying off the fixed flow we will be receiving from XYZ. This will be handled in stages, whilst responding to both market opportunities and client needs.

The next stage builds on XYZ's simple fixed/floating swap (see Exhibit 5.2).

Exhibit 5.2   Interest rate swap: 2

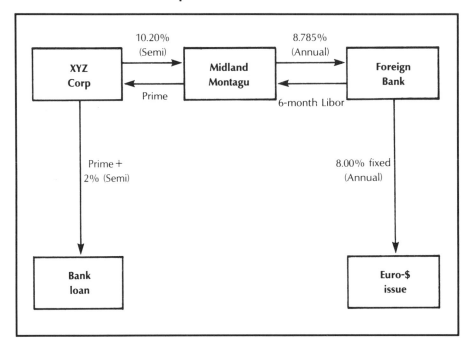

Our syndicate desk approaches us with a transaction they are structuring on behalf of Foreign Bank. Foreign Bank wants to launch a Eurobond issue on which our syndicate desk believes a coupon of 8% and the standard issuing fees for a 5-year deal of $1\frac{7}{8}$% would apply, thus providing a fixed cost to Foreign Bank of 8.476% AIBD (or annual) basis. A proposed swap transaction is attractive to Foreign Bank because of their interest in swapping out of the fixed rate of 8.476%. Foreign Bank's objective is to achieve a margin under Libor, on floating rate debt.

As dealers, we are quoting 5-year fixed rate swaps against Libor at Treasuries plus 85/95. That is, we are prepared to pay Treasuries plus 85 or to receive Treasuries plus 95. As we are bidders in this case, we will pay the Treasury rate of 7.75%, plus the margin of 85 basis points, bringing us to an 8.60% semi-annual rate. This translates into 8.785% annual (like most dealers, we are prepared to write either annual or semi-annual).

What have we accomplished? We have 'laid off' the fixed rate flow received from XYZ Corporation. However, we are still mismatched on the floating rate because of receiving 6-month Libor and paying prime. But, most importantly, we have balanced the fixed rate element of the transaction. At this point, both clients have achieved their objectives – our corporate client (XYZ) is totally balanced, and the Foreign Bank client is also balanced. Foreign Bank achieved a margin of 31 basis points under Libor and XYZ Corporation achieved a fixed rate on its floating bank loan.

Exhibit 5.3   Interest rate swap: 3

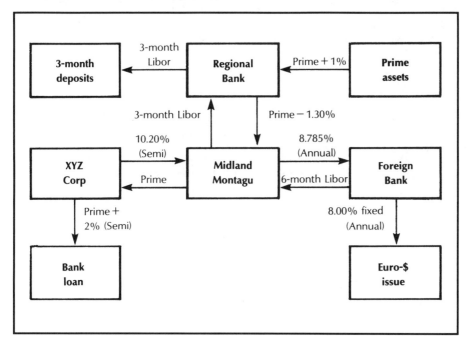

As dealers, we are left with a mismatch on the floating rate side; however, Regional Bank provides the solution to this problem (see Exhibit 5.3). Regional Bank, which has a prime rate loan book, tends to raise its funding on a 3-month deposit basis. That is, it has a block of 3-month Libor deposits, which it wants to match off with the prime based assets. In order to accomplish this objective, Regional Bank asked us for a quote on prime/Libor swaps.

The market for prime/Libor swaps is prime less 120/prime less 130. As shown in Exhibit 5.3, Regional Bank paid us prime less 130 basis points and we paid it 3-month Libor. Thus, Regional Bank achieved its objective of effectively converting prime-based loans to Libor-based loans, leaving the Bank 'matched off'.

In fact, we have achieved something else. We now have a prime inflow matched against the prime outflow we were paying to XYZ Corporation, and we have a place to use the Libor inflow that we are getting in from Foreign Bank. We still have a mismatch between 3- and 6-month Libor, but for ourselves (and for most dealers) that is not of any consequence. The 3- versus the 6-month Libor market tends to trade flat or to plus three, minus three basis points (with the differential shifting from one side to the other depending on market conditions). In order to be perfectly matched, however, we could do a 3-month Libor versus a 6-month Libor floating/floating swap.

Up to this point, we have analysed swaps primarily from the clients' point of view. Now let us consider how the dealer fared in economic terms after booking such swaps. Ignoring the fact that there is a difference in basis of 365 days verus 360 days on various elements of this transaction, we (the dealers) are receiving 10.20% semi-annual payments, and are paying the equivalent of 8.60% semi-annually. This will provide us with a net gain (on that leg of the transaction) of 160 basis points. Subtracted from this net gain is 130 basis points from the prime side of the transaction, leaving us with a 30 basis point profit – plus 'something else'.

Given that this is a prime/Libor swap pegged to 3-month Libor, the prime rate we receive will be paid quarterly. As a result, we achieve a compounding differential between the prime that we are receiving quarterly and the prime that we are paying out, which in this case is paid semi-annually. Thus, we will achieve 'something else', the exact magnitude of which we will not know until the transaction is complete, because the value of the compounding will depend on the absolute level of the prime rates over the period.

Even though we have settled the transaction, swap dealers have never *completely* settled, because of clients' demands and constant market opportunities.

Exhibit 5.4   Interest rate swap: 4

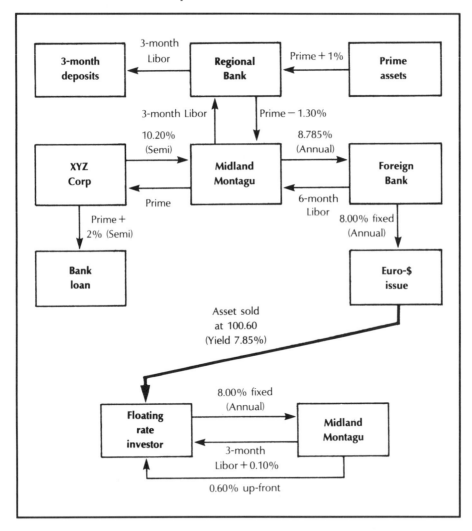

As time goes on, the Eurobond, which sourced the fixed rate we provided XYZ Corporation, has matured (see Exhibit 5.4). The situation has changed in the market because of a major rally which moved the 5-year Treasury from 7.75% to 6.80%. The swap spreads have also changed. Originally, the bid/offered spread for a Libor swap was 85/95. Now, the bid/offered spread is 65/75. Rates have come down significantly and swap spreads have also slimmed. As a result of the rally, one of the original investors in the Eurobond has a gain and would like to unload part of their securities. Our sales desk is prepared to bid that investor par 60 for his bond, for a yield of 7.85%. This compares to a 8.10% yield the investor originally achieved on the issue.

Our sales desk has a purchaser interested in taking on this position, but on a floating, not a fixed rate basis. The purchaser wants to be cash flow neutral, i.e. he wants to receive a payment equal to the premium he is going to have to pay on the bond. Expressed another way, he wants to receive a 60 basis point payment up-front. In return, the bond purchaser will pass along the annual 8% coupon flows received from the security.

The sales desk approaches us for quotes regarding the collection of flows. What is going to be left to the purchaser as a floating rate yield? What can we quote as a floating rate inflow (which is what the new investor wants to generate on this transaction), in return for paying him 60 basis points up-front and receiving from him the fixed 8% annual flows the Eurobond will generate?

Our quote is Libor plus 10 basis points, yielded from a bid/offered spread of 65/75 on fixed /Libor swaps of this maturity. The 60 basis points front-end payment on the swap has a value that, when added to the 10 basis point margin over Libor (what we are paying to the bond purchaser), equates an 8% fixed annual inflow to a 7.85% effective rate (see Exhibit 5.5).

Exhibit 5.5 Interest rate swap: 5

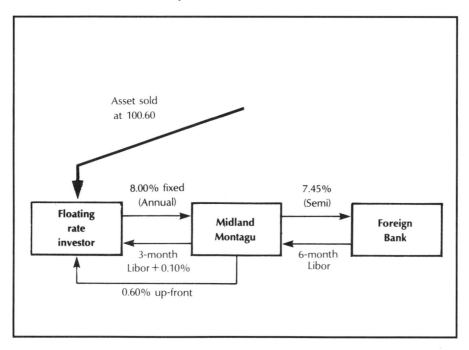

Cross-currency swap

In Exhibit 5.6, US Company requires a margin under commercial paper (CP) as their net result. They will issue in any market and in any type of security.

The dealers (we) identified an opening in the sterling market to launch a 7-year bond issue, and the opportunity to swap it back into dollars at a rate which could be appealing to US Company. However, there is no 'market', no bid/offered spread, between dollar-denominated CP floating rates and sterling-denominated fixed rates. In effect, we are making assumptions about our ability to hedge and lay off this transaction. In doing so, we arrived at a margin under CP that we are prepared to receive, in return for paying US Company the fixed rate, in sterling, needed to service their bond issue.

171

Exhibit 5.6   Cross-currency swap: 1

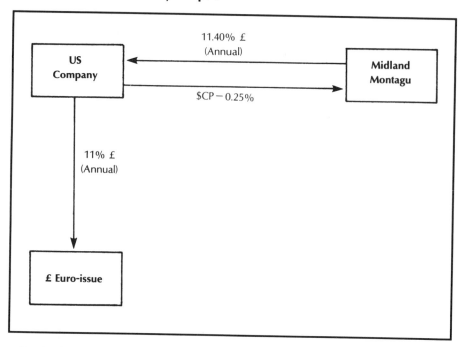

In the first leg of this particular example, UK Company approaches us with a straightforward request, very similar to the request of US Company above (Exhibit 5.6), i.e. the need to fix a rate on a bank loan (see Exhibit 5.7).

Exhibit 5.7   Cross-currency swap: 2

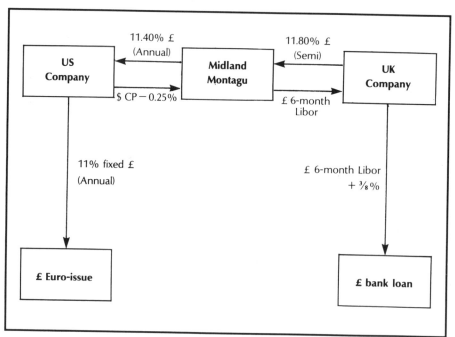

As this is a UK company, not surprisingly, their loan is sterling-denominated. We quote them a fixed rate of 11.80% semi-annually, in sterling, in return for receipt of sterling 6-month Libor. Adding their loan margin of $\frac{3}{8}$% to the 11.80% that they will pay to us on the swap, gives UK Company an all-in fixed rate of 12.175% semi-annually, in sterling. Now, they are hedged. We have laid off, or obtained a hedge for, the fixed rate payment that we are going to pay to US Company on their sterling-denominated bond issue.

Exhibit 5.8   Cross-currency swap: 3

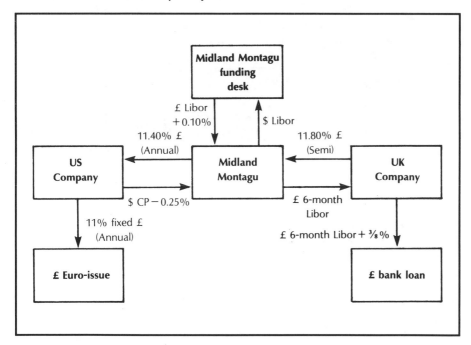

Even with the hedge, we are still mismatched on the floating rate side of the transaction (Exhibit 5.8). Receiving CP less 25 basis points in dollars and paying out sterling 6-month Libor, is not a match. However, there is an easy way to arrive at a matched position; simply swap Libor payments from sterling to dollars. This sort of swap is widely available and generally entails a premium on the sterling side of the transaction. The premium will vary, but our 10 basis point premium received from our funding desk is typically in the market.

Not only have we resolved the mismatch, but because of the 6-month sterling Libor and 6-month dollar Libor flows, we have also hedged the sterling flow needed to pay UK Company. This provided us with 10 extra basis points which we will add to our gains on the fixed rate side of the transaction (11.80% semi-annually that we received from the UK client minus 11.40% annually that we paid to the sterling bond issuer). With 11.40% annually equalling 11.09% semi-annually, the result is a 71 basis point differential on the part of the transaction. So far, we are doing well, with 71 basis points on the fixed leg, and 10 basis points on the floating leg, for a total of 81 basis points.

Let us now consider the unhedged CP inflow. A US company approaches us that has a fairly straightforward kind of a requirement which will help us out (Exhibit 5.9). US Company wants to pay fixed dollars against the receipt of dollar CP. We arrived at a 9.30% semi-annual rate based on the following: the fixed/CP market as we saw it was Treasuries plus 70/Treasuries plus 80 market for 7-year transactions, i.e. we are prepared to bid at 7-year Treasuries plus 70 basis points, or to receive at 7-year Treasuries plus 80 basis points versus CP flat. The 7-year Treasury at the time is 8.50%,

Exhibit 5.9 Cross-currency swap: 4

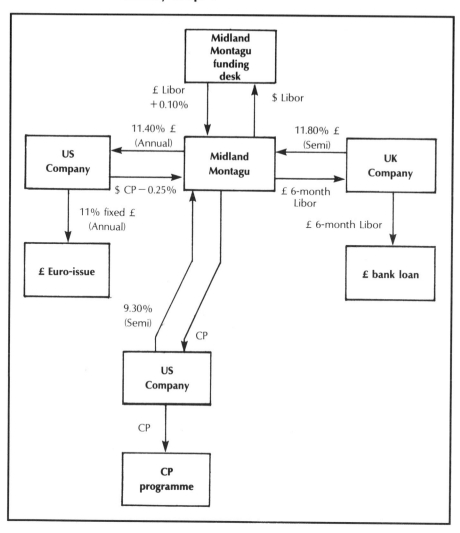

and adding the 8.50% to the 80 basis points swap is how we got to the 9.30% semi-annual rate that we are willing to receive.

To summarise: having dropped the commercial paper inflow, we have acquired something better than the CP – a fixed rate inflow at 9.30% semi-annually. We have also 'lost' 25 basis points en route to the CP leg. Before this last swap we were up 81 basis points. Now we are down 25 basis points on this swap, leaving us net up 56 basis points in this transaction so far.

The final leg is straightforward because all we are looking for is a standard market transaction, namely a dollar-fixed versus 6-month Libor swap (Exhibit 5.10). We get this swap from Foreign Bank who is a swap dealer and who has a syndicate desk that also seeks opportunities to underwrite Euro-issues in the market. The process of laying off risk while meeting clients' requirements begins all over again. Except that now, the Foreign Bank will start playing the role that we played before.

As we are anxious to complete the trade, we pay the 'wrong' side of the bid/asked spread, on this particular leg with the fixed-Libor market at Treasuries plus 80/Treasuries plus 90. That is, 9.62% annually, which is to be the equivalent of 9.40% semi-annually, so we are down 10 basis points,

Exhibit 5.10   Cross-currency swap: 5

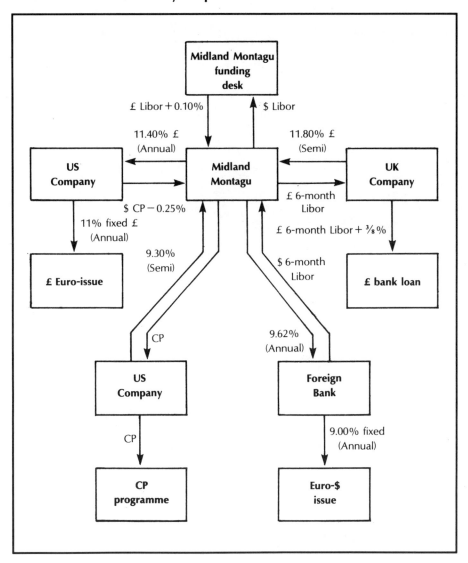

which means a deduction from our gain of 56 basis points. This brings us to a 46 basis point net gain. Unfortunately, it is not quite so simple because portions of this transaction were denominated in dollars and portions were denominated in sterling. Given the difference in interest rate levels, the discount rates are not identical for those two sets of flows. Such differences are not great, but there are an extra 10 to 15 basis points pick up that we will get out of the fact that we are receiving in, and making a profit on the sterling side of the transaction, and taking losses on the dollar side.

Finally, having worked from a plain vanilla swap to more sophisticated structures, we see that the tailoring process for clients requires not only a strong market knowledge, but also a well-established swap dealer's network.

PART V

Interest rate options

1 The mechanics of interest rate options

Ian Cooper

The market

Introduction

Interest rate options are short-term options on short-term interest rates. They are one part of the debt market option market. This market also includes medium-term options on short-term interest rates (caps, floors and collars), short-term options on bonds (bond options), and medium-term options on bonds (bond warrants).

As with other option markets, the market for interest rate options offers exchange-traded contracts and over-the-counter (OTC) contracts. Exhibit 1.1 lists some of the major contract types. The difference between the two markets is the usual one that exchange-traded contracts tend to be more liquid but offer a restricted range of contracts. OTC markets offer tailor-made transactions, but often with lower liquidity or higher cost.

Exhibit 1.1   Types of interest rate option

Type	Example
A Exchange-traded	
Calls and puts on interest rate futures	3-month Eurodollar (IMM,LIFFE)
	3-month T-bills (IMM)
	3-month Eurosterling (LIFFE)
B Over-the-counter	
1 Single calls and puts	Eurodollar, CDs, Eurosterling, FRAs
2 Hybrid	Collars, mini-max, participating forwards

Single traded puts and calls

Traded interest rate options are individual puts and calls, usually on money-market futures. Exhibit 1.2 gives, as an example, the characteristics of the CME/LIFFE option on 3-month Eurodollar futures. The underlying asset is a US$1m face value futures contract on the 3-month Eurodollar deposit rate. Quotations on both the futures contract and the option are in terms of an index price which represents 100 less the annualised interest rate.

The holder of a call option on the futures benefits if interest rates fall and the index price rises. The holder of a put option benefits if the interest rate rises and the index price falls. Borrowers wishing to hedge future borrowing rates are, therefore, natural holders of the put option. Lenders wishing to lock in a floor on future lending rates are natural holders of the call option.

Exhibit 1.2   Characteristics of an interest rate option

Option on 3-month Eurodollar futures	
Exchanges	CME(IMM), LIFFE
Underlying asset	Futures on 3-month Eurodollar deposit
Maturity months	March, June, September, December
Exercise prices	Multiples of 25 basis points
Contract size	US$1,000,000 face value futures
Option style	American puts and calls
Value per basis point	US$25 = US$1,000,000 × 0.0001 × (90/360)

Single OTC puts and calls

A standard OTC interest rate option offers borrower and lender protection similar to a traded option. It differs in that more currencies, exercise prices, tenors and maturity dates are available. It also differs in that the exercise price quoted is usually expressed as an annualised interest rate rather than a futures price index. Finally, OTC options tend to be European-style, exercisable at only their maturity date, rather than American, exercisable at any time during their life.

A slight source of potential confusion is the nomenclature used to differentiate between calls and puts. In the OTC market the equivalent of a call on a futures contract is called a lender's option (LO), as it protects against falls in the interest rate. Similarly, the equivalent of a traded put on interest rate futures is called a borrower's option (BO), as it protects the holder against a rise in interest rates.

Interest rate option payoffs

The payoffs to the holder of interest rate options can be summarised by standard option payoff tables. An example of the gross payoffs to a traded put and an equivalent borrower's option is given in Exhibit 1.3A. The net payoffs depend upon the price paid for the option and are discussed in 'Pricing models'.

Exhibit 1.3   Payoffs to interest rate options at maturity

Gross payoffs at maturity
Option on 3-month Eurodollars
Exercise price: 9% (equivalent to 91 on futures)
US$1,000,000 face value

A Put on futures (borrowers option)						
Libor	4.0	6.0	8.0	10.0	12.0	14.0
Futures price	96.0	94.0	92.0	90.0	88.0	86.0
Payoff (annual rate equivalent)	0.0	0.0	0.0	1.0	3.0	5.0
Payoff (US$1,000's)[a]	0.0	0.0	0.0	2.5	7.5	12.5

B Call on futures (lenders option)						
Libor	4.0	6.0	8.0	10.0	12.0	14.0
Futures price	96.0	94.0	92.0	90.0	88.0	86.0
Payoff (annual rate equivalent)	5.0	3.0	1.0	0.0	0.0	0.0
Payoff (US$1,000's)[a]	12.5	7.5	2.5	0.0	0.0	0.0

[a] Payoff in basis points × US$25 per basis point.

180

A put on an interest rate futures contract (a borrowers option) is equivalent to a call option on the interest rate. It is the same as a single component of the strip of options sold as a cap. Similarly, a call on the futures contract (lenders option) is a put on the interest rate. It is the same as a single component of the strip of options sold as a floor.

Non-standard and hybrid contracts

Only a limited range of contracts is available in the exchange-traded markets. Those seeking non-standard contracts in terms of currency, maturity, tenor, strike price, or underlying interest rate can solicit quotes from individual banks. In doing so, it is important to realise that this 'tailoring' does not come free. It may sometimes be the case that accepting a slight risk in terms of mismatching the cover using a traded market is beneficial in avoiding the potentially significant costs of customisation.

As well as customisation of individual puts and calls, some banks offer contracts which amount to portfolios of puts and calls. A range forward contract, for instance, offers a floating rate borrower a call option on the floating rate (borrowers option) in exchange for a put option on the floating rate (lenders option). The strike prices on the two options are set so that the value of the lenders option received by the bank is slightly greater than the value of the borrowers option received by the borrower. No payment is, therefore, necessary upon initiation of this contract.

Mechanics and key characteristics

Quotation conventions

The two dominant forms of interest rate option are exchange-traded options on interest rate futures and OTC borrower options and lender options. Futures on money market instruments are quoted as a price index equal to 100 minus the annualised interest rate expressed as a percentage. Option exercise prices are expressed in terms of this index price. Option prices are also expressed in terms of annualised percentage equivalents. To compute the amount of money paid for the option and the amount paid on settlement, the price or value of the option in basis points must be multiplied by the value of 1 basis point. Exhibit 1.4 summarises the differences between OTC and exchange-traded interest rate options.

Exhibit 1.4   Characteristics of exchange-traded and OTC options

	Exchange traded	Standard OTC
Name	Call	Lenders option (LO)
Name	Put	Borrowers option (BO)
Maturity	Specified date	Specified period
Type	American	European
Underlying asset	Interest rate futures	Interest rate
Exercise price quote	100-interest rate	Interest rate
Option quote	Annualised percentage	Annualised percentage

OTC contracts are based upon annualised interest rates rather than price indices. Exercise prices are expressed as annual percentage interest rates. Option prices are expressed also in terms of annualised percentage equivalents. As with traded interest rate options, the dollar price of the option is equal to its price in basis points multiplied by the value of 1 basis point.

Settlement

Upon exercise, traded calls on interest rate futures allow the holder to exchange the exercise price in cash for the futures price. Traded puts allow the exchange of the futures price for the option exercise price. Since the options are American, exercise can take place at any time during the option life.

By contrast, OTC interest rate options tend to be European. At the maturity date of the borrowers option, the writer of the option pays to the buyer the difference between the strike rate and the market reference rate, if the market reference rate is higher. Upon maturity of a lenders option, the writer pays to the buyer the difference between the strike rate and the market reference rate if the latter is lower.

Settlement amounts on both types of option are converted to dollar amounts by multiplying the exercise value in basis points by the value of 1 basis point. If the OTC option is based on an add-on rate such as Libor, the settlement amount is discounted over the tenor of the underlying rate.

Pricing

Parameters affecting interest rate option prices

The price of any interest rate option depends upon the parameters listed in Exhibit 1.5. Most of these are familiar to users of any option market: maturity, underlying asset price, strike price, interest rate and volatility. Those familiar with equity options markets may be slightly surprised to see that the underlying asset used is a futures or forward contract. Interest rates are not in and of themselves assets, so the 'asset' underlying the option has to be defined as a futures or forward contract on the rate.

Exhibit 1.5 Parameters affecting interest rate option values

```
1   Maturity of option contract
2   Tenor of rate
3   Futures price or FRA rate for maturity and tenor equivalent to the option
4   Strike price
5   Money rate for maturity equal to maturity of option
6   Forecast volatility of underlying interest rate over life of option
7   Other factors specific to particular models: yield curve information and assumptions about interest rate
    behaviour
```

All the inputs other than volatility required for pricing an option are easily obtained. Volatility must be forecast or implied from existing option prices, and this procedure is described in 'Time value and volatility' below. One must, however, be cautious in valuing interest rate options even with a good volatility forecast, because there are several different models in use. These are described in 'Pricing models' below.

The structure of prices

Exhibit 1.6 shows the prices for Eurodollar puts and calls on LIFFE at close of trading on 22 May 1987. As usual, the value of calls increases and the value of puts decreases as the strike price is lowered. Unlike other options markets, however, the value of options with a fixed strike price does not necessarily increase as the maturity lengthens. For instance, the September call at a strike price of 92 is worth less than the June call at 92. This reflects the upward sloping yield curve, as represented by the June futures price of 92.45 and the September futures price of 91.75. The June call at 92 is actually in the money by 45 basis points, whereas the September call is out of money by 25 basis points.

Exhibit 1.6   LIFFE Eurodollar options prices

Futures prices: June, 92.45; September, 91.75

Calls

Strike price	June price	Intrinsic value	Time value	September price	Intrinsic value	Time value
91.50	0.95	0.95	0.00	0.53	0.25	0.28
91.75	0.71	0.70	0.01	0.37	0.00	0.37
92.00	0.48	0.45	0.03	0.24	0.00	0.24
92.25	0.26	0.20	0.06	0.15	0.00	0.15
92.50	0.08	0.00	0.08	0.09	0.00	0.09
92.75	0.02	0.00	0.02	0.05	0.00	0.05
93.00	0.01	0.00	0.01	0.02	0.00	0.02

Puts

Strike price	June price	Intrinsic value	Time value	September price	Intrinsic value	Time value
91.50	0.00	0.00	0.00	0.28	0.00	0.28
91.75	0.01	0.00	0.01	0.37	0.00	0.37
92.00	0.03	0.00	0.03	0.49	0.25	0.24
92.25	0.06	0.00	0.06	0.65	0.50	0.15
92.50	0.13	0.05	0.08	0.84	0.75	0.09
92.75	0.32	0.30	0.02	1.05	1.00	0.05
93.00	0.56	0.55	0.01	1.27	1.25	0.02

Insight into the pricing structure can be obtained by splitting the option values into the immediate exercise (intrinsic) value and the remainder, which is the time value. The June call at 92 has 45 points of intrinsic value, whereas the September call has zero intrinsic value. The time value of the June call at 92 is very small, reflecting its short maturity and the fact that it is already quite a long way in the money. The higher time value for the September call reflects its longer maturity and the fact that it is closer to the money.

Put/call parity

The September futures price is 91.75. The holder of a futures contract receives or pays an amount equal to the futures price at maturity minus 91.75. An equivalent position can be constructed from options. The holder of a call at 91.75 who also writes a put has exactly the same net position as the holder of the futures contract. As the value of the futures contract is zero, this put and call must sell for equal prices. This is illustrated in Exhibit 1.7A.

For puts and calls with equal strike prices that are not equal to the market futures price, a position which is long a call and short a put is equivalent to a futures contract at an off-market rate; this is shown in Exhibit 1.7B. The put/call parity relation is then:

$$\text{Call price} - \text{Put price} = \text{Futures price} - \text{Strike price}$$

Exhibit 1.7 Put/call/futures parity

A September, 91.75 options					
Rate at maturity	4.00	6.00	8.00	10.00	12.00
Futures price	96.00	94.00	92.00	90.00	88.00
Call payoff	4.25	2.25	0.25	0.00	0.00
Put payoff	0.00	0.00	0.00	1.75	3.75
Call minus put payoff	4.25	2.25	0.25	−1.75	−3.75
Futures payoff	4.25	2.25	0.25	−1.75	−3.75

Parity: Call price − Put price = 0

B September, 92.25 options					
Rate at maturity	4.00	6.00	8.00	10.00	12.00
Futures price	96.00	94.00	92.00	90.00	88.00
Call payoff	3.75	1.75	0.00	0.00	0.00
Put payoff	0.00	0.00	0.25	2.25	4.25
Call minus put payoff	3.75	1.75	−0.25	−2.25	−4.25
Futures payoff	4.25	2.25	0.25	−1.75	−3.75

Parity: Call price − Put price = Futures price − Strike price

In this case, for the September options with strike prices of 92.25, the relationship is:

$$0.15 - 0.65 = 91.75 - 92.25$$

The value of the position which is long a call and short a put is equal to the value of a futures contract at an off-market price equal to the strike price on the two options.

These relationships are of the form that hold for LIFFE options because of the margining procedure for options on that exchange. For exchange where payment for the option is made in cash at contract initiation, the difference between the futures price and the strike price must be valued presently at the riskless interest rate.

Time value and volatility

Determining the intrinsic value of interest rate options and using put/call parity to price puts off calls or vice versa is simple. To price the time value of an option, however, requires assumptions about the way that interest rates behave and a forecast of how volatile they will be over the life of the option.

The usual assumptions about interest rate behaviour made in the standard models used to price interest rate options are shown in Exhibit 1.8A. Given these assumptions, the price of a particular interest rate option corresponds to a particular forecast of interest rate volatility over the option's life.

Exhibit 1.9 shows Eurodollar call prices on 20 September 1985. Corresponding to each call price is an implied volatility. This is the volatility forecast that would make the price 'fair' on the basis of the standard model described in 'Pricing models' below.

The implied volatility of the 89.50 strike price option is higher than the others. This is not particularly anomalous, as the time value of this option is only 0.02. The estimate of implied volatility is, therefore, very crude because the time value could only be one point higher or lower, which would give implied volatilities 50% higher or lower. (This is also true for the 90.00 option.)

Exhibit 1.8   Assumptions about interest rates used in interest rate option models

A   *Standard models*
1   Successive daily changes in interest rates are independent
2   The log of the ratio of successive daily rates is normally distributed with a constant volatility
3   The drift in interest rates is independent of the level of interest rates

B   *Alternative models*
1   The drift in interest rates depends on their level
2   The volatility of interest rates depends on their level
3   There is more than one random factor generating yield curve changes

Exhibit 1.9   Implied volatilities, 20 September 1985

December maturity calls on Eurodollar futures
Futures price for December: 91.53

Strike price	Call price	Implied volatility (%)	Change from 16 August (%)
89.50	2.05	31.8	+5.9
90.00	1.55	25.3	+1.9
90.50	1.08	21.8	−0.9
91.00	0.66	20.2	−2.7
91.50	0.35	20.6	−2.4
92.00	0.14	20.3	−3.1
92.50	0.04	20.1	−2.9
93.00	0.01	21.2	−2.7

The implied volatilities of the other options are very similar. This does not mean, however, that they are good forecasts of how volatile interest rates will actually be. The last column of Exhibit 1.9 shows the changes in implied volatilities over the previous month. Significant revisions have occurred, reflecting the decreased volatility of interest rates over this period.

Thus, the purchaser or writer of an interest rate option pays or receives a price that reflects a particular volatility. Because this implied volatility can be very different from the actual outcome, users of options must carefully consider whether the volatility forecast that is implicit in the price they are paying or receiving is reasonable.

Pricing models

The most widely used pricing model for interest rate options is based upon the assumptions about interest rate behaviour summarised in Exhibit 1.8A. This model is based upon the assumption that the logarithm of the interest rate performs a random walk. Thus the possible range of interest rates at the maturity date of the option is completely described by the expected rate at that time, the volatility of the rate, and the maturity of the option. The way that this model operates is by pricing the option as if the expected rate at the maturity date of the option is equal to the forward rate agreement (FRA) implicit in the futures contract. The expected payoff to the option is then discounted at a money market rate to give the value of the option.

There is still controversy over whether this is the correct procedure to value interest rate options.

A variety of more complex pricing models exist. These differ from the standard model in that they use more complicated assumptions about the random ways that interest rates can behave. The most sophisticated of these models allow for several sources of variation in interest rates, so that the yield curve can change shape. They also allow for interest rate trends and volatilities to depend upon the current structure of the yield curve. It is still an open question as to whether this added sophistication improves interest rate option pricing models. (The added complexity is definitely necessary, however, for pricing caps and floors.)

Uses and applications

Capping liability rates

If a borrower wishes to protect future borrowings against a possible rise in short-term interest rates, he has five alternatives. These are:

1 Borrow now and lend the proceeds until needed.
2 Buy an FRA.
3 Sell interest rate futures.
4 Buy a traded Eurodollar put.
5 Buy an OTC borrowers option.

The payoffs to the futures hedge and the traded option hedge are shown in Exhibit 1.10. The resulting net borrowing costs are also shown.

Exhibit 1.10   Payoffs to an interest rate option hedge

Situation	Rates
May 1987	Spot 3-month: Libor: $7\frac{5}{8}$
Intend to borrow US$1m in September 1987	September 3-month Eurodollar futures: 91.72
Will borrow at Libor flat	September 91.75 put on futures: 0.41

Alternatives
Unhedged
Futures hedge
Option hedge (traded put)

Rates in September					
3-month Eurodollar rate	4.00	6.00	8.00	10.00	12.00
Futures price	96.00	94.00	92.00	90.00	88.00

Settlement cash flows (US$)					
Sell 1 futures	−10,700	−5,700	−700	+4,300	+9,300
Buy 1 put (gross)	0	0	0	+4,375	+9,375
Buy 1 put (net)	−1,025	−1,025	−1,025	+3,350	+8,350

Net borrowing rate (%)					
Unhedged	4.00	6.00	8.00	10.00	12.00
Futures hedge	8.28	8.28	8.28	8.28	8.28
Option hedge	4.41	6.41	8.41	8.66	8.66

The futures hedge locks in a specific borrowing rate as long as the maturity and characteristics of the futures contract are matched to the borrowing needs. The option hedge locks in a maximum borrowing cost at a level higher than the futures hedge. As a result, the option hedger is able to keep the potential gain resulting from a fall in rates. Should the borrower have a continuing money-market borrowing programme, a sequence of option maturities can be used to cap a sequence of future borrowings. A natural extension of this strategy is the purchase of a single cap agreement.

Insuring asset returns

Investors holding variable rate instruments or rolling over money-market instruments can place a floor on the rates earned. Either a single call option on interest rate futures, or a sequence of such options can be used. Alternatively, an OTC lenders option or a strip of such options can be used if the appropriate traded contract is not available.

As with the liability hedging example, the option hedge for the investor gives up part of the rate that could be locked in using an FRA or futures hedge. In exchange the investor using the option hedge receives compensation in the form of increased returns should rates rise.

Trading volatility

The value of an interest rate option is very sensitive to the forecast volatility of interest rates over the option's life. The most sensitive options are those that are at the money in that they have strike prices close to the corresponding futures price. There are various ways to use these options to speculate that actual volatility will be different to that implied by the option prices.

The most simple speculation on volatility is a straddle that involves buying a put and a call with equal strike prices. Usually these options will be roughly at the money. This position gains whenever the interest rate at the maturity date of the options is further away from the strike rate than the sum of the prices of the two options. The straddle position is a speculation that, at some time before the maturity of the two options, the underlying interest rate will move significantly one way or the other. Other types of spread and strangle positions can be used to speculate on beliefs of this type.

A more complex speculation on volatility is given by the delta hedge strategy. A market participant who believes that the volatility forecast currently being used by the market to price the options is too high can take advantage of this belief through the delta strategy. This involves selling interest rate options and hedging the resulting exposure to the direction of interest rate moves. In this case, it would involve simultaneously selling the option and taking an offsetting position in futures with a face value equal to the hedge ratio of the option times the option face value. This hedge ratio is computed using an option pricing model, and is commonly referred to as the 'delta' of the option. This position is then rebalanced over the option's life.

Advantages and disadvantages

As 'Uses and applications' explained, interest rate options can be used to cap liability rates and to put a floor on asset returns. An example of a liability hedge is given in Exhibit 1.10. The interest cost structure resulting from the option hedge has the following features:

1   The maximum interest cost is limited.
2   If rates rise, the option hedge will perform worse than the futures hedge and better than not hedging.
3   If rates fall, the option hedge will perform better than the futures hedge and worse than not hedging.
4   If the borrowing for which cover is taken does not materialise, then the option loss is limited to the premium paid, where the futures loss is 'unlimited'.

These features of hedging with options suggest that the natural buyers of interest rate options are not those with strong views on the direction of interest rates. Such investors or borrowers should use forward and futures markets directly rather than option markets.

Option markets should, therefore, be used for hedging by those without a strong view on the direction of rates. This is very similar to the statement that options should be used for hedging by those who think that volatility will be high. A second prerequisite is, however, that they, for some reason, do not wish to use the futures or forward market to hedge. This could be the case because the hedger wishes to preserve some of the upside potential or because the forward/futures hedge would not work because the size of the risk to be covered is not known with certainty.

Thus those that should hedge with interest rate options are those who:

1   do not have a strongly held view on the direction of rates,
2   think rates will be volatile, *and*
3   wish to retain some upside potential, *or*
4   do not know with certainty the size of the risk to be hedged.

In addition, the natural speculators in interest rate options are those who have a strong view on volatility.

Summary

Interest rate options offer an opportunity to hedge interest rate risk and to speculate on interest rate volatility. As hedging instruments, they are particularly attractive for those with no strongly held view on the direction of rates and a concern that rates may be volatile. They are particularly appropriate hedges when the size of the risk to be covered is uncertain.

The traded interest rate option markets offer options on interest rate futures. The OTC markets offer tailored transactions on a variety of underlying rates.

The price paid reflects a particular forecast of the future volatility of rates. Standard interest rate option models enable the user to price the options using their own volatility forecast or to impute market expectations of volatility from option prices. Actual volatilities and market implied volatilities fluctuate considerably over time, offering possibilities for speculation by those with strongly held views on future interest rate volatility.

2 Accounting treatment: United States

Benjamin S. Neuhausen

Introduction

The accounting for interest rate options in the US is covered in AICPA Issues Paper 86–2, *Accounting for options*. Although the AICPA accounting issues paper is not authoritative and binding like an FASB Statement, it represents the best guidance available on accounting for options. The accounting called for in the AICPA accounting issues paper is based on the requirements in FASB Statement No. 80, *Accounting for futures contracts*, regarding accounting for futures (see Part III, Chapter 2), although it differs in some respects. The accounting described in this chapter generally conforms to the accounting called for in the AICPA accounting issues paper. In those areas in which other accounting practices might be acceptable, the chapter so notes.

As noted in Part II, Chapter 1, 'Accounting framework: United States', the accounting for options, along with other interest rate protection products, is the subject of a major FASB project and could change.

Overall basis of accounting

Transactions in options involve the payment of a premium for purchased options and the receipt of a premium for written options. For purchased options, the premium is recorded as an asset. For written options, the premium is reflected as a liability. Consistent with the accounting treatment for futures contracts, the gross amount of the item that may be deliverable under the option should not be reported in the balance sheet.

Generally, realised and unrealised gains and losses resulting from a change in the market value of options should be recognised currently in the income statement. This basis of accounting is commonly referred to as mark-to-market accounting. Mark-to-market accounting should be used for options that:

- are entered into for speculation;
- hedge existing or anticipated asset or liability positions that are or will be carried at market value (however, a form of hedge accounting may be used for these options); or
- do not meet the criteria for hedge accounting, which are discussed below.

The AICPA accounting issues paper recommends mark-to-market accounting for all options that do not qualify for hedge accounting. As an alternative to mark-to-market accounting, purchased options may be stated at the lower-of-cost-or-market and written options at the higher of proceeds received or market. Adjustments caused by changes in market should be included in net income.

In deciding which alternative to use, an entity should consider its accounting policies for other related items. For example, an entity that accounts for other trading positions at market should account for options positions at market. As a further example, a commodity dealer that carries its inventory at the lower-of-cost-or-market may account for options on commodities that do not qualify for hedge accounting at the lower-of-cost-or-market.

The use of over the counter options does not allow market values to be easily determined by quoted market prices. Two solutions to this problem are available. First, the option holder can use a formula valuation, such as the Black–Scholes option pricing model. Alternatively, the holder can go back to the original writer of the option and ask for a current value quotation. The market calculation can then be performed on the basis of this price.

Accounting treatment for hedges

Certain options that are hedges are accounted for differently. Options contracts may be hedges of:

- existing assets, liabilities, or firm, fixed price commitments, or
- probable future transactions that an entity expects but may not be legally obligated to enter into (commonly referred to as 'anticipatory hedges').

Hedge accounting treatment applies only if the criteria discussed below for purchased and written options are met.

Hedge accounting is based on a concept of symmetry between the accounting for the options and the assets, liabilities or transactions being hedged. As explained in more detail later, gains or losses on options entered into as hedges generally are deferred, rather than recognised currently in income. However, if unrealised changes in the market price of a hedged item are included in income or a separate component of stockholders' equity, changes in the market value of the options are recognised as they occur in income or in the separate component of stockholder's equity.

Hedge accounting requires designating specific assets or liabilities as being hedged to determine the appropriate time to recognise deferred gains and losses on options and/or to determine the amortisation period for those gains and losses. In addition, hedge accounting is appropriate if the entity can designate groups of like items (e.g. pools of loans that have similar terms) as being hedged.

Criteria for hedges of existing assets, liabilities or firm commitments

Purchased options

Purchased options qualify as hedges of existing assets, liabilities or firm commitments if the following criteria are met:

- The item to be hedged is exposed to price or interest rate risk.
- The options position reduces the price or interest rate exposure.
- The options position is designated as a hedge.

Assessing whether the hedged item is exposed to price risk desirably should be accomplished using an 'enterprise' approach; alternatively, it may be made on an individual transaction approach. In applying the enterprise approach, an entity's other assets, liabilities and commitments need to be considered to determine whether they already offset or reduce the risk exposure. For example, a company that owns fixed interest rate financial instruments would not be exposed to interest rate risk if the instruments are funded by fixed interest rate debt of similar maturity. Companies that conduct their risk management on a decentralised basis can satisfy this criterion if the hedged item exposes the particular business unit that enters into the option to price risk. In determining if this condition is met under an individual transaction approach, it is not necessary to consider whether other positions already offset or reduce the exposure to risk.

The options position reduces price risk only when high correlation is probable between changes in (1) the fair value of the hedged assets, liabilities or firm commitments and (2) the market value of the item underlying the options. When determining the probability of high correlation, the hedger should consider the correlation during relevant past periods and also the correlation that could be expected at higher or lower price levels. The option may be for an item different from the item to be hedged (a *'cross hedge'*) if there is a clear economic relationship between their prices and high correlation is probable.

Written options

Under the AICPA accounting issues paper, written options qualify as hedges if the three criteria specified for purchased options are satisfied. However, the paper concludes that, when hedge accounting is applied to a written option, only a net gain on the option should be deferred. A net loss should be reported in income as incurred.

Some believe that it also should be acceptable to account for a written option as a hedge if the three criteria specified for purchased options are satisfied *and* the option is so deep in the money that it is reasonably assured that the option will remain in the money throughout its term.

This last condition would be met, for example, when: (1) a call option with a one-year exercise period is written on a bond with a US$90 strike price, when the market value of the bond is US$100 (i.e. the option is US$10 in the money); (2) over recent one-year periods the bond's market value has not changed by more than US$10; and (3) the volatility of the bond's market value is not expected to change significantly in the future.

Such a written option will behave as if it were a futures contract; therefore, it would be reasonable to apply hedge accounting (with deferral of either gains or losses) the same as for futures contracts. Because the premiums on deep in the money options are relatively expensive, the market for them often is thin. This makes it unlikely that many enterprises would use written deep in the money options to hedge.

Criteria for anticipatory hedges

Options qualify as hedges of anticipated transactions if the criteria for hedges of existing assets, liabilities or firm commitments and both of the following additional conditions are met:

- The significant characteristics and expected terms of the anticipated transaction are identified, including its expected date, the cash item involved, the quantity and the instrument's expected maturity.
- It is probable that the anticipated transaction will occur.

Considerations in assessing the likelihood that a transaction will occur include: the frequency of similar transactions in the past; the ability of the enterprise to carry out the transaction; the length of time to the anticipated transaction date; the extent of loss or disruption of operations that could result if the transaction does not occur; and the likelihood that transactions with substantially different characteristics might be used to achieve the same business purpose (e.g. an enterprise that intends to raise cash may have several ways of doing so, ranging from short-term bank loans to common stock offerings). Sometimes an entity may have a choice among similar transactions, for example, a financial institution that plans to issue short-term obligations at a particular future date may have the choice of issuing various types of short-term obligations in domestic or foreign markets. In such cases, options qualify as a hedge if all hedge criteria are met regardless of which transaction will be undertaken.

An option that hedges a transaction whose occurrence is possible but not probable does not qualify for hedge accounting. For example, if an entity buys a call option on a commodity that it will require if it is awarded a contract on which it had bid, the option does not qualify for hedge accounting unless it is probable that the entity will be awarded the contract.

Accounting for time and intrinsic value

Purchased options

An option premium is composed of two distinct parts. The time value of a purchased option might be considered equivalent to an insurance premium, representing the cost to the purchaser of obtaining protection against the risk of loss over the option's exercise period. Such cost should generally be charged to income over the period the option provides protection from loss and, therefore, should be treated separately from the intrinsic value, if any.

The time and intrinsic values of a purchased option that qualifies for hedge accounting should be split if the option hedges an asset, liability or firm commitment carried or to be carried at other than market. The time value should be amortised and recognised as an expense over the term of the option. An alternative treatment of the time value of an option that hedges a firm commitment is discussed below. Hedge accounting should be applied to changes in the intrinsic value, as explained in more detail later.

The same accounting should be applied to a purchased option that qualifies for hedge accounting and hedges assets reported at fair value if changes in the carrying amount of those assets are reported in a separate component of shareholders' equity.

The time and intrinsic values of a purchased option *may* be split if:

- the option qualifies for hedge accounting and hedges an asset, liability, or firm commitment carried or to be carried at market, and
- gains and losses on the hedged item are included in income as they arise.

If the time and intrinsic values are split, the time value should be amortised and recognised as an expense over the term of the option and changes in the intrinsic value should be included in income as they occur. If the time and intrinsic values are not split, changes in the entire value of the option should be included in income as they occur.

As discussed earlier, an option that hedges a firm commitment or an anticipated transaction may qualify for hedge accounting. The portion of the time value of such an option that relates to the period before the related transaction occurs may be either included in the measurement of the transaction or amortised to expense over that period.

When a purchased option that qualifies for hedge accounting is closed out, the difference between the unamortised balance of the time value and the time value received on closing out the option should be treated in the same manner as was the time value prior to the close out. If the time value was being amortised to income, the difference should be recognised in income. If the time value was being deferred (i.e. in the case of a hedge of a firm commitment or anticipated transaction), the difference similarly should be deferred.

Written options

The time and intrinsic values of a written option that qualifies for hedge accounting should *not* be split. Hedge accounting should be applied to changes in the entire value of the option.

Discussion of hedge accounting

Gains and losses on options that meet the criteria described above are deferred as an adjustment to the carrying amount of the hedged item provided it is carried at other than market. If options hedge existing assets or liabilities carried at other than market, at each reporting date the deferred gains or losses are classified as an adjustment of the carrying amount of the hedged assets or liabilities. If the options hedge firm, fixed price commitments, the deferred gains or losses are included in the measurement of the transactions that satisfy the commitments. Similary, if options hedge anticipated transactions, the deferred gains or losses are included in the measurement of the transactions when they occur.

The deferred gains or losses on options are applied to adjust the carrying amount of an existing asset or liability carried at other than market, or will be applied to adjust the carrying amount of a future asset or liability to be carried at other than market. Those adjustments become an integral part of the carrying amount of the asset or liability and are accounted for as such.

Deferred gains or losses that adjust the carrying amounts of interest-bearing assets and liabilities are like discounts or premiums and are amortised to interest income or expense over the expected remaining lives of the instruments. For hedges of firm commitments and anticipated transactions for interest-bearing financial instruments, the amortisation starts when the anticipated transaction is entered into. For hedges of existing interest-bearing financial assets and liabilities, amortisation should start no later than the date that a particular option is closed out. If deferred gains or losses become part of the carrying amount of an asset carried at the lower-of-cost-or-market, they become part of cost in the cost versus market comparison.

A treatment different from that described above applies to options that qualify for hedge accounting and hedge assets reported at fair value, if changes in the carrying amounts of these assets are reported in a separate component of shareholders' equity. In these cases, the changes in the intrinsic value should be included in the separate component of shareholders' equity and should remain therein (even after the option is closed out or expires) until the sale or disposition of the assets. The time value, however, should be charged to income.

An entity should regularly assess the results of an option designated as a hedge to determine whether high correlation is being achieved between the market value of the item underlying the option and the market value of the item being hedged. If that assessment indicates high correlation has not occurred, the enterprise should cease to account for the option as a hedge and should recognise a gain or loss to the extent the changes in the option's intrinsic value (or, in the case of a written option, its entire value) have not been offset by the effects of price or interest rate changes on the hedged item since inception of the hedge. The remaining deferred gain or loss should continue to be treated as an adjustment of the carrying amount of the hedged item.

The accounting for an option that hedges a firm commitment to acquire assets or issue liabilities should be consistent with the enterprise's method of accounting for those types of assets or liabilities. For example, a loss should be recognised for an option that hedges a firm commitment to purchase securities to the extent that evidence indicates that the amount will not be recoverable.

If an option that has been accounted for as a hedge is closed before the transaction date of the related commitment, the accumulated deferred change in value (intrinsic for purchased option, entire for written option) of the option should continue to be carried forward and included in the measurement of the related transaction subject to the existence of continuing high correlation through the date of the close-out. The same accounting should be applied to any amortisation of time value that had been deferred.

Some entities (e.g. mortgage bankers) may use options to hedge a net exposure comprising inventory held for sale and firm commitments to purchase and sell essentially similar assets. If associating individual options with the assets on hand or specific commitments is impractical because of the volume and frequency of transactions, reasonable allocations of the results of options between assets or commitments on hand at the end of a reporting period and assets sold during the period may be used. The method of allocation should be consistent from period to period.

The accounting for an option that hedges an anticipated acquisition of assets or an anticipated issuance of liabilities should be consistent with the entity's method of accounting for those types of assets or liabilities. If an entity hedges an anticipated transaction and subsequently concludes that the amount of the transaction is likely to be less than originally expected, a *pro rata* portion of the option results that would otherwise be included in the measurement of a subsequent transaction should be recognised as a gain or loss. If the transaction is abandoned, all of the option results should be recognised as a gain or loss.

If the option is closed before the date of the anticipated transaction, the accumulated deferred change in value (intrinsic for purchased option, entire for written option) of the option (and any amortisation of the time value that had been deferred) should continue to be carried forward and included in the measurement of the related transaction. The deferral is subject to the existence of continuing high correlation through the date of the close-out.

Other matters

An entity can create a *'synthetic futures'* contract by buying a put and writing a call at the same strike price with the same expiration date (equivalent to a short position in a futures contract) or by buying a call and writing a put at the same strike price with the same expiration date (equivalent to a long position in a futures contract). This type of synthetic futures contract should be accounted for in accordance with Statement No. 80 (see Part III, Chapter 2).

When an entity is concerned with the risk of a limited adverse price change, it can use a combination of purchased and written options with the same expiration dates but different strike prices. For example, a bank buys a bond for 102 on 1 February 19XX, and is concerned about a modest short-term increase in interest rates. Therefore, the bank buys a put with a strike price of 102 and sells a put with a strike price of 95. The bank pays US$3 for the 102 and receives US$1 for the 95 put. Therefore, the bank is protected to the extent that the price of the bond does not decline by more than US$7 and it has decreased the cost of its hedge.

If the premium paid for the purchased option is greater than the premium received for the written option, the 'option spread' should be accounted for as a hedge if the *purchased* option qualifies for hedge accounting. Specifically:

- The excess of the time value paid over the time value received should be accounted for as the time value of a purchased option.
- Hedge accounting should be applied to changes in the excess of the intrinsic value of the purchased option over the intrinsic value of the written option.

If the premium received from the written option is greater than the premium paid for the purchased option, the spread should be accounted for as a hedge if the *written* option qualifies for hedge accounting.

Disclosure

Although the disclosure of options transactions is not addressed in the AICPA accounting issues paper, an entity should disclose (1) the nature of the items that are hedged with options and (2) the method of accounting for options (including a description of the events that result in recognising the changes in an option's value in income).

3 Accounting treatment: United Kingdom

Mark Davis

Overall basis of accounting

To date, no authoritative pronouncements have been issued in the UK concerning accounting for options, nor is there any equivalent of the US AICPA Issues Paper 86–2. Application of the basic principles outlined in Part II, Chapter 2, is somewhat more complex for options than for some other types of interest rates instruments. Currently, a wide variety of accounting policies are adopted in the UK, some of which might be considered unacceptable, were the options material in the context of the company's financial statements.

Hedging criteria

To qualify as a hedge, an option must satisfy the criteria discussed in Part II, Chapter 2:

- The transaction being hedged must expose the company to interest rate risk.
- The option must be designated as a hedge.
- The option must be effective as a hedge.
- If the option is a hedge against an anticipated transaction, it must be probable that the transaction will occur.

Options are often preferred to futures as hedges when there is doubt if a particular anticipated transaction will actually occur. Generally, this doubt does not preclude the option from being treated as a hedge, providing that the anticipated transaction is clearly identified at the outset. The problem in determining whether an option meets the criteria, generally arises when considering whether the option is effective. Consideration must be given to the degree of correlation between the effect of interest rate movements on the hedged item and their effect on the instrument underlying the option. It may be argued that consideration should also be given to whether there is sufficient correlation between changes in the value of the underlying instruments and changes in the value of the option.

Accounting for hedges

Purchased options

The value of an option or the premium paid can be split into two elements, intrinsic value and time value. The time value inherent in an option will fluctuate over the option period and reflect expectations about volatility of interest rates. Consequently, an option may change in value, even where there is no change in the fair value of the item being hedged. Prudence suggests that the time value will also decline as the option approaches its expiry date. Therefore, even if there is no change in interest rates, the company will suffer a loss equivalent to the time value inherent in the option premium. The time value should therefore be treated as the cost of hedging and either written off immediately or amortised over the period of the option, rather than the interest period being hedged. Only changes in the intrinsic value should be matched with the accounting treatment of the item being hedged. It may be argued that the matching concept suggests that the whole of the premium is deferred. In practice treating the whole of the premium as if it were intrinsic value may not give a materially different result and thus many companies adopt such an approach.

Accounting for the intrinsic value of a purchased option which qualifies as a hedge, is broadly similar to the treatment adopted for futures. If hedging an anticipated transaction or a borrowing, changes in the intrinsic value of the option will be ignored prior to the interest period being hedged. Any premium or margin payments give rise to balance sheet entries only. Any profit or loss arising on exercise of the option is deferred and amortised over the interest period hedged. If the item hedged is an asset, any provision for diminution in value of the asset should reflect changes in the intrinsic value of the option. If the asset is marked to market, then the option should be marked to market.

Written options

As indicated in the previous chapter on US accounting, there is some debate as to whether written options should qualify as a hedge, given that there may be little correlation between changes in the value of the option and the effect of changing interest rates on the item being hedged. Currently, in the UK, it is generally considered that written options may qualify as hedges. Prudence would suggest that the time and intrinsic elements of any option premium received should not be split. The whole of the premium should be deferred and amortised over the interest period being hedged.

In the absence of any equivalent to the AICPA Issues Paper, it appears that it is acceptable in the UK to defer losses on written options which qualify as hedges, even where these exceed the premium receivable.

In summary, where a written option qualifies as a hedge, the accounting treatment should be symmetrical with that of the item being hedged. If the option hedges a liability, any premium or margin payment received is credited to a balance sheet account. On expiry or exercise, any profit or loss arising on the option is deferred and amortised to the P&L account over the interest period being hedged. If a hedged asset is held at the lower-of-cost-and-market, any provision against the asset value should be arrived at after taking into account any profit arising on changes in the market value of the option. If a bank accounts for the hedged item at market value, then the option should be marked to market.

Option trading

A variety of option strategies can be adopted, involving the simultaneous purchase and sale of a number of options, each strategy having a different profit and loss profile and a different degree of risk. The extent to which a loss on one option will be offset by a profit on another in such circumstances, largely depends on the extent of interest rate movements. Similarly, the extent to which a delta neutral hedge is effective will depend on its gamma and the extent of interest rate changes. If a company is position trading or arbitraging in options it would seem more appropriate to treat all the instruments involved as speculative transactions.

Accounting for speculative transactions

If an option is speculative, it should be recorded at market value. Time and intrinsic value should not be split. Any profit or loss arising on revaluation should be credited to the P&L account (though as discussed in Part II, Chapter 2, corporates are restricted to recognising only realised profits). The corresponding balance sheet entry is normally netted against the balance on any margin accounts.

When valuing over the counter (OTC) options, a corporate will generally have to get a quote from one or more banks. In order to value their own OTC options, banks will generally have to use an option pricing model based on the Black–Scholes or Leland formulae.

Disclosure

The accounting policy adopted for options should be stated. As discussed in Part II, Chapter 2, some indication of the nature and extent of a corporate's outstanding options may be necessary, particularly if the company has written options on a speculative basis. Banks currently give little indication of the extent of their involvement with options. The best practice would be to indicate both the nature of the bank's involvement in options and the amount of options outstanding.

4 Documentation of interest rate options

Patrick Daniels and David J. Gilberg

United Kingdom

Apart from the form of the standard options contract, the documentation to cover the trading of options contracts does not differ substantially from that described in Part III, Chapter 4. Options are traded in the UK on LIFFE and on the UK Traded Options market established by The Stock Exchange. Of these markets, LIFFE provides the options of most direct relevance to interest rate futures; namely, the long gilt, Eurodollar and Treasury bill option contracts, whereas the Traded Options market provides options in short and long gilts. Because the option contract provides, in the case of contracts traded on LIFFE, for delivery of the underlying futures contract, at a stated price, it is possible for the buyer of such an option to retain the right, without a corresponding obligation, to decide whether or not to enter the futures market. This, in effect, limits the risk of the purchaser to the cost of the option purchased by him. In practice, options are subject to similar margin requirements to those required of clients who trade in futures.

United States

There are three types of interest rate options traded in the US, each of which is regulated and documented in a slightly different manner: (a) exchange-traded options on US Treasury securities, traded primarily on the Chicago Board Options Exchange (CBOE), although the market for these instruments is not substantial; (b) over the counter (OTC) options on US Treasury securities and mortgage-backed instruments, such as certificates issued or guaranteed by the Government National Mortgage Association, the Federal National Mortgage Association or the Federal Home Loan Mortgage Corporation; and (c) options on the interest rate futures contracts discussed above, traded primarily on the CBT and the IMM. Options on interest rate sensitive securities, regardless of whether they are traded on an exchange or OTC, are considered separate securities under US law, and are within the jurisdiction of the Securities and Exchange Commission (SEC).[1] For this reason, such instruments are not subject to the prohibition on off-exchange futures trading imposed by the CEA. Options on interest rate futures, however, are regulated by the CFTC and are therefore traded on regulated futures exchanges.

Broker and client

The legal relationship between a broker and client entering into exchange-traded options or options on futures contracts is virtually identical to that described above with respect to futures transac-

---

[1] It should be noted that, in contrast to the exclusive jurisdiction granted to the CFTC, the SEC's jurisdiction over securities trading in the US is exclusive only at the federal level. The states also retain authority to regulate the trading of securities, including options on securities, within their territories.

tions.[2] The parties to an OTC transaction, however, most often deal with each other as principals, although the agreements evidencing such transactions are subject to individual negotiation and their form may, therefore, vary widely.

(a) *Exchange-traded options.* SEC regulations do not require that brokers enter into written agreements with their clients regarding OTC or exchange-traded interest rate options. CBOE rules, however, require that, with respect to exchange trade options, an account agreement be entered into between the broker and the client and that the agreement contain, at a minimum, an acknowledgement that all transactions will be conducted in accordance with the rules of the CBOE and the OCC, and that the client will not violate position or exercise limits. Moreover, it is customary for such agreements to include the types of provisions described above in connection with interest rate futures trading, and to address a number of other points peculiar to options, such as the actions which must be taken by the client in order to exercise an option purchased or to make or receive delivery, and disclosures regarding the manner in which the broker will allocate option exercise notices received from the exchange.

CBOE rules also require a broker to provide each options client with a copy of a disclosure document prepared by the OCC, which describes the nature, mechanics and risks of options trading. In addition, although not expressly required, brokers generally receive from their clients a signed agreement to submit disputes to arbitration, either in the account agreement or in a separate document.

(b) *Over the counter options.* Agreements governing OTC options are, by definition, customised and subject to individual negotiation between the principals, thereby rendering generalisation more difficult. Nevertheless, an institution engaging in OTC trading typically will enter into a master agreement with each of its counterparties setting out the terms and conditions to which each option between them will be subject. Such an agreement ordinarily will establish the terms of the options to be traded, such as quantities, expirations and exercise procedures, provide for deposits of margin or collateral by option writers, specify the manner in which positions can be closed out prior to expiration, if any, grant each party a security interest in property of the other party held by it and identify the circumstances under which defaults may be declared as well as the remedies available to the non-defaulting party.

Because OTC transactions are principal-to-principal, neither party will generally carry an 'account' for the other; to the contrary, each transaction is evidenced simply by a telex or other form of written confirmation sent by one or both parties, which may reference the terms of the master agreement. Moreover, in some instances, particularly where each entity is a large and sophisticated financial institution, the parties may not even enter into a master agreement, and their respective rights and obligations will therefore be evidenced solely by the confirmation sent in connection with each transaction. Under such circumstances, it is generally understood that each such transaction is subject to commonly accepted customs and practices in the relevant OTC market. There are also no disclosure requirements expressly applicable to OTC options transactions, although many institutions include some type of disclosure in their form agreements, as well as an arbitration clause.

(c) *Options on interest rate futures.* The documentation of options on interest rate futures transactions is virtually identical to that used in connection with the underlying futures contracts, except that the particular provisions noted above regarding option exercises and allocation of notices will ordinarily be included. CFTC regulations also require that brokers provide their clients with the

---

[2] Because options on interest rate securities are themselves separate securities, however, a broker trading such instruments on behalf of clients must be registered with the SEC. As a result, a broker engaging in both an interest rate futures and interest rate options business would likely be required to register with the CFTC and the SEC. In addition, all options transactions executed on a United States securities exchange are cleared by the Options Clearing Corporation (OCC), which operates in a manner similar to the ICCH.

disclosure statements and related documents described above in connection with interest rate futures, as well as a separate Options Risk Disclosure Statement.

Broker and the clearing house

The documentation of the relationship between a broker and clearing house in connection with an exchange-traded interest rate option, or an option on a futures contract, is not materially different from that applicable to an interest rate futures transaction, as described above. The principal distinction is that, because the OCC acts as the clearing agent and guarantor of all exchange-traded options on securities, a broker need only establish a clearing relationship with that entity, rather than with a number of separate exchanges. OTC transactions ordinarily are not cleared through a common clearing facility, and it is therefore difficult to state generally the type of documentation which would be used. In most instances, however, the principals to the transactions arrange for clearance and settlement through banks or depositories with which they have existing relationships. These relationships will ordinarily be documented separately.

Standard form contracts

As in the case of interest rate futures, exchange-traded interest rate options or options on futures are not evidenced by actual written contracts, but simply incorporate by reference the terms and conditions set forth in exchange rules. OTC options may be embodied in a written agreement, although it is more common for the parties simply to refer to the terms and conditions included in a master agreement or to terms and conditions generally accepted by industry practice.

5 Case study: Treasury bond options

Carl A. Batlin

Introduction

The Consolidated Allied Bank (CAB) had been originating long-term mortgage loans and funding them with 3-month deposits for many years. Because of the normally upward sloping yield curve, this 'short-funding' strategy proved to be generally profitable until the 1979–82 period, when the sharp increase in deposit interest rates nearly put CAB out of business. In reaction to this sobering experience, the bank's management decided to try to eliminate its exposure to interest rate risk by instituting a policy of selling all newly originated mortgages as packaged certificates, rather than holding them as assets – effectively creating its own mortgage-backed securities.

Issues and assumptions

To implement the new programme, it was estimated that the bank would need to warehouse its new mortgages for periods of about three months, in order to accumulate sufficiently large principal amounts to meet minimum market denomination requirements. As CAB would continue to rely on 3-month funding, the implication was that the bank's earnings would be immune to the effects of rising deposit rates over each anticipated holding period. The bank would still have an exposure, however, that the value of its mortgages could decline between their origination dates and the time of sale. To hedge this exposure, CAB's management turned its consideration to the Treasury bond futures contracts and the Treasury bond futures options traded on the Chicago Board of Trade.

In deciding on the proper hedge strategy, CAB first recognised the trade-off between these exchange-traded instruments and the over-the-counter (OTC) hedge contracts tied to mortgage indexes (e.g. GNMA forwards or options). In comparing the greater liquidity and lower transaction costs of the exchange-traded instruments against the basis risk created by the differential price behaviour of the underlying mortgages and the Treasury bond-based futures or options, it was decided that the latter problem could be minimised by choosing the correct hedge ratio, thus making the exchange-traded instruments the preferred hedge vehicle.

The next issue concerned the choice between futures and options. If the mortgage asset was viewed simply as a long bond position whose value fluctuates inversely with mortgage interest rate movements, the best hedge would be a short futures position whose value would fluctuate inversely with Treasury bond yield movements. Some members of the CAB research staff, however, emphasised that although this futures hedge protected the bank against rising interest rates, the value of the mortgage asset was also vulnerable to falling interest rates. The reason was that mortgage borrowers could refinance whenever market mortgage rates fell sufficiently below their contractual mortgage rate, and they thus effectively held a call option with a strike rate equal to the contractual mortgage rate. As a consequence, the mortgage asset should be viewed – it was argued – as the combination of a long bond and a short call, which, as Exhibit 5.1 demonstrates by graphing the price changes of the bond and the call against the interest rate, is equivalent to a short put option. Accordingly, if this view had merit, the proper hedge of the long mortgage asset would be a long position in a put option.

Exhibit 5.1 Equivalence between long bond/short call and short put

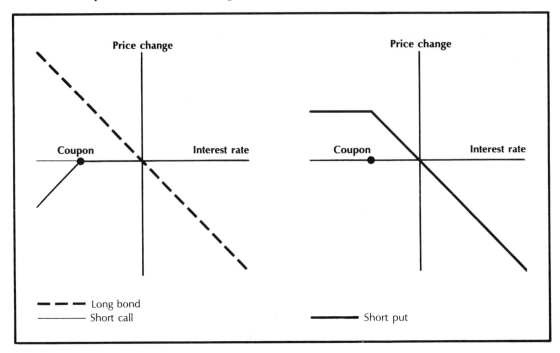

The hedging decision

Because there was some dispute about the degree of significance of the prepayment effect, CAB decided to split its mortgage portfolio, hedging half with futures and half with options, in order to test the relative hedging effectiveness of the two instruments. The mortgage sales programme began at the beginning of January 1985, so that by January 1987, eight hedge cycles had been completed. For each cycle, several decisions had to be implemented. First, CAB needed to determine the coupon on the mortgage certificate. Following the GNMA practice of allowing one-half of a percentage point for servicing costs, the coupon was set about 50 basis points below the market mortgage rates prevalent during the warehousing period. The implication was that during that period, the market value of the certificates would generally be at a discount from par.

CAB also had to establish and implement the proper futures and option hedge positions each period. The first obstacle to be crossed in this regard was to adjust for the differential price behaviour of the underlying mortgages and the Treasury bond-based hedge instruments. In order to try to equalise the changes in the market values of the bank's mortgage and hedge contract positions, it was necessary to choose an appropriate hedge ratio, or fraction of the value of the mortgage position to be hedged. Moreover, as the prepayment option imbedded in the mortgages would change in importance as market mortgage rates changed relative to the contractual mortgage rate, a new hedge ratio would need to be selected for each hedge period. Of the two methodologies available for estimating hedge ratios – the duration-matching approach and the regression approach – CAB decided that the latter would be more efficient in this case, because it alone did not require the bank to make any assumption about the rate at which prepayments would occur during the hedge period.

To calculate the hedge ratio for each 3-month period (e.g. 1 January 1985–1 April 1985 for the first cycle) using this method, CAB's research staff would collect data on daily price changes of comparable mortgage-backed securities (MBS) and Treasury bond futures contracts over the previous 2-month period (e.g. 1 November 1984–1 January 1985 for the first cycle) and perform the following statistical regression:

$$\text{MBS price change} = h \times \text{Futures price change} + \text{Error term}$$

The result is that h, the regression coefficient which minimises the statistical variance of the error term, is the hedge ratio which minimises the volatility of the mortgage-Treasury bond futures hedge position, assuming the estimation period is representative of the hedge period. To choose the specific MBS and futures price series to use in the regression, CAB decided on the MBS pool whose coupon fulfilled the bank's mortgage certificate pricing objective (i.e. the one which produced those discount MBS prices which were closest to par) and the Treasury bond futures corresponding to the first deferred contract at the start of the hedge period (e.g. the June 1985 contract for the first cycle), resolving the trade-off of the liquidity of nearby contracts versus the stability of deferred contracts.

As MBS are denominated in units of US$1m, while Treasury bond futures and options are in US$100,000 units, the bank would sell $h \times 10$ futures, or buy $h \times 10$ put options, at the start of the hedge period. Moreover, because the futures or option contracts would have 6-month maturities at the start of the period, the hedge position could be reversed at the end of the period by buying back the futures or selling the options, which would still have 3-month maturities at that time (cf. if only 3-month options were used to hedge, they could not be sold if they were out of the money, since they would expire worthless). Furthermore, since the prices are quoted as a percentage of par, the dollar gain or loss from the hedged position each period would be:

$$(\text{MBS price change} - h \times \text{Futures price change}) \times 10,000$$

for the futures hedge (as the bank would be long the mortgages and short the futures), and

$$(\text{MBS price change} + h \times \text{Option price change}) \times 10,000$$

for the option hedge (since CAB would be long both the mortgages and the options).

Although choosing the hedge ratio would be sufficient to establish the futures hedge, CAB recognised that it must also choose the strike rate of the option before it could enter into the option hedge. As the amount of the MBS price discount at the beginning of the hedge period measures the extent to which the MBS – conceptualised as a short put option – is out of the money, the strike price of the Treasury bond futures option should be the same amount above the futures price at the start of the hedge period. In other words, the option strike should be that one which came closest to satisfying the relationship:

$$100 - \text{MBS price} = \text{Option strike price} - \text{Futures price}$$

With the appropriate strike price tying the level of the mortgage 'option' price to the comparable level of the Treasury bond option price, and the proper hedge ratio tying subsequent changes in the mortgage 'option' price to changes in the Treasury bond option price, CAB had designed the hedge so that changes in the value of the option position should effectively hedge changes in the value of the mortgage position.

Exhibit 5.2   Regression results for determining hedge ratios

	Hedge period	Estimation period	GNMA	Futures	Hedge ratios	t	R²	DW
1	1/85 – 4/85	11/84 – 1/85	11.5	6/85	0.81	8.5	0.74	1.63
2	4/85 – 7/85	2/85 – 4/85	11.5	9/85	0.80	13.1	0.86	1.53
3	7/85 –10/85	5/85 – 7/85	11.5	12/85	0.76	17.3	0.90	1.53
4	10/85 – 1/86	8/85 –10/85	11.5	3/86	0.63	12.1	0.83	1.95
5	1/86 – 4/86	11/85 – 1/86	9.0	6/86	0.71	8.0	0.70	1.37
6	4/86 – 7/86	2/86 – 4/86	9.0	9/86	0.42	7.3	0.65	2.68
7	7/86 –10/86	5/86 – 7/86	9.0	12/86	0.30	8.2	0.68	1.08
8	10/86 – 1/87	8/86 –10/86	9.0	3/87	0.29	5.5	0.48	1.40

The results

Exhibit 5.2 summarises the hedge ratio results for the eight hedge cycles using actual data from Data Resources Inc. As the exhibit indicates, the $11\frac{1}{2}\%$ GNMA coupon was the representative MBS for the first four periods, and the 9% coupon was appropriate for the next four cycles. As interest rates dropped over the two-year period, the hedge ratios, R^2 statistics (measuring the explanatory power of the independent variables), and t statistics (showing the degree of significance of that explanatory power) declined, reflecting the increasing value of the prepayment option and the resulting shortening of the duration of the mortgages relative to that of Treasury bonds. All but one (period 7) of the Durbin–Watson statistics reflected an absence of autocorrelation (meaning that the t statistics were meaningful) and all the t statistics indicated that the hedge ratios were statistically significantly different from zero. For the purposes of constructing the hedges, however, CAB rounded off all hedge ratios (e.g. eight futures contracts or options were used to hedge each MBS in the first hedge period).

Exhibit 5.3   Option and futures hedge results

Period	Price change			Hedge gain/loss		
	MBS	Option	Futures	Option	Futures	Difference
1	(9/16)	5/32	(1/16)	(4,375)	(5,125)	750
2	7 1/16	(5 23/64)	8 29/32	27,750	(625)	28,375
3	(5/8)	55/64	(3/4)	625	(250)	875
4	5 5/8	(2 57/64)	10 21/32	38,906	(7,687)	46,593
5	3 3/4	(4 7/16)	12 1/4	6,438	(85,000)	91,438
6	(2 15/16)	2 3/8	(1 13/16)	(19,875)	(21,763)	1,888
7	1 13/16	(11/64)	3 11/16	17,609	7,063	10,546
8	2 3/4	(3 1/16)	5 7/16	18,313	11,188	7,126

Exhibit 5.3 shows the results of the option and futures hedges using the hedge ratios from Exhibit 5.2. The first half of the exhibit simply records the price changes of the MBS, option and futures contracts that occurred in each hedge period. All price movements were consistent; that is, every bull market period was characterised by rising MBS and futures prices and by falling put option prices, whereas in every bear market period, the reverse occurred. The magnitudes of the MBS and hedge instrument price changes were, of course, never equal, and it was this differential price behaviour for which the hedge ratios were intended to adjust.

The relative success of the option hedge and the futures hedge in achieving this objective is revealed in the second half of the exhibit. The gain or loss (in US$) from each hedged position in each period is reported for the option hedge and the futures hedge, as well as the difference between them, calculated using the equations given earlier. In every period, the option hedge out-performed the futures hedge, often by a substantial margin. The greater effectiveness of the option hedge was perhaps best illustrated in the fifth hedge period (the first quarter of 1986). Because interest rates fell, both the MBS and the Treasury bond futures prices rose. In the case of the MBS, however, the increase in value of the short call option implicit in the underlying mortgages limited the overall MBS price gains – a phenomenon known as price compression. The Treasury bond futures position, on the other hand, suffered from no such corresponding constraint, so that the losses from the short Treasury futures position overwhelmed the meagre gains from the long MBS position, producing a staggering loss. The price decline in the long put option position, in contrast, mirrored much more closely the price gain in the long MBS position (reflecting their similar economic structures), producing a small gain for the total hedged position.

Comparative analysis of futures versus options

Early in the programme, a floor broker in CAB's futures subsidiary objected that the true relative costs of the futures and option hedge programmes were not being properly taken into account. He argued that in each three-month period, CAB earned, in addition to the gain or loss on the hedged position, one-fourth of the MBS coupon times the par value of the MBS, because it owned the mortgage assets during the period. On the other hand, the bank paid out one-fourth of the 3-month Libor prevailing at the start of the period times the initial MBS price, because it had to finance the acquisition of the mortgage assets. Accordingly, its net interest earnings from holding the mortgage assets over the warehousing period were:

$$[(\text{MBS coupon} \times 100) - (\text{Libor} \times \text{MBS price})] \times 10,000/4$$

Because new mortgage assets were always priced at discount, and because the yield curve was upwards sloping, these net interest earnings were always positive (there was 'positive carry'). Moreover, as the futures position was margined and was therefore effectively costless to maintain, the floor broker argued, this entire net interest earnings should be added to the futures hedge gain or loss. In the case of the option hedge, however, the cost of the options must, like the cost of the mortgages, be financed, and the net interest earnings to be added to that hedge's gain or loss should therefore be reduced by the amount:

$$\text{Libor} \times h \times \text{Option price} \times 10,000/4$$

Although the implication was that the superiority of the option hedge would be greatly diminished after adjusting for this disadvantage, Exhibit 5.4 shows that the damage was minimal. The first half of the exhibit calculates the net interest earnings of the two hedge programmes each period, using the equations given above, and it indicates that the cost savings from futures were not very large. The second half of the exhibit then adds these net interest earnings to the hedge gain/loss of each programme from Exhibit 5.3, thus producing the 'all-in' hedge results.

Exhibit 5.4   Hedge results including net interest earnings

Period	Net interest earned			Total hedge performance		
	Option	Futures	Difference	Option	Futures	Difference
1	7,208	7,968	(760)	2,833	2,843	(10)
2	6,365	7,396	(1,031)	34,115	6,771	27,344
3	8,657	8,962	(305)	9,282	8,712	570
4	7,782	8,141	(359)	46,688	454	46,234
5	2,624	3,250	(626)	9,062	(81,750)	90,812
6	3,888	4,119	(231)	(15,987)	(17,644)	1,657
7	5,658	5,969	(311)	23,267	13,032	10,235
8	7,329	7,514	(185)	25,642	18,702	6,940

It is true that the futures hedge benefited from consideration of the net interest earnings. Previously, six of the eight periods produced losses in the futures hedging programme (as opposed to two for the option hedge). After taking account of the net interest earnings, however, only two of the periods remained ineffective for the futures hedge, whereas one of the option hedge's periods still produced a loss. In one period, the futures hedge even gained a slight advantage over the option hedge. On balance, however, the superior hedging capability of the options still more than compensated for the additional cost of carry over the futures alternative.

6 Case study: 'Delta neutral' option strategies

Paul Sutin

Introduction

The following case study demonstrates how option strategies on Treasury bond futures can provide the corporate treasurer with a dynamic and profitable way to hedge interest rate exposure. This can be achieved by applying the concept of 'delta neutrality'. A delta neutral strategy is a dynamic hedging technique which matches the relationship between the movements in the option premium with the price of the underlying asset. Delta is derived from any standard options pricing model and measures the amount by which the option premium can be expected to change for a small change in the asset price. Delta is more formally known as the 'hedge ratio'. The neutral hedge option/asset ratio reflects the optimal point at which an option hedge reduces risk to a minimum. By taking the reciprocal of delta we can solve for the exact number of option contracts required to achieve an optimal hedge.

A financial institution is long Treasury bonds. The treasurer, being concerned that the market will go down in the short term, decided that a hedge should be implemented to reduce the long Treasury bond exposure risk. Having made the decision to hedge, the treasurer must select the appropriate hedging strategy and instruments. The alternatives would be:

1   a short futures contract,
2   a short call option,
3   a long put option, or
4   a combination of call and put options and/or futures.

For the purposes of this case study other interest management instruments have not been discussed such as interest rate 'swap' strategies, and caps and collars. The alternatives presented here focus on hedging instruments traded on public exchanges. To select one of these alternatives the treasurer must define his risk parameters and his opinion on the market. At the outset purchasing puts would be the most conservative alternative because it is absolutely impossible to lose more than the initial premium paid under any potential market scenario. With a short futures contract it is also possible to create a riskless hedge; however, in the short term a large basis shift can create a situation where a substantial unrealised loss would remain for several days before the futures would realign itself with the cash position at the breakeven level. The disadvantage of the short futures hedge is that it does not give the means to delta neutralise the hedge; adjusting for profit potential. With the short call alternative, the hedge will only be effective if the market moves sideways at moderate levels of volatility; if this does not occur, the hedge will be inadequate if the market moves more than expected in either direction. The last alternative, a combination of call and put options and/or futures, is more demanding, in terms of technical monitoring and the frequency of position adjustments. After commissions, personnel and computer resource expenses, the cost-to-benefit may not pay off.

Exhibit 6.1 'Delta neutral' option strategies, December 1987 Treasury bonds

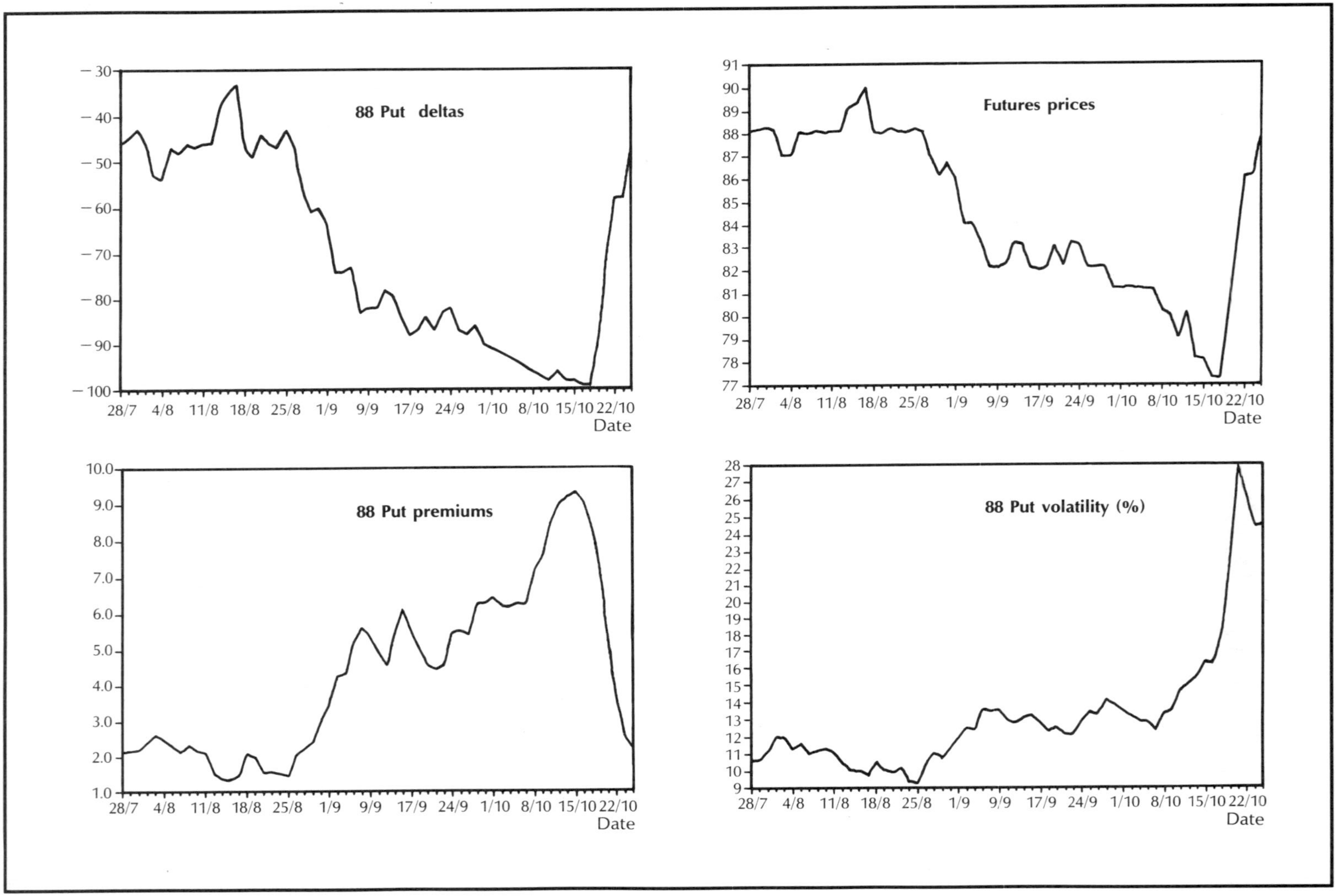

Case study

Market environment

The corporation is long US$10m in 8% Treasury bonds. In late July 1987, the treasurer observes a negative correlation between the December Treasury bond futures prices and December Treasury bond put option volatility. As volatility was reaching extremely low levels this suggested that the probability of an increase in volatility and a decrease in bond prices could be quite high. (See Exhibit 6.1.) Under these market conditions the treasurer decided that his long Treasury bond position should be hedged using long put options, delta neutralised to the market. The following condition existed at the time the hedge was initiated: the yield curve was almost flat making the cash Treasury bond prices close to the Treasury bond futures price. As the prices were almost equal at 87 the following options strategy was implemented: purchase of at-the-money long Treasury bond put options on the nearby Treasury bond future with an 88 strike price. As the options were at-the-money, their delta approximated negative 0.56. The neutral hedge ratio would therefore be $1/\text{delta}$; $\frac{1}{0.5} = 2$. This indicates that a ratio of two option contracts to one Treasury bond contract will create a risk neutral hedge. This implies that 200 puts must be purchased to match the risks associated with the US$10m face value cash bonds. (See Exhibit 6.2 for hedge performance details.) (Note: The reciprocal of delta is expressed as a positive number even though the deltas for put options are expressed as negative numbers because it would be technically impossible to hedge with a negative number of option contracts.)

The aggregate deltas of the position at the beginning of the hedge period amount to $-11,200$ deltas (200 puts multiplied by a delta of -56). These $-11,200$ deltas will represent the neutral level of the hedge, from which the treasurer sets a maximum variance. This level will reflect the treasurer's attitude towards risk and the size of the position. In the case of a long put position, a 15% deviation or 1,500 deltas away from the $-11,200$ variance from neutrality, would be an optimal level between being too conservative to adjust for profits and being too aggressive to let the profits run.

Strategy

27 August 1987
> Long US$10m face value
> 8% cash bonds @ $87 - \frac{2}{32}$
> Buy 200 88 puts @ $2 - \frac{24}{64}$, or US$2375.12 a piece
> US$475,024 debit

Over the next six market days, the Treasury bond futures price declined to $84 - \frac{2}{32}$% of par. At that point, the put premium advanced to $4 - \frac{24}{64}$, or US$4437.64 a piece. As a result, the value of the cash holdings dropped by US$300,000. The value of the 200 puts, however, advanced to US$411,485 in the aggregate. Thus, on 2 September the options hedge had preserved the value of the cash holdings and had generated some incremental profit.

2 September 1987
> Long US$10m face value 8% bonds @ $\frac{84 \cdot 02}{32}$ US$300,000 paper loss
> Long 200 84 puts @ $4 - \frac{28}{64}$, or US$4,437.64 a piece
> US$426,571 paper gain

At that point, the delta associated with the long puts had gone from -0.56 to -0.74. That amounted to an aggregate $-2,600$ delta deviation from neutrality. As maximum delta variance was set at 1,500 (see Exhibit 6.2), this required the treasurer to delta neutralise the position again. The new hedge ratio will become -50 (Current delta, -74 divided by the aggregate deltas of the position, 14,800). This

211

Exhibit 6.2 Hedge performance

Date	T-bond price	Vola-tility (%)	Pre-mium	Δ	Mark to market cash 8% T-bond (US$)	Net cash bond balance (US$)	No. put ops (US$)	Put option value (US$)	Option position (US$)	Net option balance (US$)	Net hedge balance (US$)	Δ neutral adjust-ment	Δ maximum variance set at 1,500	No. options to sell/buy	Realised P&L from options
27/8	87.02	11.06	2.24	−56	8,706,250		200	2,375.12	475,024			−11,200	−1000	Buy 200	0
29/8	86.13	10.82	2.43	−61	8,640,625	(65,625)	200	2,672.09	534,418	59,394	(6,231)	−12,200	−1000	Hold 200	0
31/8	86.71	11.35	3.03	−60	8,821,875	(115,625)	200	3,046.89	609,378	134,354	249,979	−12,000	−800	Hold 200	0
1/9	86.01	11.94	3.48	−63	8,603,125	(103,125)	200	3,748.80	749,760	274,736	171,611	−12,600	−1400	Hold 200	0
2/9	84.02	12.52	4.28	−74	8,406,250	(300,000)	150	4,437.64	665,646	412,504	112,504	−14,800	−2600	Sell −50	221,882
3/9	84.05	12.39	4.34	−74	8,415,625	(290,625)	150	4,531.42	679,713	426,571	135,946	−11,100	0	Hold 150	0
4/9	83.31	13.55	5.17	−73	8,396,875	(309,375)	150	5,265.71	789,857	536,715	227,340	−10,950	150	Hold 150	0
8/9	82.11	13.47	5.63	−83	8,234,375	(471,875)	150	5,984.69	897,703	644,561	172,686	−12,450	−1350	Hold 150	0
9/9	82.12	13.58	5.37	−82	8,237,500	(468,750)	150	5,578.31	836,747	583,605	114,855	−12,300	−1200	Hold 150	0
10/9	82.26	12.92	4.92	−82	8,281,250	(425,000)	150	5,437.96	815,694	562,552	137,552	−12,300	−1200	Hold 150	0
11/9	83.20	12.78	4.56	−78	8,306,250	(400,000)	150	4,875.28	731,292	478,150	78,150	−11,700	−600	Hold 150	0
14/9	83.15	13.11	5.46	−79	8,346,875	(359,375)	150	5,718.98	857,847	604,705	245,330	−11,850	−750	Hold 150	0
16/9	82.16	13.25	6.12	−84	8,250,000	(456,250)	93	6,187.56	575,443	673,487	217,237	−12,600	−1500	Sell −57	351,186
17/9	82.00	12.72	5.50	−88	8,200,000	(506,250)	93	5,781.50	537,680	635,723	129,473	−8,184	0	Hold 93	0
18/9	82.11	12.31	5.06	−87	8,234,375	(471,875)	93	5,093.78	473,722	571,765	99,890	−8,091	93	Hold 93	0
21/9	83.05	12.54	4.58	−84	8,315,625	(390,625)	93	4,906.54	456,308	554,352	163,727	−7,812	372	Hold 93	0
22/9	82.21	12.09	4.46	−87	8,265,625	(440,625)	93	4,718.98	438,865	536,909	96,284	−8,091	93	Hold 93	0
23/9	83.18	12.07	4.56	−83	8,356,250	(350,000)	93	4,875.28	453,401	551,445	201,445	−7,719	465	Hold 93	0
24/9	83.14	12.83	5.49	−82	8,343,750	(362,500)	93	5,765.87	536,226	634,270	271,770	−7,626	558	Hold 93	0
25/9	82.12	13.45	5.53	−87	8,237,500	(468,750)	93	5,828.39	542,040	640,084	171,334	−8,091	93	Hold 93	0
28/9	82.11	13.28	5.43	−88	8,234,375	(471,875)	93	5,672.09	527,504	625,548	153,673	−8,184	0	Hold 93	0
29/9	82.16	14.14	6.29	−86	8,250,000	(456,250)	93	6,453.27	600,154	698,198	241,948	−7,998	186	Hold 93	0
30/9	81.22	13.83	6.30	−90	8,168,750	(537,500)	93	6,468.90	601,608	699,652	162,152	−8,370	−186	Hold 93	0
1/10	81.22	13.45	6.45	−91	8,168,750	(537,500)	93	6,703.35	623,412	721,455	183,955	−8,463	−279	Hold 93	0
2/10	81.24	13.17	6.21	−92	8,175,000	(531,250)	93	6,328.23	588,525	686,569	155,319	−8,556	−372	Hold 93	0
5/10	81.23	12.90	6.20	−93	8,171,875	(534,375)	93	6,312.60	587,072	685,116	150,741	−8,649	−465	Hold 93	0
6/10	81.19	12.82	6.29	−94	8,159,375	(546,875)	93	6,453.27	600,154	698,198	151,323	−8,742	−558	Hold 93	0
7/10	81.19	12.35	6.26	−95	8,159,375	(546,875)	93	6,406.38	595,793	693,837	146,962	−8,835	−651	Hold 93	0
8/10	80.23	13.37	7.20	−96	8,071,875	(634,375)	93	7,312.60	680,072	778,116	143,741	−8,928	−744	Hold 93	0
9/10	80.03	13.45	7.58	−97	8,009,375	(696,875)	93	7,906.54	735,308	833,352	136,477	−9,021	−837	Hold 93	0
12/10	79.08	14.66	8.48	−98	7,925,000	(781,250)	93	8,750.24	813,772	911,816	130,566	−9,114	−930	Hold 93	0
13/10	80.16	15.04	9.03	−96	8,050,000	(656,250)	93	9,046.89	841,361	939,405	283,155	−8,928	−744	Hold 93	0
14/10	78.21	15.43	9.22	−98	7,865,625	(840,625)	93	9,343.86	868,979	967,023	126,398	−9,114	−930	Hold 93	0
15/10	78.14	16.34	9.36	−98	7,843,750	(862,500)	93	9,562.68	889,329	987,373	124,873	−9,114	−930	Hold 93	0
16/10	77.30	16.20	9.08	−99	7,709,375	(996,875)	93	9,125.04	848,629	946,673	50,202	−9,207	−1023	Hold 93	0
19/10	77.25	17.93	8.43	−99	7,778,125	(928,125)	93	8,672.09	806,504	904,548	23,577	−9,207	−1023	Hold 93	0
20/10	80.25	22.92	7.18	−88	8,078,125	(628,125)	93	7,281.34	677,165	775,208	147,083	−8,184	0	Hold 93	0
21/10	83.22	27.90	5.10	−71	8,368,750	(337,500)	141	5,156.30	727,038	577,719	240,219	−6,248	1936	Buy −48	(247,363)
22/10	86.12	26.18	3.63	−58	8,637,500	(68,750)	141	3,984.69	561,841	907,248	838,498	−8,178	0	Hold 141	0
23/10	86.18	24.46	2.52	−58	8,656,250	(50,000)	141	2,812.76	396,599	742,006	692,006	−8,178	0	Hold 141	0
26/10	88.06	24.53	2.20	−47	8,818,750	(112,500)	141	2,312.60	326,077	671,483	783,983	−6,627	1551	Hold 141	0

Put option market value US$651,781

Put option cost US$475,024

Put option net profit US$176,757

Δ = Delta

required the treasurer to liquidate 50 of the 200 puts, bringing the total down to 150 long puts, and a new 11,100 aggregate amount of deltas from which the maximum variance will be measured from.

Sell 50 88 puts @ $4-\frac{28}{64}$, or US$4,437.64 a piece for a credit of US$221,882

On 16 September, the Treasury bond futures prices have declined to $82-\frac{16}{32}$. By this time the treasurer had a US$456,250 paper loss in the value of the cash bonds and the 150 long puts increased in value to $6\frac{12}{64}$, or US$6187.56 a piece, for a US$451,605 paper gain and a realised gain of US$221,882 in the option premiums. In total, the option position has now increased to US$673,487. That brought the net hedge balance up to an unrealised US$217,237 gain.

On 16 September, the position also reached the 1500 maximum delta variance, requiring another hedge ratio adjustment of -57. The liquidation of 57 puts amounted to a US$351,186 credit bringing the long put option position down from 150 to 93 contracts.

Results

The purchasing of the put options resulting from the delta neutralising had amounted to US$573,068 which exceeded the US$475,024 cost of the hedge by US$98,044.

As of 16 September the treasurer enjoyed a free insurance policy on his long Treasury bond cash position and, in addition, he was able to place the US$98,004 of his realised put option profits in Treasury bills during the life of the hedge. This favourable situation resulting from delta neutralisation remains cost-efficient and yet the integrity of the hedge is preserved at no increase in risk. As bond prices continued to decline the options position did not require any more delta adjustments until 20 October, when a market anomaly occurred. (See Exhibit 6.1.)

Exhibit 6.3   Treasury bond long put option, 27 August – 20 October 1987

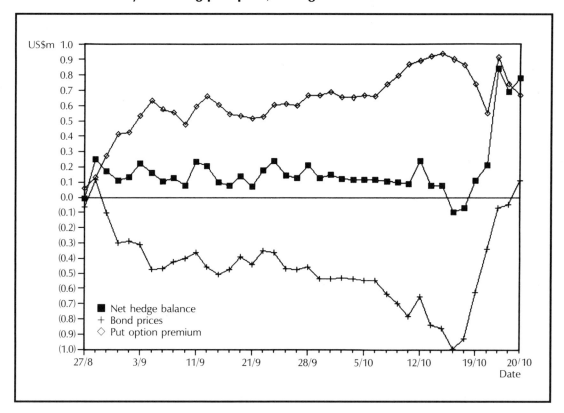

213

On 19 October, the US equities market suffered a 500 point crash, followed by an unexpected $\frac{1}{2}$% downward adjustment in the US discount rate, causing bond prices to swing around and increase dramatically by three points on 20 October and an additional three points on 21 October. Under these conditions of unprecedented volatility and market nervousness the net hedge position performed remarkably well. On 21 October, the position required a delta adjustment of 0.48, i.e. the purchase of 48 puts bringing the put option position up from 93 to 141. This amounted to a US$247,363 debit which was more than compensated for by the appreciation in the Treasury bond cash position. The net hedge balance still shows a credit of US$240,219.

On 26 October, at the end of the period observed in this case study, the market had suffered a considerable shock; however, the position was winning on all sides. A large portion of the profits from put option appreciation had already been realised, volatility had kept option premiums overvalued, and the long cash bond position was up US$112,500. (See Exhibit 6.3.)

Conclusion

We have seen how this application of an interest rate management strategy, using options on futures, has given the treasurer a considerable degree of flexibility. The outcome of the 'long put/delta neutral' strategy is that it allows the treasurer to:

1 minimise hedging costs and exposure,
2 profit from overvalued premiums on the downside without limiting the upside appreciation potential of the assets and,
3 insulate the position against a severe market anomaly.

Appendix: Option on US Treasury bond future
Summary of contract

Unit of trading	1 US Treasury bond futures contract
Delivery months	March, June, September, December
Delivery day/Exercise day/Expiry day	Exercise by 17.00 on any business day; extended to 20.30 on last trading day. Delivery on the first business day after the exercise day. Expiry at 20.30 on the last trading day.
Last trading day	First Friday preceding by at least six Chicago Board of Trade working days the first delivery day of the US Treasury bond futures contract
Quotation	Multiples of 1/64
Minimum price movement	1/64
(Tick size and value)	(US$15.625)
Initial margin (straddle margin)	See below
Trading hours	08.17–16.10

Contract standard

Assignment of one US Treasury bond futures contract for the delivery month at the exercise price.

Exercise price intervals

US$2, e.g. 86–00, 88–00, etc.

Introduction of New Exercise Prices

Seven exercise prices will be listed for new series. Additional prices will be introduced on the business day after the US Treasury bond futures contract settlement price is within US$1 of the third highest or lowest existing price.

Initial margin

Initial margin for long and short options positions is calculated with reference to daily published risk factors and the level of initial margin for the related futures contract which it cannot exceed. Initial margin is reduced for all options and options futures combinations which include offsetting positions.

Option price

The contract price is payable by the buyer to the seller on exercise or expiry of the option, **not** on purchase. Positions are marked to market daily.

Last trading day

The last trading day is defined to coincide with the last trading day for the Chicago Board of Trade Option on US Treasury futures, where this is a LIFFE trading day.

PART VI

Forward rate agreements and forward/forward agreements

1 Mechanics of forward rate agreements

R.D. Bown

Introduction

Forward rate agreements (FRAs) have existed in one form or another for about five years. However, it was only in 1984 that a fully fledged interbank market began to develop and its subsequent growth has been impressive. It is estimated that the daily turnover in London alone has now reached approximately US$4bn, DM500m and £500m. In addition, prices are available, admittedly on an *ad hoc* basis, in virtually every currency for which there is a Euromarket with indigenous banks making prices in London for their national currencies. There has also been a considerable improvement in the periods which can be dealt in. Both in length of time (up to 24 months is now freely available), and in the number of non-standard, or broken date, periods which can be priced.

Of course, none of this would have been possible without the increased turnover in the Eurodollar futures contract as this is the mechanism which is most frequently used for the short-term hedging. Banks have found it a useful tool both for hedging and also for speculative purposes and indeed with the overall growth in off-balance sheet trading the FRA has been at the forefront. It is worth examining why the FRA has suddenly become acceptable.

Financial futures versus the FRA

For many years there has been considerable disappointment over the relative lack of interest shown by the non-financial institution to the use of financial futures as a hedging mechanism. This applies equally to all exchanges worldwide and seems to stem from problems such as the following.

- There is a considerable amount of back office work required to cope with the initial margin and daily margin calls. Although the calculations are basically simple, they nevertheless involve considerable time and, therefore, expense. The reporting procedure can quite easily involve additional staff requirements.
- The daily margin calls involve cash payments to and from the exchange which obviously involves a possible funding cost and subsequent effects on cash flow.
- Very few commercial deposits/loans actually come up for renewal on dates which coincide with the futures settlement dates. This means that a hedging programme has to compensate for the difference between the deposit/loan period and the futures period available. Also the concept of basis risk must be acknowledged. Futures prices tend to trade cheaper than their cash equivalents and only to converge in the last two to three weeks before settlement. Unfortunately, there is no set rule as to how much the differential between cash and futures should be at any given time and it more often reflects the bullish or bearish tone prevalent in the market as to whether futures are trading 'rich' or 'cheap' to cash.

Although not a problem for banks with fully developed settlement offices these are enough to preclude all but the largest corporates from becoming heavily involved in the futures markets. By using FRAs commercial users have found that these problems have been overcome.

The structure of an FRA

Essentially an FRA is a futures contract without the troublesome elements which have hampered the growth of the futures market as a corporate hedging market. (See Part III, Chapter 1 for an examination of interest rate futures.) In its interbank form an FRA is a contract between two banks for a stated sum of principal at a stated price of interest for a stated period. Unlike financial futures which have fixed settlement dates, the FRA can be dealt from any date in the future until any other date. Although the most commonly dealt periods are those which start one, two, three or six months from the current spot value date, in fact virtually any dealing period is now readily available. It should be noted that there is no commitment, on either side, to physically transfer the principal sum involved; unlike a forward/forward deposit, it is only the rate on a given amount which has been dealt in. See Exhibit 1.1 for an example.

Exhibit 1.1   The structure of an FRA: an example

1   On 7 January 1986 Bank A 'lends' (or sells an FRA) via an FRA to Bank B £5,000,000 from 10 October 1986 until 10 April 1987 at 11.20%

2   For value date 10 October 1986, the Libor rate is established as $10\frac{7}{8}$

3   The difference between the rate on the FRA of 11.20% and the settled rate of $10\frac{7}{8}$ is in favour of Bank A

4   Because the differential is paid up-front it is calculated on a discount to yield basis. The formula for working out how much should be paid by Bank B is:

$$\frac{\text{Rate differential} \times \text{No. of days of deal} \times \text{Principal}}{360 \text{ or } 365 \text{ (in case of domestic sterling} \times 100)} = \text{Interest}$$

$$\text{Settlement figures} = \frac{\text{Interest}}{1 + \frac{(\text{Libor} \times \text{days})}{(360 \text{ or } 365) \times 100}}$$

In this example Bank B owes Bank A £7,685.96

Advantages to banks

The Euromarkets are made up of commercial deposits and loans being transacted by banks on a daily basis. Due to increasing uncertainty about the future direction of interest rates, more and more customers are asking banks to quote on a forward/forward basis and the FRA provides the perfect marketplace within which to satisfy their needs. In Exhibit 1.1 Bank A may have had a depositor who wishes to lock in a rate for part of his available funds on a forward basis and Bank B wished to cover a similar commitment to a borrower. Previously both banks would have been forced into an asset/liability position to create a forward cash rate. This would have involved a commitment of funds which would not only block credit limit lines but also would increase the usage of the balance sheet. By dealing in the FRA market they are able to achieve considerable savings which can be passed on to the client. The main advantages of an FRA are:

- There are no margin calls to be monitored and, therefore, no funding costs attached to dealing in FRAs.
- Because the FRA is a 'clean' rate constructed from actual market rates there is no basis risk. This has probably been the biggest drawback in hedging through financial futures and although numerous computer programs have been developed to reduce basis risk, no one has successfully eliminated it. When an FRA is settled it is at the exact cash market Libor. This has been helped by the acceptance of FRABBA as a standard for all dealings undertaken in London. The British Bankers Association (BBA) gathers together rates in US dollars, sterling, Deutschmarks, Swiss

francs and Japanese yen from eight BBA designated banks each day at 11.00 am on the relevant fixing date for settlement date value. After eliminating the two highest (or, in the event of equality, two of the lowest) it takes the average of the remaining four and then, if necessary, rounds the resulting figure upwards to five decimal points. The settlement rates for one through 12 months are published on Telerate p. 3750. In the event of broken date periods being dealt in, then the counterparties agree to accept reference banks as referees at the commencement of the deal.

- It is possible for commercial customers to lock in a long-term rate (up to two years) even though their lines of credit may only be for six months. This would be done by simply borrowing under their cash lines for six months and 'buying' the rate for six months – 24 months via an FRA. This can be done as the credit risk on an FRA is considerably less than that of a straight loan, since no principal sum is exchanged on settlement. General market practice is to allow for a credit line usage of about 3% of the total principal sum dealt in. Also, because the FRA is settled on a discounted basis at the beginning of the six months versus 24 months period, the credit line is only used for six months from the date of dealing and will cease once a settlement figure is paid. This is a very valuable source of medium-term interest rate protection at minimal cost to the client. It has also meant that a customer can, for the first time, insure against his interest rate risk from a different source to his cash line provider. With the many available quotations in FRAs he can call several banks to determine the finest price and deal where he wishes.
- The FRA market is now quoted on a 24-hour basis around the world and is not restrained by the opening hours of any given exchange.

Conclusion

The FRA market has made it possible for interest rate protection to be taken out on a forward basis which is more adequately tailored to the customers' requirements, more competitively priced, and also more easily defined on a basis which can be understood, than has hitherto been available through either the futures or cash forward/forward market.

2   Accounting treatment: United States

Benjamin S. Neuhausen

Introduction

The authoritative accounting literature in the US contains no rules specifically applicable to accounting for forward rate agreements (FRAs). Accordingly, practice has evolved based on analogies to similar areas in accounting, such as accounting for interest rate futures contracts. However, practice is not uniform in all respects. This chapter describes the accounting practices that are most supportable based on generally accepted accounting principles. The reader should be aware that other, less supportable practices, may be followed by some companies.

As noted in Part III, Chapter 1, 'Accounting framework: United States', the accounting for FRAs, along with other interest rate protection products is the subject of a major FASB project and could change.

Accounting by buyer

Forward rate agreements and forward/forward agreements are economically similar to futures contracts. A buyer would typically use a forward rate or forward/forward agreement to hedge a firm commitment or an anticipated transaction. Accordingly, to qualify as a hedge, a forward rate or forward/forward agreement should meet the same criteria required for a futures contract to qualify as a hedge – the three basic criteria (risk, designation, and effectiveness) and the two additional criteria for hedges of anticipated transactions (identification and probability). The only difference is that the risk criterion could be measured on an individual transaction basis rather than on the enterprise basis required for a futures contract.

If an FRA qualifies as a hedge, the net settlement amount would be treated as discount or premium on the investment or borrowing that was hedged and amortised by the interest method over the life of the investment/loan. If it does not qualify as a hedge for accounting purposes, perhaps because the anticipated transaction is only possible and not probable, the forward rate agreement would be accounted for on a market value or lower-of-cost-or-market value basis.

A forward/forward agreement will, almost by definition, qualify as a hedge for accounting purposes. If the investment or borrowing does not take place, the forward/forward agreement becomes null and void. Any termination penalty from failing to consummate the transaction would be charged to expense as soon as it became probable.

Accounting by seller

Forward rate and forward/forward agreements ordinarily would be speculative positions from the seller's perspective. Depending on the seller's accounting for similar speculative positions, they should be accounted for on either a market value or lower-of-cost-or-market value basis.

3 Accounting treatment: United Kingdom

Mark Davis

Overall basis of accounting

There is no authoritative guidance on accounting for forward rate agreements (FRAs) in the UK. Initially, banks generally tried to draw analogies with forward deposits or placings and consequently ignored FRAs for accounting purposes until the settlement date. With the development of the FRA market, a more acceptable form of accounting has emerged. Normal practice is now to treat an FRA as a hedge or a speculative transaction.

Hedging criteria

If an FRA is to be treated as a hedge it must satisfy the criteria outlined in Part II, Chapter 2. Because FRAs can be tailored to the particular hedging requirements of a company, there is usually no problem in determining the effectiveness of an FRA as a hedge.

Accounting treatment for hedges

Corporates will normally use FRAs as hedges. Any arrangement fees paid are usually written off. If the FRA hedges a liability, any receipt or payment under the FRA is amortised over the interest period being hedged. The interest differential payment under the FRA is discounted and consequently will not match exactly the change in the interest cost on the hedged liability. This difference, however, is normally immaterial and can be ignored for accounting purposes. Prior to the interest period being hedged, the FRA is ignored, since there are no margin payments. Alternatively, the FRA may be marked to market and any profit or loss shown as deferred income or expense. This simply adds entries either side of the balance sheet, with no effect on the P&L account until the settlement date.

Where an FRA hedges an asset, then the accounting should follow the treatment discussed in the futures chapter. If the asset is maintained at cost, the FRA can be ignored or its market value can be included on either side of the balance sheet. Any adjustment to the value of the asset such as a provision for diminution in value, should be arrived at after taking into account changes in the fair value of the FRA.

Accounting for speculative transactions

Most speculative transactions are undertaken by banks. An FRA can be revalued by obtaining a quote for a second FRA to close the position. The rate difference between the two FRAs can then be discounted back to arrive at an estimated payment or receipt on settlement day. Alternatively, forward forward rates can be calculated by interpolation from existing forward rates and the payment or receipt due on settlement day calculated from the standard settlement formula. When a bank's treasury book is comprised mainly of placings, deposits and FRAs, it seems inconsistent to market value the FRAs when interest rate positions inherent in the loan and deposit book are ignored. In such cases a bank may be justified in ignoring FRAs for accounting purposes and amortising the settlement payments over the term of each FRA. As discussed in Part II, Chapter 2, a more sensible, alternative accounting approach would be to fair value the whole treasury book.

Disclosure

Minimum disclosure requirements include an indication of the accounting policy adopted. Corporates should normally indicate the nature and extent of outstanding FRAs. Banks usually indicate only that FRAs have been undertaken in the normal course of business with no indication of the magnitude of such transactions. As with other forms of interest rate instruments, the European Community bank accounts directive will require greater disclosure in the future.

4 Documentation of forward rate agreements

Anthony C. Gooch and Linda B. Klein

Introduction

By 1984, given the growth in the FRA interbank market in London from its inception in the previous year, major participants in the market realised the need to standardise documentation; as the volume of transactions increased, so too did documentation backlogs. The response, through working parties of the British Bankers' Association and the Foreign Exchange and Currency Deposit Brokers' Association, was to develop the FRABBA terms – *Recommended terms and conditions* for London interbank forward rate agreements in specified currencies – which were published in 1985.

Like the BBAIRS terms for short-term fixed/Libor interest rate swaps in the London interbank market, the FRABBA terms were designed as a complete agreement and meant to be the standard that banks in that market would be presumed to accept in their dealings with each other unless they stated otherwise at the time they entered into an FRA. Those terms were not, however, intended as a model for agreements between those banks and their customers or banks outside that market, and attempts to standardise terms for such agreements, or for FRAs generally, have not occurred as they have for rate swaps. However, the FRABBA terms, which are governed by English law, are a helpful handbook on how conventional FRAs are generally documented.

Like swaps, FRAs are often agreed to over the telephone, with the documentation to follow. Under the FRABBA terms, the parties are presumed to have a binding contract at the time they reach their agreement, although they later record the financial terms of the transaction in an exchange of simple confirmations. The other provisions of their agreement are those set forth in the FRABBA terms, which are presumed to apply. A similar procedure will generally be followed for FRAs not governed by the FRABBA terms, although the exchange of confirmations may be followed by execution of a short document like the sample agreement included in Appendix A to this chapter. When parties contemplate entering into a series of FRAs with each other, they may avoid repetition of the effort involved in multiple agreements by entering into a master agreement that sets forth the basic terms of their understanding, and under which they may document each transaction through a simple confirmation. The advantages to master agreements can go beyond this; for example, if a party becomes involved in bankruptcy proceedings, they may enhance the other party's ability to treat a series of transactions with the insolvent party as offsetting assets and liabilities (depending on their respective market values at the time), thus reducing the solvent party's total risk to the insolvent party. These and other issues related to the use of master agreements are discussed in Part IV, Chapter 4.

Many institutions had already developed their own forms of documentation before the FRABBA terms were published and since that time have modified their forms to adopt the FRABBA terms supplemented by other provisions that reflect their particular concerns and policies. An institution that engages in cross-border transactions, for example, may wish to address in some detail the parties' agreement about how to handle situations in which it becomes illegal for one of the parties to perform its obligations under the FRA or in which a party would be required to make a withholding on account of taxes from a payment to be made by it under the FRA and, pursuant to the terms of the agreement, would be required to pay additional amounts to make the payee whole. Forward rate agreements involve only a single payment, and generally it is due within three, six or nine months from the date on which the FRA is done. Given that short-term frame of reference, such situations are of less concern than they are in interest rate swaps, which involve a series of payments over a term that may be as long as ten years, or occasionally longer. Nevertheless, many institutions deal in their FRA agreements with these and other concerns not addressed by the FRABBA terms, in particular in master agreements that may cover a series of transactions with a party.

As the concepts underlying forward rate transactions are quite similar to those applicable in rate swaps, forward rate agreements in many ways resemble rate swap agreements; the sample agreement included in Appendix A is therefore quite similar to Appendix A in Chapter 4, Part IV on documenting rate swaps. However, even though the concepts are the same, convention dictates that some of the terminology be different. For example, 'Contract Amount' and 'Contract Period', which are used in the FRA market, mean the same things as 'Notional Amount' and 'Calculation Period', which are generally used in rate swap agreements. Other, more fundamental, differences in the documents are highlighted below. The reader is referred to Part IV, Chapter 4, for discussion of provisions of Appendix A not dealt with in this chapter.

Special provisions of forward rate agreements

Definitions

As is true in the documentation of rate swaps, caps, collars and similar agreements, in forward rate agreements the basic provision on payments cannot be understood without the definitions. In a classic forward rate agreement, the 'buyer' will have entered into the transaction seeking protection against rising rates between the date the agreement is reached and a date in the future (the 'Settlement Date'), for a period (the 'Contract Period') beginning on that future date. Appendix A, for example, assumes a single forward rate transaction involving a period of approximately six months between the date of the agreement and the Settlement Date. The buyer in a classic FRA might be a corporate borrower with a Libor-based loan obligation using an FRA to protect itself against the possibility that Libor for the six-month interest period scheduled to begin three months later might be above, say, 11%. An FRA should provide that protection through an obligation of the 'seller' to make a payment to the buyer if Libor – the agreed floating rate – for the same period exceeds the agreed level of 11% in our example, which the FRA is likely to define as the 'Contract Rate' and state the same way as one would a fixed rate in a swap.

As the convention in the FRA market is to settle any amount payable in respect of the Contract Period at the beginning of the period, in our example the payment to be made by the seller under the FRA should be defined to be the present value on that future Settlement Date, discounted back from the last day in the Contract Period (the 'Maturity Date'), of the amount that would accrue on the agreed 'Contract Amount' during the Contract Period at a rate equal to the difference between Libor and the Contract Rate. This amount, called the 'Settlement Amount', should be discounted to present value at the same floating rate used in its calculation (Libor). Thus, if the buyer invested the payment made to it for the protected period at Libor, it would have an amount of interest that it could apply at the end of the Contract Period to service its Libor-based loan obligation for the same period, adding to that amount interest computed at the Contract Rate (at and below which it felt it did not need protection) plus any spread over Libor payable under the loan agreement. In exchange for that protection, the seller of the FRA obtains protection against (or the benefit of) falling rates from the buyer, through the buyer's promise to make a payment to the seller if Libor for the period falls below the Contract Rate. As illustrated in Appendix A, the amount payable by the buyer will be determined in similar fashion, and no additional terms need be defined to express the buyer's payment obligation, as 'Settlement Amount' is a neutral term that can be applied to the buyer and the seller alike in the appropriate circumstances. This chapter does not illustrate a different approach sometimes used in which the buyer pays the seller a single, initial fee in exchange for the FRA protection; however, a one-way payment transaction of that kind could easily be documented by combining techniques used in the appendix to this chapter and Appendix A in Chapter 4, Part VII on documenting rate caps and collars.

The definitions required in a conventional FRA like the one illustrated in this chapter can be quite simple, and they and other definitions relating to computation of the FRA Settlement Amount will involve concerns similar to those relevant in computing payment obligations under rate swap agreements. There will also be areas of concern in the definitions that distinguish FRA documentation from swap documentation. One is the appropriate expression of the concept of the present value; this is irrelevant in conventional rate swaps, which call for payments at, or near, the end of each calculation period. Appendix A takes a simple approach to referring to the present value computation, on the theory that the methodology used for such computations is widely understood and should not give rise to dispute so long as four elements are clearly stated: the relevant discount rate, the dates from and to which the amount is to be discounted and the computation basis (e.g. the actual number of days in the relevant period and a year of 360 days). An alternative, illustrated in the FRABBA terms, is to include a formula to be followed for the computation.

A second important difference from rate swap agreements relates to the definition of the FRA Contract Period. Since payment for the protection of an FRA must be made at the beginning of the relevant period and the parties' contractual duties (except for ancillary obligations) will end when that payment is made, in our view the Contract Period should be defined without regard to the possibility that the final day of the period may later be declared a holiday. On the other hand, if the buyer of the FRA wishes to ensure that Libor for the agreed period under the FRA is set on the same day, and for value on the same day, as Libor for the relevant period of the underlying obligation or instrument in respect of which protection is bought, holidays declared between the date the FRA is agreed and the Settlement Date should be taken into account. The definitions of 'Settlement Date' and 'Maturity Date' and the final sentence of Section 3(a) in Appendix A illustrate the kinds of provisions that may be used to accomplish this result. In contrast, as illustrated in the definition of 'Calculation Period' and Section 3(b) in Appendix A, Chapter 4, Part IV, holidays will generally be taken into account in computing floating rate amounts payable throughout the term of a rate swap, except perhaps for the final payment, and adjustments will be payable if the number of days in a calculation period changes because of an unexpected holiday declared between the date the payer is notified of the amount due and the date it becomes payable.

Payments

Because only one party will be required to make a single payment in a conventional FRA, this section can be much simpler than its counterpart in rate swap agreements, which often include terms relating to netting of payments and the rights of the parties to suspend or defer their payment obligations in certain circumstances. Provisions of this kind can, however, be appropriate in master agreements for forward rate transactions. In an FRA for a single transaction, like the one illustrated in Appendix A, the principal concern, as noted, will be precision in the defined terms used to state the payment obligation.

Defaults, termination events and remedies

As we have noted elsewhere in this book, rate swap agreements tend to have fewer events of default than other kinds of agreements involving credit risk. Still fewer default events may be used in documenting an FRA and, indeed, as illustrated in Appendix A, an agreement for a single FRA between two banks may not include any at all, although we note that the FRABBA terms for interbank FRAs include three events of default – two relating to a party's insolvency or bankruptcy and the third triggered by a material misrepresentation. These and other events of default, of course, may be appropriate in master forward rate agreements and FRAs with certain counterparties.

The difference in approach between FRAs and rate swaps in this area is a function of the fact that the former involve short-term risk, whereas rate swaps are done for periods of as long as 10 years, and sometimes longer. The need for events of default in FRAs should be examined in this light, and in light of special considerations relating to the counterparty and, often, the insolvency or bankruptcy laws to which it is subject. For example, if proceedings under the US Bankruptcy Code are commenced with respect to a party to an FRA of the kind illustrated in Appendix A, since the FRA can involve performance on the Settlement Date from either party, it may constitute an executory contract of a kind that the bankruptcy trustee might be free to elect to keep in place, assign or reject, notwithstanding a provision in the agreement that entitles the other party to treat the commencement of the proceedings as an event of default that allows it to terminate, or that automatically operates to terminate, its obligations under the agreement and collect damages, and notwithstanding a prohibition in the agreement against assignments without consent. Exceptions to these rules of the US Bankruptcy Code apply to certain forward contracts involving commodities and their byproducts but apparently not to the kinds of FRAs dealt with in this volume. (Further discussion of these questions as they relate to rate swaps is included in Part IV, Chapter 4. When applicable bankruptcy law presents this kind of problem, given the short-term nature of the risk involved, the utility of an event of default relating to insolvency or bankruptcy may be outweighed by a desire to minimise the length and complexity of the FRA documentation.

Similarly, 'no-fault' termination events of the kinds generally included in rate swap agreements may not be included in FRAs. Sections 7 and 8 of Appendix A deal with situations of the kinds that in a rate swap agreement might entitle a party to give notice of early termination (as illustrated in Appendix A, Chapter 4, Part IV). However, in the sample FRA, the first of these circumstances – supervening illegality – merely results in an obligation of the affected party to use reasonable efforts to attempt to avoid the problem through an assignment or transfer or other arrangement agreed upon with the other party to the FRA. Given the relatively short period between the date a conventional FRA is entered into and the Settlement Date it contemplates, the parties may well choose this kind of approach, if they address the subject at all (the FRABBA terms do not), since the benefits to be gained from provisions on early termination may be small: early termination will require a provision regarding computation of any damages payable as a result of the parties' loss of their bargain, but that step (and any dispute over the amount determined under the provision) can be avoided if the parties wait the relatively short period until determination of the floating rate relevant for computing the Settlement Amount; at that time precise damages will be determinable.

Similarly, in Appendix A a party's obligation to make 'gross-up' payments in respect of taxes it may be required to withhold would not entitle that party to call for early termination, although that would generally be permitted under a rate swap agreement, after suitable efforts to avoid the problem. The sample FRA simply places the burden of the gross-up for the single payment on the affected party. Some institutions may choose an approach more similar to the one they use in rate swaps; others may leave the appropriate treatment of such matters to future agreement. For example, the FRABBA terms simply include a provision to the effect that the parties may opt to terminate their agreement at any time, assuming they so agree and also agree on the appropriate amount to be paid as a result. That kind of provision may be helpful as a reflection of the market's positive view of consensual cancellation of FRAs but technically, under New York law, it would be an unenforceable agreement to agree (although perhaps it would be viewed as resulting in an obligation to negotiate in good faith).

If there is any question under the law chosen to govern an FRA about the legal rights of the parties (outside the contract) to collect damages in the event one of the parties repudiates the contract or cannot perform because of a change in law, the parties will probably wish to include a provision on damages in their agreement. In such circumstances, and when FRAs do include provisions stating grounds for early termination, there is no reason why the provisions cannot be modelled after those used in rate swap agreements. Where events of default are concerned, the FRABBA terms provide for payment of damages pursuant to a general indemnification clause. The market-based agreement value approach described in our chapter on rate swap documentation, similarly, could be adapted for use in an FRA. As noted, the FRABBA terms do not specify how 'no-fault' termination events are to be handled, but here too institutions wishing to include provisions on such matters may adopt any of the approaches used in the rate swap market (the most common of which are described in Chapter 4, Part IV).

Conclusion

The FRA for a single transaction can be a very simple document, because of the simplicity of the transaction itself and the short-term risk it involves. Somewhat more complexity can be expected in master FRAs, and there is likely to be greater use of such agreements in the future, and of master agreements that will accommodate a variety of rate protection arrangements, including FRAs, swaps, caps and collars. If more institutions do choose to integrate their rate risk management arrangements with any given counterparty under a single umbrella agreement, further attempts at standardisation of FRA documents may be expected to build on the achievements of the FRABBA terms.

Appendix A: Forward rate agreement

This agreement is a sample of the kind of documentation that might be used for a two-way US dollar forward rate agreement in which a bank organised under the laws of the United States is the 'buyer' of the contract (the party seeking protection against a rise in rates) and a bank organised under the laws of Switzerland is the 'seller'.

This sample is merely an illustration and should not be used for an actual transaction; each transaction will have its own special features, and the agreement drafted to document it should be carefully tailored to address the legal and business problems that it presents.

FORWARD RATE AGREEMENT dated as of July 1, 1987 between BIG BANK, N.A. (the 'Buyer') and EUROPEAN BANK S.A. (the 'Seller'), whereby the parties agree as follows.

1. *Definitions.* For purposes of this Agreement, the following terms shall have the meanings indicated.

'Banking Day' means a day on which banks are not required or authorized by law to close in New York City that is also a London Banking Day.

'Contract Amount' means $80,000,000.

'Contract Period' means the period commencing on the Settlement Date and ending on the Maturity Date.

'Contract Rate' means __% per annum.

'Dollars' or *'$'* means lawful money of the United States.

'LIBOR' means the rate (expressed as an annual rate) equal to the arithmetic mean (rounded up, if necessary, to the nearest 1/100,000 of 1%) of the rates shown on the 'LIBO' page display (or any substitute display) of the Reuter Monitor Money Rates Service as the London interbank offered rates of the banks named on that display at approximately 11:00 a.m. (London time) on the second London Banking Day before the Settlement Date for deposits in Dollars for a period of six months, subject to Section 3(c).

'London Banking Day' means a day on which dealings in deposits in Dollars are carried on in the London interbank market.

'Maturity Date' means June 30, 1988 or, if by the time for setting LIBOR that day has been declared a bank holiday in London or New York City, the following Banking Day, unless that following Banking Day is in a different calendar month, in which case the Maturity Date shall be the preceding Banking Day.

'Present Value of the Settlement Amount' means the amount determined by discounting the Settlement Amount from the Maturity Date to its present value on the Settlement Date at a rate per annum equal to LIBOR.

'Settlement Amount' means the amount that would accrue during the Contract Period on the Contract Amount at the difference between LIBOR and the Contract Rate, computed as provided in Section 3(a).

'Settlement Date' means December 31, 1987 or, if by the time for setting LIBOR that day has been declared a bank holiday in London or New York City, the following Banking Day, unless that following Banking Day falls in a different calendar month, in which case the Settlement Date shall be the preceding Banking Day.

'Taxes', with respect to payments hereunder by either party, means any present or future taxes, levies, imposts, duties or charges of any nature whatsoever that are collectible by withholding except for any such tax, levy, impost, duty or charge that would not have been imposed but for the existence of a connection between the party receiving the payment and the jurisdiction where it is imposed.

'United States' means the United States of America.

2. *Payments.* On the terms and subject to the conditions set forth herein, on the Settlement Date (a) if LIBOR is greater than the Contract Rate, the Seller shall pay the Present Value of the Settlement Amount to the Buyer, and (b) if the Contract Rate is greater than LIBOR, the Buyer shall pay the Present Value of the Settlement Amount to the Seller.

3. *Computations and Determinations.* (a) The Settlement Amount and Present Value of the Settlement Amount and any interest payable pursuant to Section 5 shall be computed on the basis of a 360-day year and actual days elapsed from and including the first day of the relevant period to but excluding the last day thereof. Holidays declared by the time for setting LIBOR shall be taken into account in computing the Settlement Amount. No adjustment shall be payable if the first or last day of the Contract Period is later declared to be a holiday in London or New York.

(b) The Buyer shall determine LIBOR and the Present Value of the Settlement Amount payable pursuant to Section 2(a) and, no later than the second London Banking Day before the Settlement Date, shall give notice to the Seller specifying that amount and the party required to make it and indicating how that amount was computed.

(c) For purposes of determining LIBOR, the rules set forth below shall apply if the 'LIBO' page (or a substitute) is not being displayed by the Reuter Monitor Money Rates Service at the time for the determination.

(i) LIBOR shall be the rate (expressed as an annual rate) equal to the arithmetic mean (rounded up, if necessary, to the nearest 1/100,000 of 1%) of the rates at which deposits in Dollars in an amount substantially equal to the Contract Amount would be offered at that time by the principal London offices of Barclays Bank PLC, The Bank of Tokyo, Ltd., Bankers Trust Company and National Westminster Bank PLC to major banks in the London interbank market for a period of six months, as quoted to the Buyer; or

(ii) if at least one but not all of the London offices of those institutions supplies the Buyer with the necessary quotation at that time, the Buyer shall determine LIBOR on the basis of the quotation or quotations supplied to it; or

(iii) if none of those offices supplies the Buyer with the necessary quotation, LIBOR shall be the arithmetic mean (rounded as provided above) of the rates quoted to the Buyer by the principal lending offices of four major banks in New York City selected by the Buyer as their respective lowest lending rates for loans in Dollars to leading European banks for that period and in that amount at approximately 11:00 a.m. (New York City time) on the Settlement Date.

4. *Making of Payments.* All payments hereunder shall be made to the account specified for the intended recipient in Exhibit 4A.1, or to such other account in New York City as that party may have last specified by notice to the other party, and shall be made in funds settled through the New York Clearing House Interbank Payments System or such other same-day funds as are customary at the time for the settlement in New York City of banking transactions denominated in Dollars.

5. *Default Interest.* If any amount due hereunder is not paid when due, interest shall accrue on that amount to the extent permitted by applicable law at a rate per annum equal for each day that amount remains unpaid to the sum of 1% and the rate quoted by the principal London office of the Buyer at 11.00 a.m. (London time) for overnight deposits in Dollars, in an amount substantially equal to the overdue amount, for value on that day or, if that day is not a London Banking Day, on the preceding London Banking Day. Interest hereunder shall be payable from time to time on demand.

6. *Supervening Illegality.* If it becomes unlawful for either party to make any payment to be made by it hereunder, or to receive any amount to be received by it hereunder, as a result of the adoption of, or any change in, or change in the interpretation of, any law, regulation or treaty, that party shall give notice to that effect to the other party and shall use reasonable efforts (a) to assign or transfer its rights and obligations under this Agreement, subject to Section 12, to another of its branches, offices or affiliates, or to any leading participant in the forward rate agreement market, that may make those payments and receive those amounts lawfully and without withholding for or on account of Taxes or (b) to agree with the other party to modify this Agreement or change the method of payment hereunder so that the payment or receipt will not be unlawful.

7. *Taxes.* Except as otherwise required by law, each payment hereunder shall be made without withholding for or on account of Taxes. If either party is required to make any withholding from any payment under this Agreement for or on account of Taxes, it shall (a) make that withholding, (b) make timely payment of the amount withheld to the appropriate governmental authority, (c) forthwith pay the other party such additional amount as may be necessary to ensure that the net amount actually received by it free and clear of Taxes (including any Taxes on the additional amount) is equal to the amount that it would have received had no Taxes been withheld and (d) on or before the thirtieth day after payment, send that other party the original or a certified copy of an official tax receipt evidencing that payment; *provided, however,* that if the representation and warranty made by a party in Section 8(e) proves not to have been true when made or, if repeated on the Settlement Date, would not then be true, or if a party fails to perform or observe its covenant set forth in Section 9 or Section 10, the other party shall be under no obligation to pay any additional amount hereunder to the extent that the withholding would not have been required if the representation and warranty had been true when made, or would have been true when repeated, or if the failure had not occurred.

8. *Representations and Warranties.* Each of the parties makes the representations and warranties set forth below to the other as of the date hereof.

(a) It is duly organized and validly existing and has the corporate power and authority to execute and deliver this Agreement and to perform its obligations hereunder.

(b) It has taken all necessary action to authorize its execution and delivery of this Agreement and the performance of its obligations hereunder.

(c) All governmental authorizations and actions necessary in connection with its execution and delivery of this Agreement and the performance of its obligations hereunder have been obtained or performed and remain valid and in full force and effect.

(d) This Agreement has been duly executed and delivered by it and constitutes its legal, valid and binding obligation, enforceable against it in accordance with the terms of this Agreement, subject to all applicable bankruptcy, insolvency, moratorium and similar laws affecting creditors' rights generally.

(e) It is, in the case of the Seller, a Swiss corporation and a Swiss enterprise, and, in the case of the Buyer, a United States corporation and a United States enterprise, for purposes of the income tax convention between the United States and Switzerland, and, in each case, it is fully eligible for the benefits of that convention with respect to any payments receivable by it under this Agreement.

9. *Covenants.* If either party is required at any time to execute any form or document in order for payments to it hereunder to qualify for exemption from withholding for or on account of Taxes or to qualify for such withholding at a reduced rate, that party shall, on demand, execute the required form or document and deliver it to the party required to make those payments.

10. *Closing Documents.* On or before July 15, 1987, the Seller shall deliver to the Buyer Internal Revenue Service Form 1001, duly completed and executed in duplicate.

11. *Costs and Expenses.* (a) Each of the parties shall pay, or reimburse the other on demand for, all stamp registration, documentation or similar taxes or duties, and any penalties or interest that may be due with respect thereto, that may be imposed by any jurisdiction in respect of its execution or delivery of this Agreement. If any such tax or duty is imposed by any jurisdiction as the result of the conduct or status of both parties, each party shall pay one half of the amount of the tax or duty.

(b) A party that fails to perform any of its obligations hereunder shall pay, or reimburse the other on demand for, all reasonable costs and expenses incurred by the other in connection with the enforcement of its rights under this Agreement, including, without limitation, fees and expenses of legal counsel.

12. *Non-Assignment.* Neither party shall be entitled to assign or transfer its rights or obligations hereunder or any interest herein to any other person or any of its other branches or offices without the written consent of the other party to this Agreement, and any purported assignment or transfer in violation of this Section shall be void. The parties are acting for purposes of this Agreement through their respective branches or offices specified in Exhibit 4A.1. Neither party shall withhold its consent to an assignment or transfer proposed pursuant to Section 6 if (a) the proposed assignee or transferee meets the criteria set forth in Section 6(a) and (b) the policies of the party whose consent has been sought, as then in effect, would permit it to enter into a forward rate transaction with the proposed assignee or transferee without credit support.

13. *Interpretation.* The section headings in this Agreement are for convenience of reference only and shall not affect the meaning or construction of any provision hereof.

14. *Notices.* All notices in connection with this Agreement shall be given by telex or cable or by notice in writing hand-delivered or sent by facsimile transmission or by airmail, postage prepaid. All such notices shall be sent to the telex or telecopier number or address (as the case may be) specified for the intended recipient in Exhibit 4A.1 (or to such other number or address as that recipient may have last specified by notice to the other party) and shall be sent with copies as indicated therein. All such notices shall be effective upon receipt, and confirmation by answerback of any notice sent by telex as provided herein shall be sufficient evidence of receipt thereof.

15. *Amendments.* This Agreement may be amended only by an instrument in writing executed by the parties hereto.

16. *Currency.* Each reference in this Agreement to Dollars is of the essence. The obligation of each of the parties in respect of any amount due under this Agreement shall, notwithstanding any payment in any other currency (whether pursuant to a judgment or otherwise), be discharged only to the extent of the amount in Dollars that the party entitled to receive that payment may, in accordance with normal banking procedures, purchase with the sum paid in such other currency (after any premium and costs of exchange) on the Banking Day immediately following the day on which that party receives that payment. If the amount in Dollars that may be so purchased for any reason falls short of the amount originally due, the party required to make that payment shall pay such additional amounts, in Dollars, as may be necessary to compensate for that shortfall. Any obligation of that party not discharged by that payment shall, to the fullest extent permitted by applicable law, be due as a separate and independent obligation and, until discharged as provided herein, shall continue in full force and effect.

17. *Jurisdiction; Governing Law; Immunity.* (a) Any action or proceeding relating in any way to this Agreement may be brought and enforced in the courts of the State of New York or of the United States for the Southern District of New York, and the Seller irrevocably submits to the nonexclusive jurisdiction of each such court in connection with any such action or proceeding.

(b) The Seller hereby irrevocably appoints _____, which maintains an office in New York City on the date hereof at _____, as its agent to receive service of process or other legal summons in connection with any such action or proceeding. So long as the Seller has any obligation under this Agreement, it shall maintain a duly appointed agent in New York City for service of such process or other summons, and if it fails to maintain such an agent, any such process or other summons may be served by mailing a copy thereof by certified or registered mail, or any substantially similar form of mail, addressed to the Seller as provided for notices hereunder. Any such process or other summons may be served on the Buyer by mailing a copy thereof by certified or registered mail, or any substantially similar form of mail, addressed to the Buyer as provided for notices hereunder.

(c) The Seller irrevocably waives to the fullest extent permitted by applicable law all immunity (whether on the basis of sovereignty or otherwise) from jurisdiction, attachment (both before and after judgment) and execution to which it might otherwise be entitled in any action or proceeding related in any way to this Agreement.

(d) This Agreement shall be governed by, and construed in accordance with, the law of the State of New York.

18. *Counterparts; Integration of Terms.* This Agreement may be executed in counterparts, and the counterparts taken together shall be deemed to constitute one and the same agreement. This Agreement contains the entire agreement between the parties relating to the subject matter hereof and supersedes all oral statements and prior writings with respect thereto.

IN WITNESS WHEREOF the parties have caused this Agreement to be duly executed and delivered as of the day and year first written above.

BIG BANK, N.A.   EUROPEAN BANK S.A.

By:_____   By:_____

Title:_____   Title:_____

Exhibit 4A.1   Addresses for Notices and Accounts for Payments

---

BIG BANK, N.A.

Address:	One Financial Center
	New York, NY 00000
Attention:	Swaps Group Leader
Telex No.:	00000 BB
Telecopier No.:	(000) 000–0000

Account for Payments

Account No.:	00–000
Depositary:	Big Bank, N.A.
	One Financial Center
	New York, NY 00000

EUROPEAN BANK S.A.

Address:	1, Gnomestrasse
	Zurich, Switzerland
Attention:	Rate Risk Management Group
Telex No.:	00000 EBSA
Telecopier No.:	(000) 000–00000

Account for Payments

Account No.:	00–000
Depositary:	Other Big Bank
	Big Bank Plaza
	New York, NY 00000

---

5 Case study: Future rate agreements

Daniel-Yves Treves and Graham Wandrag

Introduction

Tradition developed the interbank future rate agreement (FRA) market in mid-1984 after having cleared all the legal aspects associated with its use, and although the FRA is thus a fairly new financial instrument, it has become rapidly popular.

The instrument was originally conceived for use in the dollar market but has now spread to most, if not all, major currencies, and although the dollar market is still by far the largest (the latest BIS volume issued in April 1986 indicated that by late-1985 the monthly volume had grown to at least US$7bn). The sterling market has also grown at an amazing rate to become the second largest in terms of volume. The Tradition Group capital market section in London, Tradition Treasury Services, is among the leading three brokers in domestic FRAs with the most sophisticated in-house computer system. This system has been used to produce the examples used later in this chapter.

The volume of these markets reflects the fact that a tailor-made interest rate hedging mechanism was simpler to use than the already well-developed financial futures area. The latter has standard features necessary to be traded on an organised exchange, whereas the FRA provides the possibility to choose the periods exactly needed to match an interest rate risk.

Its fields of application are unlimited. They can be used by anyone wishing to lock in a fixed rate, for example, an investor who is more particularly concerned with falling rates in the future or, on the other hand, the borrower desirous to protect himself against rising rates ahead.

Explained below are three examples of how FRAs are best applied in arbitrage situations and how, in various instances, they compare favourably with other interest rate hedging instruments.

1   Situations linked to deposits or borrowings (cash markets).
2   Positions completing financial futures operations.
3   Positions linked to interest swap operations.

The cash market

Increasing yields on deposits

A bank has received a one-year (365 days) deposit on to its balance sheet for which it pays $9\frac{1}{8}$%. The bank wishes to lend this money straight back out to the market which it can do at $9\frac{3}{16}$, however, it feels that $\frac{1}{16}$% is not enough to cover the costs and credit risk exposure.

By lending the money for 6 months (182 days) at $8\frac{7}{8}$% and selling the 6- against 12-month FRA at 9.22%, the bank can effectively lend the money at $9\frac{1}{4}$% for the year providing a more comfortable $\frac{1}{8}$% profit.

The effect of the FRA is to insure that the bank can lend the returned 6-month loan at 9.22% regardless of the Libor in 6 months time.

Reducing borrowing costs

A bank wishes to borrow 6-month interbank against a loan to a customer. The current offered rate in the market is 9% but the bank sees the opportunity to borrow 3-month money at $8\frac{7}{8}$%, which is easier than borrowing for 6 months; and to buy the 3- versus 6-month FRA at 8.83% giving the bank a 6-month borrowing cost of only 8.95%, an improvement of 5 basis points.

Improving short cash position using FRA and longer cash

A bank has short 3-month (92 days) position which it wishes to close by borrowing for that period. To close the position without making a loss the bank must borrow at no more than $8\frac{13}{16}$% but the best offer in the market is $8\frac{15}{16}$%. However, the bank is able to borrow for 6 months at $8\frac{15}{16}$% from a fellow national, effectively a better rate, and to sell the 3- versus 6-month FRA (91 days) at 8.90%. This has the effect of leaving the bank long of 3-month cash at almost $8\frac{25}{32}$% (see diagram), enabling a cut in the position with a small profit instead of a loss.

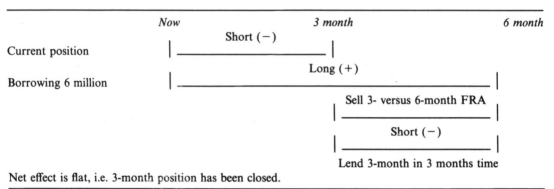

Net effect is flat, i.e. 3-month position has been closed.

Note: The bank could achieve the same result by borrowing for 9 months at $9\frac{1}{8}$% and selling the 3- versus 6-month FRA at 9.09%.

Pure CD – cash – FRA arbitrage

A bank can issue its one-year certificate of deposit (CD) at $9\frac{1}{8}$%. It can then lend the funds raised for 6 months at $8\frac{15}{16}$%. In 6 months time the bank will be long of those funds again and must ensure an income from them at least sufficient to cover the cost of issuing the CD. To do this the bank must lend the funds at, at least, 8.91%. Fortunately, 6- versus 12-months is well bid at 9.30% giving a net profit of 39 basis points over the final 6 months, equivalent to $19\frac{1}{2}$ points over the year. This profit must be weighed against tying up credit limits by issuing the CD, by trading the FRA and against all the transaction and back office costs.

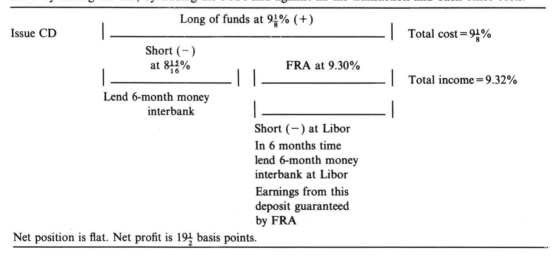

Net position is flat. Net profit is $19\frac{1}{2}$ basis points.

238

Financial futures

The following is an example of a simple arbitrage between a futures contract traded on LIFFE and the view of 3-month Libor expressed by the FRA market.

If the dealing date is mid-April then the start date of 2- versus 5-month FRA will be the date on which the near June futures contract will settle.

Suppose the June contract is offered at 91.35 (equivalent yield approx. $100 - 91.35 = 8.65\%$) and the 2-versus 5-month FRA with matched dates, is offered at 8.55 and that both contracts are bought and held till settlement on 15 June, say. By buying the FRA the bank has agreed to pay 8.55% and receive the 3-month Libor of 15 June.

For the sake of this analysis we shall assume the 3-month Libor settles at $9\frac{1}{2}\%$ and that the futures contract settles at 90.51.

Then, on 15 June:

Loss on futures contract $= (91.35 - 90.51)$
$= 84$ basis points (ignoring effects of daily marginal adjustments)

Profit on FRA $= 95$ basis points, equivalent to approx. 93 basis points after discounting at Libor of $9\frac{1}{2}\%$ for the duration of the FRA.

Thus, the net profit is $93 - 84 = 9$ basis points, which was locked in at the start of the transaction.

Interest rate swaps

A bank sees an arbitrage in a one-year interest rate swap (IRS) with fixed interest paid quarterly against 3-month Libor. The IRS is bid at 9.15%. Three-month Libor is $8\frac{7}{8}\%$ and the following FRAs are offered at the levels shown below:

$$3\text{- versus 6-month FRA at } 8.88\%$$
$$6\text{- versus 9-month FRA at } 9.09\%$$
$$9\text{- versus 12-month FRA at } 9.27\%$$

If the bank gives (sells) the IRS at 9.15% and takes (buys) all the FRAs at the levels stated above it will receive a 15 basis point profit off-balance sheet through the arbitrage between these markets. This profit is calculated as follows:

First fixing: For the first three month period the bank receives 9.15% from the IRS and pays $8\frac{7}{8}\%$ which is the 3-month Libor fixing. It is therefore gaining 27.5 basis points for the first 3 months.

Second fixing: For the second 3 months the bank receives 9.15%, pays 3-month Libor on the IRS, pays 8.88% and receives 3-month Libor on the FRA. The Libor payments cancel each other and the bank gains 27 basis points (see diagram).

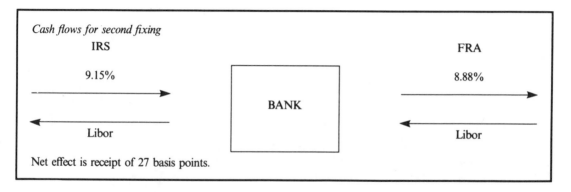

Cash flows for second fixing

IRS

FRA

9.15%

8.88%

BANK

Libor

Libor

Net effect is receipt of 27 basis points.

Third fixing: For the third 3 months the bank receives 9.15%, pays 3-month Libor on the IRS, pays 9.09% and receives 3-month Libor on the FRA. The Libor payments cancel each other and the bank gains 6 basis points.

Fourth fixing: For the final 3 months the bank receives 9.15%, pays 3-month Libor on the IRS, pays 9.27% and receives 3-month Libor on the FRA. The Libor payments cancel each other and the bank loses 2 basis points.

The total profit is therefore $27.5 + 27 + 6 - 2 = 58.5$ basis points. However, these are quarterly points profit and, to equate to an annual profit, we must divide the total by 4 giving 14.625 basis points. But if this is to be assessed at the end of the year, assuming reinvestment of any differences at the FRA rates, then the annual profit is 15.45 basis points, a generally acceptable off-balance sheet profit.

The above is a simplistic analysis. It should therefore be regarded as a generalised view of this kind of transaction and not a definitive illustration of actual calculations.

Conclusion

A corporation or an institution with a hedging requirement will see from these examples how it can at times act more advantageously through the FRA route rather than in the cash market, financial futures or an interest rate swap.

Note: An assumption has been made in all the examples that the points profit are sufficient for the bank to enter 'off-balance sheet trading'. All banks require slightly differing margins to enter into arbitrage transactions. In addition, accounting practices may give rise to different results from similar arbitrage transactions.

PART VII

Caps and collars

1 Mechanics of caps and collars

Steve Oakes

Introduction

Caps, floors, collars, corridors, piras, swaptions – all these interest rate option products have attracted a great deal of attention recently as they comprise the fastest growing area of the interest rate protection market.

These products have come a long way from their origination in 1984/85 when traders began to 'strip out' the option element of a capped FRCD and FRN and traded them separately. Estimates of market volume for caps are from virtually nothing in 1984 to $60–70bn in 1986, and $100–150bn in 1987. Many players are predicting a $200-250bn market for 1988 – almost half the size of the total swap market.

US dealers still dominate the market, and probably 75% of cap business is still in New York. The 25% in Europe is split equally across the three major currencies – dollars, Deutschmarks and sterling. French francs enjoy a reasonable market, predominantly out of Paris, and there are occasional trades in Swiss francs, ECUs, Dutch guilders and pesetas. Tokyo remains an unknown quantity – it is just beginning to feel its way into the market and much depends on the attitude taken by the authorities towards option products.

The market is driven now more by funding books rather than asset managers. Much of the growth is attributable to the increased sophistication of corporate treasurers as they begin to get behind what at first appears to be complicated products. However, once understood, they offer a range of new possibilities in order to design any asset portfolio or hedging book to match perfectly any given view on interest rates.

This chapter will attempt to address those areas most frequently questioned by end users. First, a description of each product and how it works; second, an explanation of how a cap price is derived; third, an examination of how to evaluate when to use a swap or an option depending on your view of future interest rate movements; and a brief review of the risks involved in trading and hedging a dynamic option book.

Product description

Cap

A buyer of a cap buys the right to be paid the interest rate differential between the strike rate and the then current rate at certain times during the life of the cap. For example, if you buy from me a 5-year 11% cap on 3-month Libor on a notional principal of $100m, that would cost you a one time up-front payment of $2,460,000. In return, every three months (i.e. on each 'reset day') if the 3-month Libor reference rate is above 11% I will pay you the difference for that interest rate period, e.g. on the reset day of 15 March 1991; say 3-month Libor is 13.5%, I will pay you $100,000,000 \times (0.135 - 0.11) \times 91/360 = \$631,945$. You have this right on each 3-month roll date, i.e. 15 times during the life of the cap.

A typical user of a cap would be a corporate treasurer concerned about his borrowing on a floating index, such as Libor, which is open to the risk of an upward shift in interest rates, but finds the fixed rate of a swap too expensive: this is why a cap is often referred to a a type of 'fire insurance'.

Exhibit 1.1 Examples of option products

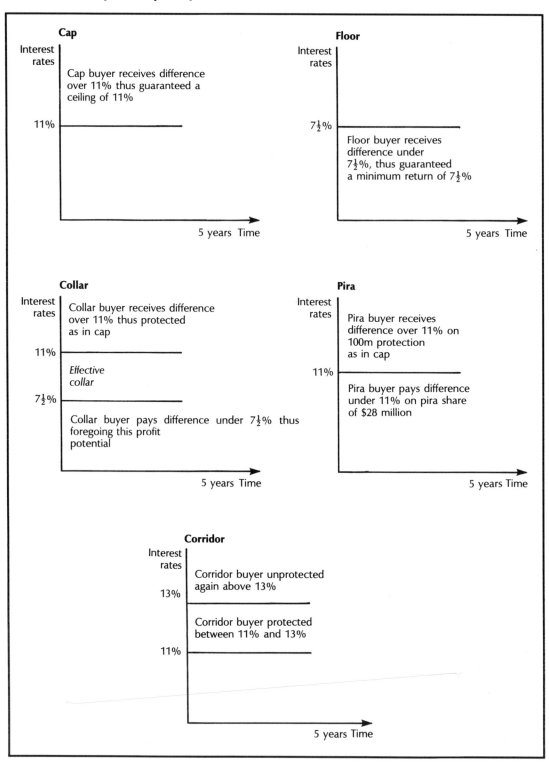

Cap

Interest rates

Cap buyer receives difference over 11% thus guaranteed a ceiling of 11%

11%

5 years Time

Floor

Interest rates

$7\frac{1}{2}$%

Floor buyer receives difference under $7\frac{1}{2}$%, thus guaranteed a minimum return of $7\frac{1}{2}$%

5 years Time

Collar

Interest rates

Collar buyer receives difference over 11% thus protected as in cap

11%

Effective collar

$7\frac{1}{2}$%

Collar buyer pays difference under $7\frac{1}{2}$% thus foregoing this profit potential

5 years Time

Pira

Interest rates

Pira buyer receives difference over 11% on 100m protection as in cap

11%

Pira buyer pays difference under 11% on pira share of $28 million

5 years Time

Corridor

Interest rates

Corridor buyer unprotected again above 13%

13%

Corridor buyer protected between 11% and 13%

11%

5 years Time

The price (premium) is generally paid as a one time up-front payment to the cap seller. Exhibit 1.2 illustrates a cross section of prices by maturity and variety of strike price when the US 30-year long bond was trading at a yield of 9.28% in May 1988. Prices are normally quoted on up-front basis points of notional principal, although premiums are also occasionally amortised over the life of the cap.

Exhibit 1.2   Indicative prices for caps and floors on US dollar 3-month Libor

Caps					Floors	
Maturity (yrs)	8%	9%	10%	11%	7%	8%
1	42	15	5	1	3	21
2	167	91	48	25	15	55
3	330	208	130	81	34	97
4	498	336	227	154	61	149
5	685	485	345	246	88	196
7	1,073	806	609	463	137	281
10	1,517	1,178	919	721	209	399

1. Prices quoted as one time up-front premium in basis points.
2. Prices as of May 1988 with 3-month Libor at 7.5% US 30-year long bond yield 9.28% and volatility of the front CME contract at 18%.
3. Typical trade size US$25–100m.
   Source: Manufacturers Hanover Reuters, p. CAPS.

Floor

A floor is very similar to a cap, except that it functions the other way round. A floor buyer buys the right to be compensated if rates fall below the strike level. Some representative prices are provided in Exhibit 1.2. Payments and mechanics are identical to the cap.

Typical floor users, on the asset side, are investors which buy floors to cover their concern that the return on floating assets will fall below a certain level, or, on the liability side, large fixed rate issuers who swap into floating and sell a floor to enhance their level of sub-Libor funding: the risk assumed here is that if rates fall below the strike level, say $6\frac{1}{2}$%, they give up potential for lower rates and lock in their funding at $6\frac{1}{2}$%.

Collar

Most corporate treasurers are strongly attracted to using a cap instead of the swap, as it allows them to enjoy the lower funding rate in the immediate future instead of the higher fixed rate (i.e. to 'ride the curve'). However, they do not want to pay the up-front premium for it. One way to avoid this is using the collar, which involves buying the cap to provide the protection required, but in the same transaction to sell a floor at a lower strike rate to reduce the up-front premium. The risk is that whilst the downside of higher rates is still protected, some of the potential gain from lower rates is foregone and the buyer of the collar accepts a maximum gain if rates fall.

In our example where you bought a 5-year 11% cap for $2,460,000 up-front, if you simultaneously sold me a $7\frac{1}{2}$% floor, the cost is reduced to $1,120,000 to you, the liability manager; it forms a *maximum* rate of 11% and a *minimum* rate of $7\frac{1}{2}$% for 5 years, i.e. a 'collar'.

This product is extremely popular with corporates because of the reduction in premium. In fact, some even trade 'zero cost collars', where the strike level of the floor is so high that it equals the value of the cap bought, i.e. at the net cost of zero. However, the most treasurers view the strike rates of a zero cost collar as too tight to be practical.

Pira (participating interest rate agreement)

With a pira, the buyer buys a cap on a notional *x* and sells back a floor *at the same strike level* but on a notional principal of only a proportion of *x* such that the whole transaction nets to a zero cost. However, under this transaction on the buyer must begin to pay out immediately on the floor with a strike already above current strikes ('in-the-money') albeit on a reduced notional principal.

Refering to Exhibit 1.1 and 1.2, in order to buy the 5-year 11% cap on $100m for zero cost via the pira, you would have to sell me a 5-year 11% floor on $28m. The pira is really another ingenious way of reducing the up-front premium, and rarely trades because once the end user better understands option products, he more readily accepts the payment of the up-front premium in relation to his profit expectation (or savings) over the life of the transaction.

Corridor

The cap buyer buys a cap at one level, say 5-years at 11%, and in the same transaction sells a 5-year cap at a *higher* strike, say 13%. The risk is that if rates rise above 11% he is protected as before, but as they go above 13% he becomes unprotected. This is merely another way of reducing the up-front premium when the buyer has a strong view on rates at certain levels.

Options on forward rate agreements (FRAs)

Options on FRAs, such as 3 × 6s, 6 × 12s or even a period further out the curve, such as 2 year × 3 year are often marketed as a 'new product'.

In fact they are simply a one time setting cap, and are extremely easy to price, see below. The cap FRA is often referred to as a 'borrower' option and the floor FRA as a 'lender' option. This market is active up to maturities of one year and introduces many customers from the cash deposit market.

Variations

Numerous variations on the above option products are possible in order to tailor a product to the client's needs:

- *Amortising/accreting* schedule (or both) of notional principal of the trade to match, for example, loan repayments.
- *Indices:* the bulk of the market trades on 3-month Libor, although caps on 1-, 6-, and 12-month Libor are readily available and there is a liquid market also in prime rate, commercial paper, certificates of deposit, Federal funds and Treasury bills.
- *Delayed caps/forward caps:* dates can always be matched to the customer's requirements, even if this means the transaction not starting for several months or years.

How a cap is priced

To understand the make-up of a cap price, we need to refer to previous chapters in this book.

A cap, conceptually, is a simple string of *put options* (a put option on the price, not the rate). Thus, if we can price each individual option separately, then the cap price is simply the sum total of all these prices.

Refering to Exhibits 1.1 and 1.2 the 5-year 11% cap on 3-month Libor of $2,460,000, this price is simply the sum total of the price of an 11% option in the first 'time bucket' from 'spot' today to three months (obviously zero as Libor is 7½% at May 1988) added to the price of the 11% strike for months 3 to 6, added to the price of the option for the 6- to 9-month bucket, and so on, until the price of the option for the 57- to 60-month bucket.

Given our knowledge of option pricing using the Black–Scholes or binomial method, our only problem is defining two of the fundamental constituents of the option price:

1. what is the 'underlying rate' (i.e. the expected rate 'at-the money') for, say, the 57- to 60-month bucket; and
2. what is the volatility assumption for that period?

In answer to the first problem I now introduce the most important concept in this chapter: 'the implied forwards curve'. This area has created much confusion in the past and accounts to a large extent for the more rapid acceptance of options in the foreign exchange world. A forward rate in foreign exchange is an easier concept to grasp as most market users are familiar with forward exchange contracts, but how do we observe a forward in interest rates? What we effectively need is a string of FRAs all the way to 54×57 and 57×60. Fortunately, the answers are obvious, but they are hidden in swap rates and need to be deduced by simple mathematics.

First, we can easily assess the 3-month FRA rates out to 3 years by interpolation between the Eurodollar futures on the Chicago mercantill Exchange (CME). A future price is in itself a 3-month FRA from the contract date. For example, the June 1990 contract currently trading (May 1988) at 90.61 is essentially a 24×27 FRA at a rate of $(100-90.61) = 9.39\%$. Secondly, we know the 3-year swap rate is mathematically equal to the weighted average of the futures (FRAs) in all 'buckets' out to 3 years (otherwise any mismatch can be arbitraged). The 4-year swap rate is also a weighted average of all the FRA buckets out to 4 years. Thus, as we already know the 12 values out to 3 years, we can 'back out' using the 4-year average rate to solve for x being the values for the 4-month buckets in the 3–4 year period. Then we can take the 5-year swap rate to derive the 4–5 year values, and so on, out to 10 years and beyond. We call this process 'bootstrapping up the curve'. In this process we need to convert the YTM (yield-to-maturity) swap rates into clean zero coupon rates, work out the implied forward rates by bootstrapping, then use a 'smoothing' technique to the curve where necessary.

The result is the 'implied forwards curve', i.e. where the market readily indicates where it expects 3-month Libor to be trading in any time bucket you care to choose in the next 10 years. it is reasonable for us to price off this curve as it represents where there is currently an equal number of buyers and sellers of all-in swap rates (which, of course, includes the yield of the widely traded underlying Treasury note) at each point on the maturity curve. More importantly, it represents levels at which the cap market-maker can hedge.

Regarding the second problem of what volatility assumption to use, this, of course, effectively controlled and traded by the market-makers themselves in caps and floors. Whilst volatilities in the first four buckets to one year are easily observed with options traded on the Eurodollar futures at the CME, volatility levels further out the curve are more difficult to observe, and even now different market-makers use various approaches to price and control this 'grey area'.

The point to grasp is that all option products, from caps and floors to piras or swaptions, are *all* priced off the implied forwards curve as the mean market expectation of future interest rates.

When to use a swap or a cap

All newcomers to the market make the fundamental error of comparing swap rates or strike rates of caps to the current 3-month Libor. Tempted to use a cap and considering the Libor rate of, say $7\frac{1}{2}\%$ buyers request a quote of 5-year 8% cap. However, on learning the understandably large up-front premium the buyer is surprised. Why? In fact, they have just requested a strike that is considerably in-the-money. The current rate of $7\frac{1}{2}\%$ is only relevant to the first 3-month bucket, but the 20- × 3-month buckets need to be considered and the prices of each totalled. The implied forward curve for the 57- × 60-month bucket, for example, is 10.25%. Obviously 8% is well 'in-the-money' here, so one would expect the 8% cap to be expensive.

Many people compare strike rates (and prices) to swap rates but often in the wrong context. The swap rate is the weighted average of all the implied forwards rates from today until maturity. In a normal upward sloping curve, this will mean implied forwards will be lower at the start but higher at the end.

It follows, therefore, that as the 'at-the-money' rate for any one bucket (e.g. an option on an FRA) is the implied forwards rate, then the 'at-the-money' rate for a maturity run from today (e.g. a 5-year cap) will be the weighted average of all the buckets, i.e. the 5-year swap rate. Only the implied forwards curve tells you where the market is trading its current expectation of what it expects Libor to be in any bucket you care to choose. (You should base your decisions on your view of future rates as compared to the implied forwards curve.)

It follows that a 5-year 8% will be expensive, 5-year 10%, whilst out-of-the-money today, is in-the-money in 5 years time. Thus, it is not such a high strike rate to choose. Similarly, a 7½% floor, which looks like a high rate today does not appear such a good deal compared to the implied forwards curve over 5 years and could be a wise sell as part of a collar. Always choose stike rates carefully, bearing in mind the shape of the curve.

Refering to Exhibits 1.1 and 1.2, where you have floating rate debt of $100m for 5 years and consider four scenarios of future interest rates:

1   *Rates move exactly in line with the implied forwards curve.* That is, the unlikely event that for the next 5 years, 3-month Libor happens to be exactly as predicted by the implied forwards curve. Because the swap rate equals the weighted average of the implied forwards curve, the bottom line effect had you transacted a swap or done nothing is exactly the same. If you had transacted a cap, you would simply lose your premium, then the lower the strike you choose, the more you would lose.

2   *Rates move up higher than the implied forwards curve.* You could have locked in the implied forwards curve by transacting a swap then if rates moved higher than this, the swap must be the most efficient choice.

3   *Rates go down.* Locking into the swap would hurt as you are paying high implied forward rates whilst you could be paying increasingly lower rates. Of course, the most efficient method would have been to do nothing, but most users would have at least bought a cap as the company's P&L may not have been able to sustain a dramatic increase in rates had they been wrong. Thus, choose a cap with as high a strike rate as possible to minimise your premium payment but at a level which your P&L can absorb in case rates do move against your view.

4   *Rates go up but not as fast as the implied forwards curve.* The scenario which often suits the majority of views but which always causes most confusion. The answer is really quite clear – if you had transacted a swap, you are paying the fixed implied forwards rate in each bucket, i.e. rates higher than this scenario and as such the *swap loses*. In fact, rather than a cap this time, a collar is better as whilst rates did not fall you might as well have sold a floor at current rates to reduce your up-front premium. In summary:

- If you view Libor rising more quickly than the implied forwards curve, transact a swap.
- If you view Libor dropping, do nothing, on-buy some 'disaster' insurance in the form of any option.
- If you view Libor rising but not as fast as the implied forwards curve buy a collar.

Finally, in a scenario where rates move wildly up then down analysis is more difficult but again will depend on where rates were 'on average' compared to the implied forwards curve.

It is clear that many corporates, especially in the United States, have re-evaluated decisions in the last three years to fix with swaps, and in view of the above analysis have reversed transactions and moved at least a good section of their portfolio into option products.

The risks in trading a dynamic options book

Long dates options and the implicit concept of long dated volatility is a new area, and as market-players gain in experience in knowledge in this highly sophisticated area of the market, we learn of new risks and new efficient methods of hedge and arbitrage. However, there are several basic risks we can more easily categorise and discuss in terms of the risk recognition and some hedging techniques.

Interest rate risk: delta

If you trade an option or cap assuming a given implied forwards curve as the mid-point, then if the curve shifts you will make or lose money depending on its direction. We can hedge against this using a hedge ration called 'delta'. For example, if, as an option trader, we were the seller of a $100m 5-year cap at a strike of the 5-year swap (9.42%), then with an 'at-the-money' delta of 0.5, on appropriate hedge could be to sell $50m 5-year Treasuries. However, this raises two separate risks, curve risk and swap spread risk, discussed below.

Gamma risk

'Gamma' is the 'rate of change of delta'. It measures how much the trader makes or loses due to re-adjusting his hedge to delta as the underlying market (the implied forwards curve) moves.

Take the $100m 5-year cap we sold at the 0.5 delta strike of 9.42% hedged with a $50m short of the 5-year Treasury. Suddenly rates move up 50 basis points, we lose on the cap (as rates move 'in-the-money' we sold it too cheaply) but we are covered as our short hedge position makes money as prices go down. One problem, the cap is now 'in-the-money', delta can no longer be 0.5, say it is now 0.6. We need to 'adjust to delta' and sell another $10m Treasuries (to total $60m) at a lower price (yields went up). We are now neatly delta hedged at 0.6 until suddenly rates drop back again to exactly where we sold the cap, i.e. delta is now 0.5 again, we must buy back the extra $10m Treasuries. Unfortunately, however, if yields are down, prices are up and we buy back at higher levels. See Exhibit 1.3 for a typical example.

We can measure gamma risk by marking the portfolio to market and then repeating the process with an assumed fixed move in rates either up or down. If you sell an option, you will always lose money by delta adjusting if the market moves up then down or vice versa, however if you buy an option and delta adjust you will always *profit* from any such movement.

Exhibit 1.3 Gamma risk: an example

To $100m 5-year cap at the swap rate of 9.42%.
Hedge = delta 0.5 = sell $50m 5-year Treasuries at $99^{15}/_{32}$.

T1 yields move up and cap goes against you in the money.
Hedge = delta 0.6 = sell another $10m Treasuries at $99^{00}/_{32}$.

T2 yields drop back to levels where the cap was sold.
Hedge = delta 0.56 = buy back $10m Treasuries at $99^{15}/_{32}$.

Net result:
Sold $10m at $99^{00}/_{32}$.
Bought back at $99^{15}/_{32}$.
Loss = $\$312.50 \times 10 = \$46,875$.

Volatility risk: vega

Vega is 'sensitivity to a change in volatility levels'. If you buy an option with an implied valatility of, say, 20% annual movement, then if volatility assumptions in the market drop to 15%, your option is already worth less than you paid even though underlying interest rates have not moved. We can measure this risk simply by marking a portfolio to market at current volatility rates, then repeating the process by shifting the volatility assumption in the model by some realistic fixed percentage.

We can hedge volatility risk only by both buying *and* selling options, controlling the vega of each option and trying to net the bottom line to zero. If you are short on options you will always make money if volatilities fall and lose if they rise: the opposite is true if you are long on options.

Changes in the shape of the yield curve

Most hedging and risk control techniques assume parallel shifts in the yield curve. Of course, we only need a shift in *one* of the implied forwards buckets and we would still win or lose money. The curve is constantly changing shape and we should, therefore, choose carefully our hedge positions to include a mixture of maturities for each bucket of the portfolio carrying its own delta and gamma profile. Such methods can be complex when one considers the many scenarios of curve movements, and market-makers use various risk analysis techniques. We can be certain of one fact, that if a curve shifts against you, and you delta adjust hedges accordingly, then you suffer 'curve shape gamma' exposure.

Changes in the volatility curve

Volatilities trade at different levels in different maturities and vega risks of each bucket must be controlled just as we control individual deltas and gammas. Again, methods of quantifying such risks can be complex and systems are still generally well protected by leading market-makers.

Time value: theta

Whilst it is important to quantify the day-to-day change in the net bottom line 'theta' value of any portfolio, active daily management of the portfolio will itself adequately control theta risk.

Swap spread risk

The majority of caps and floors trade on Libor, but traders often hedge with Treasuries and are open to the risk of a move in the spread over Treasuries. This would increase the all-in swap rate, which is used to calculate the implied forwards curve, although the Treasury yield and price are unchanged. A better hedge would be a swap. However, in a large portfolio, both buying and selling caps, some consider it justifiable to assume this swap spread risk themselves rather than pay the large transaction costs of hedging and delta adjusting with swaps.

Basis risk

Trading a portfolio involving, for example, a Libor cap on one side against a commercial paper cap; or 1-month Libor cap against a 6-month Libor cap, involves considerable basis risk which again must be managed separately.

Summary

The above discussion should have illustrated the considerable risks involved when trading options outright rather than using them as a hedging tool. The best way to manage these risks is by running a large well-balanced dynamic book trading both sides of the market. For example, we have identified gamma risk as a big potential money loser. The two main factors affecting gamma are : (1) gamma is highest when 'at-the-money', it is zero when deep in *or* 'out-of-the-money'; and (2) it gets increasingly higher as the option approaches maturity. Thus, if we sell a 1-year 10% cap, it has high gamma due to maturity and low gamma due to strike being 'out-of-the-money'. A good gamma hedge might be to buy a 5-year 9% cap – high gamma as close to the money but low gamma as a longer maturity. However, each will have very different theta and vega risks. Running a large dynamic book allows the trader maximum flexibility to control these various risks.

In addition to this, an options trader must, by definition, take views of future movements in the market he is trading: both the short-term and long-term end of the market, both a parallel shift in rates, or just a change in the shape of the curve. For example, consider the problem of gamma risk, should you delta adjust to the new delta of 0.6 and risk losing money if rates revert to the 0.5 delta? Or wait for rates to move back? If so, how long do you wait unhedged? The trader is also implicitly trading theta values, swap spreads, indices like Libor to commercial paper, and, above all, volatility risk. For this reason, all major options traders use in-house developed models for pricing and trading caps. To develop a model to price such products is less than 10% of the work. The real value in an option model is how it reports to you the various risks involved, how it categorises them, the presentation of maturity profile and suggests alternative methods of hedging each category of risk.

Conclusion

This chapter has approached the cap and options market in two ways, First, to explain the products and their uses from an end users point of view. As corporate treasurers become more comfortable with option products, they are discovering new areas of opportunity profit potential and more flexible methods of tailoring products to take advantage of interest rate views rather than simply to pay the fixed or remain unhedged. Similarly, managers on both the asset and liability side are finding many ways of enhancing returns by assuming limited risk in line with budget forecasts of interest rate movements. Retail users quick to understand these products have already enjoyed considerable benefits and other potential users around the world are hungry for 'option knowledge' in order to catch up. In 1988 any sophisticated portfolio or hedging strategy must include consideration of option products.

The second part of this chapter appraoches caps and collars more from the professionals' point of view and discusses some of the risks involved in running and hedging a dynamic portfolio of options. Risks and potential rewards are high. It is a highly sophisticated area where new more efficient techniques are constantly being developed and always at an ever increasing pace. Some names have been tempted by the high rewards but were forced out of the business in the wake of October 1987 as they clearly did not either fully understand or properly control the complexity of the risks involved. However, as we continue to push into unchartered territory with an increasing degree of experience, sophistication and understanding, all major banks are racing to develop a presence in options in all major trading currencies worldwide.

2 Accounting treatment: United States

Benjamin S. Neuhausen

Introduction

From the perspective of the buyer, an interest rate cap is like a series of purchased put options. If interest rates rise above the cap (an option moves into the money), the seller of the cap will reimburse the buyer for the excess of interest rates above the cap. An interest rate collar is like entering into a series of option spreads (simultaneous purchase of a put option and sale of a call option with the same expiration dates but different strike prices – see Part V, Chapter 2 on accounting for interest rate options in the US). If interest rates rise above the cap (a purchased option moves into the money), the seller of the collar will reimburse the buyer for the excess of interest rates above the cap; if interest rates fall below the floor (a written option moves into the money), the buyer of the collar reimburses the seller for the savings it is enjoying. From the perspective of the seller, an interest rate cap is like a series of written put options and an interest rate collar is like entering into a series of option spreads. As a result, the accounting for caps and collars is similar to the accounting for options discussed in Part V, Chapter 2.

As noted in Part II, Chapter 1, 'Accounting framework: United States', the accounting for caps and collars, along with other interest rate protection products, is the subject of a major FASB project and could change.

Accounting by buyer

A cap or collar is ordinarily entered to hedge the repricing of interest rates on variable-rate debt, an anticipated transaction. To qualify as a hedge, therefore, it must satisfy all of the basic criteria for hedge accounting (risk, designation and effectiveness) and the two additional criteria for hedges of anticipated transactions (identification and probability).

Caps and collars are ordinarily out of the money at issuance. Accordingly, the entire premium paid represents time value and, assuming the hedge criteria are satisfied, is amortised to expense over the life of the contract. If the contract moves into the money – rates rise above the cap or, for a collar only, fall below the floor – the payments from or to the seller are accrued as adjustments to interest expense in each settlement period. In option terminology, the change in intrinsic value is deferred and is recognised in income when the hedged transaction – the interest payment – is accrued as interest expense.

If a cap/collar is terminated, any gain or loss may be either included in income currently or deferred and amortised over the original contract period. If the debt is extinguished, any deferred gain or loss from the cap/collar termination would be included in measuring the extinguishment gain or loss. If the debt is extinguished but the cap/collar remains outstanding, the cap/collar becomes a speculative option position unless it can be designated as a hedge of another borrowing.

Accounting by seller

From the standpoint of the seller, caps and collars are accounted for like written options or spreads in which the premium received exceeds the premium paid. As noted in Part V, Chapter 2, views differ on whether hedge accounting can be applied to written options. Under the AICPA accounting issues paper approach, only gains could be deferred; losses would be recognised in income currently. Under the alternative approach described in Part V, Chapter 2, caps and collars would not qualify for any form of hedge accounting because they are not deep in the money at issuance. If a cap or collar does not qualify for hedge accounting, changes in its value would be included in income currently.

Because caps and collars do not have quoted market prices, determining market value will require estimates or the use of mathematical models. For collars, regardless of which method is used to estimate market value, the estimate should include the effect of credit considerations, such as the current credit standing of the buyer in assessing whether the buyer could perform if interest rates fell below the floor.

Some sellers of caps do so in conjunction with issuing debt with a cap. They issue variable-rate debt with a cap providing that the variable rate cannot exceed a stated maximum. They then sell a cap contract with the same stated maximum to another entity (referred to as 'stripping' the cap from their debt). Economically, the debtor/seller is in the same position as if he had issued variable-rate debt without a cap, and the fee received from selling the cap reduces the overall financing cost. If the writing of the cap contract is clearly linked to the borrowing and is entered into at the time of the borrowing – i.e. the two constitute an integrated transaction – the fee received should be amortised over the life of the contract as a reduction of interest expense on the debt and any payments under the cap contract should be charged to interest expense as they accrue.

Alternatively, if the cap contract is not clearly linked to the borrowing or is not entered into at the same time, the cap contract should be treated like a series of written put options.

3   Accounting treatment: United Kingdom

Mark Davis

Overall basis of accounting

Caps, floors and collars can take a variety of forms and the accounting treatment to be adopted should reflect the substance of the transaction in each case. These instruments exhibit similar characteristics to options in many respects. As with options, there is no authoritative guidance in the UK on the accounting treatment to be adopted and one must therefore rely on the basic principles outlined in Part II, Chapter 2.

Corporates

Corporates normally use these instruments to hedge borrowings. They purchase for a premium, a cap which effectively sets a ceiling on interest costs. If the relevant Libor rate is above the preset ceiling at the start of the interest period, the counterparty will reimburse the corporate the excess funding cost. This amount should be accrued as interest receivable over the interest rate period (as it is normally received as a single payment at the end of the interest period). The cap agreement will normally cover a number of interest rate periods on the borrowing and thus the cap premium is similar to the premium paid for a series of interest rate options. As the ceiling is normally above current rates the premium is all time value. It is generally not practical to allocate the premium over the various interest periods concerned. Amortisation of the premium on a straight line basis over the life of the cap, provides a simpler and more prudent accounting policy. Any arrangement fees are normally written off immediately.

A collar involves a floor as well as a cap. If interest rates fall below the floor, the corporate will pay the difference to the counterparty and such payments should be accrued as interest payable over the relevant interest period. The floor is similar to writing an option. Instead of a premium, the corporate receives a reduction in the premium it pays for the cap. As indicated in the chapter on options, premiums purchased are normally amortised over the option period whereas premiums receivable are amortised over the interest period being hedged. It is generally impossible to account separately for the different elements of the premium paid for a collar. It is normally acceptable, therefore, to simply amortise the premium evenly over the life of the collar.

Banks

Banks may buy or sell caps and collars. If a bank purchases a cap or collar in order to hedge a borrowing, the accounting treatment described above should be adopted. If the bank is hedging an option or swap position, the correct accounting treatment is more debatable. While they may satisfy the basic hedge criteria, it seems generally more appropriate to mark to market all the transactions involved.

Where a bank sells a cap, it has effectively written a series of options. A collar is akin to a series of written and put options with matching maturities but different strike prices. Both forms of instrument are difficult to value. Estimating the net present value of likely future payments on the basis of existing forward rates, in the manner adopted for swaps, will generally be unsatisfactory. It will result in the time value inherent in the premium received (and thus generally the whole premium) being taken to income at the outset of the transaction. It would seem more appropriate, therefore, to estimate the cost of closing out the position using a series of options on the basis of the Black–Scholes or an equivalent formula.

As a simpler alternative the premium received can be amortised over the period of the cap or collar, and any payments or receipts under the collar amortised over the relevant interest periods. Such a policy should only be adopted if it does not result in the deferral of material losses.

Disclosure

Corporates which purchase a cap or collar to hedge borrowing costs should normally indicate, in the note to the accounts which details borrowings, the existence and nature of the transaction and the amount of any deferred premium.

Banks should indicate the accounting policy they have adopted. As with most instruments of this type, banks currently indicate little more than the existence of such transactions in a contingencies note.

4 Documentation of caps and collars

Anthony C. Gooch and Linda B. Klein

Introduction

In a straightforward rate cap agreement, the seller, or 'writer', of the cap agrees to make payments to the buyer when a designated interest rate rises above an agreed level, in return for a fee paid by the buyer at the time the parties enter into the rate cap transaction. The documentation for this kind of cap can be very simple when the buyer of the cap has no other obligation than to pay an initial fee to the seller. From the point of view of the seller of the cap, there is no credit risk once that fee has been paid. Therefore, if the fee is paid at or before execution of the agreement, most contractual provisions relating to the buyer may be dispensed with completely and, indeed, in some circumstances the cap agreement can be a one-party instrument made by the seller for the benefit of the buyer. There does not seem to be a market consensus on what contractual provisions relating to the seller of the cap should be included for the benefit of the buyer.

In some cases the seller of the rate cap may agree to receive its fee in periodic payments (e.g. quarterly) during the term of the agreement. The documentation for a cap agreement of that kind, with ongoing payment obligations on both sides, could be expected to resemble the documentation for a collar (also called a 'floor/ceiling') agreement.

Collars, like rate swaps, can be done as short-, medium- or long-term transactions, and they, like rate swaps, require payments from each of the parties over the term of the transaction. Whenever actual rates for the chosen floating rate index (e.g. Libor) fall outside the collar framed by the chosen cap and floor rates, one or the other of the parties will be required to make a payment: the seller of the cap portion of the collar will be required to make payments to the extent that actual market rates for the index on the relevant dates, or for the relevant periods, exceed the cap rate; the seller of the floor portion of the collar will be required to make payments to the extent that actual market rates for the index on the relevant dates, or for the relevant periods, are below the floor rate. In addition, the buyer of the cap portion of the collar will pay a fee to the cap seller. The documentation for collars should therefore be quite similar to that used for rate swaps, in so far as each of the parties will have the same kinds of credit concerns that it would as a party to a swap.

As noted in our chapter on interest rate swaps in this volume (Part IV, Chapter 4), in the swap market those concerns have led to a consensus that, at least where medium- and long-term agreements are involved, something more than a deal ticket is appropriate to document the transaction, as precision is desirable on such matters as events of default, the measure of damages if the agreement is terminated prematurely and other credit-related questions.

There may well be a drive to standardise documentation for rate-caps and collars, as it would be a logical extension of the work that has already been done for swaps. Indeed, the International Swap Dealers Association, Inc. has begun work on standard cap documentation. In the meantime, it is only natural that the benefits of the standardisation efforts described in our chapter on swaps in this volume should spill over into the documentation of these other kinds of rate protection agreements;

the underlying concepts are the same, as are the rate indexes used, so much of the terminology found in swap agreements should be transferable to cap and collar agreements. There is also no reason why a single master agreement similar to the one included as Appendix B to the chapter on interest rate swaps (Part IV, Chapter 4) cannot be done to accommodate swaps, caps and collars, as well as other rate protection transactions. Indeed, at least one major participant in the market has developed such an agreement.

The remainder of this chapter will deal only with the features peculiar to caps and collars that make the Appendices to this chapter different from the sample rate swap agreement included as Appendix A to the chapter on documenting interest rate swaps. The reader is referred to that chapter for discussion of the other provisions.

The examples included in this chapter illustrate documentation for simple cap and collar transactions in which the cap and floor protection relates to movements in 6-month Libo rates for US dollar deposits. A cap agreement similar to the example in Appendix A might be used by a borrower in a conventional Eurodollar loan transaction if it wished to put a limit on its exposure to rising interest rates without losing any of the benefit of cost reduction that would come with a decline in rates. However, if the borrower were willing to forego some of that benefit in exchange for obtaining the cap at a lower cost, it might enter into a collar documented in an agreement similar to the example in Appendix B, in which it would buy the cap and sell the floor. Another user of the cap agreement is the issuer of a capped floating rate instrument, which then sells the cap to reduce the all-in cost of the issue below the cost of a straight floating rate issue. The instrument, in a case like this, would have been made attractive to the investor by a spread over, say, Libor, somewhat higher than that available on a straight floating rate note or certificate of deposit. The financial intermediary that purchases the 'stripped' cap from the issuer may in turn sell the protection to another buyer.

Before describing the principal features and concerns in documenting caps and collars, we should note that floor transactions can be entered into independently of collars. For example, the holder of a floating rate asset who is concerned about falling interest rates might wish to buy a floor in which it would pay a fee to the seller in exchange for protection should, say, 6-month Libor fall below a specified strike level. This chapter does not consider documentation of such agreements since, except for the definition of the differential payment to be made by the floor seller, a floor agreement could be identical to a cap agreement. A simple way of stating the differential payment amount and obligation is illustrated in the floor portion of the relevant provisions in the sample collar agreement included in Appendix B to this chapter.

Special provisions of cap and collar agreements

Definitions

In cap and collar agreements, the section on definitions is just as important as it is in rate swap agreements. Cap and collar agreements will have to define the floating rate that will be compared for each relevant calculation period to the cap rate or the cap and floor rates. This means, as it does for floating rates in interest rate swaps, that the agreement will have to specify the appropriate source for the rate (a published source or reference banks or dealers), any appropriate maturity for the instrument used to determine that rate (e.g. 6-month London interbank deposits), the reset dates as of which the rate must be determined periodically and, where the rate is reset more than once per period, whether compounding is to apply and whether any rates to be averaged should be weighted or averaged simply. It will also have to set forth the cap rate, and, in a collar, the floor rate, as a rate swap agreement would for the fixed rate payer.

As illustrated by the definitions of the term 'Settlement Amount' in Appendices A and B, assuming payment of the cap and floor differential amounts at the end of each period for which they are measured, defined terms used to refer to these amounts can be stated quite simply.

Payments

The basic payment obligations – including the obligation of the cap buyer to pay a fee to the seller of the cap – as well as the settlement mechanics would be treated in the provisions on payments in cap and collar agreements. The transactions illustrated in Appendices A and B provide for payment of the fee at the beginning of the term of the agreement, which seems to be the prevailing practice. However, as noted above, these transactions are sometimes structured to provide for payment of the fee in instalments.

Appendices A and B also contemplate payment of the cap, or cap and floor, differentials at the end of each calculation period. However, some cap and floor transactions are structured so that these payments (like those in a forward rate agreement) are due at the beginning of the period, shortly after it becomes possible to determine the floating rate for the period. There are several important factors to be considered in choosing and documenting this alternative structure.

First, if the differential amount in respect of a period is payable at the beginning of the period, the drafter should be careful to ascertain whether the amount should be the full amount computed in the manner described above or instead should be the present value on the payment date of an amount so determined (discounted back from the last day of the relevant period). A second, and related, question is whether the structure for payment at the beginning of the period was chosen after due consideration for any reinvestment risk to the party receiving the payment, if it expects to apply that payment to meet an obligation to make interest payments at the end of the relevant period.

Interest payments under loan agreements and on bonds and other conventional forms of borrowing are generally payable in arrears. If a party to the cap or collar is engaging in the transaction as a hedge in connection with such an agreement or instrument, payment of a differential at the beginning of a calculation period may be inappropriate, both because of the reinvestment risk and because the actual number of days in the relevant period for which interest must be paid to the lender or investor may ultimately turn out to be different from the number of days covered by the differential amount prepaid for the period if an unexpected holiday occurs at the end of the period. The chances may be small, but this can occur, and although adjustment mechanisms can be devised to deal with the contingency, they of course add to complexity of the agreement.

Secondly, payment at the beginning of a period involves greater short-term credit risk than payment at the end of a calculation period. To illustrate, let us assume that a party to a collar receives a cap differential amount in respect of a period at the beginning of the period and that a default (e.g. under a cross-default clause) in respect of that party occurs before the end of the period. In this case, if the non-defaulting seller of the cap decides to give notice of early termination under the agreement, its damages will have to include both settlement for the loss of its bargain in respect of future calculation periods and an amount to compensate it for a portion of the cap differential that it paid for the period during which the default occurred (that is, a portion relating to the days between the early termination date and the end of the period). Concerns about recovery of both of these amounts would exist in the event of bankruptcy. If differential payments are due at the end of each calculation period, however, the need for the second element does not arise. Of course, if the differential amounts involved are likely to be small, so may be the parties' concerns for the unaccrued portion of a prepaid differential amount. From the point of view of documentation, however, payment at the end of the period is simpler to handle, so all else being equal, prepayment is less desirable.

Finally, collar agreements should include appropriate protections for each of the parties if an event of default with respect to the other party exists or would exist with the giving of notice or the lapse of an applicable grace period. Similar protections would be required in cap agreements providing for payment of the cap fee by the buyer in instalments.

Covenants

In addition to any other covenants it might deem desirable, the seller of cap or floor protection may wish its counterparty to agree that it will not represent to any third party that the arrangements contemplated in their cap or collar agreement in any way constitute a guaranty, assurance or assumption by the seller of any obligation the buyer of the protection may have to a third party. A similar commitment sometimes included in these documents is that the buyer of the cap or floor will not, without the seller's consent, use the seller's name in connection with any other agreement or proposed transaction of the buyer.

Calculation of payments upon early termination

Where measurement of loss of bargain on early termination is concerned, cap and collar agreements can be patterned after interest rate swap agreements.

As illustrated in Appendices A and B, the market-based 'agreement value' approach can be used to quantify loss of bargain for a cap or collar. If agreement value cannot be determined, a party's damages for loss of its bargain are dealt with in general indemnification clauses in the Appendices. The reader is referred to a discussion of these subjects in the chapter on documenting interest rate swaps (Part IV, Chapter 4).

However, when collar transactions are structured to provide for payment of the cap and floor differential amount for any relevant calculation period at the beginning of the period, as noted above, the agreement should also entitle the payer to compensation in respect of the unaccrued portion of the prepaid amount at the early termination date (i.e. a portion in respect of the period beginning on the early termination date and ending on the last day of the period).

Cap and collar agreements sometimes provide that if early termination occurs, the damages of the payer of the cap fee should include refund of a pro-rated portion of the fee, determined on the basis of the part of the term of the agreement remaining after the early termination date, as well as compensation for loss of bargain. The agreement value approach to damages would not separate the two elements; rather, as the amount computed as agreement value would reflect the cost of a replacement transaction for the remaining term of the cap or collar being terminated, it would be assumed to offset payment of the initial fee. Underlying the alternative approach that calls for refund of a portion of the fee is apparently an assumption that equal portions of the fee are attributable to the protection provided for each day in the term of the agreement. The cost of cap protection seems, however, not to increase arithmetically; rather, coverage for the earlier parts of the term are generally said to cost less than coverage for the later parts – because, except in an extremely volatile rate environment, the earlier coverage is likely to be less necessary and, therefore, worth less. (Evidence of this are the increasing reports of caps purchased with delayed commencement dates.) The parties to a collar agreement may wish to weigh this question if they are considering this alternative approach to computing damages which involves a refund mechanism.

If amounts would be payable by each of the parties in connection with early termination of a collar, the agreement should provide for their netting, with only the net amount payable by the party with the larger payment obligation. Finally, it should be noted that, as is the case in swap agreements, the early termination provisions of collar agreements may not be enforceable under the bankruptcy and insolvency laws of some jurisdictions. This subject is discussed in our chapter on documenting interest rate swaps (Part IV, Chapter 4).

Assignment

The provisions in a collar agreement dealing with this subject will generally be similar to those used in interest rate swap documentation, as could be expected since collars and rate swaps involve ongoing payment obligations of both parties. The cap, however, does not involve mutual ongoing payment obligations when the cap fee is paid at the outset by the buyer. As illustrated in Appendix

A, this provision in a cap agreement may therefore give the buyer almost complete freedom to assign its rights, assuming such freedom does not give rise to legal problems under, say, the securities laws of the cap seller's jurisdiction.

Conclusion

The move toward standardisation of swap documents began rather quickly as the number of participants in the market and volume of transactions increased. The substantial growth in the cap market that is reported to have occurred since 1985 may well provide sufficient incentive for standardisation of cap and collar agreements. The nature of the cap itself may provide additional incentive since, in circumstances where the cap is written to involve no obligations of the buyer after it pays an initial fee, the buyers' desire to trade these facilities may make standard terms very attractive. The question of trading itself will require analysis in the market, in light of the securities laws of relevant jurisdictions.

Much of the necessary work on standardisation should be readily transferable from the market's accomplishments with swaps, but not all the thinking that has been done about swaps is, or necessarily should be, equally applicable to caps and collars. For example, there are likely to be divergent views over granting the writer of a cap the right to give a notice of early termination if it is required to make 'gross-up' payments in respect of taxes it must withhold from the cap differentials it agreed to pay.

In the meantime, the parties to rate caps and collars can at least be expected to begin to use master agreements, and perhaps to develop master agreements that can accommodate these transactions as well as swaps. This will be a first step towards simplifying the documentation and, at least with respect to collars, which involve ongoing obligations and therefore credit concerns of both parties, should be considered in the light of the potential benefit to be derived from an integrated master agreement in the event of an insolvency of one of the parties.

Appendix A: Interest rate cap agreement

This agreement is a sample of the kind of documentation that might be used for a single US dollar interest rate cap in which a bank organised under the laws of the United States is the seller of the cap and a corporation organised under the laws of Switzerland is the buyer.

This sample is merely an illustration and should not be used for an actual transaction; each transaction will have its own special features, and the agreement drafted to document it should be carefully tailored to address the legal and business problems that it presents.

INTEREST RATE CAP AGREEMENT dated as of July 1, 1987 between BIG BANK, N.A. (the 'Bank') and HEDGED CORPORATION (the 'Company'), whereby the parties agree as follows.

1. *Definitions.* For purposes of this Agreement, the following terms shall have the meanings indicated.

'Agreement Value', means an amount determined as provided in Section 15.

'Banking Day' means a day on which banks are not required or authorized by law to close in New York City that is also a London Banking Day.

'Calculation Period' means the period commencing on July 1, 1987 and ending on January 4, 1988 and thereafter each period beginning on the last day of the preceding Calculation Period and ending on the first day of the sixth month thereafter, subject to the following exceptions: (i) if a Calculation Period would otherwise end on a day that is not a Banking Day, it shall be extended to the following Banking Day, unless that Calculation Period would, as a result, extend into the following calendar month, in which case the Calculation Period shall end on the preceding Banking Day, and (ii) the final Calculation Period shall end on July 1, 1994, whether or not it is a Banking Day.

'Contract Rate' means ____% per annum.

'Damages', with respect to the Company, means an amount determined as provided in Section 14(b).

'Dollars' or *'$'* means lawful money of the United States.

'Early Termination Date' has the meaning given to that term in Section 13(b).

'Event of Default' has the meaning given to that term in Section 12.

'LIBOR', for each Calculation Period, means the rate (expressed as an annual rate) equal to the arithmetic mean (rounded up, if necessary, to the nearest 1/100,000 of 1%) of the rates shown on the 'LIBO' page display (or any substitute display) of the Reuter Monitor Money Rates Service as the London interbank offered rates of the banks named on that display at approximately 11.00 a.m. (London time) on the second London Banking Day before the first day of that Calculation Period for deposits in Dollars for a period of six months, subject to Section 3(c).

'London Banking Day' means a day on which dealings in deposits in Dollars are carried on in the London interbank market.

'Notional Principal Amount' means $80,000,000.

'Payment Date', for each Calculation Period, means the last day of that Calculation Period.

'Reference Market-maker' has the meaning given to that term in Section 15(a).

'Settlement Amount', for each Calculation Period, means the amount that would accrue during that Calculation Period on the Notional Principal Amount at a rate determined by subtracting the Contract Rate from LIBOR for that Calculation Period.

'Taxes', with respect to payments hereunder by the Bank, means any present or future taxes, levies, imposts, duties or charges of any nature whatsoever that are collectible by withholding except for any such tax, levy, impost, duty or charge that would not have been imposed but for the existence of a connection between the Company and the jurisdiction where it is imposed.

'United States' means the United States of America.

2. *Payments.* On the Payment Date for each Calculation Period, if LIBOR for that Calculation Period is greater than the Contract Rate, the Bank shall pay the Company the Settlement Amount for that Calculation Period; *provided, however,* that, if any payment due hereunder is scheduled to be made on a day that is not a Banking Day, that payment shall be made on the following Banking Day.

3. *Computations and Determinations.* (a) Each Settlement Amount and any interest payable pursuant to Section 5 shall be computed on the basis of a 360-day year and actual days elapsed from and including the first

day of the relevant period to but excluding the last day thereof.

(b) The Bank shall determine LIBOR for each Calculation Period and the amount of each payment (if any) to be made pursuant to Section 2 and, no later than the second Banking Day before such a payment is due, shall give notice to the Company specifying the amount of the payment. If a change in the number of days in a Calculation Period occurs after the Bank has given a notice relating to that period under this Section, as soon as practicable thereafter the Bank shall give the Company notice of the change and of any resulting change in an amount payable pursuant to Section 2.

(c) For purposes of determining LIBOR for each Calculation Period, the rules set forth below shall apply if the 'LIBO' page (or a substitute) is not being displayed by the Reuter Monitor Money Rates Service at the time for the determination.

(i) LIBOR for that Calculation Period shall be the rate (expressed as an annual rate) equal to the arithmetic mean (rounded up, if necessary, to the nearest 1/100,000 of 1%) of the rates at which deposits in Dollars in an amount substantially equal to the Notional Principal Amount would be offered at that time by the principal London offices of Barclays Bank PLC, The Bank of Tokyo, Ltd., Bankers Trust Company and National Westminster Bank PLC to major banks in the London interbank market for a period of six months, as quoted to the Bank; or

(ii) if at least one but not all of the London offices of those institutions supplies the Bank with the necessary quotation at that time, the Bank shall determine LIBOR for that Calculation Period on the basis of the quotation or quotations supplied to it; or

(iii) if none of those offices supplies the Bank with the necessary quotation, LIBOR for that Calculation Period shall be the arithmetic mean (rounded as provided above) of the rates quoted to the Bank by the principal lending offices of four major banks in New York City selected by the Bank as their respective lowest lending rates for loans in Dollars to leading European banks for that period and in that amount at approximately 11.00 a.m. (New York City time) on the first day of that Calculation Period.

4. *Making of Payments.* All payments hereunder shall be made to the account specified in Exhibit 4A.1, or to such other account in New York City as the Company may have last specified by notice to the Bank, and shall be made in funds settled through the New York Clearing House Interbank Payments System or such other same-day funds as are customary at the time for the settlement in New York City of banking transactions denominated in Dollars.

5. *Default Interest.* If any amount due hereunder is not paid when due, interest shall accrue on that amount to the extent permitted by applicable law at a rate per annum equal for each day that amount remains unpaid to the sum of 1% and the rate quoted by the principal London office of the Bank at 11.00 a.m. (London time) for overnight deposits in Dollars, in an amount substantially equal to the overdue amount, for value on that day or, if that day is not a London Banking Day, on the preceding London Banking Day. Interest hereunder shall be payable from time to time on demand.

6. *Fee.* At or before the time of the execution of this Agreement by the Bank, the Company has paid a fee to the Bank in the amount separately agreed between the parties.

7. *Supervening Illegality.* If it becomes unlawful for the Bank to make any payment to be made by it hereunder, as a result of the adoption of, or any change in, or change in the interpretation of, any law, regulation or treaty, the Bank shall give notice to that effect to the Company and shall use reasonable efforts (i) to assign or transfer its rights and obligations under this Agreement, subject to Section 17, to another of its branches, offices or affiliates, or to any leading participant in the interest rate cap market, that may make those payments lawfully and without withholding for or on account of Taxes or (ii) to agree with the Company to modify this Agreement or change the method of payment hereunder so that the payment will not be unlawful. If an assignment or agreement is not made as provided herein on or before the tenth day after that notice becomes effective, either party may give notice of termination as provided in Section 13.

8. *Taxes.* (a) Except as otherwise required by law, each payment hereunder shall be made without withholding for or on account of Taxes. If the Bank is required to make any withholding from any payment under this Agreement for or on account of Taxes, it shall (i) make that withholding, (ii) make timely payment of the amount withheld to the appropriate governmental authority, (iii) forthwith pay the Company such additional amount as may be necessary to ensure that the net amount actually received by it free and clear of Taxes (including any Taxes on the additional amount) is equal to the amount that it would have received had no Taxes been withheld and (iv) on or before the thirtieth day after payment, send the Company the original or a certified copy of an official tax receipt evidencing that payment; *provided, however,* that if the representation and warranty made by the Company in Section 9(c) proves not to have been true when made or, if repeated on each Payment Date, would not then be true, or if the Company fails to perform or observe any of its covenants set forth in Section 10 or Section 11, the Bank shall be under no obligation to pay any additional amount hereunder to the extent that the withholding would not have been required if the representation and warranty had been true when made, or would have been true if so repeated, or if the failure had not occurred.

(b) If the Bank would be required to make any withholding for or on account of Taxes and pay any additional amount as provided in Section 8(a) with respect to any payment to be made by it in accordance with Section 2, it shall give notice to that effect to the Company and shall use reasonable efforts (i) to assign or transfer its rights and obligations under this Agreement, subject to Section 17, to another of its branches, offices or affiliates, or to any leading participant in the interest rate cap market, that may make the payments to be made by it hereunder lawfully and without withholding for or on account of Taxes or (ii) to agree with the Company to modify this Agreement or change the method of payment hereunder so that those payments will not be subject to the withholding. If an assignment or agreement is not made as provided herein on or before the tenth day after that notice becomes effective, the Bank may give notice of termination as provided in Section 13.

9. *Representations and Warranties.* (a) Each of the parties makes the representations and warranties set forth below to the other as of the date hereof.

(i) It is duly organized and validly existing and has the corporate power and authority to execute and deliver this Agreement and to perform its obligations hereunder.

(ii) It has taken all necessary action to authorize its execution and delivery of this Agreement and the performance of its obligations hereunder.

(iii) All governmental authorizations and actions necessary in connection with its execution and delivery of this Agreement and the performance of its obligations hereunder have been obtained or performed and remain valid and in full force and effect.

(iv) This Agreement has been duly executed and delivered by it and constitutes its legal, valid and binding obligation, enforceable against it in accordance with the terms of this Agreement, subject to all applicable bankruptcy, insolvency, moratorium and similar laws affecting creditors' rights generally.

(b) The Bank makes the following additional representations and warranties to the Company.

(i) No event or condition that constitutes (or that with the giving of notice or the lapse of time or both would constitute) an Event of Default with respect to it has occurred and is continuing or will occur by reason of its entering into or performing its obligations under this Agreement.

(ii) There are no actions, proceedings or claims pending or, to its knowledge, threatened, the adverse determination of which might have a materially adverse effect on its ability to perform its obligations under, or affect the validity or enforceability against it of, this Agreement.

(c) In addition, the Company represents and warrants to the Bank that it is a Swiss corporation and a Swiss enterprise fully eligible for the benefits of the income tax convention between the United States and Switzerland with respect to any payments receivable by it under this Agreement and, in reliance on that representation and warranty, the Bank represents and warrants to the Company that it is not required by applicable law to make any deduction or withholding for or on account of Taxes from any payment (other than interest payable pursuant to Section 5) that it is required to make under this Agreement.

10. *Covenants.* If the Company is required at any time to execute any form or document in order for payments to it hereunder to qualify for exemption from withholding for or on account of Taxes or to qualify for such withholding at a reduced rate, the Company shall, on demand, execute the required form or document and deliver it to the Bank.

11. *Closing Documents.* On or before July 15, 1987, the Company shall deliver to the Bank United States Internal Revenue Service Form 1001, duly completed and executed in duplicate, in form and substance satisfactory to the Bank.

12. *Events of Default.* For purposes of this Agreement, the term 'Event of Default' shall mean any of the events listed below:

(a) The Bank fails to pay any amount payable by it hereunder as and when that amount becomes payable and does not remedy that failure on or before the third Banking Day after notice from the Company of the failure.

(b) Any representation or warranty made by the Bank in this Agreement, other than in Section 9(c), proves to have been incorrect, incomplete or misleading in any material respect at the time it was made.

(c) The Bank becomes the subject of any action or proceeding for relief under any bankruptcy or insolvency law or any law affecting creditors' rights that is similar to a bankruptcy or insolvency law or seeks or becomes subject to the appointment of a receiver, custodian or similar official for it or any of its property.

13. *Early Termination.* (a) At any time while an Event of Default is continuing, the Company may, in its absolute discretion, give notice of termination in accordance with this Section. If the Bank gives notice of supervening illegality, either party may give notice of termination in accordance with this Section in the circumstances described in Section 7. If the Bank is required to pay any additional amount pursuant to Section 8, it may give notice of termination in accordance with this Section in the circumstances described in Section 8.

(b) Any notice of termination hereunder (i) shall state the grounds for termination, (ii) shall specify a date that is not before, nor more than ten days after, the date the notice of early termination is given on which the payments required by Section 14 shall be made as provided therein (the 'Early Termination Date') and (iii) shall declare the obligations of the Bank to make the payments required by Section 2 that are scheduled to be made after the Early Termination Date to be terminated as of that date, and those obligations shall so terminate and be replaced by the parties' obligations to make the payments specified in Section 14.

14. *Payments upon Early Termination.* (a) If notice of termination is given hereunder, the Bank shall pay the Company its Damages.

(b) The Company's Damages in the event of early termination shall be the Agreement Value, if it can be determined. If it cannot be determined, the Company's Damages shall be an amount in Dollars equal to the sum of the losses (including loss of bargain) that it may incur as a result of the early termination or as a result of the event that served as the ground for early termination.

(c) Payments to be made in accordance with this Section shall be made on the Early Termination Date. If the Company is entitled to be paid any amount in respect of its Damages in accordance with this Section, it shall submit to the Bank a statement in reasonable detail of those Damages.

15. *Agreement Value.* (a) For the purpose of determining Agreement Value, the Company shall select four leading participants in the interest rate cap market (each a 'Reference Market-maker'), in its sole discretion and in good faith, with a view to minimizing that Agreement Value; *provided, however,* that in doing so the Company shall be entitled to select market participants that are of the highest credit standing and that otherwise satisfy all the criteria that the Company applies generally at the time in deciding whether to enter into an interest rate protection transaction.

(b) The Company shall request from each of the Reference Market-makers it has selected a quotation of the amount in Dollars which that Reference Market-maker would charge on the Early Termination Date as a flat fee for entering into an agreement, effective on the Early Termination Date, pursuant to which it would make all the payments scheduled to be made by the Bank under Section 2 of this Agreement after the Early Termination Date.

(c) Agreement Value shall be the arithmetic mean (rounded up, if necessary, to the nearest cent) of the fees described in Section 15(b) that are quoted to the Company by the Reference Market-makers it has selected or, if only one Reference Market-maker will quote such a fee, Agreement Value shall be the amount of the fee quoted by that Reference Market-maker.

16. *Costs and Expenses.* (a) Each of the parties shall pay, or reimburse the other on demand for, all stamp, registration, documentation or similar taxes or duties, and any penalties or interest that may be due with respect thereto, that may be imposed by any jurisdiction in respect of its execution or delivery of this Agreement. If any such tax or duty is imposed by any jurisdiction as the result of the conduct or status of both parties, each party shall pay one half of the amount of the tax or duty.

(b) The Bank shall pay, or reimburse the Company on demand for, all reasonable costs and expenses incurred by the Company in connection with enforcement of its rights under this Agreement or as a consequence of an Event of Default, including, without limitation, fees and expenses of legal counsel.

17. *Non-Assignment.* Neither party shall assign or transfer its rights or obligations hereunder or any interest herein to any other person or any of its other branches or offices without the written consent of the other party to this Agreement, and any purported assignment or transfer in violation of this Section shall be void. The parties are acting for purposes of this Agreement through their respective branches or offices specified in Exhibit 4A.1. The Company shall not withhold its consent to an assignment or transfer proposed pursuant to Section 7 or Section 8 if the proposed assignee or transferee meets the criteria set forth in Section 7(i) or Section 8(b) (as the case may be) and the credit policies of the Company at the time would permit it to purchase an interest rate cap from the proposed assignee or transferee without credit support. The Bank shall not withhold its consent to an assignment or transfer proposed by the Company if the Bank would be entitled to make the payments it is required to make pursuant to Section 2 to the proposed assignee or transferee lawfully and without withholding for or on account of Taxes and the proposed assignee or transferee assumes the obligations of the Company under Section 10 of this Agreement to the satisfaction of the Bank.

18. *Waivers; Rights Not Exclusive.* No failure or delay by a party in exercising any right hereunder shall operate as a waiver of, or impair, any such right. No single or partial exercise of any such right shall preclude any other or further exercise thereof or the exercise of any other right. No waiver of any such right shall be effective unless given in writing. No waiver of any such right shall be deemed a waiver of any other right hereunder. The right to terminate provided for herein is in addition to, and not exclusive of, any other rights, powers, privileges or remedies provided by law.

19. *Interpretation.* The section headings in this Agreement are for convenience of reference only and shall not affect the meaning or construction of any provision hereof.

20. *Notices.* All notices in connection with this Agreement shall be given by telex or cable or by notice in writing hand-delivered or sent by facsimile transmission or by airmail, postage prepaid. All such notices shall be sent to the telex or telecopier number or address (as the case may be) specified for the intended recipient in

Exhibit 4A.1 (or to such other number or address as that recipient may have last specified by notice to the other party). All such notices shall be effective upon receipt, and confirmation by answerback of any notice sent by telex as provided herein shall be sufficient evidence of receipt thereof.

21. *Amendments.* This Agreement may be amended only by an instrument in writing executed by the parties hereto.

22. *Survival.* The obligations of the parties under Section 8, Section 14 and Section 16 shall survive payment of the obligations of the parties under Section 2 and Section 5 and the termination of their other obligations hereunder.

23. *Jurisdiction; Governing Law; Immunity.* (a) Any action or proceeding relating in any way to this Agreement may be brought and enforced in the courts of the State of New York or of the United States for the Southern District of New York, and the Bank irrevocably submits to the nonexclusive jurisdiction of each such court in connection with any such action or proceeding.

(b) This Agreement shall be governed by, and construed in accordance with, the law of the State of New York.

24. *Counterparts; Integration of Terms.* This Agreement may be executed in counterparts, and the counterparts taken together shall be deemed to constitute one and the same agreement. This Agreement contains the entire agreement between the parties relating to the subject matter hereof and supersedes all oral statements and prior writings with respect thereto.

IN WITNESS WHEREOF the parties have caused this Agreement to be duly executed and delivered as of the day and year first written above.

BIG BANK, N.A.   HEDGED CORPORATION

By:_____   By:_____

Title:_____   Title:_____

Exhibit 4A.1   Addresses for Notices and Accounts for Payments

BIG BANK, N.A.

Address: One Financial Center
                  New York, NY 00000
Attention: Rate Risk Management Group
Telex No.:   00000 BB
Telecopier No.:   (000) 000–0000

HEDGED CORPORATION

Address: 1, Gnomestrasse
                  Zurich, Switzerland
Attention: Corporate Treasury Group Officer
Telex No.:   00000 HC
Telecopier No.:   (000) 000–00000

Account for Payments

Account No.:   00–000
Depositary: Other Big Bank
                  Big Bank Plaza
                  New York, NY 00000

Appendix B: Interest rate collar agreement

This agreement is a sample of the kind of documentation that might be used for a single US dollar interest rate collar in which a bank organised under the laws of the United States is the seller of the cap and a corporation organised under the laws of Switzerland is the seller of the floor portion of the collar.

This sample is merely an illustration and should not be used for an actual transaction; each transaction will have its own special features, and the agreement drafted to document it should be carefully tailored to address the legal and business problems that it presents.

INTEREST RATE COLLAR AGREEMENT dated as of July 1, 1987 between BIG BANK, N.A. (the 'Bank') and HEDGED CORPORATION (the 'Company'), whereby the parties agree as follows.

1. *Definitions.* For purposes of this Agreement, the following terms have the meanings indicated.

'Affiliate', with respect to either party, means any entity that is controlled by that party, any entity that controls that party or any entity under common control with that party. For purposes of this definition, 'control' of an entity means direct or indirect ownership of a majority in voting power of the shares or other ownership interests in that entity.

'Agreement Value', with respect to a party, means an amount determined as provided in Section 16.

'Banking Day', means a day on which banks are not required or authorized by law to close in New York City that is also a London Banking Day.

'Calculation Period' means the period commencing on July 1, 1987 and ending on January 4, 1988 and thereafter each period beginning on the last day of the preceding Calculation Period and ending on the first day of the sixth month thereafter, subject to the following exceptions: (i) if a Calculation Period would otherwise end on a day that is not a Banking Day, it shall be extended to the following Banking Day, unless that Calculation Period would, as a result, extend into the following calendar month, in which case the Calculation Period shall end on the preceding Banking Day, and (ii) the final Calculation Period shall end on July 1, 1994, whether or not it is a Banking Day.

'Cap Rate' means ____% per annum.

'Damages', with respect to a party, means an amount determined as provided in Section 15(c).

'Defaulting Party' has the meaning given to that term in Section 12.

'Dollars' or *'$'* means lawful money of the United States.

'Early Termination Date' has the meaning given to that term in Section 14(b).

'Event of Default' has the meaning given to that term in Section 12.

'Floor Rate' means ____% per annum.

'Indebtedness', with respect to either party, means any present or future indebtedness of that party, as debtor, borrower or guarantor, in respect of money borrowed (other than indebtedness in respect of deposits received), including interest on any Indebtedness.

'LIBOR', for each Calculation Period, means the rate (expressed as an annual rate) equal to the arithmetic mean (rounded up, if necessary, to the nearest 1/100,000 of 1%) of the rates shown on the 'LIBO' page display (or any substitute display) of the Reuter Monitor Money Rates Service as the London interbank offered rates of the banks named on that display at approximately 11.00 a.m. (London time) on the second London Banking Day before the first day of that Calculation Period for deposits in Dollars for a period of six months, subject to Section 3(c).

'London Banking Day' means a day on which dealings in deposits in Dollars are carried on in the London interbank market.

'Merger Event' has the meaning given to that term in Section 13.

'Notional Principal Amount' means $80,000,000.

'Payment Date', for each Calculation Period, means the last day of that Calculation Period.

'Reference Market-maker' has the meaning given to that term in Section 16(a).

'Settlement Amount', for each Calculation Period, means the amount that would accrue during that Calculation Period on the Notional Principal Amount at a rate equal to the difference between LIBOR for that Calculation Period and (i) in the case of a Settlement Amount payable by the Bank, the Cap Rate, and (ii) in the case of a Settlement Amount payable by the Company, the Floor Rate, computed as provided in Section 3(a).

'*Taxes*', with respect to payments hereunder by either party, means any present or future taxes, levies, imposts, duties or charges of any nature whatsoever that are collectible by withholding except for any such tax, levy, impost, duty or charge that would not have been imposed but for the existence of a connection between the party receiving the payment and the jurisdiction where it is imposed.

'*United States*' means the United States of America.

2. *Payments.* (a) On the terms and subject to the conditions set forth herein, on the Payment Date for each Calculation Period, if LIBOR for that Calculation Period is greater than the Cap Rate, the Bank shall pay the Company the Settlement Amount for that Calculation Period, and, if LIBOR for that Calculation Period is lower than the Floor Rate, the Company shall pay the Bank the Settlement Amount for that Calculation Period; *provided, however*, that, if any payment due hereunder is scheduled to be made on a day that is not a Banking Day, that payment shall be made on the following Banking Day.

(b) The obligation of each party to make each payment to be made by it pursuant to Section 2(a) is subject to the condition that no event or condition that constitutes (or that with the giving of notice or the lapse of time or both would constitute) an Event or Default with respect to the other party shall be continuing; *provided, however*, that for purposes of Section 15 the foregoing condition shall be deemed to have been satisfied; *provided further, however*, that the foregoing condition shall no longer be applicable when that other party has performed all its payment obligations hereunder.

3. *Computations and Determinations.* (a) Each Settlement Amount and any interest payable pursuant to Section 5 shall be computed on the basis of a 360-day year and actual days elapsed from and including the first day of the relevant period to but excluding the last day thereof.

(b) The Bank shall determine LIBOR for each Calculation Period and the amount of each payment to be made pursuant to Section 2(a) and, no later than the second Banking Day before such a payment is due, shall give notice to the Company specifying the amount of the payment and the party required to make it and indicating how the amount was computed. If a change in the number of days in a Calculation Period occurs after the Bank has given a notice relating to that period under this Section, as soon as practicable thereafter the Bank shall give the Company notice of the change and of any resulting change in an amount payable pursuant to Section 2(a).

(c) For purposes of determining LIBOR for each Calculation Period, the rules set forth below shall apply if the 'LIBO' page (or a substitute) is not being displayed by the Reuter Monitor Money Rates Service at the time for the determination.

(i) LIBOR for that Calculation Period shall be the rate (expressed as an annual rate) equal to the arithmetic mean (rounded up, if necessary, to the nearest 1/100,000 of 1%) of the rates at which deposits in Dollars in an amount substantially equal to the Notional Principal Amount would be offered at that time by the principal London offices of Barclays Bank PLC, The Bank of Tokyo, Ltd., Bankers Trust Company and National Westminster Bank PLC to major banks in the London interbank market for a period of six months, as quoted to the Bank; or

(ii) if at least one but not all of the London offices of those institutions supplies the Bank with the necessary quotation at that time, the Bank shall determine LIBOR for that Calculation Period on the basis of the quotation or quotations supplied to it; or

(iii) if none of those offices supplies the Bank with the necessary quotation, LIBOR for that Calculation Period shall be the arithmetic mean (rounded as provided above) of the rates quoted to the Bank by the principal lending offices of four major banks in New York City selected by the Bank as their respective lowest lending rates for loans in Dollars to leading European banks for that period and in that amount at approximately 11.00 a.m. (New York City time) on the first day of that Calculation Period.

4. *Making of Payments.* All payments hereunder shall be made to the account specified for the intended recipient in Exhibit 4B.1, or to such other account in New York City as that party may have last specified by notice to the other party, and shall be made in funds settled through the New York Clearing House Interbank Payments System or such other same-day funds as are customary at the time for the settlement in New York City of banking transactions denominated in Dollars.

5. *Default Interest.* If any amount due hereunder is not paid when due, interest shall accrue on that amount to the extent permitted by applicable law at a rate per annum equal for each day that amount remains unpaid to the sum of 1% and the rate quoted by the principal London office of the Bank at 11.00 a.m. (London time) for overnight deposits in Dollars, in an amount substantially equal to the overdue amount, for value on that day or, if that day is not a London Banking Day, on the preceding London Banking Day. Interest hereunder shall be payable from time to time on demand.

6. *Fee.* At or before the time of the execution of this Agreement by the Bank, the Company has paid a fee to the Bank in the amount separately agreed between the parties.

7. *Supervening Illegality.* If it becomes unlawful for either party to make any payment to be made by it hereunder, or to receive any amount to be received by it hereunder, as a result of the adoption of, or any change

in, or change in the interpretation of, any law, regulation or treaty, that party shall give notice to that effect to the other party and shall use reasonable efforts (i) to assign or transfer its rights and obligations under this Agreement, subject to Section 18, to another of its branches, offices or Affiliates, or to any leading participant in the interest rate products market, that may make those payments and receive those amounts lawfully and without withholding for or on account of Taxes or (ii) to agree with the other party to modify this Agreement or change the method of payment hereunder so that the payment or receipt will not be unlawful. If an assignment or agreement is not made as provided herein on or before the tenth day after that notice becomes effective, either party may give notice of termination as provided in Section 14.

8. *Taxes.* (a) Except as otherwise required by law, each payment hereunder shall be made without withholding for or on account of Taxes. If either party is required to make any withholding from any payment under this Agreement for or on account of Taxes, it shall (i) make that withholding, (ii) make timely payment of the amount withheld to the appropriate governmental authority, (iii) forthwith pay the other party such additional amount as may be necessary to ensure that the net amount actually received by it free and clear of Taxes (including any Taxes on the additional amount) is equal to the amount that it would have received had no Taxes been withheld and (iv) on or before the thirtieth day after payment, send that other party the original or a certified copy of an official tax receipt evidencing that payment; *provided, however,* that if the representation and warranty made by a party in Section 9(g) proves not to have been true when made or, if repeated on each Payment Date, would not then be true, or if a party fails to perform or observe any of its covenants set forth in Section 10(b) or 11(a), the other party shall be under no obligation to pay any additional amount hereunder to the extent that the withholding would not have been required if the representation and warranty had been true when made, or would be true if so repeated, or if the failure had not occurred.

(b) If either party would be required to make any withholding for or on account of Taxes and pay any additional amount as provided in Section 8(a) with respect to any payment to be made by it in accordance with Section 2(a), that party shall give notice to that effect to the other party and shall use reasonable efforts (i) to assign or transfer its rights and obligations under this Agreement, subject to Section 18, to another of its branches, offices or Affiliates, or to any leading participant in the interest rate products market, that may make the payments to be made by it hereunder and receive the amounts to be received by it hereunder lawfully and without withholding for or on account of Taxes or (ii) to agree with the other party to modify this Agreement or change the method of payment hereunder so that those payments will not be subject to the withholding. If an assignment or agreement is not made as provided herein on or before the tenth day after that notice becomes effective, the party required to make the withholding may give notice of termination as provided in Section 14.

9. *Representations and Warranties.* Each of the parties makes the representations and warranties set forth below to the other as of the date hereof.

(a) It is duly organized and validly existing and has the corporate power and authority to execute and deliver this Agreement and to perform its obligations hereunder.

(b) It has taken all necessary action to authorize its execution and delivery of this Agreement and the performance of its obligations hereunder.

(c) All governmental authorizations and actions necessary in connection with its execution and delivery of this Agreement and the performance of its obligations hereunder have been obtained or performed and remain valid and in full force and effect.

(d) This Agreement has been duly executed and delivered by it and constitutes its legal, valid and binding obligation, enforceable against it in accordance with the terms of this Agreement, subject to all applicable bankruptcy, insolvency, moratorium and similar laws affecting creditors' rights generally.

(e) No event or condition that constitutes (or that with the giving of notice or the lapse of time or both would constitute) an Event of Default with respect to it has occurred and is continuing or will occur by reason of its entering into or performing its obligations under this Agreement.

(f) There are no actions, proceedings or claims pending or, to its knowledge, threatened the adverse determination of which might have a materially adverse effect on its ability to perform its obligations under, or affect the validity or enforceability against it of, this Agreement.

(g) It is, in the case of the Company, a Swiss corporation and a Swiss enterprise, and, in the case of the Bank, a United States corporation and a United States enterprise, for purposes of the income tax convention between the United States and Switzerland, and, in each case, it is fully eligible for the benefits of that convention with respect to any payments receivable by it under this Agreement.

(h) It has delivered to the other party its financial statements specified below:

(i) the Bank: the Bank's annual report for the fiscal year ended December 31, 1986, containing the Bank's financial statements as at that date and for that fiscal year prepared in accordance with generally accepted accounting principles in the United States, consistently applied (except insofar as any change in the application thereof is disclosed in those financial statements and is concurred in by the accountants that certified those financial statements), and certified by independent public accountants as fairly presenting the Bank's financial condition as at that date and the results of its operations for that fiscal year; and

(ii) the Company: the Company's financial statements as at December 31, 1986 and for the fiscal year ended December 31, 1986, prepared in accordance with generally accepted accounting principles in Switzerland, consistently applied (except insofar as any change in the application thereof is disclosed in those financial statements and is concurred in by the accountants that certified those financial statements), and certified by independent public accountants as fairly presenting the Company's financial condition as at that date and the results of its operations for that fiscal year.

10. *Covenants.* (a) Each of the parties shall give the other notice of any event or condition that constitutes (or that with the giving of notice or the lapse of time or both would constitute) an Event of Default with respect to it, other than one referred to in Section 12(a), not later than the third Banking Day after learning of that event or condition.

(b) If either party is required at any time to execute any form or document in order for payments to it hereunder to qualify for exemption from withholding for or on account of Taxes or to qualify for such withholding at a reduced rate, that party shall, on demand, execute the required form or document and deliver it to the party required to make those payments.

(c) So long as it has any obligations under Section 2, the Company shall deliver to the Bank, as soon as available and in any event on or before the ninetieth day after the end of each of the Company's fiscal years, its financial statements for that fiscal year, prepared in accordance with generally accepted accounting principles in Switzerland, consistently applied (except insofar as any change in the application thereof is disclosed in those financial statements and is concurred in by the accountants that certified those financial statements), and certified by independent public accountants as fairly presenting the Company's financial condition at the close of that fiscal year and the results of its operations for that fiscal year.

11. *Closing Documents.* On or before July 15, 1987, each party shall deliver to the other a duly executed certificate substantially in the form set forth in Exhibit 4B.2, together with the attachments referred to therein, and the Company shall deliver to the Bank (i) United States Internal Revenue Service Form 1001, duly completed and executed in duplicate, and (ii) an opinion of counsel for the Company with respect to the matters addressed in subsections (a) through (f) of the Company's representations and warranties set forth in Section 9. The opinion may be to the best of counsel's knowledge insofar as it relates to the matters addressed in subsections (e) and (f) of Section 9. The documents required hereunder shall be in form and substance satisfactory to the recipient.

12. *Events of Default.* For purposes of this Agreement, the term 'Event of Default' shall mean any of the events listed below in respect of a party (the 'Defaulting Party').

(a) That party (i) fails to pay any amount payable by it hereunder as and when that amount becomes payable and does not remedy that failure on or before the third Banking Day after notice from the other party of the failure or (ii) fails duly to give any notice to be given by it pursuant to Section 10(a), or to cure the event or condition that should have been reported in that notice, on or before the fifth day after that notice should have been given.

(b) That party fails duly to perform any covenant to be performed by it hereunder, other than those set forth or referred to in Section 10(b), Section 11(i) or Section 12(a), and does not remedy that failure on or before the thirtieth day after notice from the other party of the failure.

(c) Any representation or warranty made by that party in this Agreement, other than in Section 9(g), proves to have been incorrect, incomplete or misleading in any material respect at the time it was made.

(d) That party (i) is dissolved, (ii) fails or is unable to pay its debts generally as they become due, (iii) makes a general assignment for the benefit of its creditors, (iv) commences, or consents to the commencement against it of, any action or proceeding for relief under any bankruptcy or insolvency law or any law affecting creditors' rights that is similar to a bankruptcy or insolvency law, (v) is the subject of an order for relief or a decree in any such action or proceeding, (vi) has commenced against it without its consent any action or proceeding described above, if that action or proceeding is not dismissed on or before the sixtieth day after it is commenced or if any dismissal thereof ceases to remain in effect, or (vii) seeks or becomes subject to the appointment of a receiver, custodian or similar official for it or any of its property.

(e) That party or any of its Affiliates fails to pay when due any amount owing in connection with any other interest rate protection transaction, however described, between that party or that Affiliate, on the one hand, and the other party to this Agreement or any of its Affiliates, on the other, if the failure is not remedied during any applicable grace period.

(f) An event of default (however described) takes place that has the effect (or that, with the giving of notice or the lapse of time or both, would have the effect) of causing or permitting Indebtedness of that party in an aggregate amount exceeding 2% of that party's stockholders' equity to become due before the scheduled maturity date of that Indebtedness, or that party fails to pay when due Indebtedness in an aggregate amount exceeding 2% of its stockholders' equity.

270

13. *Mergers and Transfers of Assets.* For purposes of this Agreement, a 'Merger Event' shall be deemed to have occurred with respect to the Company (i) if the Company merges or consolidates with another entity and the Bank's policies in effect at the time would not permit it to enter into an interest rate protection transaction with the entity that is produced by or survives the merger or consolidation or (ii) the Company sells or otherwise transfers all or substantially all its assets.

14. *Early Termination.* (a) At any time while an Event of Default with respect to a Defaulting Party is continuing, the other party may, in its absolute discretion, give notice of termination in accordance with this Section. If a party gives notice of supervening illegality, either party may give notice of termination in accordance with this Section in the circumstances described in Section 7. If a party is required to pay any additional amount pursuant to Section 8, it may give notice of termination in accordance with this Section in the circumstances described in Section 8. If a Merger Event occurs with respect to the Company, the Bank may give notice of termination in accordance with this Section.

(b) Any notice of termination hereunder (i) shall state the grounds for termination, (ii) shall specify a date that is not before, nor more than ten days after, the date the notice of early termination is given on which the payments required by Section 15 shall be made as provided therein (the 'Early Termination Date') and (iii) shall declare the obligations of the parties to make the payments required by Section 2 that are scheduled to be made after the Early Termination Date to be terminated as of that date, and those obligations shall so terminate and be replaced by the parties' obligations to make the payments specified in Section 15.

15. *Payments upon Early Termination.* (a) If notice of termination is given hereunder on the ground of an Event of Default, the Defaulting Party shall pay the other party that other party's Damages if they exceed zero.

(b) If either party gives notice of termination on the ground of supervening illegality, because it is required to pay an additional amount pursuant to Section 8 or because of the occurrence of a Merger Event, each party shall pay the other one half the other's Damages (if they exceed zero) and, if a party would realize any gain or benefit as a result of the termination, it shall also pay to the other party one half of that gain or benefit.

(c) A party's Damages in the event of early termination shall be its Agreement Value, if that party's Agreement Value can be determined. If a party's Agreement Value cannot be determined, its Damages shall be an amount of Dollars equal to the sum of the losses (including loss of bargain), if any, that it may incur as a result of the early termination or as a result of the event that served as the ground for early termination.

(d) Payments to be made in accordance with this Section shall be made on the Early Termination Date, together with all other amounts then due hereunder, and shall be payable on a net basis. A party entitled to be paid any amount in respect of its Damages in accordance with this Section shall submit to the other party a statement in reasonable detail of those Damages. A party required under Section 15(b) to pay any amount in respect of its gain or benefit as a result of early termination shall submit to the other party a statement in reasonable detail of that gain or benefit.

16. *Agreement Value.* (a) For the purpose of determining a party's Agreement Value, that party shall select four leading participants in the interest rate products market (each a 'Reference market-maker'), in its sole discretion and in good faith, with a view to minimizing that Agreement Value; *provided, however,* that in doing so the party shall be entitled to select market participants that are of the highest credit standing and that otherwise satisfy all the criteria that party applies generally at the time in deciding whether to enter into an interest rate protection transaction.

(b) A party that is seeking to determine its Agreement Value shall request from each of the Reference Market-makers it has selected a quotation of the amount in Dollars which that Reference Market-maker would charge or pay that party on the Early Termination Date as a flat fee for entering into an agreement, effective on the Early Termination Date, pursuant to which that party would make all the payments scheduled to be made by it under Section 2 of this Agreement after the Early Termination Date and that Reference Market-maker would make all the payments the other party to this Agreement is scheduled to make under Section 2 of this Agreement after the Early Termination Date. If a Reference Market-maker would pay a flat fee to enter into such an agreement, the quotation obtained from that Reference Market-maker shall be expressed as a negative number for the purpose of determining Agreement Value, and if it would charge a flat fee, the quotation shall be expressed as a positive number for that purpose.

(c) A party's Agreement Value shall be the arithmetic mean (rounded up, if necessary, to the nearest cent) of the fees described in Section 16(b) that are quoted to that party by the Reference Market-makers it has selected or, if only one Reference Market-maker will quote such a fee to that party, that party's Agreement Value shall be the amount of the fee quoted by that Reference Market-maker.

17. *Costs and Expenses.* (a) Each of the parties shall pay, or reimburse the other on demand for, all stamp, registration, documentation or similar taxes or duties, and any penalties or interest that may be due with respect thereto, that may be imposed by any jurisdiction in respect of its execution or delivery of this Agreement. If any such tax or duty is imposed by any jurisdiction as the result of the conduct or status of both

parties, each party shall pay one half the amount of the tax or duty.

(b) A party that fails to perform any of its obligations hereunder shall pay, or reimburse the other on demand for, all reasonable costs and expenses incurred by the other in connection with enforcement of its rights under this Agreement including, without limitation, fees and expenses of legal counsel.

18. *Non-Assignment.* Neither party shall assign or transfer its rights or obligations hereunder or any interest herein to any other person or any of its other branches or offices without the written consent of the other party to this Agreement, and any purported assignment or transfer in violation of this Section shall be void. The parties are acting for purposes of this Agreement through their respective branches or offices specified in Exhibit 4B.1. Neither party shall withhold its consent to an assignment or transfer proposed pursuant to Section 7 or Section 8 if (i) the proposed assignee or transferee meets the criteria set forth in Section 7(i) or Section 8(b) (as the case may be), and (ii) the policies of the party whose consent has been sought, as then in effect, would permit it to enter into an interest rate collar transaction with the proposed assignee or transferee without credit support.

19. *Waivers; Rights Not Exclusive.* No failure or delay by a party in exercising any right hereunder shall operate as a waiver of, or impair, any such right. No single or partial exercise of any such right shall preclude any other or further exercise thereof or the exercise of any other right. No waiver of any such right shall be effective unless given in writing. No waiver of any such right shall be deemed a waiver of any other right hereunder. The right to terminate provided for herein is in addition to, and not exclusive of, any other rights, powers, privileges or remedies provided by law.

20. *Interpretation.* The section headings in this Agreement are for convenience of reference only and shall not affect the meaning or construction of any provision hereof.

21. *Notices.* All notices in connection with this Agreement shall be given by telex or cable or by notice in writing hand-delivered or sent by facsimile transmission or by airmail, postage prepaid. All such notices shall be sent to the telex or telecopier number or address (as the case may be) specified for the intended recipient in Exhibit 4B.1 (or to such other number or address as that recipient may have last specified by notice to the other party). All such notices shall be effective upon reciept, and confirmation by answerback of any notice sent by telex as provided herein shall be sufficient evidence of receipt thereof.

22. *Amendments.* This Agreement may be amended only by an instrument in writing executed by the parties hereto.

23. *Survival.* The obligations of the parties under Section 8, Section 15 and Section 17 shall survive payment of the obligations of the parties under Section 2 and Section 5 and the termination of their other obligations hereunder.

24. *Currency.* Each reference in this Agreement to Dollars is of the essence. The obligation of each of the parties in respect of any amount due under this Agreement shall, notwithstanding any payment in any other currency (whether pursuant to a judgment or otherwise), be discharged only to the extent of the amount in Dollars that the party entitled to receive that payment may, in accordance with normal banking procedures, purchase with the sum paid in such other currency (after any premium and costs of exchange) on the Banking Day immediately following the day on which that party receives that payment. If the amount in Dollars that may be so purchased for any reason falls short of the amount originally due, the party required to make that payment shall pay such additional amounts, in Dollars, as may be necessary to compensate for that shortfall. Any obligation of that party not discharged by that payment shall, to the fullest extent permitted by applicable law, be due as a separate and independent obligation and, until discharged as provided herein, shall continue in full force and effect.

25. *Jurisdiction; Governing Law; Immunity.* (a) Any action or proceeding relating in any way to this Agreement may be brought and enforced in the courts of the State of New York or of the United States for the Southern District of New York, and the Company irrevocably submits to the nonexclusive jurisdiction of each such court in connection with any such action or proceeding.

(b) The Company hereby irrevocably appoints Eternal Mail Box, which maintains an office in New York City on the date hereof at Broad and Narrow Streets, New York, New York 00000, as its agent to receive service of process or other legal summons in connection with any such action or proceeding. So long as the Company has any obligation under this Agreement, it shall maintain a duly appointed agent in New York City for service of such process or other summons, and if it fails to maintain such an agent, any such process or other summons may be served by mailing a copy thereof by certified or registered mail, or any substantially similar form of mail, addressed to the Company as provided for notices hereunder. Any such process or other summons may be served on the Bank by mailing a copy thereof by certified or registered mail, or any substantially similar form of mail, addressed to the Bank as provided for notices hereunder.

(c) The Company irrevocably waives to the fullest extent permitted by applicable law all immunity (whether on the basis of sovereignty or otherwise) from jurisdiction, attachment (both before and after judgment) and execution to which it might otherwise be entitled in any action or proceeding relating in any way to this Agreement.

(d) This Agreement shall be governed by, and construed in accordance with, the law of the State of New York.

26. *Counterparts; Integration of Terms.* This Agreement may be executed in counterparts, and the counterparts taken together shall be deemed to constitute one and the same agreement. This Agreement contains the entire agreement between the parties relating to the subject matter hereof and supersedes all oral statements and prior writings with respect thereto.

IN WITNESS WHEREOF the parties have caused this Agreement to be duly executed and delivered as of the day and year first written above.

BIG BANK, N.A.   HEDGED CORPORATION

By:_____   By:_____

Title:_____   Title:_____

Exhibit 4B.1   Addresses for Notices and Accounts for Payments

---

BIG BANK, N.A.

Address:	One Financial Center
	New York, NY 00000
Attention:	Rate Risk Management Group
Telex No.:	00000 BB
Telecopier No.:	(000) 000–0000

Account for Payments

Account No.:	00–000
Depositary:	Big Bank, N.A.
	Big Bank Plaza
	New York, NY 00000

HEDGED CORPORATION

Address:	1, Gnomestrasse
	Zurich, Switzerland
Attention:	Corporate Treasury Group Officer
Telex No.:	00000 HC
Telecopier No.:	(000) 000–00000

Account for Payments

Account No.:	00–000
Depositary:	Other Big Bank
	Big Bank Plaza
	New York, NY 00000

Exhibit 4B.2 Certificate

Pursuant to Section 11 of the Interest Rate Collar Agreement dated as of July 1, 1987 between Big Bank, N.A. and Hedged Corporation (the 'Agreement'), _____[a] hereby certifies to _____[b] as follows:

(1) _____[c] is a _____ _____[d] of _____[a] duly appointed, and a specimen or facsimile of [his] [her] genuine signature is set forth on Appendix A hereto.

(2) [He] [She] was in office on the date of [his] [her] execution of the Agreement and at that time was authorized to execute the Agreement and all documents to be delivered thereunder on behalf of _____ .[a]

(3) Also attached, as Appendix B hereto, are certified copies of all documents evidencing all necessary corporate and other authorizations and approvals required for the execution and delivery by_____[a] of the Agreement and the performance of its obligations thereunder.

IN WITNESS WHEREOF, this certificate has been executed on and as of _____ , 1987.

[NAME OF PARTY]

By:_____

Title:_____

Notes: [a] Name of party delivering certificate; [b] Name of party receiving certificate; [c] Name of officer; [d] Title of officer.

5   Case study: Caps and collars as alternatives to interest rate swaps

Michael L. Hein

Introduction

The following case study illustrates how a floating rate bank borrower used an interest rate collar agreement as a hedge to reduce rate exposure while achieving significant cost savings compared to its fixed rate alternative, an interest rate swap.

Background

In 1985, a media company had entered into an agreement to purchase five broadcasting stations, with closing expected in the autumn. The acquisition would be financed by a combination of bank borrowings, public issues of convertible debt and sales of certain assets. The company's leverage would be significantly increased during the early years following the acquisition until the cash flow from the acquisition could reduce the outstanding bank loans to manageable levels, and the company would be exposed to the risk of rising interest rates because of the floating rates on the bank loans. The chief financial officer (CFO) had calculated breakeven levels of interest rates which could be comfortably serviced by the projected cash flows from the acquisition. A number of financial institutions had made presentations to the CFO explaining how the rate on the bank loans could be fixed with interest rate swaps. Citicorp Investment Bank suggested that he consider achieving his objectives by using interest rate caps and collars. At that time, Citicorp was the only financial institution offering collars.

Structure of the alternatives

By 1985 interest rate swaps had become a well-known device for converting the floating rate on bank loans into a fixed rate for nearly any maturity from two to 10 years. Using interest rate caps to limit rate increases on the upside had been used since 1983, and collars were not widely known. The economics of caps and collars were not well understood by most borrowers, and maturities beyond three years were not widely available. The borrower here was primarily interested in 5- and 7-year maturities. Citicorp was quoting prices for these maturities.

Interest rate swaps are agreements to exchange a floating rate for a fixed rate. At the time, a 5-year interest rate swap could be arranged in which the company would pay about 10.2% in exchange for receiving Libor payments which would be used to make interest payments on the company's bank loans. The company would then know with certainty that its interest cost for five years would be 10.2% plus the credit spread on its loans. This was about 2.6% per annum more than Libor at the time. If rates increased less than 2.6% on average over the life of the loan, fixing would be more expensive than remaining unhedged. As remaining unhedged was an unacceptable risk, the CFO had a strong inclination to enter into interest rate swaps.

Citicorp proposed two alternatives. The first was an interest rate cap. The company would pay a front-end premium in return for which Citicorp would ensure that the company's floating Libor rate would not exceed a specified level. During any period when Libor exceeded that level, Citicorp would pay the difference to the company. For example, at the time, for a premium of 4.2%, the company could obtain a cap at 10.125% for five years. How should the company evaluate this alternative? With a cap, the company's borrowing cost would float with market rates *up to* the level of the cap. Therefore, the company would know that its *maximum* borrowing cost would be 10.125% (plus its credit spread) and that its actual borrowing cost would be whatever market rates turned out to be over five years, perhaps much less than 10.125%. Therefore, it would not be possible to predict in advance what the cost would be. Rather, the company would have to make a judgement on the future course of rates. In addition, there is the substantial front-end fee to be taken into account. To calculate the all-in cost of borrowing with a cap in place, it is necessary to amortise the fee. For accounting purposes, the fee is amortised on a straight-line basis, but this ignores the time value of money. For comparison purposes it would be better to convert the fee to a per annum basis using an assumed discount rate or solving for the per annum cost on an internal rate of return basis, which is simple to do with a calculator or personal computer. Thus, for example, the per annum cost of a 4.2% fee over five years if the borrowing rate were 10% is 1.11% and the all-in cost of borrowing is 11.11%. Now it is possible to make some comparisons:

Market rate (%)	4.0	6.0	8.0	10.0	12.0	14.0
Fixed rate (%)	10.2	10.2	10.2	10.2	10.2	10.2
Cap rate (%)						
Market rate (%)	4.0	6.0	8.0	10.0	12.0	14.0
Cap refund (%)	–	–	–	–	(2.0)	(4.0)
Fee per annum (%)	1.1	1.1	1.1	1.1	1.1	1.1
All-in cost (%)	5.1	7.1	9.1	11.1	11.1	11.1

It is clear that at market rates current at the time of our example (7.625%), borrowing with a cap in place would be cheaper than fixing and if rates were to decline, the advantage would increase. At worst, if rates rose to high levels, the all-in cost with a cap could be as much as 1.1% more expensive than fixing. There is the trade-off: the risk of paying 1.1% more on the upside compared to the savings possible if rates do not rise. What to do is a matter of judgement. In our case, the borrower did not feel comfortable with the all-in cost in the worst case. What other alternatives did he have? Citicorp proposed a collar.

A collar is the same as a cap except that the borrower has a floor on his borrowing rate in addition to a cap on his rate. When market rates fall below the floor, the borrower must pay the difference to the provider of the collar, effectively restricting his borrowing cost to a band between the floor and the cap, e.g. 7.625% and 10.125%. What is the advantage of this? The front-end premium is lower – 2.6% in the example here – because the borrower gives up some of his downside savings potential and the provider has the potential benefit of it. The all-in cost of borrowing with a collar in place may be attractive compared to fixed rate alternatives. How can the borrower evaluate this? As with a cap, the front-end fee must be amortised, then comparisons can be made. Two convenient reference points are the all-in cost at the floor and at the cap:

	All-in cost at the floor	All-in cost at the cap
Borrowing rate (%)	7.625	10.125
Fee per annum (%)	0.690	0.690
All-in cost (%)	8.315	10.815

These results can now be compared to the fixed rate alternative. At worst, the cost with a collar would be about 62 basis points higher than the fixed rate alternative; at best, the cost with a collar would be 190 basis points cheaper than the fixed rate alternative. Depending upon what the company's outlook for rates is, this could be a very attractive trade-off. We can now also compare the collar with the other alternatives, as shown above, remembering that the company's borrowing cost can not fall below the floor rate.

Results

In actual fact, the company in this case hedged its bets. The CFO decided to hedge US$100m at that time, doing a US$50m swap and a US$50m collar. Libor rates rose slightly in the second half of 1985 before dropping to below 6% in 1986. Consequently, the company's borrowing rate on the portion of debt hedged with the collar has been 8.13% all-in compared to the 10.2% paid on the swapped portion. The company has saved a substantial amount of money since the deal was completed. In the light of hindsight, the company would have done better during some periods had it used a cap agreement, even though the front-end fee would have been higher, but the CFO was unwilling to live with the possibility of a higher all-in worst-case cost at the time of the decision.

Conclusion

It is important to note that the economic trade-offs among the available hedging alternatives do not always follow the pattern in the example above. During 1986, with a rapidly flattening yield curve, fixed rates looked much more attractive than caps, and far fewer caps were done than in the previous year. Collars did not provide attractive trade-offs because little value was given to the prospect for further rate declines. During the first part of 1987, caps regained their attractive trade-off characteristics compared to fixed rates, whereas collars continued to provide little incremental benefit.

PART VIII

Conclusions

1 A comparative analysis: A treasurer's perspective

John Wisbey

Introduction

Interest rate risk is a phenomenon which affects almost every company in the world. It also affects very many individuals, as anyone with a floating rate mortgage will know only too well. Unlike exchange risk, which has been increasingly well managed ever since the end of fixed exchange rates, it is only in the last five years or so that companies have paid increasing attention to their interest rate exposure as well. They have been greatly helped by an explosion in the number of financial instruments available to them from the banking community, in particular the interest rate swap and the interest rate cap.

Any treasurer of a medium-sized or large company is unlikely to be short of information on the various instruments available. In addition to becoming more active in the area of Treasury products, many banks have put greater emphasis on marketing them as the return on risk for more traditional areas such as lending has continued to decline. The most difficult decisions that a treasurer has to make are those of when to hedge an exposure, and then which of the array of instruments to use. While there are no easy answers, this article sets out a framework for how to make the decision. The principal choices that a borrower has are the following:

1 Not to hedge the interest rate exposure at all.
2 To fix the interest rate cost through a swap or fixed rate borrowing.
3 To fix the maximum interest rate cost through buying a cap or other option product but to retain the ability to benefit from rates falling.

No hedge

Factors that might induce a borrower not to hedge at all are various. The exposure might be very small in relation to the company's size, or the treasurer might have a strong view that rates were going down anyway – at least not going up by enough to justify the usually higher cost of funding further up the yield curve. Another valid reason for not hedging would be if cash flow projections showed a very quick paydown of existing debt – whether through generated profit, through asset disposals, or through the raising of capital through a rights issue; clearly it would not be a very good hedge to enter into a five-year swap for borrowings that were not likely to be on the balance sheet for more than the next year.

There are many sound reasons, therefore, why a company with a strong balance sheet might decide not to hedge. Some relate to knowledge of cash flow, others to taking a market view. As always, taking a market view can bring rewards but also carries risk. Provided that the company is strong enough to carry some interest rate risk as well as the trading risks in its normal business, there is a fair risk/reward ratio.

Fixing the rate

Other than fixed rate loans, the two principal methods by which a rate on a floating rate loan can be fixed are the forward rate agreement (FRA) and the interest rate swap. An FRA covers one interest rate period only (although, of course, a whole strip of FRAs can be executed at the same time), whereas a swap covers a series of interest periods typically at semi-annual intervals over a number of years. Although the settlement procedure is normally different (FRA interest equalisation payments are discounted and payable at the beginning of an interest period, whereas swap payments are not discounted and are payable at the end of an interest period), the end result is effectively the same. If short-term interest rates subsequently go up to above the swap rate, then having done the swap will be seen to have been a profitable decision; on the other hand, if rates fall (or even if they stay unchanged in a currency with a positive yield curve) then there will have been an opportunity loss from having done the swap. This is usually clear with the benefit of hindsight but far from clear at the time that a hedging decision needs to be made.

The advantages of a swap to a borrower are:

- Overall interest costs are known exactly in advance.
- There is no up-front premium.

The disadvantages of a swap to a borrower are:

- There is usually an immediate increase in the cost of funds (assuming a positive yield curve).
- There is an opportunity loss if rates stay the same or fall.
- A bank treats a swap as a credit risk. This may therefore reduce its ability to conclude other transactions with the borrower.

Interest rate options

The principal interest rate option products available to a borrower are the following:

1   Interest rate caps.
2   Hybrid products such as interest rate collars and participation caps.
3   Swaptions (also known as swap options).
4   Interest rate guarantees (options on individual FRAs).

Although all option products have a number of features in common, all have important differences. Features of interest rate options are discussed below.

Interest rate caps

An interest rate cap (also known as a ceiling) is an arrangement whereby in return for a premium normally payable on the deal date the seller (writer) of the cap undertakes over an agreed period to compensate the buyer of the cap whenever a reference interest rate (e.g. 3-month Libor) exceeds a pre-agreed maximum interest rate (the 'cap rate').

An interest rate cap can be thought of as a one-sided interest rate swap. The method of rate fixing and calculating interest equalisation payments is identical for swaps and caps whenever the reference rate is above the cap rate. The difference arises when the reference rate is fixed below the cap rate. In this case, for a swap the borrower (the fixed rate payer) would have to pay the difference between the short-term rate and the swap rate; however, for a cap the buyer of the cap is not required to pay anything out at all. Obviously, as for any option, the seller of the cap has to be compensated for this one-sided arrangement and this is achieved through the initial payment to the seller by the buyer of a premium. The level of this premium depends, rather like insurance, on the period for which cover is required and on the level of cover required. Obviously, the lower the interest rate above which the buyer wishes to be compensated, the more expensive the cap premium will be.

Example A buyer of a cap requires three-year protection and decides on 1 February 1988 to buy a three-year 9% cap at a cost of 1.85% of the principal amount. The total to be capped is US$100m and the reference rate used is 6-month Libor. Using a hypothetical interest rate scenario, payment flows might appear as follows:

Rate fixing date	Interest period	Days in period	Interest rate (% p.a.)	Interest differential to be paid (% p.a.)	Amount paid by seller to buyer
1.2.88	3.2.88–3.8.88	182	7.5	–	–
1.8.88	3.8.88–3.2.89	184	8.0	–	–
1.2.89	3.2.89–3.8.89	181	9.5	0.5	251,388.89
1.8.89	3.8.89–5.2.90	186	10.75	1.75	904,166.67
1.2.90	5.2.90–3.8.90	179	9.25	0.25	124,305.56
1.8.90	3.8.90–4.2.91	185	8.75	–	–
					US$1,279,861.12

The advantages of using an interest rate cap are numerous:

- The buyer (borrower) retains the ability to fund at the short-term rate while always enjoying full protection if rates rise above the cap rate.
- If the yield curve is a steep one, then provided that short-term rates do not rise immediately it is often possible for the cost of the cap to be effectively paid for in the first one to two years by the interest rate saving through not doing a swap.
- Bid/offer spreads are often narrower than in the swap market (to make a valid comparison it needs to be remembered that cap prices are usually expressed in per cent flat, whereas swap rates are expressed in per cent per annum).
- As the bank selling a cap has no credit risk after receipt of the initial premium, selling a cap does not use up a bank's credit lines (although it should be noted that this is not the case for a collar – described further below). There is therefore no need for differential pricing for a cap between a weak and a strong borrower. Whereas this does not mean that strong companies should not use caps, it does mean that weaker or more highly geared companies will often get better value from the cap market than from the swap market – assuming that the swap market is open to them at all. This same argument holds true for major borrowers in countries where country risk rather than commercial risk is the major factor affecting a bank's pricing.
- Any borrower which for credit reasons needs to pay a differential of more than about 20 basis points per annum over the market swap rate would almost certainly achieve the same result more cheaply by buying a deep in the money cap. With US dollar short-term rates at 7% per annum and the five-year swap rate at around 9% per annum, an appropriate cap rate for achieving this might be, say 6% per annum – such a cap's value would be primarily intrinsic value with very little time value.

The disadvantages of using caps are:

- The cost of the initial premium must be weighed up against the expected interest saving through being able to fund at the short-term rate rather than at the swap rate.

- If there is an immediate sharp rise in short-term rates (and no subsequent fall), it is likely to be cheaper to enter into a swap and to avoid paying a cap premium.

A further point that should be borne in mind for any Treasury product is taxation. For example, if under the borrower's country's tax laws cap premiums are fully deductible against the current year's income, it may be additionally beneficial to buy a cap because of the resultant deferral of tax. However, if a cap premium is not deductible for tax purposes at all, and if swap or interest payments are deductible, then a cap would not be as good value after taxation is taken into account.

Interest rate floors and collars

So far this chapter has dealt with the situation for a borrower. Naturally there are many companies with cash surpluses, or insurance companies which need to obtain a minimum return on funds, which are more concerned with the possibility of rates falling. For them the interest rate floor is an appropriate product.

Interest rate floor Whereas an interest rate cap guarantees a maximum rate for a reference rate over a chosen period, an interest rate floor guarantees a minimum rate. The mechanism of payment is similar to that for a cap, in other words the buyer of an interest rate floor pays a premium on the deal date, and receives payments at the end of each interest period during the life of the floor if the rate for that period was below the floor rate.

Interest rate collar An interest rate collar is an arrangement whereby simultaneously:

- *A* buys an interest rate cap from *B*.
- *A* sells an interest rate floor to *B*.

Typically, a borrower might want to buy an interest rate cap at 9% per annum, but be prepared to forego the benefit of rates falling below 6.5% per annum. Taking *A* in the above example to be the borrower, and using rates of 9% per annum for the cap and 6.5% per annum for the floor, the effect on *A*'s Libor cost will be as follows:

Libor	Adjusted Libor as paid by A
Less than 6.5% p.a.	6.5% p.a.
6.5 – 9% p.a.	Libor
Above 9% p.a.	9% p.a.

The principal advantages of an interest rate collar are:

- It is always cheaper than an interest rate cap because the buyer is giving up the ability to benefit if rates fall below the floor rate.
- It is possible to construct 'zero cost' collars provided that the cap rate is above the swap rate.

The disadvantages of an interest rate collar are:

- In an interest rate environment with a steeply upward sloping yield curve (such as the US dollar yield curve in early 1988), the value of a floor is very low and hence the cost saving over a cap not very great.
- A collar negates the principle of buying an option to achieve unlimited benefit with limited downside potential. This is because as well as buying an option (the cap), the borrower is also selling an option (the floor).
- If in the above example rates were to fall below 6.5% per annum, the buyer of the collar (the borrower) would need to reimburse the bank. The possibility of this means that a bank, if it is

prudent, must treat the collar as a credit risk. In practice this means that most banks will pay less than the perceived 'fair value' for the floor as the return on perceived credit risk has to be taken into account when using up a credit line – just as in the swap market.

The author's experience at Kleinwort Benson Limited has been that we have sold only a few collars in relation to the number of caps that we have sold or the number of swaps that our swap group has concluded.

Participation caps

As described above, it is possible to generate a collar at zero cost provided that the cap rate is higher than the swap rate for the relevant period. However, the resultant band of interest rates is often so narrow that companies decide to do a swap instead. One other product which is worth considering is the participation cap.

If we take any interest rate above the swap rate, we can calculate the relative current values of a cap or a floor struck at those levels. Let us suppose that the five-year US dollar swap rate is currently 9.19% per annum. In this case the relative values of a five-year 10% per annum cap and a five-year 10% per annum floor might be, say, 3.4% flat and 6.6% flat. It follows that a zero cost combination could be achieved by the following:

- Bank sells to borrower US$66m of 10% per annum caps at 3.4% flat.
- Bank buys from borrower US$34m of 10% per annum floors at 6.6% flat.

If the borrower's total borrowings were US$66m the net effect of this combination would be as follows:

- For Libor rates above 10% per annum the borrower would enjoy full protection at zero cost.
- For Libor rates below 10% per annum the borrower would enjoy 48.48% $= 100 \times \dfrac{66-34}{66}$ of the benefit of rates below 10% per annum.

A table of effective costs in this example would therefore be as follows:

Libor (% p.a.)	All-in cost (% p.a.)
13	10
12	10
11	10
10	10
9	9.5152
8	9.0304
7	8.5456
6	8.0608
5	7.5760

The advantages of participation caps are:

- The protection if rates rise is similar to that for a cap, but with no up-front premium payable.
- Unlike a zero cost collar, there is continued ability to benefit if rates fall.
- They are easier for a bank to hedge than a collar, and should consequently be better value for a borrower.

The disadvantages of participation caps are:

- If there is an immediate sharp rise in Libor, it would still have been better to have done a swap.
- If rates stay the same or go down, it would have been better to have bought a cap.
- As for swaps and collars, they use up part of a bank's credit limits.

Swaptions

A swaption (also known as a swap option) is an option to enter into an interest rate swap. In return for a premium payable in advance, the borrower has the right *but not the obligation*, to enter into a swap at a pre-agreed level.

A swaption is a valuable tool when a borrower has decided to do a swap but is not sure of the best timing of the swap. The typical structure would be for a borrower to buy a six-month or one-year option to conclude an interest rate swap at or near current market levels. Clearly, a borrower buying a swaption would buy in the hope that swap rates would in fact go down. Although, if rates went down, this would involve losing most of the option premium, this loss would be more than outweighed by the benefit of locking into a swap at a significantly lower rate.

A swaption is not directly comparable to a cap, as the period of protection is very different. For example, a one-year option to enter into a four-year swap gives the right to exercise within one year; after one year the borrower has either exercised the swaption, in which case he is locked into a swap, or has allowed the swaption to expire, in which case no protection is in place for the next four years. The swaption is a valuable product, however, and has a useful role in liability management – particularly where a borrower prefers the certainty of paying fixed rate through a swap, and is not concerned about the opportunity loss if interest rates fall in, say, three years' time.

Interest rate guarantees

Interest rate guarantees (IRGs) are the simplest type of interest rate option. An IRG is an option to buy or sell a forward rate agreement (FRA). This is effectively identical to concluding a cap with only one interest period. There is a minor difference in settlement procedures between the two as FRAs are settled at the beginning of an interest period while caps are settled at the end of a period.

Summary of the relative benefits of interest rate protection products

In order to analyse the relative advantages of the various instruments, it is necessary to compare both their cost and their payout over time in different interest rate scenarios. A full analysis over a long period would break down that period into, say, quarterly intervals, and would use a good estimate of the cost of the hedge broken down by interval rather than using an average swap rate or an average annualised cost of a cap. Although Kleinwort's hedging models make a precise theoretical estimate of FRA rates going out to 10 years and the value of individual options on those FRAs (which when combined for a full period make up a cap), it is not practical to do a full analysis here. However, reviewing average rates usually gives similar results and the following courses of action are considered below:

1 No hedging.
2 Five-year interest rate swap at current rate of 9.19% per annum.
3 Purchase of five-year interest rate cap at 9% per annum at the current cost of 4.72% flat (equivalent to 1.18% per annum).
4 Purchase of a five-year interest rate cap at 10% per annum at the current cost of 3.40% flat (equivalent to 0.85% per annum).

5   Purchase of five-year interest rate collar at 10% per annum (cap rate) and 7% per annum (floor rate) at the current cost of 2.75% flat (equivalent to 0.69% per annum).

6   Conclusion of five-year zero cost participation cap with the cap rate at 10% per annum and a 48.48% benefit for rates below this.

The table below shows the all-in cost using the above six strategies. All figures are expressed in per cent per annum.

Libor % p.a.	Cost if no hedging	Cost if swap at 9.19% p.a.	Cost if buy 9% cap	Cost if buy 10% cap	Cost if buy 10%/7% collar	Cost if buy 10% partici-pation cap
15	15	9.19	10.18	10.85	10.69	10
14	14	9.19	10.18	10.85	10.69	10
13	13	9.19	10.18	10.85	10.69	10
12	12	9.19	10.18	10.85	10.69	10
11	11	9.19	10.18	10.85	10.69	10
10	10	9.19	10.18	10.85	10.69	10
9	9	9.19	10.18	9.85	9.69	9.52
8	8	9.19	9.18	8.85	8.69	9.03
7	7	9.19	8.18	7.85	7.69	8.55
6	6	9.19	7.18	6.85	7.69	8.06
5	5	9.19	6.18	5.85	7.69	7.58
4	4	9.19	5.18	4.85	7.69	7.09
3	3	9.19	4.18	3.85	7.69	6.61

As can be seen, although similar protection is achieved if rates rise sharply (although in this case the swap is the best value), when rates are the same or lower there can be a large difference in the overall interest rate cost. If rates in fact fall, then the best strategy would be the traditional one of not hedging an interest rate exposure at all, followed by concluding an out of the money interest rate cap.

One general conclusion of any study on these lines is that with the benefit of hindsight the best course of action would normally either have been to conclude a swap or not to have hedged at all. The interest rate cap and other option products in such a study are usually not as profitable as the 'best' course of action but are invariably a great deal better than the worst course of action. In fact, a more sophisticated analysis by interval can produce scenarios where an interest rate cap is the best solution, e.g. when rates rise sharply for a relatively short period (e.g. 1980/81) but then fall equally sharply.

Conclusion

It can be seen that all the above hedging strategies give very different all-in interest costs in different interest rate scenarios. The swap offers the most cost-effective hedge if US dollar rates rise above 10% per annum and stay at high levels; on the other hand, anything other than a cap involves substantial opportunity losses if rates in fact fall sharply. Libor in the past six years has ranged from a high of 21% per annum to a low of 5.75% per annum. There must be very few people, whether economists, bankers or corporate treasurers, who were able correctly to forecast anything like these extremes. Only time will tell whether the next few years will bring swings of similar magnitude, but with all the hedging tools now available we can at least be sure that there will be less and less acceptance by company chairmen and shareholders of 'unforeseen interest rate movements' as an excuse for poor results.

2 Interest rate protection techniques: An accounting perspective

R. Kilsby and Chris Taylor

Introduction

There are various specific accounting frameworks in different sovereign states around the world. Many of these are further modified or influenced by specific statutory requirements or central bank or other regulatory body regulation. They range from environments in which there are specific rules, such as in the US, with detailed guidance in the form of FASB pronouncements which are mandatory and other guidance with a lesser degree of compulsion, to those such as in the UK where there is specific guidance in certain restricted areas but generally a broader approach may be adopted in trying to reflect the economic substance of transactions rather than the strict legal form. None-the-less, the vast majority of financial reporting throughout the world is based on the historical cost concept which, as discussed below, is largely driven by a traditional view of external financial reporting as a statement of stewardship and not a true indication of the performance of management in adding to the overall economic wealth of the entity.

However, if corporations are to manage financial risk properly, it is imperative that they have the base information to do this and typically much of this base information will be drawn from the accounting records of the corporation. Thus, the accounting system reporting forms part of the overall financial risk management process. However, it is part only of this system and in many cases the information drawn from the accounting records is inadequate by itself because exposure is frequently only identified at too late a stage when a transaction is actually booked into the accounting records. None-the-less, accounting is effectively the ultimate measure of performance in assessing the degree of success or otherwise in managing, for example, the interest rate exposure of a corporation.

Once the concept of accounting being part of the financial risk management information systems is accepted, it follows that the accounting practices and policies adopted and the accounting reports produced should facilitate the making of decisions on such matters. In other words, if 'accounting' is to provide useful risk management information, then it must be based on a framework and concepts which assist in evaluating decisions and performance. This concept of accounting conflicts to some extent with the more traditional view expressed above. It may be argued that from a risk management perspective, performance evaluation is a more important purpose for accounting. Accordingly, the basis on which accounting information is prepared for risk management purposes should be one that attempts to match the risks/costs of a transaction with the rewards derived from that transaction in order to obtain a true measure of profitability and performance.

Accounting should not be a set of rules engraved on stone; rather it should be a management tool and should be flexible enough to reflect the realities of the business. Devising products which, whilst commercially similar to other products, 'get around the letter' of accounting rules is a fruitless task certainly for performance measurement and risk management purposes. A treasurer who seeks to boost accounting profits by choosing to release locked in mismatch profits on the money market book through the use of, say, swaps is fooling no one but himself if he thinks that this actually makes him more profitable. Indeed, if such profit manipulation is possible, then perhaps the accounting is *not* truly reflecting the business.

The purpose of this chapter is to explore more fully the traditional ways of accounting for interest rate products and to highlight some of the anomalies and inconsistencies which arise from these methods. I will then attempt to establish an alternative accounting framework which matches risks/costs with rewards and perhaps provides a better structure for performance evaluation than some of the practices currently employed. The chapter will also examine the role of the balance sheet and will attempt to suggest ways in which the balance sheet can be made into a more useful risk management tool.

It may be that some of the techniques described in this chapter will not be acceptable for financial accounting purposes in some territories. This aspect is explored in more detail later. However, just because a set of external rules prohibits the use of a specific accounting methodology for external reporting purposes, this does not necessarily mean that such a methodology cannot be employed for internal reporting purposes, particularly if that methodology provides more useful risk management information.

It is not the aim of this chapter to be dogmatic and to provide definitive methods by which all interest rate products should be accounted for. If accounting is to provide useful risk management information then it must be flexible enough to adapt to differing environments. Rather, the purpose is to attempt to provoke thought and discussion on alternative methods of accounting which could be adopted for interest rate products. It is hoped that in this way the quality of accounting information for risk management purposes can be improved and made more relevant to the decision-makers.

Purpose of accounting

In determining the purpose of accounting it is necessary to look at the different uses to which accounting information is put. In relation to this it is useful to split accounting into two main types – financial accounting and management accounting.

Financial accounting is the term used to cover reporting to the outside world. Although such information is typically addressed explicitly to the shareholders in the corporation, in practice this externally published accounting information is often used by a wide range of different parties who in turn put it to a large number of different uses. Indeed, it is often difficult for the corporation publishing external accounting information to be certain precisely who will ultimately use the information and for what purpose. Accordingly, it is necessary to state explicitly the basis on which the accounting information is produced and to detail the more significant policies adopted in the preparation of the information.

In order to ensure consistency between the published information of different corporations, it is necessary for there to be generally accepted rules which are followed by all corporations in the preparation of their external accounting information. In some countries these rules have been codified into law whilst in others they take the form of pronouncements by the accounting bodies within the countries. The existence of such external rules clearly restricts the types of accounting policy which may or may not be adopted by a corporation. In other words, a corporation is forced to prepare its external accounting information in a prescribed manner even if that corporation feels that the policies imposed upon it do not allow it to report on its business in the most appropriate way. Additionally, there is no opportunity to supplement externally published accounting information or to correct any misunderstandings which the readers of the accounts may have.

In contrast, management accounting is the term applied to the accounting information used internally within a corporation. Here the range of users and uses for the information are much better defined and, accordingly, the information may be prepared in the manner which is most meaningful for a particular use or user. Where a particular user requires further information this can be prepared and any misunderstandings are more easily identified and rectified. As such, management accounting techniques can be much more flexible than financial accounting techniques and thus the policies adopted can be tailored more closely to the individual business.

One issue to stress at this point is that accounting can no longer be considered, as it is in some circles, as mere 'bean counting' or 'score keeping', passively recording the results of what has happened. I believe a better term might be 'performance measurement', because in order for the accounting or performance measurement to realistically reflect the economic substance of what is happening to the business it must be linked to the risk management criteria adopted as part of the detailed application of the overall business strategy of the entity. Thus, it is not merely the total profit which is to be earned from a transaction which is relevant but the degree of exposure to risk which is incurred by the organisation in earning that profit and the relationship between the two. In simplistic terms from a financial institution's perspective, this means that it is not merely the profit and loss which matters but also the consumption and allocation of capital reflected in the balance sheet or such extended measure of this aspect as might be developed to replace or supplement the traditional balance sheet.

In looking at profit measurement, consideration is first given to management accounting, as this allows a 'green field' site for developing performance evaluation and risk management techniques. The applicability of these techniques to financial reporting can then be reviewed.

The profit and loss account

In exploring the role of the profit and loss account in the management accounting process, the aim should truly be to match the risks/costs of a transaction with the rewards derived from the deal. This should reflect the commercial reality, and indeed the pricing of the transaction. This leads to a simple three-stage approach to profit measurement for interest rate products in the management accounting environment:

1   Identify all risks/costs inherent in the transactions.
2   Identify all rewards arising out of the transaction (including all reinvestment income).
3   Match the rewards to the risks/costs so as to obtain a proper compensation for the risks/costs involved.

In examining different accounting methodologies it is necessary to bear the above steps in mind and to assess how closely an individual methodology reflects these steps.

Historical cost accounting

The majority of corporations still use a basic historical cost method of accounting in reporting the results of interest rate transactions. This basic framework records assets and liabilities at cost, and in general accrues the income and expense derived from those assets and liabilities over a period of time. In the case of an asset or a liability with a finite redemption date, the income or expense is usually recognised relatively evenly over the period to redemption. Thus, under the historical accounting method, it is the effluxion of time which gives rise to income or expense.

All liabilities are stated at cost and are not revalued to reflect the relative expense or cheapness of their rate compared to current market rates. This is on the basis that one cannot sell a liability; only with the consent of the person to whom the liability is due may the obligation be transferred fully to a third party. In addition, assets held for the medium and long term are stated at their historical cost (together with amortisation of any premium or discount against their final maturity value) unless there is considered to be a permanent impairment in their value. If it can be proved that it is intended that the items are to be held until maturity, then no account is taken of intervening movement in interest rates even though this may significantly affect the yield on the assets versus the current market yield.

As far as so-called trading assets are concerned these are usually carried at market or in certain environments at the lower-of-cost-or-market value. Accordingly, this has led to the need to designate all assets as either trading assets or investment assets. Trading assets are usually defined as those assets which are held with the intention of reselling them in the near future in order to realise short-term holding gains.

Whilst these definitions seem fine in theory, in practice it can be extremely difficult to differentiate between a dealing and an investment situation. The definition of where the short term ends and the long term begins can be very subjective. For example, individual assets within an investment portfolio may from time to time be sold and the proceeds reinvested in new assets. Under the historical cost convention it would be usual for the profits and losses on such disposals to be recognised currently even though they may be partly offset by a changed yield on the new assets which will be spread over a period of time. The question arises as to whether it is right to view an investment portfolio on an asset by asset basis or whether it would be better to view the portfolio on a basket basis. Indeed, to take this argument to its logical conclusion, one would expect there to be no difference between a corporation participating in an investment fund and investing in the individual assets and liabilities of the fund itself. However, under the first structure the corporation would account for its participation at cost and would only accrue income distributed to it by the investment fund. Any capital growth would not be recognised until the participation were disposed of. However, under the second structure, profits and losses would be recognised each time an individual asset were disposed of.

Having differentiated between trading and investment assets, a further differentiation is then required when one goes on to look at interest risk management products. Here the differentiation is between trading instruments and hedging instruments. Basically, trading instruments are those purchased and sold with a view to making short-term holding gains whilst hedging instruments are those held in order to provide protection against the effect of interest rate movements on other assets and liabilities held by the corporation. Under the historical cost convention trading instruments are marked to market and profits and losses recognised currently. The profits and losses on hedging instruments are usually accumulated in a balance sheet account and taken to income in order to match the losses or profits on the related asset or liability. Again, although this sounds fine in theory, in practice it can be difficult to differentiate between trading and hedging instruments. Whilst the three hedging criteria of intent, certainty and correlation have been introduced to try and provide guidance on this, these again can be difficult to apply in practice. For example, how close must correlation be in order for a transaction to qualify as a hedge and how certain must a cash flow be before a hedging transaction can be treated as such?

Disadvantages of historical cost accounting

The main disadvantages of the historical cost accounting method from a management accounting/performance evaluation perspective may be summarised as follows:

- The recognition of income and expense over a period of time does not necessarily reflect the results of a decision in the same period as that in which the decision was taken. For example, the profits in respect of an open position taken in a money market book with a subsequent advantageous movement in rates then locked in by matched funding would normally be taken on the accruals basis over the period of the matched funding. However, the profits do not actually result from activity over this period but from the taking of the position and closing it out at advantageous rates.
- One corollary of the above point is that the reported results for any one period may both exclude the full effects of some of the decisions taken within that period and include the effects of some of the decisions taken in prior periods. This makes performance evaluation extremely difficult, as it is

possible for a poor performance in the current period to be masked by good performances in prior periods. This is particularly so in respect of transactions which occur over a significant length of time but which, apart from carrying credit and operational risk, have 'locked in' profits. Many examples can be found in the swap dealing area or in some of the earlier arranged swaps. Here, the swaps team may well be remunerated on a discounted cash flow basis but the corporation accounts for the profits on an accruals basis. The remuneration is attempting to assess performance currently and reward it whereas the accounting treatment is spreading such profits over a more conservative and prudent period.

- The accruals method of accounting does not really reflect the economic reality of the underlying transactions. In particular it does not achieve the objectives of matching risks/cost with rewards. Indeed, the rewards derived from a transaction are recognised by reference to the effluxion of time rather than by reference to the risks inherent in the transaction. As such the accruals basis of accounting does not reflect either the pricing of the transaction or the understanding of the transaction held by the people undertaking it.

- The historical cost accounting basis as modified by the revaluation of trading assets leads to a number of anomalies and inconsistencies. For example, if a trader wishes to open and close an interest rate position, this can be done through the use of say the money markets or by using say futures or forward rate agreements (FRAs). If the position is either opened or closed using the money markets then under the historical cost convention the results of the transaction are spread over the period of the money market loan or deposit. However, if the position is opened and closed using futures and FRAs for both legs then the transaction can be marked to market and any resultant profits and losses recognised immediately. From the dealer's perspective, if all the markets are in line, there is no difference between using any of the methods to open and close an interest rate position. However, the accounting for such products is clearly inconsistent and differs depending on the precise mechanism used within the transaction. Anomalies and inconsistencies such as this allow profit figures to be manipulated through the choice of instrument.

- Finally, and perhaps most important of all – viewed simply – historical cost accounting just does not recognise the so-called time value of money. Interest rate exposure and protection techniques, however, are fundamentally concerned with costs associated with such time value of money. It would therefore seem almost axiomatic that conventional or historical cost accounting will be unable to cope with such aspects and techniques. For example, if a corporation receives a bill due in six months time in settlement of a debt arising on sale of goods, it will normally show this receivable at full value in the balance sheet and reflect the results of this in the profit and loss account. However, if the bill is discounted, a lesser amount will be received and the difference can either be amortised over the period as financing cost or reduce the amount of profit taken on the sale. I believe that in reality such issues have not been fully addressed in the past, as the distorting effects have not been significant given low nominal interest rates and low inflation. In times of high inflation and high nominal interest rates, interest has been rekindled in certain aspects of so-called inflation accounting but the fundamental issues have not realistically been addressed.

Market value based accounting

One proposed solution to the drawbacks of historical cost accounting is to adopt a 'mark-to-market' basis of accounting for all assets and liabilities except those of an infrastructural nature. This clearly eliminates the need to differentiate between trading and investment assets and trading and hedging transactions.

Whilst this method has a certain appeal, it does assume that there is a deep liquid market for all assets and liabilities owned by a corporation. This is difficult enough to justify for assets as there are a number of markets which could in no way be described as deep and liquid. When one goes on to consider liabilities the argument appears even stronger. There are very few, if any, markets in which a bank can dispose of its liabilities. The only practical way in which an obligation can be avoided is by full legal defeasance or in substance defeasance through the use of trusts. Under the latter method an independent trust is set up and sufficient risk-free assets are transferred to the trust to enable all servicing and repayment obligations under the liability to be met. However, the applicability of such techniques is fairly restricted.

The market value based accounting method leaves unanswered the question of how to mark an asset or a liability to market when there is no market there in the first place. Even where markets do exist, unless they are deep and liquid it is likely that there will be temporary aberrations in the prices quoted in these markets. Is it right for a corporation, who has no intention of disposing of an asset in an abnormal market, to be judged on the basis of prices quoted in such markets?

Discounted cash flow (DCF) based accounting

An alternative solution to the problems which exist under historical cost accounting is to apply some sort of DCF based accounting methodology which may be regarded as looking at intrinsic rather than market value. This accounting methodology does not attempt to look at activity on a transactional basis but rather breaks each individual transaction in to a series of cash flows and aggregates these cash flows with those arising from other assets and liabilities. It then attempts to measure the changing values to the corporation of these aggregated cash flows. In practical terms this DCF based accounting methodology can be summarised as follows:

- All transactions are broken down into their individual cash flows and aggregated with the cash flows arising out of other instruments so as to form an overall cash flow ladder for the corporation as a whole.
- Cash flows arising at the same point of time are netted and discounted to their net present value.
- An amount is eliminated from the net present value to compensate for the credit risk and ongoing operational costs and risk elements inherent in the transactions.

The resulting net present value of the book as a whole is compared with that at the last revaluation and any difference is booked as a profit or loss in the current period.

This methodology can be illustrated by considering a deposit taken by a bank in the money markets. This is demonstrated in the simplified example below. The deposit taken can be split into two separate cash flows; an inflow equivalent to the principal at time zero and an outflow equivalent to the principal plus interest in three months time. The example demonstrates that where the rates of interest prevailing in the market are equal to the rate charged on the deposit then the transaction has a zero net present value. However, where the deposit has been taken at a rate more favourable than the rates generally prevailing in the market, then the discounted value of the principal plus interest is less than the value of the principal inflow at time zero, thus generating a profit. Under the DCF method of accounting this profit arises at the time that the deal is undertaken albeit on a discounted basis. This contrasts with the historical cost accounting method where the profit would have been spread evenly over the three month period of the deposit.

Money market deposit

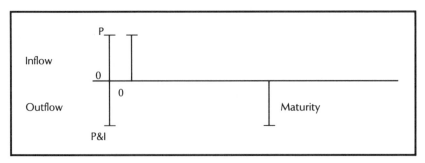

Example of DCF accounting for a money market deposit

A bank takes a three-month deposit of US$1,000,000 at a rate of interest of 8%. Current interest rates are: (a) 8%; (b) 10%.

(a) The deposit can be split into two cash flows:

Time 0:	1,000,000	inflow
Time 3 months:	(1,020,000)	outflow

At current rates of 8% the NPV =

$$1,000,000 - \frac{1,020,000}{1.02} = 0$$

(b) At current rates of 10% the NPV =

$$1,000,000 - \frac{1,020,000}{1.025} = 1,000,000 - 995,122 = US\$4,878$$

As interest rates move, the profits and losses derived from the deposit will fluctuate. For example, a movement in interest rates from 10% down to 8% would eliminate the profit previously booked. This movement in profits reflects the fact that, considered in isolation, the money market deposit represents an open interest rate position. If this position had been closed using, say, a money market loan, then any decrease in the profits derived from the deposit would be offset by a similar increase in the profits derived from the loan.

The above example illustrates the natural advantage which the DCF based method of accounting has over the historical accounting method. The DCF based method reflects the results of transactions in the period in which the transaction is undertaken thus providing a better method of performance evaluation. The calculations described above will be familiar to anyone who has dealt in interest rate products as they represent the same type of methodology as applied in pricing the transactions. As such the DCF based method of accounting can be said to more closely reflect the economic realities of the transactions which it is trying to record.

Although the DCF based method of accounting clearly has some advantages over the more traditional methods, there are a number of practical problems which need to be addressed if such a method is to be introduced. These problems may be summarised as follows:

- Arguably the most difficult aspect of introducing a DCF based method of accounting is deciding which discount rate to use. Clearly the choice of discount rate is crucial as it can significantly affect the profits and losses derived under this method. If one makes a separate allowance for credit risk as discussed below, then it would appear logical for the discount rate to be based on some sort of risk-free rate such as US Treasuries, for example, for dollar based cash flows. In addition, a zero coupon based rate would seem appropriate as the cash flows being discounted are single inflows or outflows at a period of time in the future. However, deciding upon precisely which risk-free zero coupon based rate to use is somewhat more difficult. For dollar based money market transactions it is possible to derive from the US Treasuries yield curve an equivalent risk-free zero coupon rate yield curve which can perhaps be applied to money market transactions. For other markets there may not be an exact equivalent, e.g. UK and gilts, or no definitive rate at all, e.g. in Switzerland. For other types of transaction, such as swaps, it may be necessary to add to the rate a margin to reflect the differences in pricing between the two markets.
- If the methodology is to work effectively in practice then it will be necessary to amalgamate cash flows arising within similar periods of time. It is clearly not desirable for cash flows to be split into individual days for the entire portfolio. Accordingly, some type of compromise needs to be reached in amalgamating the cash flows. For shorter dated cash flows the intervals within which cash flows are amalgamated clearly need to be shorter than for longer dated cash flows. Thus, some sort of grouping similar to the traditional interest rate maturity ladder may be appropriate with cash flows being classified by day or by week for shorter dated cash flows, gradually

lengthening to say three month intervals for longer dated cash flows. The precise interval must depend upon the individual organisation. The danger in imposing such arbitrary intervals is that cash flows which are in reality only a few days apart may end up being treated as being months apart if they happen to fall either side of a dividing line between two time intervals. Accordingly, in performing a DCF based calculation it may be necessary to vary the time intervals to check that this does not have a significant effect on the results.

- One of the most difficult areas to address in respect of DCF based accounting is how to take account of the credit risk inherent in many interest rate based transactions. For example, a loan to a triple-B counterparty will clearly tend to carry a higher rate of interest than a loan to a triple-A counterparty. To recognise the effects of this more favourable rate at the time that the transaction is undertaken would not be matching the rewards from the transaction with the inherent risks. The credit risk on a transaction clearly extends throughout its life and, accordingly, any compensation for that credit risk should also be accrued throughout the life of the transaction. Although this may seem ideal in theory, the practicalities are much more difficult.

The main difficulty is in identifying what part of the rewards derived from a transaction are compensation for the credit element. Indeed, perhaps the question should be how much compensation should be received for the credit element of a transaction and if that amount is not received then there is an argument for booking a loss to reflect the fact that the transaction has been underpriced. The development of a methodology in order to take account of the credit risk in interest rate based transactions must clearly be done on an individual basis by banks and must involve the participation of the credit department.

This is a relatively new area where few banks and virtually no corporates have any in-depth experience. The issue is being addressed with a new vigour following the proposed convergence principles on capital adequacy which are addressing the parallel issue of how much capital is required to support the credit aspects of cash flow based instruments such as swaps, etc. In practice, there is nothing new about this; the market has been well aware of the credit implications of longer dated foreign exchange transactions but is unclear how these have been reflected in the pricing. None-the-less, I believe it is essential that research continues and the ability of the banking community and others to address and quantify these issues is enhanced. This is essential, since all that is proposed is that the method of recognising profit and measuring performance reflects the economic realities of the transaction and, in turn, be reflected in the pricing of such a transaction. It is unfortunate that in all probability many of the transactions have been entered into without adequate consideration in the pricing of the full credit cost potential.

A further difficulty is that the development of such methodologies almost inevitably involves the use of statistical mathematical methods. This arises because the exposure at a point in time reflects not only (i) the current exposure, which is a measure of the difference between current market rates at which a replacement transaction would have to be put in place and the original transaction rate if the counterparty failed now, but also (ii) the potential exposure, that is the risk that market rates will move such that there will be a difference between the contracted rate and the market rate at some future point in time that a counterparty might fail, giving rise to the need to cover the resultant open position.

Although the above practical problems clearly demand the development of new techniques by banks, the benefits of the DCF based method of accounting are apparent. Such a method also has the advantage that it provides a clear link with risk management techniques in that it addresses to some extent the fundamental question of whether the rewards derived from a transaction are adequate to compensate for the risk inherent in the transaction. A number of banks are increasingly moving towards a DCF based method of accounting, at least for management accounting purposes. As interest rate products become increasingly complex, it may be that more and more banks turn to this solution.

Financial accounting

The DCF based method of accounting represents a radical departure from the accounting methodologies traditionally employed. Although the logic of such a departure can be defended and new accounting policies can be implemented fairly easily for management accounting purposes, the situation becomes more difficult when one moves on to consider financial accounting. Ideally, there should be no difference between management accounting and financial accounting. However, the imposition of rules on financial accounting by bodies external to the organisations preparing those accounts means that it may not be possible to apply new management accounting techniques in the preparation of financial accounts. These rules are frequently designed to apply to all types of businesses and cannot therefore be expected to fit easily into banks and other financial institutions. However, if accounting is to be used really as a true measure of performance in an organisation, it is important that the accounting policies are not dictated by external rules but are formulated within the organisation itself. As such it may be necessary for there to be different accounting policies for management accounting purposes and for financial accounting purposes if the external rules do not allow the same policies for both.

Just how prescriptive the external financial accounting rules are will depend upon the territory in which a bank is operating. Generally, the less prescriptive the financial accounting rules, the more acceptable will be the management accounting techniques for financial accounting purposes. In the UK, for example, I do not believe that there would be any impediment to the use of a DCF based method of accounting for external reporting purposes. In the US, however, the situation is likely to be more difficult as the revaluation of liabilities is not permitted. However, many of the financial accounting practices in the US are prescribed by the accounting bodies themselves and, hence, as long as a logical case can be made for a particular accounting methodology which enjoys a reasonable level of support there is a chance that the accounting bodies can be persuaded to change the financial accounting rules.

The situation is likely to be much more difficult in countries where the financial accounting rules are enshrined in legislation and particularly where tax law and accounting law have been meshed together. This state of affairs exists in many European countries and here there is a strong case for adopting management accounting policies which are different from those adopted for financial reporting. Clearly, if accounting is to be used as a risk management tool, it would appear incongruous to apply accounting policies laid down in statute to management accounts where such policies will lead to the organisation avoiding transactions which add to the overall economic wealth and are the most beneficial when viewed in the medium term. None-the-less, it is recognised that it is extremely difficult to do this if it means that the entity under its existing historical cost reporting may report depressed results in the short term.

If different policies are adopted for financial accounting purposes than for management accounting purposes it is necessary to be able to reconcile the two profit figures. At the end of the day the externally reported profit figure is still important and if this differs, for whatever reason, from the profit figures which management believe to be the true amount then management must be able to explain how the differences have arisen.

This is particularly important as management will, of course, be concerned to manage the business with a view at least partially to the externally reported results. It is essential to ensure that there is congruence between what is trying to be achieved at the senior management level and any bonus or remuneration schemes aimed at those actually transacting the individual transactions.

The balance sheet

So far we have considered only the profit and loss implications of interest rate products. However, one of the big advantages quoted for products such as futures, FRAs, options and swaps is that they are off-balance sheet. But why is it that these products, which carry many of the same risks as money market transactions, are off-balance sheet and indeed why is this an advantage? In this part of the chapter I explain why such products are off-balance sheet, why this is important and suggest a way in which the balance sheet could perhaps be made into a more useful risk management tool.

The first question that needs to be addressed is what is the purpose of a balance sheet? The traditional explanation is that a balance sheet gives a 'snapshot' of the assets and liabilities of a business at a given point in time. In other words, a balance sheet shows the assets of a business and the way in which those assets have been funded – the keyword here is 'funded'. Assets that do not require funding do not appear on the balance sheet. In particular, agreements to acquire assets at a future point in time are not reflected on the balance sheet until that future point in time is reached and the asset is actually funded. Thus, contracts such as futures, FRAs, swaps, etc., that clearly fall into the category of agreements to perform actions in the future do not appear on the balance sheet.

In essence, the balance sheet reflects the stewardship concept of accounting. The balance sheet shows the assets which the company has under its stewardship at a given point in time. It does not reflect the effects of any agreements to either acquire more assets or to dispose of assets contained in the balance sheet.

Despite this rather straightforward aim, the balance sheet has come to be used for a wide variety of purposes. For example, by calculating return on assets ratios which compare profit with the gross assets on the balance sheet, investment analysts have effectively used the balance sheet as part of a performance evaluation methodology. The problem here is that, as discussed earlier, profit represents compensation for risk. The balance sheet in no way purports fully to reflect risk. It must therefore be possible to generate profit without affecting the balance sheet by undertaking transactions which, although they bear risk, have no funding effect. In this way it is possible to improve ratios such as return on assets. This is what many banks have achieved through the use of various off-balance sheet transactions such as swaps, futures, FRAs, etc.

In the past, the designation of a transaction as on- or off-balance sheet also had another advantage. The capital adequacy calculation of many central banks relied heavily on examining the assets of the bank as disclosed in the balance sheet. Items that did not appear in the balance sheet therefore did not come within the scope of the capital adequacy calculations and could therefore be undertaken without any additional capital. This advantage now appears likely to disappear as the central banks revise their capital adequacy methodologies to be based more on risk exposures than on balance sheet classification. To this extent, it may be said that the central banks have recognised that the balance sheet does not at present reflect fully the risks to which an organisation is exposed.

Having established that the balance sheet is not a measure of risk in any way, two questions that become apparent are: Should the balance sheet reflect risk in some way? Does the balance sheet in its current form really provide anyone with any useful information? It may be argued that as accounts increasingly become used for performance evaluation there is an argument for reflecting at least some element of risk on the balance sheet. However, in practice, this is likely to be difficult to achieve. A bank is exposed to many different types of risk and it would be very difficult to change the format of the balance sheet in such a way as to reflect all these different risks. However, one possible compromise is to change the balance sheet such that it reflects at least all the credit risk to which a bank is exposed. This argument would take the balance sheet along the same track as the capital adequacy calculations imposed by the central banks. Thus, all transactions entered into by a bank would result in a credit equivalent figure being reflected on the balance sheet with a contra account on the funding side of the balance sheet for those items which were not actually funded. Whilst this practice would not allow a true assessment of credit risk, in that it would not reflect the differing degrees of credit risk attaching to individual counterparties, it would at least move the balance sheet on to a more risk based basis and perhaps produce a more meaningful piece of information.

The adoption of such a change to the structure of the balance sheet is unlikely to happen in the near future. Such a change would represent a fundamental change in the basis of preparing financial accounts and could not therefore be undertaken rapidly. However, I believe that there is an argument for reassessing the information given by a balance sheet certainly for banks and other financial institutions where the whole business is dependent upon the assumption of risk.

Summary

Clearly, accounting has a very important role to play in the risk management systems of a bank. However, accounting is only a way of reporting what is happening in a business and should not take precedence over commercial and business reasons in determining courses of actions. Ideally, the decision as to whether a transaction is or is not worth undertaking should not be affected by the accounting treatment of the transaction. This can only be so if the accounting treatment truly reflects the economic reality of the transaction.

As interest rate instruments become increasingly complex it is becoming more difficult to sustain a historical cost accounting basis within banks. Frequently, anomalies and inconsistencies are arising between the treatment of what are basically similar instruments. Additionally, as performance evaluation becomes more important, management and external reviewers are being forced to look towards new accounting techniques.

The DCF based method of accounting and the inclusion of all credit risk on the balance sheet are suggestions as to the way accounting may develop in the future to take account of the changing demands put upon it. The need to change has been highlighted by the new interest rate products developed over the last few years. As further new products are developed, it is likely that the pressure to change will increase. If accounting is to remain relevant then it must react to these changes.

3 The future: A banker's perspective

Brian Leach

Introduction

If risk managers could be perfect forecasters of interest rates, then there would be no need for the intricate strategies which characterise risk management. Instead, their jobs would consist solely of the decision to fix rates or float with market rates. If, for example, rates were projected to rise, then all liabilities would be fixed and all assets would float. Alternatively, if rates were falling, then all assets would be fixed and all liabilities would float. Exhibit 3.1 illustrates, from the liability manager's perspective, that the optimal decision always lies in either fixing or floating. Conversely, from an asset manager's perspective, the best and worst case in Exhibit 3.1 would be reversed.

Exhibit 3.1 Interest rate exposure

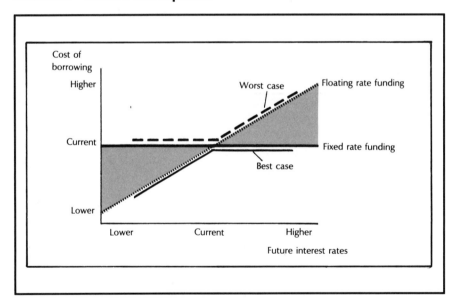

Unfortunately, no one forecasts interest rates perfectly. Therefore, it is the job of risk managers to position the firm's interest rate exposure to exploit favourable interest rate moves and avoid unfavourable moves. This favourable position is reflected in the shaded area of Exhibit 3.1. The most common strategy used by risk managers to achieve this balance is to create a portfolio that combines fixed and floating rate liabilities and assets. The appropriate combination will be determined based on the principles of gap management, duration analysis or sensitivity analysis. Issuing an assortment of fixed and floating rate assets and liabilities is an averaging strategy which, although quite effective, is available only to those firms that have access to many of the world's capital markets and can rapidly expand and contract their balance sheets. Few firms can meet these criteria and, therefore, must rely on interest rate risk management products as a means of controlling rate exposure.

Risk management products

Selecting the appropriate risk management product is further complicated by the considerable number of choices. It is essential that the risk manager compare the attributes of the various products in order to make the optimal decision. Risk management products can be fundamentally differentiated based upon two broad categorisations. First, is where they are traded; either on listed exchanges or with financial intermediaries who have created the product. Second, is what type of market exposure they create; either a two-sided exposure to the market (e.g. if rates increase, then there is a gain or a loss, whereas if rates decrease there is a loss or gain, respectively) or a one-sided exposure (e.g. if rates increase, then there is a gain or loss, whereas if rates decrease there is no gain or loss). Exhibit 3.2 displays many of the products currently offered in the market based upon these two broad categorisations. In addition to these differences, enhancements can be added to the products further customising interest rate exposure and/or reducing cost.

Exhibit 3.2   Essential differences between products

	Listed market	Packaged products
Two-sided market exposure	Futures	Interest rate swaps Money market swaps Interest rate guarantees Forward rate agreements
One-sided market exposure	Options	Caps Floors Collars

Exhibit 3.3   Detailed differences between products

Product	Liquidity	Attributes Bid offer spread	Credit exposure	Simplicity
Futures	High	Narrow	No	Difficult
Interest rate swap	Limited	Wide	Yes	Moderate
Money market swap	Limited	Wide	Yes	Moderate
Interest rate guarantee	Limited	Wide	Yes	Easy
Forward rate guarantee	Medium	Medium	Yes	Easy
Options	High	Narrow	No[a]	Difficult
Caps	Limited	Wide	No[a]	Easy
Floors	Limited	Wide	No[a]	Easy
Collars	Limited	Wide	Yes	Moderate

Seller has only an overnight credit exposure.

Exhibit 3.2 is intended to function strictly as a summary of the most essential differences among products. These products have other, more subtle, differences, as summarised in Exhibit 3.3. Understanding the interplay among these subtle attributes and a risk manager's resources and risk objectives is essential in selecting the optimal risk management product. The breadth of products available have been created to meet the needs of the full spectrum of risk managers, ranging from the highly leveraged small industrial corporation, for example, to the triple-A rated large financial institution. The motivation behind choosing a product requires users to decide which attributes, as summarised in Exhibit 3.4, are best suited to the characteristics of their particular firm.

Exhibit 3.4   Choice of product

Attribute	Implications	User characteristics
Liquidity	Response time	Highly rate sensitive users must be able to reposition their risk exposure rapidly.
	Size limitation	Large users need to be able to transact in quantity.
Bid/offer	Adjustment expense	Frequent adjusters of rate forecasts cannot afford a wide bid/offer spread.
Credit exposure	Credit fee	Low quality credits should avoid products with credit exposure fees.
Simplicity	Management time	Firms with limited resources may elect to use products requiring less management time.

Selection of strategy – examples

This section examines how a small highly leveraged industrial company and a large high quality finance company might begin to select an appropriate risk management product. It is illustrative of the typical internal review of corporate characteristics, as completed by a potential user of risk management products, and the subsequent selection of a product with symbiotic attributes.

Caps

The characteristic which is generally most critical to a highly leveraged firm is the minimisation of the cost of credit extension. Caps, which have virtually no credit exposure, may be the leveraged firm's most useful risk management product. This type of firm, due to its weak credit rating, has limited available borrowing sources. The long-term fixed rate funding market may be fully closed to this firm or, at best, open at uneconomic levels. Therefore, the highly leveraged firm's most advantageous funding alternative is usually a floating rate bank loan. Unfortunately, a bank loan exposes the firm to rising rates, which a highly leveraged firm can least afford. Interest rate swaps could be used to convert the floating loan to a fixed loan, but this market, if not fully closed, may be prohibitively expensive after paying for credit intermediation.

Caps, in contrast to the above alternatives, enable the leveraged firm to use attractively priced bank loans, reduce exposure to rising rates, extend maturity and to limit management time. They can also be purchased for a very economical price. Caps should be economically attractive to any firm that has a large disparity between short- and long-term borrowing spreads. If, for example, a firm could borrow 10-year fixed rate funds at a spread of 350 basis points over the 10-year Treasury, and a bank loan at Libor plus 100 basis points, then the firm could spend as much as 250 basis

Exhibit 3.5 Cap funding costs

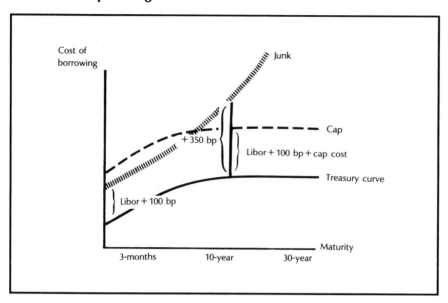

points (the differential in short- and long-term spreads, e.g. 350 basis points less 100 basis points) to cap Libor at the current 10-year Treasury rate level and still attain a funding cost that will not exceed the current 10-year fixed rate borrowing cost. Exhibit 3.5 shows an example of these funding costs. This financing advantage exists whenever the present value of the credit premium charged by the market (i.e. the present value of the 250 basis point per year incremental credit premium) exceeds the cost of buying the cap. The most significant drawback in the use of caps is that the purchase price is an up-front fee. A leveraged firm can sometimes find it difficult to allocate its most limited resource – cash – for the payment of this fee.

Futures

Futures, much like swaps, could also be used to convert the floating rate loan to a fixed rate. Futures would be cheaper than swaps because of the lack of a credit intermediation fee. This characteristic of futures is linked to the mark-to-market provisions which exist on futures exchanges that virtually guarantee the credit integrity of the transaction. However, the same mark-to-market provision exposes the firm to significant cash flow timing risks. If, for example, the firm used futures contracts to extend its bank borrowing for two years and rates immediately fell, then the firm would instantly incur two years of interest rate losses generated by the futures contracts. Furthermore, the benefits that would result from rolling over the bank loan at lower rates would take two years to materialise. Additionally, the futures market may not allow the borrower to extend the maturity of the loan for the desired period of time because of the limited number of months in which the contracts trade. Eurodollar futures, for example, have only three years of contracts traded and borrowers are thus limited to fixing bank loans for a maximum of three years. Finally, futures require more frequent monitoring, and thus a greater time commitment by the finance staff – a limited resource in a lean, highly leveraged industrial corporation.

One reason why a high-quality finance company might elect to use futures is because of its access to a variety of resources. This type of firm, in contrast to a highly leveraged firm, is best served by using its balance sheet as the primary means of managing interest rate risk and by supplementing the balance sheet adjustments with listed futures. The balance sheet can involve a full range of financing alternatives including fixed rate borrowings, bank loans and swaps. The cap market is usually inappropriate for this sort of firm, because the premium price paid to have only a one-sided market exposure cannot be justified in a large company that has many two-sided risk exposures booked over time. A high-quality finance company has been, and will be, in the market so frequently that its most reasonable goal is to achieve an average funding cost, i.e. the shaded area referred to in Exhibit 3.1. This company may, however, frequently change its rate forecast requiring an adjustment to its risk exposure; the futures market is an excellent tool which may be used to accomplish this adjustment. A large company has the systems, the personnel with the financial acumen and the long-term needs sufficient to warrant an investment in this product. A similar but smaller finance company may not have all of these resources to implement a futures program and, therefore, might be better advised to use forward rate agreements and swaps as a means of managing risk.

Summary

A highly leveraged industrial company and a large, high-credit quality finance company are just two examples of the different types of firms that should be using risk management products. Other firms, with alternative characteristics, might use different products. Regardless of which product is selected, risk managers must assess objectives, measure risk, examine product attributes and, most importantly, act. Active users become skilful at identifying and dealing with rate exposure. Familiarity with these products enables users to find new and innovative methods of employing the products. Whether this means offering purchasers new financing arrangements, accepting innovative investment opportunities, or drawing down an exceptional financing package, each firm's unique needs can be met through the creative use of risk management products. It is precisely due to the versatility of these products that these markets have, over a short period of time, evolved into highly liquid markets.

Authors' biographies

Boris Antl is the President of Finexis Inc, the Managing Partner of Swap Services International, a software company in Silicon Valley producing analytical systems for the swap industry. He is a graduate of the University of California in Berkeley and the Columbia Graduate School of Business. He has previously worked with Chemical Bank's Foreign Exchange Advisory Service in New York, J. Henry Schroder Wagg & Co in London and New York, and the Capital Markets Division of Crocker Bank in San Francisco and Tokyo. He has edited and written a number of books and articles on the subject of exposure and financial risk management.

Carl A. Batlin is Vice President and Director of Risk Management Research at Manufacturers Hanover Trust Company. He has also worked at Chase Manhattan and Chemical Banks and as Professor of Finance at The University of Michigan. He holds a PhD in Financial Economics from Columbia University and has published articles on various financial topics in a number of academic and trade journals.

R.D. Bown joined J. Henry Schroder Wagg & Co Ltd in 1960. He became a foreign exchange dealer in 1967 and subsequently was made Chief Dealer for both Treasury and Foreign Exchange in 1972. In 1982 he also took responsibility for establishing JHSW's Financial Futures unit. He was appointed a Director in July 1985.

Horace Brock holds five degrees from Harvard and Princeton Universities. From 1974 to 1980 he was senior member of Stanford Research Institute's International Management and Economics group. In 1980, Dr Brock founded Strategic Economic Decisions, of which he is President. His company specialises in applications of the modern 'economics of uncertainty' to world capital and currency markets. He is a frequent contributor to the *New York Times* and *International Herald Tribune*.

Ian Cooper is Senior Lecturer and Baring Brothers Research Fellow in Finance at the London Business School. He has also taught at the University of Chicago. He received his PhD in Financial Economics from the University of North Carolina at Chapel Hill.

Patrick Daniels graduated from the University of Durham with a Degree in Law and is a Partner in the firm of Simmons & Simmons. He has lectured on the law and tax implications relating to futures contracts and futures funds and serves on the Taxation Committee of the Federation of Commodity Associations in London.

Mark Davis is a Senior Manager in the UK banking industry group of Deloitte Haskins & Sells and specialises in risk and control, regulatory and accounting issues facing banks and other financial institutions.

Roger Emerson is a taxation Partner of Coopers & Lybrand London, leading the UK firm's financial sectorgroup. He is a frequent speaker at financial conferences and is co-author of the Euromoney *Guide to financial instruments*. He is a mathematics graduate of University College Oxford.

Victor J. Farhi has been involved in the securities industry for several years working with Merrill Lynch in a variety of functions starting as a stockbroker and moving on to Bond Trading and Investment Banking. He joined Citicorp and was Product Manager for Interest Rate Options in London, advising major government and corporate relationships on interest rate risk management. He is currently with the Hongkong Bank Group and is Manager of the Financial Engineering unit in London.

M. Desmond Fitzgerald is currently Group Chief Economist and Head of Planning for Alexanders Laing and Cruickshank Holdings Limited, the international securities division of Mercantile House Holdings. He is also Visiting Professor of Finance at the City University Business School.

David J. Gilberg studied at the University of Pennsylvania, from which he received a BA and an MA and at Harvard Law School from which he received a JD. He has been practising as an attorney with Rogers & Wells since 1981 and he is currently an Adjunct Professor at Georgetown University Law Center in Washington where he is teaching a course on the regulation of financial instruments.

Anthony C. Gooch is with the New York office of Cleary, Gottlieb, Steen & Hamilton. He is the co-author of Euromoney's books on *Loan agreement documentation* and *Swap agreement documentation* and a frequent lecturer on topics in the international financial area.

Michael L. Hein is a Senior Vice President of Capital Markets Assurance Corporation (CapMAC), a financial guaranty insurance company wholly owned by Citicorp. A graduate of the University of Wisconsin, he previously worked in the Interest Rate Risk Management group of the Citicorp Investment Bank.

Robert Henrey is a Partner of Coopers & Lybrand in New York. He directs the firm's international tax consulting group.

Richard A. Hutchison is a Vice President within the Strategic Risk Management Division of Chase Manhattan's Treasury Department responsible for marketing interest rate risk management instruments. Prior to his present appointment, Mr Hutchison was manager in charge of Chase Manhattan's International Financial Management Consulting Division in London providing consulting services to major international companies.

Richard Kilsby joined Charterhouse Bank Limited, part of The Royal Bank of Scotland Group, as Managing Director, in January 1988 to establish a capital markets operation. Previously, he was a partner in Price Waterhouse London responsible for coordinating their services to clients involved in dealing, capital markets and securities operations.

Linda B. Klein is with the New York office of Sidley & Austin. She is the co-author of Euromoney's books on *Loan agreement Documentation* and *Swap agreement Documentation*. She is a frequent lecturer on topics in the international financial area.

Charles Kolstad is a tax Partner at Coopers & Lybrand in Tokyo.

Brian Leach joined Morgan Stanley in 1981. He has a Masters degree in Business Administration from Harvard Business School. After several years in Morgan Stanley's Corporate Finance Department and Capital Markets Services group, he joined the Futures and Options group with responsibilities for Morgan Stanley's corporate hedging services. Recently, his responsibilities have changed to include marketing Morgan Stanley's Over the Counter Options in US Treasuries, Mortgage Securities and Foreign Denominated Government Securities.

Irrene S. Leibowitz is Managing Director of Samuel Montagu Capital Markets Inc and an Executive Director of Samuel Montagu & Co Limited. She joined Montagu in September 1984 to build a New York based origination and execution capability in interest rate and currency swaps, rate options and US debt and equity placements. She also coordinates the marketing to US clients of the firm's international capital raising services.

Mike Mason is a specialist in the international tax consulting group of Coopers & Lybrand in New York.

Ben Neuhausen is an Audit Partner at Arthur Andersen & Co. He joined the firm's New York office in 1973, where his responsibilities were primarily with clients in the financial services and oil and gas industries. From 1979 to 1981, he took a leave of absence from Arthur Andersen to work as a Project Manager at the Financial

Accounting Standards Board. In 1985, he transferred to the Accounting Principles group at Arthur Andersen's Chicago headquarters. His principal areas of responsibility include accounting issues relating to pensions, financial instruments, financial institutions, insurance and leasing.

Steve Oakes graduated in 1983 with a BA Honours in economics to join Midland Bank International for a general training in credit analysis, international banking and corporate marketing and overseas assignments. He joined Manufacturers Hanover in October 1986 to trade interest rate swaps before moving into options trading.

W.P. Ridley is with Wood Mackenzie and his major responsibility is to formulate investment strategy for those running institutional funds. After leaving Oxford he qualified as a chartered accountant. He then worked with international organisations including a two-year term in Nigeria. Subsequently, he joined a management consultancy, Merrett Cyriax transferring to Wood Mackenzie in 1973.

Rick Solway is a Manager in Cooper & Lybrand's international tax consulting group based in New York.

Cory N. Strupp is a Vice President and Assistant Resident Counsel of Morgan Guaranty Trust Company of New York. Prior to joining Morgan in 1984, he was an attorney with Winthrop, Stimson, Putnam & Roberts, a New York City law firm. Mr Strupp is a graduate of the University of Wisconsin–Madison and holds a law degree from Boston University.

Paul Sutin is with Security Pacific (Switzerland) SA, where he is in charge of options, futures and swap strategy development. He is also on the faculty of Economics and Computer Science at Webster University, Geneva. Prior to this he has been a research analyst for First Chicago National Bank, a consultant and assistant market maker on the floor of the Pacific Options Exchange for Chicago Research and Trade, Inc, and project manager for Options Research, Inc.

Chris Taylor is a specialist banking manager in the London office of Price Waterhouse. He specialises in foreign exchange, money market activities and international capital markets as well as developing various technical materials relating to banks and financial institutions. He has also undertaken reviews of the treasury operations of a number of corporates.

Tony Thurston graduated from the University of Warwick with a Masters Degree in Economics. His first step into the financial markets was as currency economist for Marine Midland Bank NA. He subsequently assumed responsibility for major account relationships advising multinational companies on how to manage their currency and interest rate risk while he worked for International Treasury Management. He has been managing the Options unit of James Capel Bankers Limited and has more recently become Senior Options Manager at the HongkongBank in London.

Daniel Treves, a graduate MBA from the Wharton School, Philadelphia, spent 13 years with Nestlé; for the last five of these he was Group Treasurer. Joining Tradition Group in 1984 as Executive Vice President he pioneered development of the Interbank FRA and over the counter currency and interest rate options.

Randy Vivona is with National Westminster Bank plc in their London office.

Graham Wandrag joined City Deposit Brokers from James Capel & Co in 1974. When the company merged with Tradition in 1981 he assumed responsibility for the Sterling Operations of the group. He was appointed Joint Managing Director in 1987 where he has special responsibilities for Treasury Services and Capital Markets.

John Wisbey was a scholar at Winchester College and Trinity College, Cambridge. He joined the Banking Division of Kleinwort Benson Limited in 1976 and worked on the Japanese desk before being posted to Kleinwort's Hong Kong and Singapore offices. On returning to London he established a new Financial Products unit attached to the North American Department. In early 1986 Mr Wisbey transferred to the Treasury Division as Head of the Options group, with particular responsibility for interest rate options. He is now Director, Swaps and Options, at Kleinwort Benson Securities Ltd.